THE I TATTI
RENAISSANCE LIBRARY

James Hankins, General Editor

ITALY ILLUMINATED

VOLUME I

ITRL 20

BIONDO FLAVIO

✦ ✦ ✦

ITALY ILLUMINATED

VOLUME I ✦ BOOKS I–IV

EDITED AND TRANSLATED BY

JEFFREY A. WHITE

THE I TATTI RENAISSANCE LIBRARY
HARVARD UNIVERSITY PRESS
CAMBRIDGE, MASSACHUSETTS
LONDON, ENGLAND
2005

Series design by Dean Bornstein

Library of Congress Cataloging-in-Publication Data

Biondo Flavio, 1392–1463.
[Italia illustrata. English & Latin]
Italy illuminated / Biondo Flavio ; edited and translated by Jeffrey A. White.
v. <1> — (ITRL ; 20)
Latin text with English translation.
Includes bibliographical references and index.
Contents: v. 1, bks. 1–4.
ISBN 0-674-01743-9 (cloth : alk. paper)
1. Italy — Description and travel — Early works to 1800.
2. Italy — History — To 1500 — Early works to 1800.
3. Humanism — Italy — Early works to 1800.
4. Italy — Biography — Early works to 1800.
5. Italy — Genealogy — Early works to 1800.
I. White, Jeffrey A.   II. Title.   III. I Tatti Renaissance library ; 20.
DG422.B56 2005
945 — dc22   2005046070

Contents

꿍꿍꿍

Introduction

꙰ꙮ꙰

Biondo Flavio of Forlì (1392–1463), the humanist civil servant and scholar, was young in an age when education in Italy was both medieval and at the same time brand new.[1] Education in Biondo's youth can be imagined as embracing the old *auctores* and *ars dictaminis* of medieval tradition alongside the developing *studia humanitatis*, not yet institutionalized in schools as they were to become by mid-century. In Lombardy §23 of the *Italy Illuminated*, Biondo says that Giovanni Balestreri of Cremona was his teacher of grammar, rhetoric and poetry, which at least shows that Biondo's Forlivese family were able to provide him with advanced literary training, one which, according to Biondo himself, was expert and thorough. To speak strictly, he had no Greek, and though of a lawyerly disposition,[2] there seems to be nothing to suggest any formal training in law.[3] As a boy, Biondo would have just missed the pervasive atmosphere of humanistic learning, with its emphasis on Ciceronian eloquence, that he extols in the *Italy Illuminated*:

> We can see that the benefit brought to our countrymen by so many books—the tinder of eloquence itself—resulted in our age having richer and finer resources of expression at its disposal than Petrarch enjoyed. The arrival of Greek letters was no small help in the acquisition of eloquence: and it was actually a stimulus to doing so, because, quite apart from the sheer knowledge and the huge supply of historical and moral material they gained from it, those who knew Greek attempted a good many translations into Latin, and so by constant practise in composition, their skill in writing improved, if they had any to begin with; or if they hadn't, they acquired some. And so academies all over Italy have long been hives

of activity, and they are more and more active now with each passing day. The schools are generally in the cities, where it is a fine and pleasant spectacle to see pupils surpassing their teachers in the polish of their speech or writing, and not just when the class is dismissed but while they are actually declaiming and composing under the teacher's very rod (Romagna §30).

But Biondo did not entirely miss this fervor of classical learning: as he grew into manhood he would have absorbed the full force of its energies right out of the Italian air, as he carried on the life of a bureaucrat and scholar, and particularly as he developed a network of relationships with other learned men of the day — humanists like Guarino da Verona, Leonardo Bruni, Leonardo Giustiniani, Francesco Filelfo, Panormita, and with powerful patrons of the humanities such as Alfonso d'Aragona, King of Naples; Borso d'Este, the Marquis of Ferrara; and Francesco Barbaro, the eminent Venetian diplomat and statesman.

From the first, Biondo combined vocation and avocation. While he was in Milan as the agent of his native city Forlì in the autumn of 1422, for example, he played a crucial (if not entirely clear) rôle in the rediscovery and publication of Cicero's lost *Brutus*: "When I myself was in Milan as a young man, carrying out official business on behalf of Forlì, I was the very first to copy the *Brutus*, which I did with extraordinary excitement and speed, and from my transcription (sent first to Guarino in Verona, then to Leonardo Giustiniani in Venice) the whole of Italy was similarly filled with copies of the book" (Romagna §29).[4]

Like so many of his era, Biondo became an exile, at thirty, from the city he loved.[5] He married Paola Michelini, of a respectable family of Forlì, and eventually they had ten children. The humanistic education of their five sons filled him with an obvious pride:

"And by the grace of God I see high hopes lodged in my five Biondo sons, all well-stocked in literature, so far as their years allow" (Romagna §34). Pride, hope and intellectual passion apart, what must have been a heavy financial investment in his sons' studies was a manifestation of the same drive for personal and family advancement that fueled the forward movement of his class, Cicero's old *ordo equester*. He owned a house on the Via Flaminia in Rome, one country property at San Biagio (Romagna §67) and perhaps another at Monte Scudo (Romagna §6). His brother Matteo was abbot of the monastery of S. Maria in Rotonda in Ravenna (Romagna §23), which again shows that his family enjoyed a certain position in the world; in the medieval social hierarchy an abbot was the equal of a bishop, and attaining such positions ordinarily required financial resources and influence.

Biondo served as secretary to Francesco Barbaro at Vicenza (1425), to Pietro Loredan at Brescia (1427), to Cardinal Domenico Capranica at Forlì, to Barbaro (again) at Bergamo (1430), and to Giovanni Vitelleschi, later archbishop of Florence, in the March of Ancona (1432).[6] By 1433, in the troubled pontificate of Eugene IV, he had joined the papal curia in Rome, where he was quick to establish himself as more than capable. Indeed, he become an insider, and remained with the papal bureaucracy — with one unsettling interruption — for the rest of his life, serving popes Eugene IV, Nicholas V, Callixtus III, and Pius II.[7] He held the positions of protonotary (composer of documents), abbreviator (or drafter of papal correspondence) and Apostolic Secretary (or composer of papal bulls).

He began his career as a writer in 1435 with *On the Expressions of Roman Speech (De verbis Romanae locutionis)*, an important contribution to the debate about the historical relationship between Latin and Italian, which he addressed to Leonardo Bruni.[8] In 1439 he began his massive *Three Decades on the History of the Romans Begin-*

ning with the Decline of Their Empire (Historiarum ab inclinatione Romani imperii decades III), covering the period from 410 AD to 1441, though with a disproportionate concentration on the first half of the Quattrocento. From 1444 to 1446 he worked to complete the Three Books on Rome Restored (De Roma instaurata libri tres), a typologically organized survey and guidebook of the Eternal City, which attempts through a scientific and judicious sifting, evaluation and interpretation of manifold evidence (textual, archaeological, numismatic, epigraphic, cartographical, etc.) to bring the physical appearance of the ancient city back from the ruin of time into contemporary consciousness.[9] He busied himself with Italy Illuminated — inter alia a peninsular expansion of the Rome Restored — from 1447 to 1453, though he had probably begun it earlier and never really regarded it as finished. In Rome Triumphant (Roma triumphans), ca. 1453–1460, Biondo surveyed Roman institutions, religious, civic, and military.[10] In addition he wrote four crusading tractates over 1452–1454,[11] sincere yet self-recommending; an unfinished Venetian history, One Book on the History of the Venetian People (Populi Veneti historiarum liber unus) in 1459–1460 — again self-recommending; and in 1460 an essay, Borso, or On Military Service and Jurisprudence (Borsus sive de militia et juris prudentia), dedicated to his patron, Borso d'Este.[12]

Biondo's admiration for Pope Eugene IV was genuine and unreserved. He expressed it frankly, both in the Italy Illuminated[13] and elsewhere; indeed, in 1446 Biondo dedicated his Rome Restored to him and gratefully described there the nature of their relationship.[14] Eugene IV died on 23 February 1447. For some time afterwards Biondo's status in the Curia was delicate, then took a turn for the worse. It may be that, over-anxious in his efforts to win patronage and preferment elsewhere, he wanted discretion, and that this, together with that pope's death, encouraged enemies. He took altogether seriously the commonplace humanist hope that

princes cherish the learned, and perhaps felt that his expectations in this regard had been disappointed.[15] In any case, it is obvious that Biondo became completely estranged from the Curia from 1449 on, and he passed the next four years disobliged financially and professionally—though friends in Rome were working on his behalf—until Nicholas V restored him to the Curia on 30 September 1453. Throughout the period, which he defines as one of ruinous idleness (*otium perniciosissimum*),[16] Biondo promoted himself through literary work and through correspondence with wealthy potential patrons and other learned men, chiefly to acquire materials and support for his literary work. To this period belongs the greater part of the composition of his *Italy Illuminated*[17] and its publication.

In 1447 a patron worth gratifying, Alfonso I of Aragon ("the Magnanimous"), King of Naples, had urged Biondo to "illuminate Italy" under his auspices, i.e., to follow his own tastes and nature to produce a work that would reconcile authoritatively the names of places and peoples of ancient Italy with modern.[18] Clearly he had established a reputation for antiquarian research. Again and again in the *Italy Illuminated*, Biondo speaks of his researches for the *Rome Restored* (which had been very well received) and for the *Decades* as fit and convenient preparation for his present task. So the work would constitute a kind of logical progression of his various interests. It would be the most complete, most vivid and most original expression of himself as humanist antiquarian and historian.

Biondo's *Italy Illuminated* is an essentially bookish (rather than cartographical[19] or eyewitness[20]) review of the fixed settlements—city-states, towns, and castles (*castelli*)—of the Italian peninsula in the mid-fifteenth century. Technically it falls into the contemporary genre of chorography, comprising the genealogy of the ruling houses of each settlement (or, in Biondo's case, genealogical

tidbits), their chronology, antiquities, local history, and topography.[21] Initially it compartmentalizes Italy (without her islands) into eighteen *regiones*, though as the work progressed this division was adjusted downwards to fourteen.[22] These divisions represent modifications of ancient Roman provinces[23] and have little to do with contemporary sovereignties. In the original order they are (1) *Liguria* (or the Republic of Genoa); (2) *Etruria* or Tuscany; (3) *Latina* (modern Lazio and northern Campania); (4) *Umbria* (roughly, the early medieval Duchy of Spoleto, modern Umbria); (5) *Picenum* (or the March of Ancona); (6) *Romandiola* or Romagna (comprising ancient Flaminia and Aemilia); (7) *Gallia Cisalpina* (or Lombardy); (8) *Venetiae* (Venice and part of the Veneto); (9) *Italia Transpadana* (or the March of Treviso); (10) *Aquileia* or *Foroiuliana* (the ancient Christian patriarchate); (11) *Histria* (the modern Istrian peninsula); (12) *Samnium* (the land of the ancient Samnites, modern Abruzzo); (13) *Campania* (the Terra di Lavoro or *Campania Vetus*, the region around Naples); (14) *Lucania* (modern Basilicata); (15) *Apulia* (the northern part of modern Puglia), (16) the land of the Salentini (or Terra d'Otranto, in southern Puglia), (17) *Calabria* (the north and central part of modern Calabria); (18) the land of the ancient Brutii (now the parts of southern Calabria facing Sicily). Each region is defined, its name justified, its borders established, its cities and towns surveyed, its interesting topographical features remarked. And each regional survey is oriented to water: to rivers and their tributary systems principally, to the seacoast, and to lakes.[24] So far, so good.

But Biondo was haunted by the idea of the failure of history to transmit the Italian past (Preface §2 and Liguria §5), and by the consequent interruption of Italian cultural continuity and identity between the barbarian incursions of the fifth century and his own times — an interruption he variously refers to as a period of loss, of murk and of shipwreck. Thus he makes his chorographical survey broaden out, in a process of enlightenment and recovery, to in-

clude much more. It becomes a scientific reconciliation, across the discouraging trough of *medium aevum* — Biondo's new term for what has become known as the Middle Ages[25] — of the ancient with the modern Italian landscape and its nomenclature, a catalogue of famous men (dead and living) of Italy, learned men particularly, and a compendium of much of Italian history. The intellectual heart of *Italy Illuminated* comes in §§25–31 of Romagna,[26] an extraordinary stemma of the propagation outwards from John of Ravenna, i.e., Giovanni Malpaghini, of the new humanistic learning and the new attitude to classical antiquity. Humanism makes the reintegration of classical past and Italian present possible, and a strong and persistent leitmotif of the *Italy Illuminated* is its triumphal procession of humanists.[27]

Throughout the *Italy Illuminated* Biondo registers his deep love of humanistic and pre-humanistic learning (e.g. in his remarks on the prehumanist Gerardo of Sabbioneta, at Lombardy §23), his sincere, orthodox Christian piety (e.g. in his treatment of St. Bernardino of Siena, at Tuscany §44, or the Church of the Virgin at Loreto at Piceno §17), his abhorrence of civil strife (e.g., in the discussion of the "Mercorini" and "Muffati" factions of Orvieto, at Tuscany §53), his dread of tyranny and anarchy both (e.g. in his account the triumvirate of Octavian, Lepidus, and Antony, at Romagna §38), his hatred of mercenaries and foreign encroachment (see his sketch of the rise of mercenary armies in Italy, at Romagna §§42–44), and his fascination with engineering (note for example the description of vented conduits at Lazio §33).

This hyper-learned chorography of Italy has another novel feature, for sometimes it is enlivened by authorial comment on contemporary developments (or by comment on certain historical matters with contemporary relevance to a humanist sensibility) that lends the work an agreeable piquancy and helps mark it, I think, as great. Among the more interesting authorial comments are his description of the Council of Union in Florence (1438–

39) — without mention of its ultimate failure (Tuscany §30; cf. Romagna §§72–73); of fowling at Nettuno (Lazio §7); of the barbarity of the fate of the Emperor Conradin at the hands of the Angevin kings — linked, through the place-name Torre Astura, to Cicero's fate (Lazio §9); of the self-destructive goodness and simplicity of Pope Celestine V (Lazio §28); his odd excursus on snakes and magic in the country of the Marsi (Lazio §35); his account of the conversion of Cicero from War to Art (Lazio §36); of the shameful beggars of Cerreto (Umbria §10); of the limitless poetic potential of Giovanni Gioviano Pontano (Umbria §11); of St John of Capistrano and the prosecution of the abominable Fraticelli (Piceno §13); of human credulity, the useless hunger for sensationalism and the demon-haunted Lago di Pilato (Piceno §24); of the condottiere Alberico da Barbiano's Order of St. George and the "balance of payments" (Romagna §§50–51); of mercy and the Lombard king Alboin I's entrance into Pavia (Lombardy 32); of the chastisement of the thirteenth-century heretics Dolcino and Margharita (Lombardy §35); of the minstrelsy of the young Leonardo Giustiniani (Venice §22).[28]

In short, *Italy Illuminated* is a work of some significance, still not fully explored or appreciated, for Renaissance historiography and antiquarianism, for the history of classical scholarship in particular and indeed for the Italian Renaissance as a movement of cultural revival in general.[29]

Like so many Renaissance Latin texts, the *Italy Illuminated* has in part the character of a *cento* or assemblage of quotations. The body of its citations (mainly of ancient Latin authors)[30] is very large, and there is sometimes needless repetition and irrelevance. Over some stretches the citations seem almost to comprise the text of the work as much as to support it. Staple authorities include Livy, the elder Pliny, Vergil with Servius's commentary, Cicero, Biondo himself (his *Histories* and *Rome Restored*), Suetonius, Andrea Dan-

dalo's *Chronica* for Venice, the *Scriptores Historiae Augustae,* Giacomo Bracelli's *Description of the Ligurian Coastline (Descriptio orae ligusticae)* for Liguria, the eighth-century Paulus Diaconus' *History of the Lombards (Historia Langobardorum)* for Romagna and Lombardy, Justin, Strabo for Lazio, Lucan, Martial, Eusebius, Ptolemy, Horace, Ovid, and Propertius.[31]

Biondo's use of his sources often detaches passages from their context (particularly when paraphrased) or customizes them, often so strenuously that, though his geographical or historical point is superficially buttressed, the author quoted is actually misrepresented. Biondo asserts (Liguria §5) that the historians of his own era miss a grandeur *(dignitas)* that might come to them from quoting ancient sources, because the correspondence between the names of ancient and modern Italian places has been lost;[32] he remedies this with his scholarship, reclaiming the lost grandeur of Roman names for *his* text by layering his *Italy Illuminated* with the special authority and magic of pagan authors. The more citations from the ancients, the better.[33] In citing classical authors, however, he worked from memory to an extent that would astonish us now: at Tuscany §54, he paraphrases from memory a passage from Ammianus Marcellinus, about the noble Persian Hormizd and the emperor Constantius II on their way to Rome, that has disappeared from our extant MSS of Ammianus.[34] Such reliance on memory naturally leads to lapses.

This is not to say, however, that Biondo's use of sources was careless. He is too fervent a worshipper of books and their power (Romagna §§26 and 30) for that. But not so fervent as to be uncritical. For example at Lazio §28, considering the source of the Fucine Lake, he accepts the possibility of textual deficiencies in Pliny *(Natural History* 2.224); at Umbria §15, he takes Donatus elaborately to task for placing the Virgilian Vale of Amsanctus, the umbilicus of Italy, in Lucania; and he disputes his friend Giacomo Bracelli's fanciful mythological etymology of *Genua* (Liguria §24),

as well as received wisdom on Charlemagne's re-foundation of Florence (Tuscany §27) and on the etymology of *Mediolanum* (Lombardy §37).

We must remember, though, that the quality of the texts he had at his disposal inevitably differs very much from what is available to us,[35] and that his interpretation of them could be peculiar, for example at Umbria §2 (on the cities of Spina and Ravenna), where his text allowed a convenient interpretation of Martial (*Ep.* 13.21.1).[36] Sometimes his interpretation might well be subtle wordplay, as in the case of his pun on the name of Stefano Colonna at Lazio §40. Also, the still-evolving state of classical scholarship leads him to make false connections. For example, in Umbria §17, describing the city of Amelia, he concludes a deft, economical account of Cicero's defense of Sextus Roscius as follows: "Roscius later attained such pre-eminence in the actor's craft that Cicero and the other men of that brilliant age would listen rapt to his recitals. He was so accomplished that he wrote a book comparing the actor's art to oratory," thus conflating Roscius of Amelia with Roscius the comic actor, both defendants in separate speeches of Cicero discovered by Poggio a few decades previously.

At other times the coincidence of text, Biondo's understanding of it, and his purpose in using it is perfect. At Umbria §24 Biondo's description of the valley of the river Farfa and Horace's Sabine Farm there, laced with Horatian texts, projects an unmistakable heart's ease and peace: his own state of mind, as owner of the villa of San Biagio. And to his description of the neighborhood of Mola on the coast near the Campanian river Garigliano (Lazio §15) as "the pleasantest land, not just of Italy, but of all the world," Biondo has Cicero's *On the Orator* (2.6, 22–23) to lend perfect believability: "Scipio and Laelius would always go off into the country together and would become marvellously boyish again, once they had flown to the countryside from the city as if slipping their shackles. At Gaeta and Laurentum they used to gather sea-

shells and cockles, and indulge themselves in all manner of diversions and mental relaxation."[37]

Biondo had wealth enough to own books. His station and his friends gave him access to the best libraries and scholarly help. He enjoyed a wonderful memory — even for his era. His learning, energy, and unselfishness were profound. He used these, honestly, methodically, originally — though not without error or immoderation — to combine texts with his own discourse into an absolutely new creation, the *Italy Illuminated*.

Ottavio Clavuot's work on Biondo's sources[38] shows that the greatest number of his citations comes from Livy (the model and darling of Renaissance Latin historians), and that from Pliny the Elder's *Natural History* there are considerably fewer quotations, though still an ample number. Yet the *Italy Illuminated* follows, overall, a Plinian scheme and methodology. It has also, in its love of the curious, a Plinian psychology and feel. The sketchy account (at Lombardy §6), of Countess Matilda's babying of Pope Gregory VII and, when we get to Canossa, of the discomfiture of Henry III, is *de rigueur* in such a survey, but why, apart from Biondo's Plinian love of curiosities, should we learn (at Lombardy §18) that Charles the Bald was murdered at Mantua, poisoned by a bribed Hebrew physician, or (Umbria §8) that at Spoleto (according to Livy 24.10.10), among other prodigies, a woman was once turned into a man? The influence (beyond mere citation) of Strabo's method is fairly obvious, too, and not just where it would be expected: in the section on Lazio. Biondo's study of Ptolemy of Alexandria also makes itself felt. Other geographical writers and writings whose presence is tangible include Pomponius Mela's *On Chorography (De chorographia)*; Gaius Julius Hyginus, cited from Servius; Gaius Julius Solinus' *Collection of Things Memorable (Collectanea rerum memorabilium)*, reinforcing Pliny and Mela; Jordanes in his *Book on the Succession of Kingdoms and Ages (De regnorum ac*

temporum successione liber); the seventh-century Geographus Ravennas (called "Guido Presbyter of Ravenna" by Biondo),[39] and the
third-century *Journey of Antoninus Pius (Itinerarium Antonini Pii).*[40]

Biondo of course also read and used the writings of his fellow
humanists. At Piceno §15, Biondo gives us a simple, wistful (and
deceptively graceful) memoir of his brother antiquarian, Cyriac of
Ancona, lately dead: "she has recently lost Cyriac of Ancona, who
by his investigation of ancient monuments restored the dead to
the memory of the living, as he used to put it." Cyriac had discov-
ered the *Journey of Antoninus Pius* (see Lombardy §4) in 1453,[41] and
Biondo would have read the *Travels of Cyriac of Ancona (Kyriaci
Anconitani itinerarium)*, which surveys the learned men of cities.[42]
And he would have known Boccaccio's geographical work, *On
Mountains, Forests, Fountains, Lakes, Rivers, Marshes [and] On the
Names of the Sea (De montibus, silvis, fontibus, lacubus, fluminibus,
stagnis seu paludibus, de nominibus maris liber)* as well as his work
On the Fates of Illustrious Men (De casibus virorum illustrium) and
Petrarch's *Syrian Journey (Itinerarium Syriacum)*. Probably he also
knew the travelogue of the Camaldolese monk and humanist
Ambrogio Traversari, the *Hodoeporicon*, a survey of the convents of
his order. Like humanism, learned geography was in the air.

In the Quattrocentro, the Italians were superior in geography to
the rest of Europe; at the beginning of the next century, thanks to
the work of Italian explorers and navigators, even more so. After
Biondo, Italy became the home of a species of ethnographic literature describing the cities of Italy (for example Giovanni Gioviano
Pontano's *Antonius*, an imaginary journey through Italy, dedicated
to the Latin poet and humanist Panormita). Biondo's contemporary, Pius II (Enea Silvio Piccolomini), both in his *Notes on Things
Worthy of Memory (Commentarii rerum memorabilium)* and in his
Cosmography, surpasses him as historian and geographer. Biondo
also had direct epigones, for example Leandro Alberti, who in his

Descrizione di tutta l'Italia (1582), is a Biondo magpie and transmitter in the *volgare*, although he could be critical of Biondo as well.[43] Despite its considerable influence, however, the *Italy Illuminated* remains in the end *sui generis*. It is not only a proto-Baedeker, but loose notes for an Italian history, as well as a kind of history of classical scholarship. It has successors to its parts but none quite to its whole.

A brief word about the work's Latinity. Leaving aside any discussion of the relative merits and demerits of the rhetorical-stylish versus the erudite schools of Renaissance historical writing,[44] we must admit right away that Biondo's Latin is not gorgeous. This is not always so in the *Italy Illuminated*, but mostly. It is surprising when we consider his deep respect for Ciceronian eloquence and elegance expressed everywhere in the work and particularly in Romagna §§25–31, and Biondo's criticisms of writers who lacked those qualities. To be sure, Biondo could deploy Ciceronian periods on occasion: in the Preface §5, for example, a formal context, we have genuinely complex Ciceronian periods. And there is much other respectable Ciceronian and neo-classical Latinity in Biondo that is well up to humanistic prose standards. But the encyclopedic format of the *Italy Illuminated* did not encourage elegance. Nor did the author's practice of interweaving bits of ancient authors with his own exposition: for example Tuscany §35, on the ordeal of Hannibal in the Casentino, where the language and argument seem to pass out of Biondo's control. Technical passages, obviously, can create difficulties for him (and us), as in Lazio §49, on Leon Battista Alberti and the raising of the Roman galleys from the Lago di Nemi, where his account of the smelting processes for ships' interiors suffers from an incomplete mastery of technical terminology. That probably he had not been exercised deeply enough and early enough in the would-be-classical Latin prose of the humanists (as I think) means that, in the economy or balance of

efforts between the substance of expression and style of expression, he veered away from style.

We know that Biondo's indebtedness to collaborators and patrons in the composition of the *Italy Illuminated* was great, and complicated.[45] For the Romagna region, he asked Malatesta Novello to review and correct his account, in return for which he would dedicate the *regio* to Novello.[46] This was not simply a conventional politeness: Biondo would have been looking for corrections of localized errors as well as for new material. He made similar arrangements with Alfonso of Aragon and the learned men of his court for the whole Kingdom of Naples, with Cardinal Prospero Colonna for the Lazio region, with Piero de'Medici for Tuscany, with Giacomo Bracelli for the Ligurian region, and the Udinese Jacopo Simeoni for the region of Aquileia.[47] And so, probably, with the remaining *regiones*. When the texts of all were combined into a whole, he removed the dedications. And it was probably the insufficiency of such patronage and collaboration—together with a sense of political and economic urgency—led him, ultimately, to abbreviate the work as we have it.

In 1451 Biondo gave the *Italy Illuminated*—probably in eleven *regiones* minus those dealing with the Kingdom of Naples—to representatives of Alfonso in Venice, to get their help for a further revision. This in effect constituted the first publication of the whole work. Then in 1453, encouraged by friends and aware that Pope Nicholas had read and approved the work (now expanded to fourteen *regiones*) and that he was to be restored to the Curia, he published it again with a formal dedication to Nicholas—a second edition. We know from a number of manuscript witnesses (particularly B) that, after Nicholas's death in 1455, Biondo excised the dedication and all mention of Nicholas and other associations with him from the text (in a kind of *damnatio memoriae*) and added other passages to make another, third recension. And we know

from manuscript E and other sources that finally, after 1458 and until his death in 1463, he appended longer *supplementa* to the regions Liguria and Tuscany at the end of his text (after 1462) and scattered marginal *additiones* (including some rewrites of the excised Nicholas passages, with the pontiff's name removed) throughout. In a letter to Pius II,[48] Biondo explained that the work had been published prematurely to forestall publication of an unauthorized edition of it by a nameless treacherous bishop to whom he had lent a copy and who had altered the text shamelessly. This was the last recension published in the author's lifetime, but after his death his son Gaspare supervised the publication of the first printed edition (1474), which contains still more new material, apparently derived at least in part from papers Gaspare inherited from his father. It is this final edition which is offered here.[49]

This is the first of two volumes. A second will complete the *Italy Illuminated*, with the *regiones* Lombardy, the Veneto, the March of Treviso, Friuli, Istria, Abruzzo, Campania, and Apulia.

For my introduction into classical and Renaissance studies, I am indebted to Leendert Westerink, Paul Oskar Kristeller, Robert Renehan, Ernst Badian (who suggested a dissertation topic that brought me to Biondo Flavio), John M. Duffy, Giuseppe Billanovich, and Steven J. Brown.

To undertake and complete this volume, I was given generous gifts of money and time from St. Bonaventure University (particularly by James P. White, the Dean of the School of Arts and Sciences), the American Philosophical Society, the Gladys Krieble Delmas Foundation, and the Newberry Library, all of which I acknowledge gratefully. Robert K. Sherk, Bruce W. Swann, John Mulryan, and Theresa Shaffer helped me to improve it.

I am happy to acknowledge indebtedness to Martin Davies, who read my translation with great care, removing many errors

and infelicities. James Hankins induced me to see a new pattern for the lines of transmission of the Latin text of the work, much truer and more useful than the one I had discerned. He, the Villa I Tatti, and Harvard University Press have established a series to which one feels lucky to belong.

J.A.W.
St. Bonaventure University
September 2004

NOTES

1. The best general introduction to him in English remains Hay, "Flavio Biondo." Indispensable are: Nogara, *Scritti inediti*; Fubini, "Biondo Flavio"; and Masius, *Flavio Biondo*. (Full references may be found in the Bibliography.)

2. See, e.g., his informed reflections on the "new branch of the Po" at Ficarolo, in Romagna §77.

3. But see Clavuot, *Biondos Italia Illustrata*, p. 9.

4. Bishop Landriani's famous and difficult codex Laudensis had already been deciphered by Gasparino Barzizza's student, Cosimo Raimondi of Cremona (as Biondo notes, at Romagna §29), and there is other evidence suggesting that Biondo did not copy his manuscript directly from the Laudensis. So his claim to be *primus omnium* to copy the work is troublesome language, not fully excused by Biondo's casual use of the superlative of eminence.

5. See, e.g., the encomium of his city at Romagna §§34–35.

6. Nogara, *Scritti inediti*, pp. XLIV–LVI.

7. At Piceno §18, e.g., consider his pride and satisfaction in handling the documentation for the canonization of Nicholas of Tolentino.

8. He appends a revisionist coda to this work, at March of Treviso §3 of the *Italy Illuminated*: "For the Lombards, haughtiest of all the foreigners who invaded Italy, sought to uproot and utterly destroy the prestige of the Roman Empire and of Italy: they laid down new laws (which are still

in force everywhere in Italy), customs, rituals; and they changed the words for peoples and institutions, so that I would venture to say that the change into Italian (now called the *volgare*) worked upon the Latin vocabulary of the speech of the Romans began in the times of the Lombards. And this I did not know when I published my work *On Roman Speech* to Leonardo Bruni."

9. See, particularly, Philip Jacks, *The Antiquarian*, pp. 114–117.

10. See Mazzocco, "Some Philological Aspects."

11. *Oratio . . . coram imperatore Frederico et Alphonso Aragonum rege* (*Speech before the Emperor Frederick and King Alfonso of Aragon*); *Ad Alfonsum Aragonensem . . . de expeditione in Turchos* (*To Alfonso of Aragon . . . on an Expedition against the Turks*); *Ad Petrum de Campo Fregoso . . . Genuae ducem* (*To Pietro da Campofregoso . . . Doge of Genoa*); and *De gestis Venetorum* (*On the Accomplishments of the Venetians*) or *Consultatio an bellum vel pax cum Turcis magis expediat rei publicae Venetorum* (*A Consideration of the Question Whether War or Peace with the Turks Would Be to the Greater Advantage of the Venetian Republic*).

12. The smaller works and a handful of letters are in Nogara, *Scritti inediti.*

13. In the *Italy Illuminated* Eugene's usual epithet is *gloriosus*, and passages like that in Tuscany §42 (on the Venetian monastery of S. Giorgio d'Alga built by the young Condulmer out of his patrimony), or Tuscany §44 (on the pope's assistance to San Bernardino of Siena in his revitalization of the Franciscan rule), or Lazio §25 (on Eugene's help to the Cistercians with the re-establishment of the Abbazia di Fossanova) are not untypical and accurately describe Eugene's character.

14. In his Prologue, he says: "Ego omnia quae mihi adsunt tuae Sanctitati debeo" ("Everything that I have I owe to your Holiness"). And he reminds us of this dedication in Lazio §1 of the *Italy Illuminated.*

15. See his remarks on M. Aurelius Severus Alexander at Preface §1, or Giangaleazzo Visconti at Lombardy §40.

16. See his letter to Bracelli of 10 November 1454 in Nogara, *Scritti inediti*, p. 168.

17. In addition to Hay, Nogara, Fubini and Masius, cited in note 1, above, for the *Italy Illuminated* one may add Husslein, *Flavio Biondo als Geograph.* Clavuot's erudite and exhaustive *Biondos Italia Illustrata* has done more to illuminate every aspect and phase of the work than anyone else. See also White, "Towards a Critical Edition," and Lucarini-Pontari, "Nuovi passi inediti."

18. The text is in A. M. Quirini, *Diatriba praeliminaris* (Brescia: Rizzardi, 1741–43), p. clxxi f.

19. Notwithstanding his mention of the map of Italy (*pictura*) of King Robert of Sicily and Petrarch (at Romagna §68), with a narrative survey (*descriptio*) attached, which he follows "primarily" (i.e., among others). Cf. also his mention of Ptolemaic (Romagna §58) and other earlier maps (Liguria §37). He could hardly have conceptualized the work without maps, of course. See Clavuot, *Biondos Italia Illustrata*, plates 1–8.

20. Consider (at Romagna §12) his treatment of the statute, supposedly in marble — though in fact a forgery (Clavuot, *Biondos Italia Illustrata*, p. 194, n. 218) — that Caesar violated when he crossed the Rubicon: Biondo gives a clear (but impossible) impression of having inspected it *in situ.* See White, "Towards a Critical Edition," p. 274f. with note 28; Castner, "Direct Observation;" see also J. D'Amato, "Cicero's Villa in the Phlegraean Fields," *Viator* 24 (1993): 385–419 (cited by Castner, p. 104, n. 10).

21. On chorography see the *Encyclopedia of the Renaissance*, Paul F. Grendler, ed. (New York: Scribners, 1999), 3: 31–34 (*s.v.* "Geography and Cartography"); and Domenico Defilippis, *La rinascita della corografia.*

22. Region XII (Abruzzo) subsumes Aprutium, Samnium, Lucania, Salentini, Calabria, and Brutii. Region XIII then becomes Campania, and Region XIV, Apulia.

23. Except for Etruria: see Tuscany §1.

24. When Biondo changes this orientation (as at Lazio §19), he feels the reader is owed an explanation: "In describing this inland region, we shall not be able to adhere to the plan used in other regions, orienting ourselves by the mouths, sources and course of rivers. We shall adopt an-

other method (one suited to this region alone) which will meet our needs better, by proceeding along three roads, the Appian, Latin, and Tiburtine, which lead in different ways to the river Liri and to Sinuessa and Gaeta."

25. See Wallace K. Ferguson, *The Renaissance in Historical Thought* (Boston: Houghton Mifflin, 1948), pp. 12ff.

26. "All that is of general significance seems to be hooked on to the province of Romagna . . . This extraordinary mixture of the parochial and the broad view exactly fixes the ablest Renaissance attempt to view Italy as a unit." See Denys Hay, *The Italian Renaissance in Its Historical Background* (Cambridge: Cambridge University Press, 1961), p. 35 and pp. 37–38.

27. Necessarily strung out over all *regiones*, unlike Romagna §§25–31: but see, e.g., the surveys of the humanists of Florence (Tuscany §§28–32), Siena (Tuscany §44), Milan (Lombardy §§40–42), and Venice (Venice §§21–28).

28. "Leonardo Giustiniani, a man of great and lordly character, who, his cultural pursuits in Latin and Greek apart, was in youth and young manhood devoted to music and filled all of Italy with the prettiest songs wittily composed in the *volgare* . . ."

29. White, "Towards a Critical Edition," p. 268 and n. 4.

30. And a few Greek, like Strabo, Ptolemy, Eusebius, Plutarch, in Latin translation. Clavuot, *Biondos Italia Illustrata*, pp. 138–302, on Biondo's sources, ancient, medieval, contemporary and near-contemporary, repays study, and his careful "Verzeichnis der von Biondo gekennzeichneten Zitate" (pp. 307–322) is invaluable.

31. Other, less frequently cited sources are given in the Notes to the Translation, and in Clavuot's "Verzeichnis" (as above in note 30).

32. Here he is perhaps alluding to his older contemporary, Leonardo Bruni, who in the preface to his *History of the Florentine* remarks that he was discouraged from undertaking the work by the necessity of violating taste and employing barbarous names; see his *History of the Florentine*

People, ed. James Hankins, I Tatti Renaissance Library 3 (Cambridge, Mass.: Harvard University Press, 2001), vol. 1, p. 3.

33. At Lazio §24, Biondo's confusion of Atina with Aricia (and his misreporting of Virgil and Servius [*A.* 7.630]; but cf. Lazio §8, where he has it right) must be the result of the desire for inclusiveness—though, lacking Greek, he would not have known that Servius' fanciful etymology of Atina could not apply to Aricia.

34. See Cameron, "Biondo's Ammianus," which builds on Cappelletto, *Recuperi ammianei* and idem, "Passi nuovi."

35. See White, "Towards a Critical Edition," p. 269 and n. 9.

36. Which raises a further question, for at Romagna §32, speaking of Ravenna, he repeats the verse in the proper understanding.

37. The passage was made famous in the Renaissance by its citation in Pier Paolo Vergerio's *De ingenuis moribus*; see *Humanist Educational Treatises*, ed. Craig Kallendorf, I Tatti Renaissance Library 5 (Cambridge, Mass.: Harvard University Press, 2002), p. 85.

38. Above, note 31.

39. After "Quido of Pisa," who excerpted him in the twelfth century (see Husslein, *Flavio Biondo als Geograph*, p. 14).

40. Ibid., with note 6.

41. Remigio Sabbadini, *Le scoperte dei codici latini e greci ne' secoli XIV e XV* (Florence: Sansoni, 1914), 2: 201.

42. On Cyriac's life and writings, see the introduction to Cyriac of Ancona, *Later Travels*, ed. Edward W. Bodnar, I Tatti Renaissance Library 10 (Cambridge, Mass.: Harvard University Press, 2003).

43. Jacob Burckhardt, *The Civilization of the Renaissance in Italy*, tr. S. G. C. Middlemore, 2 vols. (New York: Harper and Row, 1958), pp. 281f., 297, 234–236; Georg Voigt, *Enea Silvio als Papst Pius der Zweite und sein Zeitalter*, 2 vols. (Berlin, 1856–63), pp. 302–309 (cited by Burckhardt, p. 281 n. 3); Husslein, *Flavio Biondo als Geograph*, p. 5f.

44. See Hay, "Flavio Biondo," p. 98f.

45. See Clavuot's reconstruction of the work's collaborative composi-

tion and complicated publication history in his *Biondos Italia Illustrata*, pp. 46–56. See also White, "Towards a Critical Edition," pp. 276–279; Lucarini-Pontari, "Nuovi passi inediti"; and Pontari, "Ancora su passi inediti."

46. Campana, "Passi inediti."

47. Bracelli's *Description of the Ligurian Coast* has been mentioned above. Like Simeoni's *On the Nobility and Antiquity of the City of Aquileia (De nobilitate et antiquitate civitatis aquileinsis)*, it was occasioned by Biondo's request. For the dedication of Tuscany to Piero de'Medici, son of Cosimo, see Lucarini-Pontari, "Passi inediti."

48. Text in Nogara, *Scritti inediti*, p. 227f.

49. See further in the Note on the Text.

ITALY ILLUMINATED

BLONDI FLAVII FORLIVIENSIS
ITALIA ILLUSTRATA

Praefatio

1 Cum multi historiam, *beatissime pater,*[1] variis celebrent extollantque sententiis, tum maxime Alexander Antoninus, Mamaea genitus christiana, imperator Romanus omnium iudicio optimus, unica illa ratione eam amplissime videtur laudasse, qui historicos et suos appellavit et habere voluit consiliarios, quorum prudentia et exemplorum copia gerendis imperii rebus quam maxime uteretur. Clarissimi etiam plerique senatores, consularesque viri, et nonnulli gloriosissimi principes, qui bellicis artibus res gesserunt aeterna dignas memoria, delectati sunt historia, usque adeo ut non solum historias libenter legerint, sed eas quoque scribendo tam praeclari muneris gloriam cum rerum scriptoribus communem habere voluerint. Nam, ut ceteros taceam, Fabius, patriciae gentis decus, cognomento Pictor, Lucius Lucullus, Aulus Albinus, Asinius Pollio, Cornelius Nepos, et Gaius Caesar, eiusque nepos Octavius Augustus, ac Hadrianus scripsere historias.[2]

2 Sed tantum hoc tam clarumque munus praeteritorum longe saeculorum malitia et infelicitate maximam accepit iniuriam, quod, urbe Roma a variis gentibus (sicut in *Historiis* accuratius a nobis est scriptum) oppressa, etsi bonarum artium studia inter-

BIONDO FLAVIO OF FORLI
ITALY ILLUMINATED

Preface

While many, *Most Holy Father*, variously extol and sing the praises
of writing history, it is Alexander Antoninus, by universal consent
the best of the Roman emperors (and the son of a Christian
mother, Mamaea), who was apparently unique in the abundance
of his praise when he placed historians under his own patronage
and sought to have them as his advisors, so that he might make
the maximum use, in conducting the affairs of empire, of the practical wisdom with which their wealth of models and precedents
drawn from history could provide him.[1] Furthermore, many famous men of senatorial rank, as well as men of consular rank, too,
and a number of illustrious princes, the successes of whose policies
in the military sphere merit eternal memory, were fascinated by
the accounts of the historians, so much so that not only did they
take pleasure in these accounts, but they sought as well to share
with the historians — by composing histories, too — the renown of
so distinguished an office. To give but a few examples, Fabius, surnamed Pictor, the glory of the patricians, Lucius Lucullus, Asinius
Pollio, Cornelius Nepos, Gaius Caesar and his nephew Octavius
Augustus,[2] as well as Hadrian, all wrote history.

But this great office today encounters a most severe impedi-
ment owing to the vices and to the simple ill luck of generations of
men long dead. For with the inundation of the City of Rome by a
succession of different peoples (as I recounted in considerable detail in my *Histories*), while the cultivation of the liberal arts was
only temporarily allowed to lapse, the art of writing history alone
failed utterly and was snuffed out. And because the barbarians

1

2

3

missa fuerunt, sola in primis omnino cessavit extinctaque est historia. Quo factum est ut, barbaris omnia evertentibus et nullo interim ea quae gerebantur litterarum monumentis ad posteros transmittente, nedum mille qui effluxerunt annorum gesta sciamus, sed Italiae regiones, urbes, oppida, lacus, flumina, montesque, quorum nomina a vetustis frequentantur scriptoribus, ubi sint magna ex parte ignoremus, et, quod maiorem nobis affert admirationem, multorum oppidorum et potentissimarum civitatum, quas interea in magnam amplitudinem crevisse cernimus, conditarum tempora nos lateant et ipsi etiam conditores.

3   Itaque, postquam propitiore nobis deo nostro meliora habet aetas nostra, et cum ceterarum artium tum maxime eloquentiae studia revixerunt, ac per ea historiarum diligentius noscendarum amor nostros homines cepit, tentare volui an per eam quam sum nactus Italiae rerum peritiam vetustioribus locis eius et populis nominum novitatem, novis auctoritatem, deletis vitam memoriae dare, denique rerum Italiae obscuritatem illustrare potero.

4   Nec tamen ipsam omnem nominum mutationem temeraria et inani arrogantia indicare spoponderim; sed gratias mihi potius de perductis ad litus e tanto naufragio supernatantibus, parum autem apparentibus, tabulis haberi, quam de tota navi desiderata rationem a me exposci debere contenderim.

5   *Tibi autem, beatissime pater Nicolae quinte pontifex Romane,[3] ut hos dedicem libros, non me magis movit spes intentioque tibi (sicut debeo*

confounded everything and because no one, meanwhile, sough
transmit to posterity via the literary record what was being d
we as a result are in great part ignorant of the very location of
regions of Italy, of the cities, towns, lakes and mountains, wh
names appear so frequently in the ancient authors, to say noth
of the historical events of the millennium that has elapsed; a
what causes me the greater astonishment, the dates of the esta
lishment of many towns and mighty cities, which we perceive
have grown in the interim to great consequence, are hidden fro
us, as are the names of their founders.

And so, seeing that the times have changed for the better, ou
God being more gracious to us now; and seeing that the cultivation of the rest of the arts and of eloquence, especially, has come
alive again; and seeing that, because of these developments, a passion to study history in greater depth has caught up the men of
our time, I wanted to discover if, through the practical experience
of the history of Italy I have gained, I shall be able to apply the
names of current coinage to the appropriate places and peoples of
Italian antiquity, to settle the authenticity of the new nomenclature, to revive and record the names that have been obliterated,
and in a word to bring some light to bear upon the murkiness of
Italian history.

Nevertheless, I should prefer not to pledge myself to give infor-   4
mation regarding the full extent of the transformation of names,
which would be rash and vainglorious, but I would propose that I
be thanked for having hauled ashore some planks from so vast a
shipwreck, planks which were floating on the surface of the water
or nearly lost to view, rather than be required to account for the
entire lost ship.

It is not so much the hope and the conscious design of finding favor with   5
you (as is my duty and desire) that impels me to dedicate this book to you,
Most Holy Father, Roman Pontiff Nicholas V.[3] *A greater motive is your*
sure mastery of all learning, of the whole of antiquity, of universal history

optoque) placandi, quam notissima mihi ac longissima consuetudine intellecta omnis doctrinae, omnis vetustatis, omnis historiae, et dignitatis Italiae peritia tua, in qua ceteros saeculi nostri homines vel peritissimos facile antecellis: quae profecto efficiet ut, si mea scripta a te laudatissimo et rei ipsius callentissimo laudabuntur, nihil[4] maius solidiusque scriptorum ipsorum dignitati et gloriae possit accedere; ut certior esse possim hoc ipso in munere nec operam mihi, ut aiunt, ullatenus iri perditum nec impensam, qui, dum nil aliud ago, sim in otio negotiosus; ut in Italia a me tuis auspiciis illustrata, pro intermortua temporum culpa vetustarum rerum memoria, cum doctissimorum huius aetatis virorum catalogo in lucem renovata, tecum in futurum et cum praesentis aevi posterisque praestantioribus quibusque hominibus doctis vivam.

6   *Tu praeterea primarias urbis Romae basilicas, Petri Apostolorum principis, Lateranensemque, et Virginis Dei nostri genetricis maiorem, Stephanique[5] protomartyris rotundam alteramque superbissimam olim Pantheon rotundam, et minores aliquot multa instaurasti decorastique[6] impensa. Tu primarium orbis papale palatium altissimis communitum crassissimisque turribus atque muris, sic omnes orbis publicas aedes magnificentia operis et vario splendidissimoque ornatu superare fecisti, sicut ipse ceteros principes dignitate et virtutibus antecellis.*

7   *Tu denique beati Petri, cuius a Deo commissas vices in orbe geris, altare suis sacratissimum ossibus absida pergis tanto numini sua celsitudine responsura decorare. Unde est decens, ut tu, inquam[7], qui urbem Romam, rerum et orbis decus, fabrorum manibus tantopere exornasti,[8] eiusque et*

and of the greatness of Italy; your mastery most well known to me and understood by reason of long familiarity; your mastery, in the matter of which you easily surpass the rest of the men of our century, even the most learned; your mastery which, should you praise my writing (given that you yourself are highly praised and accomplished in this subject), will undoubtedly ensure that nothing greater or of more substance can attach to the prestige and renown of these very writings. As a result I can be the more assured in the case of this very task that I shall lose neither care nor expense in any respect whatsoever, as they say; I who, while doing nothing else, keep busy in the midst of my leisure.[4] As a result, I shall live on with you into the future, together with all the more distinguished learned men both of this era and of the eras to come, in my Italy Illuminated, which under your auspices, instead of being an historical account of antiquity destined to perish owing to the fault of the times, shall be renewed in the light of day, listed in the catalogue of the most learned men of this age.[5]

Besides, you have at great expense restored and embellished the chiefest 6
basilicas of the City of Rome: the Basilica of St. Peter, Prince of the Apostles; of St. John Lateran; the Greater Basilica of the Virgin Mother of Our Lord;[6] the Rotunda of St. Stephen Protomartyr;[7] and a second superb rotunda, formerly the Pantheon,[8] and a number of lesser structures. By your orders the chiefest papal palace of the world, secured by innumerable lofty turrets and by walls, now surpasses in the magnificence of its workmanship and in its manifold and most splendid embellishments all the public buildings of the world, just as you yourself surpass all other princes in your station and in your virtues.

Finally, the altar of Blessed Peter, the altar made holy by his bones — the 7
Peter whose role, as ordained by God, you discharge in the world — you strive to embellish with an apse that will match the loftiness of so great a divine spirit. Hence it is fitting that you, I say — who have so greatly ornamented the City of Rome by the skill of craftsmen, making her the glory of the world and of the universe, and who have restored the walls, the beautifully fortified citadel, and the roads of Rome and of the Vatican — should illuminate, as it were, Italy too, on this account: because the Italy Illumi-

Vaticani moenia, arcem perpulchre munitam, et vias restituisti, Italiam quoque vel ea ratione illustres, quod ea, servi tui manuum opus, tuo dicata nomini, in tuamque suscepta protectionem, simul cum praedictis tuum opus censeri poterit. Diu bene valeat Sanctitas tua.[9]

nated, *the work of the hands of your servant, dedicated to your name, by being taken under your protection can be counted as your own work, along with the works previously mentioned. May Your Holiness prosper long and well.*

LIBER I

Regio prima. Liguria[1]

1 Italiam describere exorsi, provinciarum orbis primariam, a laudibus suis incipere debuimus, quod quidem pro ampla parataque materia tam faciliter quam libenter fecissemus, nisi ab eximio poeta Vergilio, et post a Plinio Veronense, demum a Francisco Petrarcha insigni poeta ornatissimae illius laudationes exstarent. Itaque a suo nomine et situ duximus inchoandum.

2 Nomen pro temporum diversitate nacta est varium. Nam Plinius et Solinus ab Italo rege quosdam, et nonnullos a bobus quos gigneret multos prisca lingua Italiam dici voluisse scripserunt; cum tamen eam Graeci Magnam interea Hesperiam appellarint, quod secutus est in VII Vergilius: 'Hesperia in magna'. et Servius exponit: 'Hesperia in magna dixisse Vergilium ad Hispaniae discretionem'. Iustinus autem in *Trogi epitomate* scribit: 'Italiae cultores primos fuisse aborigines, quorum rex Saturnus tantae iustitiae fuerit, ut neque serviret quisquam sub illo neque quicquam privatae rei haberet, sed communia et indivisa fuerint omnia: unde Italia regis nomine Saturnia fuerit appellata'.

3 Ea vero, sicut Plinius ex Octavio Augusto tradit, querno folio adsimilis, mari gemino maxima parte cingitur, quod ab oriente Adriatico, sive Supero, et a meridie atque occasu Tyrrheno, sive

BOOK I

Region 1. Liguria

Having undertaken to write a description of Italy, the foremost of 1
the provinces of the world, I ought to begin with her praises, and
given the wealth of material at hand I should have done so with
ease and good will did there not exist already most splendid enco-
mia in her honor by the excellent poet Vergil, and later by Pliny of
Verona, and finally by the distinguished poet Francesco Petrarca.[1]
So I decided that I ought rather to begin with her name and her
geography.

Italy has acquired at different times a variety of names. Pliny 2
and Solinus[2] wrote that certain authorities had held that she was
named *Italia* for Italus, the king, while some others thought she
was called after the name (in the ancient tongue) for the cat-
tle which she produced in abundance.[3] Nevertheless, the Greeks
called her Magna Hesperia, a practice which Virgil followed in
Book VII [of the *Aeneid*]: "in great Hesperia."[4] (And Servius explains: "Vergil wrote 'in great Hesperia,' to distinguish her from
Spain.")[5] Justin, moreover, in his *Epitome* of Trogus, writes that
"the first inhabitants of Italy were the Aborigines, whose king,
Saturnus, was a figure of such great righteousness that no one
toiled as a slave during his reign or held any private property, but
everything was shared and held in common. For this reason, Italy
was called Saturnia, after the name of the king."[6]

Now the Italian peninsula is for the most part encompassed 3
like an oak leaf[7] (as Pliny says, handing on the *mot* of the Emperor
Octavius) by a twin sea, in that she is washed on the east by the
Adriatic (or Upper Sea), and on the south and on the west by the
Tyrrhenian Sea (or Lower Sea). But where she stretches north-

Infero, abluitur. Qua vero in septentrionem vergit, montes altissimi, Alpes lingua Gallica a celsitudine dicti, illam a barbarorum, ut inquit Cicero, incursu naturae benignitate communiunt. Longitudo eius ab Alpino sinu Praetoriae Augustae ad Hydruntum decies centena et viginti passuum milia extenditur. Latitudo, ubi est amplior, a Varo ad Arsiam, quadringenta et quinquaginta. Et circa urbem Romam ab ostiis Aterni, nunc Piscariae, in Adriaticum defluentis, ad Tiberina ostia, centum et viginti sex milia. Totusque ambitus a Varo ad Arsiam tricies centena et insuper triginta octo milia complectitur. Habet vero Italia dorsum et, ceu in piscibus esse videmus, a capite in infimam partem spinae formam, Apenninum, qui mons ex Alpibus qua ab infero mari recedunt oriundus, cum recto propemodum cursu Anconae urbi, ut vult Plinius, appropinquavit, in mare superum ferri et ibi finiri videtur; et tamen inde rursus, ab eo mari recedens, per mediam Italiam in Bruttios ac Siculum fretum fertur.

4   Situ mensuraque ostensis, ad regionum divisionem locorumque descriptionem veniamus.

5   Est vero perdifficile in tanta mutatione rerum regionumque (quantam vident factam qui Romanas historias attente legunt) modum adinvenire dividendis regionibus, recensendisque ordine civitatum, oppidorum, montium, fluminumque vocabulis. Et quidem quantum attinet ad ipsa vocabula, eximius scriptor Livius Pa-

ward, very high mountains, called "Alps" in the Gallic tongue because of their loftiness, provide her with a bulwark, thanks to the
beneficence of nature, as Cicero says, against the assault of the
barbarians.[8] She extends, lengthwise, from the Alpine valley of
Aosta to Otranto for 1,020 miles; in breadth, at her widest, from
the Var to the Arsa, she extends for 450 miles. And on the lati-
tude of the City of Rome, from the mouth of the Aternus, now
the Pescara, which flows down into the Adriatic, to the mouth of
the Tiber, she extends for 126 miles. The perimeter of the Italian
peninsula in its entirety, from the Var to the Arsa, measures 3,038
miles.[9] Italy has a kind of backbone, like the one we see in fish,
running from her head to the tip of the tail: the Apennine Ridge.
This mountain range arises in the Alps where they march away
from the Tyrrhennian Sea, and after it has come down to the city
of Ancona (almost in a straight line, according to Pliny) it seems
to continue on towards the Adriatic and to come to an end there;
and yet from that point it again marches away from that sea,
straight across the middle of Italy to the land of the Bruttii and
the Straits of Messina.[10]

Now that I have set out the dimensions and situation of Italy   4
for examination, let us next consider the delimitation and the topography of her regions.

To be sure, it is extremely difficult, amidst such enormous   5
changes in the history and geographical subdivisions of Italy (and
those who read Roman history carefully realize the scale of the
changes), to devise and to apply a means for delimiting these regions and for reviewing systematically the nomenclature of their
cities, towns, mountains and rivers. And, indeed, as for the names
themselves, Livy of Padua, the Father of Roman history, in the
portion of his work which is left to us, uses the names of peoples
who barely survived into his day, to say nothing of our own. For
the fact that many towns and very many peoples have perished
whose names appear again and again in Livy, in that most pains-

tavinus, Romanae pater historiae, qua in parte nobis superest, populorum nominibus utitur, qui nedum ad nostram, sed parva ex
parte ad suam pervenerunt aetatem. Quod enim ex Strabonis Cre-
tensis *Geographia* ac ex Plinii Veronensis *Naturali historia* conicere
facile est, in Octavii Augusti, cuius temporibus et adiumento
scripsit Livius, descriptione Italiae quam fecit accuratissimam, in-
terierant multa oppida plurimique populi, quorum nomina apud
Livium celebrantur. In ea vero descriptione, quam Plinius ipse
anno vix octogesimo post functum vita Octavium diligenter fecit,
maior quam pro temporum brevitate et florentium tunc Italiae rerum condicione par fuerit, mutatio est facta. Quae autem ex Strabonis primum, post ex Plinii enumeratione, et Pomponii Melae ac
Ptolemaei descriptionibus, haud quaquam multum distantibus inter se aetatibus factis, desint nobis, horrendum infinitumque fuerit
referre; et quamquam multos interiisse populos, multa excisa oppida, multas deletas urbes non negaverim, plurimas tamen ex ipsis
simul cum regionibus, montibus, et fluminibus mutasse nomina
constat: quo fit, ut nec prisca legentes intellegant, neque possit novus scriptor illis uti uocabulis, magnam vel eo ipso, quod apud illustres vetustosque scriptores frequentia habentur, dignitatem historiae allaturis.

6   Factam vero esse locorum nominumque mutationem et simul
exinanitam esse populis et urbibus ac oppidis, quorum nomina
nobis desunt, Italiam hinc tenemus, quod post habita urbis Romae
populi magnitudine, cui nihil in orbe umquam fuit estque nunc
par, iactura, nulla nunc est huius saeculi et felicium, quae stante re
publica fuerunt, saeculorum comparatio multitudinis populorum.
Picenem enim infra ex Plinio ostendemus trecenta sexaginta milia

taking description he drew up of the Italy of Octavius Augustus (whose contemporary he was and with whose assistance he wrote) is easy to surmise from the *Natural History* of Pliny of Verona and from the *Geography* of Strabo of Crete. In fact, in that survey which Pliny himself carefully put together scarcely eighty years after the death of Octavius, upheaval has taken place on a larger scale than seems reasonable, considering the brief period of elapsed time between the age of Livy and Augustus and that of Pliny, and considering the prosperous circumstances which Italy enjoyed at that time. It would be a dreadful and endless task to describe those upheavals from the enumeration first of Strabo, then of Pliny, and from the surveys of Pomponius Mela and Ptolemy, works composed at very nearly the same time; and, although I would not deny that many peoples have perished, many towns have been extirpated, many cities have been reduced in station, it is, nevertheless, a matter of fact that many of these, together with their regions, mountains and rivers, have [merely] changed their names. The result is that those who read the ancient names do not recognize them, nor can the writer of our day make use of them to impart to his historical account the grandeur that stems, precisely, from the frequency with which these names are encountered in the works of the illustrious writers of antiquity.

I maintain that Italy has been drained of peoples and cities and 6 towns whose very names are lost to us, and hence, at the same time, a transformation of places and names has taken place; and quite apart from the loss of greatness on the part of the City of the People of Rome—whose like the world has never seen, nor sees now—there is now no comparing the size of Italy's population in this present age with the population of those happy ages which flourished while the Republic endured. For example, Piceno, as I shall show below (using Pliny as a source), surrendered 360,000 men to the Republic[11]—a region which now has hardly a tithe of that amount. Pliny also, in reciting the praises of Italy of his own

in rei publicae deditionem dedisse, quod nunc vix decimam partem habet. Plinius etiam, laudes Italiae suorum priorumque temporum narrans, 'eam' dicit 'diis sacram, L. Aemilio Paulo, C. Atilio consulibus nuntiato Gallico tumultu, solam sine auxiliis externorum atque etiam tunc sine ullis Transpadanis equitum triginta, peditum octoginta milia armasse'. Nostra vero huius temporis Italia quantum sine Transpadanis externorumque auxiliis equitatum peditatumque armaret, non satis facile est nobis iudicare; sed non dubitamus quin difficile sit futurum, si tertiam quis partem conatus fuerit ita armare, ut extra fines quisque suos in bellum expeditionemque ducatur.

7   Quanta autem sit facta locorum mutatio hinc etiam apparet, quod Iginius qui de urbibus Italiae scripsit et eum secutus Guido Presbyter Ravennas prodidere septingentas fuisse Italiae civitates. Nos vero nunc Romanae Ecclesiae stilum secuti, facta per singulas regiones diligenti enumeratione, sexaginta quattuor supra ducentas tantummodo invenimus. Sed appellant Romanae Ecclesiae instituta ciuitates loca quae episcopos habent; et Iginium videmus ac Guidonem etiam multa ex oppidis, quae nostra aetate proprio carentia episcopo alterius dioceseos censentur, pro civitatibus posuisse; et tamen omnium ab ipsis positorum pro civitatibus, quae nunc exstent, numerus vix quadringenta complectitur loca, ut uel excisas esse civitates aut mutationem omnino incognitam in eis factam esse necessarium videamus.

8   Quam aliis fortasse impossibilem visam tot locorum acceptam in Italia per sexcentos annos, qui post Guidonis tempora fluxerunt, cladem nos ideo minus mirabilem ducimus, quia scimus videmusque per saeculum nostrum, quod dei nostri munere eorum quae ante patrum nostrorum aetatem fuerunt saeculorum respectu felix appellari potest, supra triginta civitates et oppida solo ae-

and of earlier times, states that "when an insurrection of the Gauls was reported during the consulship of L. Aemilius Paulus and C. Atilius, Italy, a land sacred to the gods, had armed and put into the field 30,000 horse and 80,000 infantry without any foreign auxiliaries and even without (at that time) any Transpadane Italians."[12] How many horse and infantry our Italy of the present day could arm and put into the field—excepting foreign auxiliaries and Transpadane Italians—cannot readily be judged; but, doubtless it would be difficult for anyone to try and arm a third so many in this way, as each [of the individual Italian states] leads its own forces on military campaigns.[13]

How great are the geographical changes that have occurred is   7
clear, too, from the fact that Hyginus, who wrote about the cities of Italy, and Guido Presbyter of Ravenna who followed Hyginus, both have related that there were once 700 cities in Italy.[14] Yet now, following the mode of reckoning of the Church of Rome, after making a painstaking survey of the regions of Italy one by one, I can find no more than 264. To be sure, the practice of the Church of Rome is to call cities those places that have bishops; and I observe that Hyginus, and Guido, too, designate as cities many towns that in our time are reckoned to belong to another diocese because they lack their own bishop. Yet the total of all such towns reckoned by them as cities and which are now extant comes to barely forty; so of necessity we can see that [the remaining 396] cities were destroyed or subjected to some entirely unknown transformation.

A calamity of the nature that has fallen to our lot in Italy over   8
the 600 years which have passed since the times of Guido seems impossible to many, perhaps; but I think it the less extraordinary because I know and see that in my time—which thanks to the generosity of our God can be termed fortunate by comparison with our forefathers' times—over thirty cities and towns have been razed; as a result, some of them are now inhabited by but a

quata, ut cum eorum pars paucis nunc habitetur colonis, tum pars omnino manserit derelicta. Cunium namque oppidum Romandiolae, a quo clarissima fluxit Comitum Cunii et Lugi familia, omnino derelictum, ut nunc aretur, videmus. Pariter propinquo in loco contigit Barbiano; pariter in Latio vetustissimae urbi Praenestae, Zagarolo, et Gallicano oppidis; pariter ad aliam urbis Romae partem Centumcellensi civitati Morlupoque castello nos accidisse conspeximus.

9   Par etiam affert hac in descriptione incommodum divisionis nominationisque regionum mutatio, ter quaterque in aliquibus et in quibusdam pluries facta, adeo ut solae Etruriae vetusta cum finibus suis et integra manserit appellatio. Quam ob rem decem et octo regionibus, in quot Italiam sine insulis commode divisam esse iudicavimus, describendis, illa ex multis sequemur vocabula, quae cum in aetate nostra sint notiora, tum nostrae intentioni accommodatiora videbuntur. Suntque nomina: Liguria sive Genuensis, Etruria, Latina sive Campania et Maritima, Umbria sive Ducatus Spoletanus, Picenem sive Marchia Anconitana, Romandiola sive Flaminia et Aemilia, Gallia Cisalpina sive Lombardia, Venetiae, Italia Transpadana sive Marchia Tarvisina, Aquileiensis sive Foroiuliana, Histria, Samnium sive Aprutium, Terra Laboris siue Campania Vetus, Lucania, Apulia, Salentini sive Terra Hydrunti, Calabria, Brutii.

10   Postquam vero omnem Italiam peragraturus ero, viros praestantiores qui singulis in urbibus et locis pridem geniti fuerunt, eosque qui sunt superstites, praesertim litterarum aut cuiuspiam virtutis gloria claros, enumerabo; atque res in singulis locis scribi dignas breviter enarrabo, ut non magis haec Italiae sit descriptio quam virorum eius illustrium praestantiumque catalogus ac non parvae partis historiarum Italiae breviarium.

few settlers, while others have remained altogether deserted. For example, Cunio, a town of the Romagna, the original home of the illustrious family of the Counts of Cunio and Lugo, is now so entirely derelict that we see it being used as farmland. A like fate befell nearby Barbiano; in Lazio, the same ill fortune befell the venerable city of Praeneste,[15] and the towns of Zagarolo and Gallicano; to the north of Rome, we have witnessed similar disasters befall the city of Civitavecchia and Morlupo Castella.

Changes, moreover, in the boundaries and in the names of the regions of Italy — three or four changes in some cases and more in certain others — make for the same kind of inconvenience in compiling this survey of mine. Only Etruria has kept her full ancient name along with her boundaries.[16] So in surveying the eighteen regions of Italy (excluding the islands) — for I determined that she could be most conveniently divided so — I shall follow that nomenclature (out of the many possible) that is most familiar in our era and seems best adapted to my purpose. These names are: Liguria (or the Genoese territory), Tuscany, Lazio (or Campania and the coastal region), Umbria (or the Duchy of Spoleto), Piceno (or the March of Ancona), Romagna (or Flaminia and Emilia), Cisalpine Gaul (or Lombardy), Venice, Transpadine Italy (or the March of Treviso), Aquileia (or Foroiuliana), Istria; the Sannio (or the Abruzzi); the Terra di Lavoro (or Campania Vetus), Lucania,[17] Puglia, the Salentino (or Terra d'Otranto), Calabria and the land of the Brutii.

After I have ranged over all of Italy, I shall enumerate the preeminent men born in former times in her cities and regions severally, as well as those who are living still, especially those who have distinguished themselves with a reputation for letters or for any great virtue; and I shall briefly set forth the noteworthy historical events of her individual regions. So this work will be not just a description of Italy, but also a catalogue of her famous and outstanding men, as well as a summary of no small part of Italian history.

9

10

11   Ab Liguria autem Plinium secuti duximus inchoandum. Ea regio latissimos aliquando habuit terminos, quippe cum Pisas in Liguribus conditas Trogus scripserit, et Apuanos Ligures, quos agri Pisani populos esse constat, a maioribus traditum viderimus. Quin 'Massiliam' Trogus Pompeius 'inter Ligures et feras Gallorum gentes positam' dicit. Cui opinioni concordat Livius, libro *XLVII, his verbis: 'Q. Opimius consul Transalpinos Ligures, qui Massiliensium oppidum Antipolim et Niceam vastabant, subegit'; idemque, libro²* *XLI: 'Fulvius Flaccus primus Transalpinos Ligures domuit bello, missus in auxilium Massiliensium adversus Salluvios³ Gallos, qui fines Massiliensium populabantur'.* Et plerique Lucam Liguriae ultimam posuere. Sed haec remotiora omittentes, satis fore tenemus, si divisionem Italiae, quae Romana re publica florente fuit, nostris temporibus accommodare poterimus. Igitur Liguria a Varo flumine ad Macrae amnis ostia longitudinem habet; et hinc Apennino, inde mari infero clauditur, qua ratione pars inferi maris, adiacens a Varo ad Macram, dicitur Ligusticum pelagus.

12   Populi eius provinciae, Ligures, quo tempore quibusve ducibus a Romano populo subacti fuerint, Iordanus Constantinopolitanus monachus, qui Iustiniani imperatoris temporibus rerum a populo Romano gestarum epitoma confecit, et L. Florus, T. Livii abbreviator, iisdem ferme verbis sic habent: 'Peracto Punico bello

I have determined that I ought to begin my survey with Ligu- 11
ria, following Pliny. This region once had very broad boundaries,
since in fact the city of Pisa was founded in Ligurian territory, as
Trogus has written;[18] and we have it as a matter of tradition that
the Apuani are Ligurian—the Apuani being a people of the Pisan
territory, as is well known. Indeed, Trogus Pompeius says that
"Marseilles was situated between the Ligurians and the wild, un-
civilized tribes of the Gauls."[19] With this opinion Livy, in Book
XLVII, concurs: "The consul Q. Opimius subdued the Transalpine Ligurians, who were laying waste to the town of the Massilians, Antibes and Nice."[20] And Livy says, in Book XLI: "Fulvius Flaccus was the first to humble the Transalpine Ligurians in
war; he was sent in aid of the Massilians against the Saluvian
Gauls, who were ravaging the Massilians' territory."[21] Also, most
authorities made Lucca the southernmost city of Liguria. But I
shall pass over these remoter parts of Liguria, regarding it as suffi-
cient if I adapt to our own times the regional division of Italy that
obtained while the Roman Republic was at the height of its
power. Accordingly, Liguria extends lengthwise from the river Var
to the mouth of the river Magra; she is bounded on the one side
by the Apennines, on the other by the Tyrrhenian Sea, which is
the reason that the portion of the Tyrrhenian Sea along the coast
between the Var and the Magra is called the Ligustine Sea.

As to when and under which generals the peoples of this prov- 12
ince, the Ligures, were subjugated by the Roman People, the monk
Jordanus of Constantinople, who compiled a digest of the achievements of the Roman People in the times of the emperor Justinian,
and Lucius Florus, the epitomator of Livy, give the following,
nearly verbatim, account: "At the conclusion of the first war with
Carthage the Ligustine war ensued without the briefest pause for
breath.[22] The Ligures used to subsist huddled along the Alpine
foothills between the Var and the Magra, enmeshed in woodland
thickets, and it was nearly a greater task to flush them out than to

primo nec quantulum respirato, sequitur Ligusticum. Ligures imis Alpium iugis adhaerentes inter Varum Macramque amnes impliciti dumis silvestribus victitabant, quos paene maius fuit invenire quam vincere. Tuti siquidem locis et fuga, durum atque uelox genus, ex occasione locorum latrocinia magis quam bella factitabant. Itaque, cum diu multumque eluderent Salluvii, Deciates, Oxybii et Briniates,[4] Ingauni, tandem Fulvius latebras eorum igne saepsit, Baebius vero in plana deduxit, Postumius ita exarmavit ut vix linqueret ferrum quo terra coleretur'.

13   Quod vero Iordanus summatim attigit, Ligures obstinatius iugum Romanorum recusasse et illis animose adversatos fuisse, Livius ipse in libris qui exstant multis ostendit in locis. Nam, libro IX: 'Dum haec Romae geruntur, consules ambo in Liguribus gerebant bellum. Is hostis velut natus ad continendam per intervalla bellorum Romanis disciplinam militarem erat, nec ulla provincia militem magis ad virtutem acuebat. In Liguribus enim erant quae militem exercerent loca montana et aspera, quae et ipsis capere labor erat et praeoccupatis hostem deicere: hostis levis et velox et repentinus, qui nullum umquam tempus, nullum locum quietum aut securum Romanis sineret. Oppugnatio autem munitorum castellorum laboriosa simul periculosaque insidiis. Regio, quae si penuria astringeret, militi haud multum praedae praeberet.

14   'Itaque non lixa sequebatur, non iumentorum longus ordo agmen implebat; nihil praeter arma omnem spem in armis habentibus erat. Nec deerat umquam cum his vel materia belli vel causa, quia propter domesticam inopiam vicinos agros incursabant. Numquam tamen in discrimen summae rerum pugnabant'.

conquer them. Protected by their situation and the ability to take to their heels, this rugged and mobile race used to practice banditry rather than war, profiting from the advantages of their situation. And so, although the Saluvii, the Deciates, the Oxybii, the Briniates, and the Ingauni[23] eluded Roman pursuit long and often, at last Fulvius Flaccus cordoned off their hiding places with fire; Baebius drove them down onto level ground; and Postumius disarmed them so thoroughly that he left them hardly any iron implements with which to till the earth."[24]

Indeed, what Jordanus briefly touches on—that the Ligures   13 were obstinate in resisting the yoke of the Romans and opposed them with courage and spirit—Livy himself, in the extant books, describes in numerous passages. For instance in Book IX: "While this was taking place at Rome, both consuls were waging war in the territory of the Ligures. It was as if this enemy were bred to preserve Roman military discipline over the peaceful intervals between campaigns; and no province honed the Roman soldier more finely for deeds of bravery.[25] For there were in Liguria hilly and forbidding places to train soldiers; it was a trial for the Romans to seize these places for their own use and an effort to dislodge the entrenched enemy from them; the enemy was lightly-armed, quick and unpredictable, and would never allow the Romans a moment's rest or security. Thanks to their ambuscades, besieging their strongholds was both frustrating and perilous. The stifling poverty of the region offered little to the soldier in the way of plunder.[26]

"Hence no sutler followed in the train of the Ligurians; no long   14 line of pack animals fattened their marching column; they kept nothing with them but their weapons, and in these was all their hope. Nor were they ever without an occasion or reason to go to war, since owing to indigence at home, they continually made raids on the neighboring lands. Yet they would never fight a pitched battle that would endanger their survival."[27]

15   Hannibal, post inflictam Romanis Trebiensem cladem, traiecto
Apennino, primum concessit in Ligures, et illi oppositus Sempronius, consul Romanus, se contulit Lucam. Et videmus, Livii
XXVIII: 'Magonem, Hamilcaris filium, capta Genua, diu in Liguribus restitisse Romanis, ex qua regione Romanos in Gallia Cisalpina plurimum agitavit, ad quem inter Alpinos Ligures Genuamque agentem naves Carthagine venerunt'.

16   Servius Vergilium in XI exponens, 'Apenninicolae bellator
filius', dicit: 'quia Liguria maiore sui parte in Apennino sita est. Ligures autem omnes fallaces sunt, sicut Cato in *Originibus* tradit'.
Vergilius: 'Assuetumque malo Ligurem'. Et Lucanus in primo: 'Et
nunc, tonse Ligur, quondam per colla decora crinibus effusis toti
praelate Comatae'.

17   Varus, prisci praesentisque nominis fluvius, e capite Alpium et
Salvii montis effusus, haud procul a Nicea mari se infundens,
nulla re notior est quam quod Bracatam Galliam ab Italia dister-
minat. Adiacent illi ad dexteram oppida primum Roccheta, post
Gilecta, et ad ortum fontemque Busonium.

18   Nicea inde, oppidum a Massiliensibus in litore conditum,
Alpes dorso contingit. Dehinc portus est Herculis Monoeci quondam, nunc Villa Franca, de quo Vergilius in VI: 'aggeribus socer
Alpinis atque arce Monoeci'; et Servius grammaticus exponit de
Liguria, ubi est portus Monoeci Herculis: 'dictus autem Monoecus, vel quod pulsis omnibus illic Hercules solus habitavit, aut
quod in eius templo numquam aliquis deorum simul colitur'. Cae-

Hannibal, after he had inflicted the catastrophe of the river   15
Trebia upon the Romans,[28] first crossed the Apennines and withdrew into Liguria, while Sempronius, the Roman consul, who had
countered him previously, withdrew to Lucca. And we see in Livy
XXVIII that: "Mago, Hamilcar's son, having captured Genoa,
held out for a long time against the Romans in Liguria: he used
this region between the Alpine Ligures and Genoa as a base of op-
erations (supplied by sea from Carthage) to harass the Romans in
Cisalpine Gaul to great effect."[29]

Servius, explaining Virgil's line in Book XI, "the warrior son,   16
dweller among the Apennines,"[30] says: "Because the greater part of
Liguria is situated in the Apennines. All of the Ligurians, moreover, are liars, as Cato says in his *Origins*."[31] Vergil says: "And the
Ligurian schooled to hardship."[32] And Lucan says in Book I:
"Now you too [rejoiced], O shorn Ligurian, once conspicuous in
all of Gallia Comata, your long hair tumbling elegantly about your
neck."[33]

The river Var (its name in ancient and recent times), which   17
arises in the heights of the Maritime Alps and empties into the sea
not far from Nice, is most famous for marking off Gallia Bracata[34]
from Italy. On the Var, on the hither side, are the towns of
Roquestéron first, then Gilette; and at the head and source of the
Var, Entraunes.[35]

Next Nice, a town founded by the Massilians on the sea coast,   18
touches the Alps inland. Then comes the harbor, once of Hercules
Monoecus, now Villefranche, of which Vergil says in Book VI: "A
father-in-law descending from Alpine ramparts and from the citadel of Monoecus";[36] and Servius comments on Liguria, where the
port of Monoecus Herculis is situated: "It is called Monoecus,
moreover, either because Hercules dwelt here in solitude, all others having been driven away, or because no other god is ever worshipped with him in his temple."[37] Caesar, returning from Gaul,
came down that way into Italy. And Lucan in Book I says: "And

sar ex Galliis veniens, illac descendit in Italiam. Et Lucanus libro
I: 'quaque sub Herculeo sacratus nomine portus urget rupe cava
pelagus, non Corus in illum ius habet aut Zephyrus, solus sua litora turbat Circius et tuta prohibet statione Monoeci'. Post haec
Monicus portus, ut Ptolemaeo placet, nunc Monachus, Genuensium imperii terminus. Eum sive scopulum sive collem Federicus,
cui Barbarosso fuit cognomen, Caesar Germanicus, Genuensi populo moenibus communiendum anno abhinc plus minus sexagesimo supra ducentesimum concessit.

19   Imminet Monacho castellum nunc ignobile, sola viarum asperitate notissimum, passuum prope duo milia a mari recedens, Tor-
bia appellatum, quod Iacobus meus Bracellius, vir eloquens et doctissimus, Tropaea Augusti a priscis appellatum fuisse affirmat.
Quem quidem tenemus fuisse locum patriae Helvii⁵ Pertinacis,
Romani imperatoris, de quo Iulius Capitolinus sic scribit: 'natus
est in Apennino in villa materna'. Et infra: 'iussus est praeterea
a Perenne in Liguriam secedere in villam paternam; nam pater
eius tabernam cratillariam exercuerat, sed posteaquam in Liguriam
venit'.

20   Sequuntur Mentonum ipso in litore et Rocca Bruna superius,
sterilis soli castella, et proxime Albintimilium civitas, nunc Vinti-
milium dicta, cuius latus, qua in orientem vergit solem, Rucuba
abluit fluvius, nunc Rodoria appellatus. Proximo deinceps ad mille
passus loco collis attolitur, cui Appio est nomen; et inde arx est, ex
qua primum nascentis Apennini iugum haud procul remotum cernitur.

21   Abest a Rucuba fluvio passuum decem milibus Sancti Romuli
castellum, cuius ager citri est palmaeque, arborum in Italia rarissi-
marum, ferax; unde Romanos pontifices vidimus palmarum ramos
in Dominica quadragesimalis ieiunii postrema, inde appellata,

[there was rejoicing] where the harbor made sacred under the protection of the name of Hercules bears down upon the sea with its hollowed-out cliff: over it, Corus holds no sway, nor Zephyrus, but Circius alone worries his shores and denies [ships] Monoecus' safe anchorage."[38] Next is Portus Monicus—the name that Ptolemy favored, now Monaco, which marks the limit of Genoese dominions. The German emperor Frederick, surnamed Barbarossa, ceded it (whether it be a hill or a cliff) to the Genoese people to be fortified with walls about 260 years ago.[39]

Overlooking Monaco, about two miles distant from the sea, is a now-humble stronghold called La Turbie, well-known for its inaccessibility; my friend Giacomo Bracelli, an eloquent and learned man, maintains with certainty that it was called Tropaea Augusti by the ancients.[40] For my part I believe it was the birthplace of Helvius Pertinax, the Roman emperor, of whom Julius Capitolinus writes as follows: "Pertinax was born in the Apennines, in his mother's country home."[41] And below: "Moreover, he was commanded by Perennis to retire to his family's home in Liguria; for his father had run a felt-maker's shop, but after he came to Liguria."[42]

Next comes Mentone right on the shore, and farther upwards and inland, Roquebrune-Cap-Martin, castles on barren soil; and, directly, the city of Albintimilium, now Ventimiglia, the eastern flank of which is washed by the river Rutuba,[43] now the Rodaria.[44] About a mile further on rises a hill called the Appio, from which one may first make out the ridge of the Apennines rising up not very far away.

Ten miles from the Rutuba is the stronghold of San Remo, whose land is rich in lemon trees and palms, the rarest trees in Italy. It is from this source, we observe, that the Roman Pontiffs get palm branches to be blessed and distributed to the people on the last Sunday of Lent (called, accordingly, Palm Sunday). Travelling five miles eastward from San Remo, one comes upon a small castle

19

20

21

benedicendos et populo dandos habere. Emensus inde passuum quinque milia castellum attingit exiguum, bis mille passibus mari propinquum, quod Tabia nomen habet, a vinorum fama celeberrimum, quippe cum ea, muscata appellata, nec Cypriis nec Creticis nec Falernis cedere a bonis potoribus existimentur. Decem ab eo passuum milia ad Mauritium numerantur, portum nomine verius quam re; sed data ibi iurisdictio celebrem locum reddit. Sequitur Unelia vallis aliquot habitata vicis; mox oppidum Dianae, nunc Dianum, duo prope miliaria a mari recedens, olea vitique undique consitum. Post haec ipso in litore Cervum, et ipso in edito colle Andoria, vitiferis collibus circumdatum.

22   Andorianos fines parvi admodum vici excipiunt. Hos Album Ingaunum ⟨excipit⟩, urbs opibus ac vetustate nobilis, nunc Albinga, Proculo imperatore Romano, alumno et cive, ornata, de quo Flavius Eutropius sic scribit: 'Proculo patria Albingaunum[6] in Alpibus Maritimis; domi fuit nobilis, sed maioribus latrocinantibus'. Albingae abluit latus Merula fluvius, Centa appellatus, quod centenis torrentibus augeatur. Hanc civitatem campestri loco vix passibus quingentis a mari recedentem, cum validissimi exercitus Philippi Mediolanensium tertii ducis, praefecto copiis omnibus Berardino Ubaldino, viro fortissimo, arcta obsidione cinxissent, quattuor oppugnatam mensibus omnia quae bello inferuntur mala perpeti coegerunt; et tandem constantia et fortitudine populi fatigatus, hostis re infecta obsidionem solvit.

23   Proximum in litore est Petra castellum. Inde ad duo milia passuum aberat Finarium oppidum, ab aeris, ut vulgare sonat verbum, salubritate appellatum, quod vallis in cuius faucibus erat si-

called Taggia no more than two miles inland, made famous by the reputation of its wines; and indeed these wines, called muscatel, are thought by oenophiles to yield to neither Cyprian nor Cretan nor Falernian vintages. From Taggia to Porto Maurizio is reckoned a distance of ten miles; the latter is a harbor more in name than fact, but its status as an assize-town gives it distinction. Next follows the valley of Oneglia, sprinkled with several villages; and, presently, Diana's town (now Diano) about two miles[45] inland, surrounded with plantings of olivetrees and grapevines. After these comes Cervo, right on the shore, and the hill-town Andora, ringed by vine-bearing hills.

After the borders of Andora come some very small villages, and Album Ingaunum (now Albenga) comes after these. This city, notable for its antiquity and its wealth, was graced by the Roman general Proculus, a native and a citizen of the place, of whom Flavius Eutropius writes: "Proculus' fatherland was Albingaunum in the Maritime Alps. At home he was a noble, but his ancestors had been brigands."[46] The river Merula, called the Centa because it is swelled by a hundred mountain streams,[47] washes one side of Albenga. When the mighty armies of Filippo [Maria Visconti], third duke of Milan, under the overall command of Bernardino Ubaldino, a most valiant man, had surrounded and laid this city, on a plain scarcely fifty paces from the sea, under a tight siege, they compelled it during four months of assault to endure every hardship war brings with it; yet in the end the enemy, discouraged by the determination and courage of her citizens, raised the siege without concluding a treaty.[48]

Next along the shore comes Pietra Ligure; then, two miles further down, the town of Finale Ligure, named—as the word, in the vulgar tongue, suggests[49]—for the wholesomeness of the air. The town used to shut off the passages to the valley at whose entrance it was situated. But the Fregosi and the Genoese people expelled the Del Carretti nobles from that place as enemies; in the follow-

22

23

tum angustias claudebat. Sed Fregosi et populus Genuensis, ut Charrectenses nobiles inimicos, inde eicerent; oppidum quoque proximo anno sustulerunt. Est proxima in litore Naulium civitas portu ac turribus inclita, et Vadorum Sabatiorum portus, a quo septem miliaribus distat Savona urbs, multorum populorum commercio nobilis, quam T. Livius, Magonis adventum referens, Savonam nominavit, sicut et nostra facit aetas, et tamen Plinius Sabatium, Pomponius Mela Sabatiam appellavit. Eam nunc possidet, qui et Genuensium ducatui summa cum laude bis praefuit, vir ingenti virtute et, quod aetas nostra rarum in principibus habuit, litteris ornatus, Thomas Fregosus, multa cuius belli et pacis temporibus praeclare gesta in *Historiis* scripsimus. Albissolam Cellasque vicos ignobiles in litore cernimus, deinde Viraginem oppidum, quod quidam vicum Virginis dixere. Succedit Vulturum vicus, quem Cherusa torrens influit. Porcifera dehinc, ut maior, ita violentior amnis, qui valli nomen dedit, aedificiorum pulchritudine superbiaque potius quam solo alioquin sterili amoenissimae.

24   Portusque succedit Genuae insignis, qui, mole ingenti obiecta fluctibus, ostia in Africum versa pandit. Urbs Genua, quos et quo tempore habuerit conditores, incertum nobis est. Non enim satis probamus, quam de Phaëthonte et eius socio Genuo Bracellius noster non improbat, fabulam, nullius certioris scriptoris auctoritati nixam; et insulse fictas de Iano ineptias improbamus.

25   Videmus vero ante belli Punici tempora nullam alicubi eius urbis haberi mentionem; et Iordanum Florumque, dum superius subactos Liguriae populos, Salluvios, Deciates, *Oxybios et* Briniates,[7] Ingaunos enumerant, Genuam, si condita tunc aut nota fuisset, non omissuros fuisse crediderim. Primam vero eius mentionem fa-

ing year, they destroyed the town as well.[50] Next along the shore is
the city of Noli, renowned for its harbor and for its towers, and
the port of Vado Ligure, and seven miles away is the city of
Savona, famous for the commerce there of many peoples, which
Livy, referring to the arrival of Mago, called Savona, just as we do
now;[51] and yet Pliny called it Sabatium[52] and Pomponius Mela
Sabatia.[53] Tommaso Fregoso,[54] who has twice served as Doge of
the Genoese with the highest praise, controls this city now, a man
of great virtue and literary distinction (a rare accomplishment today among rulers), whose many famous achievements in times of
war and of peace I have written about in my *Histories*. Along
the shore we see the mean villages of Albissola Marina and Celle
Ligure, then Varazze, which some call the village of the Virgin.[55]
Next comes the town of Voltri, into which runs the torrent
Cherusa. From thence comes the river Polcevera,[56] a larger and
therefore livelier stream, which has given its name to the valley, a
valley made charming by the beauty and splendor of its buildings,
rather than by its otherwise barren soil.

And next follows the famous port of Genoa, which, protected   24
from the waves by an enormous breakwater, opens the mouth of
its harbor in the direction of Africa. We are unsure about who
founded the city of Genoa, and when. Certainly I am *not* satisfied
with the tale about Phaëthon and his companion Genuus (which
my friend Bracelli does not dismiss),[57] as it relies on the authority
of no identifiable writer; and I do not endorse the dull-witted
nonsense about Janus.[58]

I observe, in fact, that before the times of the first Punic war no   25
mention is made of this city anywhere; and I should think that
Jordanus and Florus, while they were surveying the peoples of
Liguria earlier subdued, the Salluvii, Deciates, Oxybii, Briniates
and Ingauni,[59] would not have remained silent about Genoa, if the
city had been founded or known at that time. Actually, Livy
makes the first mention of the city in Book XXI, where he says

cit Livius libro XXI, ubi 'P. Scipionem dicit cum admodum exiguis copiis Genuam petiisse, cum eo qui circa Padum erat exercitu Italiam defensurum'. Primum autem incrementum habuisse videtur, de quo Livius libro XXX sic dicit: 'Lucretio prorogatum imperium, ut Genuam oppidum, a Magone Poeno destructum, exaedificaret'. Post quae tempora Romani Liguribus Genuensibusque amicioribus usi fuerunt; et tamen multitudinem considerans coloniarum, quas Romani per omnia paene Italiae loca deduxerunt, mirari soleo nec Genuam nec alium quempiam in Ligustinis locum pro colonia captum fuisse, quod a situs sterilitate, quam milites horruerint, crediderim processisse.

26   Post secundi vero belli Punici finem, Romanus populus Gallis Insubribus et Alpinis ceterisque Galliae Cisalpinae populis et inde Illyriis subigendis arma convertit; ad quae bella cum magnae copiae variaque bello usui futura mitterentur, maxime opportuna fuisse videtur Genua, loci natura tunc etiam portuosa, ex qua commodus in Mediolanenses Papiensesque, sicut nunc est, transitus etiam tunc erat. Nihil autem aeque augendis opibus conducere ac frequentiam commeantium, et quibus in locis opum quaerendarum facultas adsit, maxime populos coalescere constat; nec tamen, in mille annis qui secundum id bellum Punicum sunt secuti, caput multum attolere potuit Genua.

27   Quam anno a Lucretii instauratione plus minus septingentesimo, ad annum videlicet salutis christianae sexcentesimum atque sexagesimum, Rotharis, Longobardorum rex, Romanis, quorum imperio semper antea fuerat subiecta, abstulerit, eam tamen, a fera Longobardorum gente parum humane gubernatam, Carolus Magnus imperator, Pipinusque filius rex Italiae et qui eis successerunt Franci reges, per annos circiter centum summa cum iustitia et humanitate, sicut et ceteras Italiae urbes, gubernarunt, illi adminis-

that: "Publius Scipio made for Genoa with his very meager forces
to defend Italy with the army that was encamped along the Po."[60]
And Livy describes what seems to have been the first enlargement
of the city when he says in Book XXX: "Lucretius' command was
extended so that he might finish rebuilding Genoa, which Mago
the Carthaginian had razed."[61] Thereafter the Romans treated the
Ligurians and Genoese in a friendlier way; and yet when I reflect
on the numerous colonies that the Romans founded nearly everywhere in Italy, I am always amazed that neither Genoa nor any
other site in Liguria was acquired for a colony. I suppose this came
about because of the area's barrenness, which repelled the troops.[62]

Now, after the close of the second Punic war, the Roman peo-   26
ple directed their military apparatus to subjugating the Insubrian
and the Alpine Gauls and the rest of the peoples of Gallia Cisalpina, and after these the Illyrians. When large troop detachments
and various war materials were being sent in support of these op-
erations, Genoa seems to have been especially suitable because of
her topography, as even then she abounded in natural harbors,
from which passage to Milan and to Pavia was convenient then, as
it is now. It is obvious that nothing serves more to increase wealth
than a large concourse of travellers, and that people tend to collect
in places where there are opportunities for gain; yet, in the thousand years which followed this second Punic war, Genoa was unable to raise her head very much.

Approximately seven hundred years after Lucretius[63] rebuilt her   27
(i.e., in about the year 660 AD), Rothari, king of the Lombards,
took Genoa away from the Romans, to whose authority she had
always been subjected theretofore.[64] Though governed inhumanely
by the brutal race of Lombards, the emperor Charlemagne and his
son Pippin, the king of Italy, and their successors, the Frankish
kings, governed her for a period of roughly one hundred years eq-
uitably and humanely—just as they did the other cities of Italy—
appointing leaders to administer her known as "counts." One of

trandae ducibus qui comites appellarentur praefectis; e quibus Ademarchus Corsicam, a Mauris oppressam, liberavit, eoque ab illis postea interfecto, Corsica nihilominus per Genuenses vindicata et naves Maurorum quattuordecim captae ac demersae sunt.

28   Berengario autem tertio in Italiam unde pulsus fuerat reverso ac imperii nomen suis titulis foedante et Ugone Arelatensi Italiae regni nomine abutente, cum pessime apud omnes nostros ageretur, Saraceni, Poenis sibi subiectis immixti, anno Christi nongentesimo et trigesimo quinto, Stephani septimi pontificis Romani temporibus, Genuam ceperunt spoliaruntque; et quod raro alibi est auditum, omnibus mortalibus qui caedi superfuerant populariter asportatis, muros urbis omni humano habitatore vacuos reliquerunt. Scribit tamen Andreas Dandulus Venetiarum dux, Francisci Petrarchae amicitia clarus, impuberes omnes brevi Genuam fuisse reductos. Estque eius testimonium eo locupletius, quod Veneti Genuensesque, magna semper aemulatione contendere soliti, per Danduli ducatus tempora gravi ac periculosissimo utrisque bello conflictati sunt.

29   A quadringentis vero annis maximum Genua habuit incrementem, quae vires nacta ingentes terra sed mari longe maiores, Liguriae cui imperat nomen obscuravit, adeo ut quae pars in Varum amnem exposita occidentem spectat solem Riperia occidentalis, quae vero ad Macram pertinens in orientem est versa dicatur Riperia Genuae orientalis. Et insuper Corsicam, Cyprum, Asiam, Thraciam, Scythiam deductis coloniis ac suis victoriis illustravit; et, negotio quam otio felicior, nunc illis terrori est, quorum insidiis prius et crudelitate bis concidit.

30   Ornata fuit Genua duobus ex gente nobili Fischa[8] pontificibus Romanis, quarto Innocentio et quinto Hadriano. Habuitque ea-

them, Ademar, liberated Corsica,[65] which had been subjugated by
the Moors; and, though afterwards the Moors killed him, Corsica
was liberated by the Genoese all the same, and fourteen Moorish
ships were captured and sunk.

But when Berengar III had returned to Italy (having earlier   28
been driven out) and was befouling the good name of the empire
with his claims thereto, and when Hugh of Arles was abusing the
good name of the Kingdom of Italy, and when all of Christendom
was in a sorry state,[66] the Saracens, in league with their vassals the
Berbers,[67] in the 935th year of Our Lord, in the time of the
pontificate of Stephen VII,[68] captured and looted Genoa; and (a
thing seldom heard of elsewhere) the Saracens carried off in one
body all the souls who had survived the slaughter, leaving the walls
of the city empty of human habitation. Yet Andrea Dandolo, the
Doge of Venice, famous for his friendship with Francesco Petrarca, writes that all the children were soon returned to Genoa.[69]
And his testimony is the more valuable as Venice and Genoa, inveterate and bitter rivals, were struggling against one another
throughout his term as Doge in a war that was grievous and extremely dangerous for both sides.

Genoa has enjoyed her greatest expansion, in fact, over the last   29
four hundred years, and having become mighty on land but might-
ier far by sea, she has eclipsed the fame of Liguria (whose mistress
she has become), so that the portion of the coast of Liguria that
extends from Genoa westward to the River Var is called Genoa's
western riviera, while that portion that extends eastward to the
river Magra is called her eastern riviera. And she has won fame for
her victories and colonies in Corsica, Cyprus, Asia, Thrace, and
Scythia; and luckier in her business affairs than in her cultural
pursuits, she is now the scourge of those by whose treachery and
barbarity she was previously laid low on two occasions.

Genoa has been honored by two pontiffs of the Fieschi family: 30
Innocent IV and Adrian V; and the same family has given approx-

dem familia ad triginta Romanae ecclesiae cardinales, quorum unicus superest Georgius Praenestinus episcopus. Dux Genuae nunc est Ludovicus Fregosus, ingenti praeditus humanitate dignusque genetrice Caterina, clarissima muliere, quae ex Ordelapha Foroliviensi praeclara gente alterum quoque genuit celebris famae virum, Ianum Fregosum, de cuius virtute merito conceptam spem nobis mors nuper eripuit. Ornatur vero nunc civibus navigatione ac mercatura toto orbe notissimis, sed paucos habet egregie litteratos, e quibus notiores nobis sunt Nicolaus Ceba, et noster item Iacobus Bracellius, ac Gottardus principis scriba.

31   Genuae latus orientale Fertor[9] amnis praeterfluit, quem nunc Bisamnem appellant. Neque tamen vetusti nominis usquequaque facta videtur oblivio; namque illum paulo supra influens minor fluvius Ferisanus dicitur. Profectus a Bisamne, Nervium, Bulliacum,[10] Saulium, tenues vicos, et paulo post illis maiorem Rechum, inde Camuleium invenit.

32   Sunt vero quattuor et viginti miliaria ab amne Cherusa superius dicto ad Camuleium, quae tota regio, non modo in planitie mari exposita, sed quantum pertinentes ad eam valles ac colles longius extenduntur, magnifici et sumptuosi operis aedibus decoratur, ut, qui alto navigantes pelago eam oram intuentur, unam se urbem prospicere opinentur. A Camuleio sinuari promontorium incipit, quod Sancto Fructuoso sacrum est, cuius templum, in intimo recessu positum, magna veneratione a vicinis populis frequentatur. Id illi promontorium Caput Montis appellant, quod arduum et saxosum in mare procurrens, sinistroque latere irrumpentes aquas angustis faucibus admittens, Delphini portum efficit, quem incolae, dempta prima syllaba, quasi potius a bonitate quam a delphine nominandus sit, Portum Finum appellant.

imately thirty cardinals to the Church of Rome, of whom only Giorgio, bishop of Palestrina, is living still.[70] The current Doge of Genoa is Ludovico Fregoso, endowed with great humanity and worthy of his mother, the famous lady Caterina, of the illustrious family of the Ordelaffi of Forlì, who bore a second son as well, the famous Giano Fregoso, whose well-founded promise of virtue death recently tore from us.[71] Modern Genoa is indeed graced with citizens world famous for their explorations and commerce; but she has few exceptionally learned men, of whom those best known to me are Niccolò Ceba,[72] my friend Giacomo Bracelli,[73] and Gottardo, the prince's copyist.[74]

The river Fertor,[75] which they call the Bisagno now, flows past   31
the eastern side of Genoa. And yet its ancient name, it seems, has not been lost to memory everywhere, for a smaller river emptying into it a little above Genoa is called the Ferisano. Setting out from the river Bisagno, one comes upon Nervi, Bogliasco and Sori, villages of little consequence, and soon thereafter the larger town of Recco, then Camogli.

A distance of twenty-four miles separates the aforementioned   32
river Cherusa from Camogli. This entire region, not only its coastal plain, but the valleys and the hills belonging to it that extend far and wide, is adorned by residences of magnificent and sumptuous workmanship, so that mariners on the high seas who gaze at that shore imagine that they are viewing a single city. From Camogli a headland starts to curve outwards which is sacred to St. Fruttuoso, whose church, set in a sheltered recess there, is thronged by the peoples roundabout with great veneration. They call this headland the Capo di Monte, which juts out steep and rocky into the sea and, by admitting through a narrow inlet the waves crashing down on its left side, forms the harbor of Delphinum. Its inhabitants, dropping the first syllable, call the harbor Portofino — as though it were to be named for the word for "goodness" rather than the word for "dolphin."

33   Sequitur ab oriente alius sinus, quem Rapalli nominant. Id etiam convalli nomen est, quae, ut montana haud sterilis citrique et oleae plurimum ferax, vicum eiusdem nominis haud quaquam obscurum in litore habet. Quinque inde miliaribus abest Clavarum, novi nominis oppidum, quippe quod ante centum et quinquaginta annos nondum moenibus cinctum erat; in eoque nunc a maritimis et montanis populis fori et iurisdictionis conventus habentur. Proxime Entella fluvius mare illabitur, quem, aliquando Laboniam dictum, nunc Lavaniam appellant; habetque ad dexteram oppida Riparossam, Mulinumque et ad fontem Rochataiam. Is fluvius, Graveia, Olo et Sturla torrentibus auctus, ad dexteram orae maritimae ripam in litore Lavanium vicum habet, a quo originem traxit Fiscorum prosapia Lavaniae comitum, dicta in Italis nobilissima, quae pontificibus illis Romanis et cardinalibus ornata fuit. Et Sturlae Prozonasium, Graveiae vero ad sinistram adiace⟨n⟩t Vignolum, Garibaldum, Frelium, et ad fontem Rupsa.

34   Ab ostio Entellae quattuor miliaribus abest Sigestrum vicus in litore, apud quem Sigestam Tigulliorum a Ptolemaeo et Plinio appellatam fuisse crediderim, cui obicit se insula tenui admodum rivulo a continente divisa. Ea, praeruptis montibus quasi muro cincta, incolas ab omni maritima terrestrique incursione tutos reddit. Gemino portu dextra levaque accessibilis, quamquam qui ad orientem solem vergit tutior veriorque portus est. Huic contermina sunt Monilia, quos colles duos vitiferos Moneliam nunc appellant. Superiusque oppida sunt Banchalesium, Matuscum, Matalana. Monilianos vero fines contingit Framula, quam ob saxosos asperosque colles Ferramulam accolae putant dictam esse, quasi diligenter eo loci soleandas esse mulas viatores admoneantur.

Another bay follows Portofino on the east side which they call   33
the bay of Rapallo. This is also the name of the adjacent valley,
which, being rather fertile and rich in lemon and olive trees on its
mountainsides, has a village of the same name on the sea shore
which is by no means unknown to fame. Five miles away is
Chiavari, a town of recent nomenclature; indeed, one hundred and
fifty years ago it had not yet been ringed with walls; it is now a
market and assize town for the hill and coastal peoples. Quite near
to Chiavari, the river Entella (once called Labonia, now Lavagna)
flows into the sea; and it has on its eastern side the towns of
Riparosa, Mulino and at its source the town of Rocchetta Ligure.
This river, fed by the streams Graveglia, Olo, and Sturla, has
on the eastern bank of its estuary the coastal town of Lavagna,
whence arose the forebears, said to be the noblest in Italy, of the
Fieschi, Counts of Lavagna, the family that has those Roman
pontiffs and cardinals [mentioned above] as ornaments.[76] And
Borzonasca is situated on the stream Stura, while the towns of
Vignolo, Garibaldo, and Frelio are on the western bank of the
Graveglia, and Rupsa is at its source.

Four miles from the mouth of the Entella lies the coastal village   34
of Sestri Levante, in whose neighborhood, I tend to believe, was
the Sigesta Tigulliorum of Ptolemy[77] and Pliny;[78] opposite is an
island separated from the mainland by a very shallow channel.
This island, girt by sheer high hills, as by a wall, makes the island-
ers safe from every kind of sea and land assault. Sestri is accessible
via a double harbor, on the east and on the west, though the eastern harbor is the truer and safer. Bordering on Sestri are the
Monilia, two hills rich in vines, which they call Moneglia now.
Further inland are the towns of Bancalese, Matusco, Mattarana.
Abutting the territory of Moneglia is Framula, which its inhabitants think was called Ferramula because of its rocky and rugged
hills, as though to warn travellers that their mules should be carefully shod in this place.

35   Paululum inde abest Levantum, nobile municipium magis quam vetustum, amoenis vallibus collibusque conspicuum. Ad cuius oram quinque sunt castella, paribus prope intervallis inter se distantia: Mons Ruber, Vulnetia (vulgo Vernatia appellata), Cornelia, Manarola, Rivus Maior; quae loca non in Italia magis quam in Galliis Britanniaque (sive Anglia) a vini odoratissimi suavissimique excellentia sunt celebria. Res profecto memoratu et spectaculo digna, videre montes adeo sublimes praecipitesque ut aves volantes fatigent; quibus omnino saxosis et nihil humoris retinentibus vitium palmites, tam pretiosae feraces vindemiae, haud secus quam hedera muris, passim haereant. Eas autem vineas et alias per Liguriam aetate Plinii non fuisse hinc videmus, quod, cum ille edocendis vinis optimis quae ubique habeat Italia diligens sit ac prope nimius, nullum in Liguria ponit, nisi forte haec sint vina Lunensia, quae ipse Plinius plurimum laudat.

36   Rivum quem Maiorem appellant inde transgressos, vetustae olim et nobilissimae urbis Lunae portus excipit, a scriptoribus quidem, sed minus quam deceat, celebratus. Quantum autem ex paucis quae exstant de eo scriptis conicere potuimus, maximi quaestus commercium in ipso portu fuit. Unde Persius satiricus, avaritiam et nimiam ad rem pecuniariam Populi Romani attentionem redarguere intendens, sic ironice scribit: 'Lunai portum operae est, cognoscite, cives'. Insulam ei, quae illum ab Austro Africoque tutum reddat, natura obiecit, secus quam vastae se pandunt fauces, multis reflexibus tortuosae, in longum amplumque sinum, qui passuum quinque milibus longitudine ac latitudine protenditur, navi-

A short distance away is Levanto, a town less ancient than fine,   35
notable for its pleasant vales and hills. At its border begins a succession of five castles,[79] set at nearly identical distances from one
another: Monterosso al Mare, Vulnetia (called Vernazza in the
common tongue), Corniglia, Manarola, Riomaggiore; this district
is as celebrated in France and Britain (or England) as it is in Italy
for the excellence of its most fragrant and extremely sweet wine.[80]
It is surely a sight worth seeing and recording: mountains so high
and so precipitous that they tire out the birds that fly over them;
mountains to which, though dry and rocky, the sprouts of vines
productive of so precious a vintage cling everywhere, like ivy to
walls. That these vineyards and others throughout Liguria did
not exist in the age of Pliny we see from the fact that the latter, though almost excessively zealous to impart a comprehensive
knowledge of the superb wines with which Italy everywhere
abounds, places not a one in Liguria—unless, perhaps, these
should be identified with the wines of Luni that Pliny himself
praises so much.[81]

From here, crossing the stream that they call the Riomaggiore   36
one encounters the harbor of the ancient and once very famous
city of Luni, a harbor celebrated by [ancient] writers, certainly, but
less than it deserves. As far as may be guessed from the few extant
writings about it, trade in the harbor itself was extremely profit-
able. Hence the satirist Persius, endeavoring to criticize the greed
and the obsession of the Romans with moneymaking, writes ironi-
cally as follows: "Familiarize yourselves with the harbor of Luna,
citizens; it is worth the trouble."[82] Nature has thrown up an island
to render that harbor safe from the south wind and from the
Affrico. Along the island a great strait, twisting along with numerous inlets, opens out into a long and broad bay that extends five
miles in length and width to admit ship-borne traffic. And the
harbor proper, which is able to handle shipping of every kind, is
fed by the river Magra, a fact that Lucan, in Book II, points out

gia admittens. Portusque ipse navigiorum omnis generis capacissimus Macra augetur, quod Lucanus in secundo sic indicat: 'nullasque vado qui Macra moratus alnos vicinae prorumpit[11] in aequora Lunae'. Supremo in eius insulae fastigio, Veneris olim templum, christianis postea temporibus Sancto Venerio consecratum, portui Veneris nomen dedit. Qua vero promontorium, sive insula, occidentem spectat solem, oppidum est Portus Veneris pariter appellatum, Genuensis populi colonia et finium quondam terminus. Et e regione Ilex est castellum vel ex hoc celebrius, quod sicut illud Genuensium, ita hoc Pisanorum agri fines terminare consuevit.

37 In sinuque Lunensis sive Veneris portus intimo Spedia est, novum oppidum ab annis sexaginta muro circumdatum, secus quod, inspecta Italiae descriptione ac pictura a maioribus facta, Tigulliam[12] fuisse coniector. Idque oppidum Bartholomaeo Facio, viro doctissimo, est ornatum. Lunensisque portus ab ea orientali parte promontorio clauditur, nunc Lunensi appellato, quod praeterlabitur Macra fluvius amoenus piscosusque et, quia Liguriam ab Etruria dividit, notissimus. Adiacent Macrae amni ad sinistram Vetianum, Arbianum, Podentianum, Richum, Luciolum, et Mulatium (ex quo marchionum eius cognominis familia nobilis fluxit).

38 Eius Ligusticae orae, quam descripsimus a Varo ad Macrae ostia, longitudinem olim undecim supra ducenta miliaria fuisse veteres prodidere, quam aetate nostra vix centum octoginta miliaribus computant; pelagus autem adiacens, quod Ligusticum appellari diximus, tres habet insulas, scopulis tamen quam insulis similiores: unam Albingauno oppositam, quae trepidis navibus saepenumero tutelae fuit, aliam Naulo, tertiam Lunensis portus promontorio occidentali adeo propinquam ut continens videatur.

thus: "And the river Magra which, having hindered no alder-wood ships with its shallow stream, rushes into the calm waters of nearby Luni."[83] On the summit of this island, a temple, once Venus', consecrated afterwards in the Christian era to St. Venerio,[84] has given its name to the harbor. Here indeed, where the headland or island faces west, there is a town, likewise called Portovenere, a colony of the Genoese people and once the endpoint of their territory. And directly opposite is the castle Ilice, quite famous for precisely this reason: for just as Portovenere was once the endpoint of Genoese territory, so Ilice was once the boundary of Pisan territory.

And in the innermost portion of the bay of the harbor of Luni 37 (or Portovenere) is La Spezia, a new town, walled for not quite sixty years now, near which I surmise, from examining a survey and map of Italy made by our forebears, was Tigullia.[85] And this town [La Spezia] is ornamented by Bartolomeo Facio,[86] a very learned man. And the harbor of Luni is enclosed on the east by a headland called the headland of Luni, along which the river Magra glides, delightful and full of fish, and notable as dividing Liguria from Tuscany. Along the river Magra to the west lie Vezziano, Arbiano, Podentiano, Ricco, Luciolo, and Mulazzo (whence arose the noble family of the marquises of that name).[87]

The ancients have passed on to us a figure for the length of the 38 Ligurian coast (which we have surveyed from the Var to the mouth of the Magra) of over 211 miles,[88] but in our era the length is reckoned as scarcely 180 miles. And the sea along this coast, which we said was called the Ligurian Sea, has three islands, though they are more like rock outcroppings than islands: the first, opposite Albenga, has often served as refuge for mariners in distress; the second is off Noli; the third is so close to the western headland of the harbor of Luni that it seems to be part of the mainland.[89]

Regio secunda. Etruria[1]

1   Etruria ad Macram sequitur, regio Italiae secunda, vel inde notissima quod priscum semper servavit nomen. *Eam vero, ut omni ex parte plenam ornatamque habeamus, tibi, Petro Mediceo, ea maxime causa duximus dedicandam, quia etsi doctrina satis et historiarum peritia tibi suppetunt, tum maxime Cosmum habes genitorem clarissimum virum et summe historiis delectatum, quo adiuvante in partium Etruriae, quas omiserimus aut minus vere proprieque descripserimus, notitiam faciliter venies, nosque quid addendum corrigendumque sit, quod in primis querimus, admonebis.* Etruriae[2] sunt notissimi etiam nunc fines: Macra et Tiberis amnes, centum et septuaginta quatuor miliaribus inter se distantes, et Apenninus mons atque Inferum Mare. Eius maris pars, quae a dictorum amnium ostiis longitudine et ad Sardiniam usque latitudine terminata fuit, quandoque Tuscum, quandoque Tyrrhenum pelagus dictum[3] est.

2   Etenim Tuscorum gens, sicut Iustinus a Trogo tradit, ex Lydia Asiae provincia veniens pulsis Umbris incoluit hanc Italiae partem, quae primo Tyrrhenia ab eorum rege Tyrrheno, mox Etruria a multo ac frequentato deorum per *tura* cultu est appellata. Leonardus autem Arretinus primo *Historiarum* dicit Etruscos venisse ex Moeonia, unde Lydi, gens maxima, navibus in Italiam advecti sunt. Huius provinciae vetustatem dignitatemque Livius Patavinus libro VI sic ostendit: 'Tuscorum ante Romanorum imperium late terra marique opes patuere; Mari Infero Superoque, quibus Italia modo insulae cingitur, quantum [autem] patuerint,[4] nomina sunt argumento, quod alterum Tuscum communi vocabulo gentis, alte-

Region 2. Tuscany

Tuscany or Etruria, the second region of Italy, comes next, starting 1
at the river Magra. The region is familiar precisely because she has
kept her ancient name. *To complete and embellish this region, I decided
it should be dedicated to you, Piero de'Medici, primarily because, though
you are yourself sufficiently learned and knowledgeable about history, you
have as your father Cosimo, a most distinguished man who takes the greatest pleasure in history. With his help, you will easily bring to our notice
anything that we have left out or described inaccurately in the Tuscan region and will advise us concerning what should be added or corrected,
which is our principal request. Tuscany's*[1] borders today are the familiar
ones, too: the rivers Magra and Tiber (174 miles apart), the Apennines, and the western sea. The part of the sea which is bounded
north and south by the mouths of those rivers and east and west
by Italy and Sardinia is sometimes called the Tuscan sea, sometimes the Tyrrhenian.

The Etruscan people (as Justin tells us, from Trogus) actually 2
came from the Asian province of Lydia. They drove out the
Umbrians and settled in that part of Italy which was at first called
"Tyrrhenia", after their king Tyrrhenus, but before long "Etruria"
from their copious and frequent use of *tura*, frankincense, in the
worship of the gods.[2] Leonardo Bruni tells us in the first book of
his *Histories* that the Etruscans came from Maeonia, from where
the Lydians sailed in great numbers to Italy.[3] Livy in Book VI explains the antiquity and importance of the region as follows: "Before the Roman ascendancy, the power of the Etruscans was widespread over land and sea. How far it extended over the two seas by
which Italy is surrounded like an island is proved by the names,
for the peoples of Italy call the western one the 'Tuscan sea' from
the general designation of the people, and the eastern the 'Adriatic'
from the Etruscan colony named Adria. The Greeks, too, call

rum Adriaticum Mare (ab Adria Tuscorum colonia) vocavere Italicae gentes; Graeci eadem Tyrrhenum atque Adriaticum vocant. Et in utrumque mare vergentes incoluere duodenis urbibus terras, prius cis Apenninum ad Inferum Mare, postea trans Apenninum, totidem quot capita originis erant missis coloniis, quae trans Padum omnia excepto Venetorum angulo (qui sinum circumcolunt maris) usque ad Alpes tenuere'.

3   Duodecim autem urbes quibus dicit Livius Etruscos incoluisse Etruriam, singulis magistratibus annuis quos vocabant lucumones creatis, qui omnem provinciam gubernarent, has fuisse invenimus: Lunam, Pisas, Populoniam, Volaterras, Agillinam, Faesulas, Rusellanam, Arretium, Perusiam, Clusium, Faleriam, et Vulsiniam, ex quibus quatuor tantummodo integrae exstant.

4   Etruscorum vero dignitatem fuisse maximam hinc constat, quod Livius tradit Romanos ab his accepisse praetextam, trabeas, phaleras, annulos, togas pictas et palmatas, currus triumphales, fasces, lictores, tubas, sellam curulem. Additque Livius Romanos consuevisse in Etruriam pueros mittere ad disciplinam sicut postea in Graeciam fuerunt missi. Potentiae etiam Etruscorum maximum est argumentum quod saepius ob Etruscum quam aliud bellum Romae trepidatum est, saepius dictator est dictus.

5   Subacti vero sunt Romanis Etrusci ad annum urbis conditae septuagesimum et quadringentesimum, cum apud Vadimonis lacum ingenti proelio superati essent. Bis tamen Romano populo rebellare conati sunt, primum Hannibalis tempore ducibus Arretinis. De quibus scribit Livius XXVIII: Cornelius cos. in Etruria iudiciis agitavit eos qui ad Magonem respiciebant et animos rebelles prae se ferebant. Secunda rebellio intentata fuit bello Marsico (sive Sociali). Quae quidem rebellio Arretinorum, Faesulanorum

them the 'Tyrrhenian' and the 'Adriatic'. The lands on both sea-
boards were settled by them, at first in twelve cities by the western
sea on this side of the Apennines, afterwards with the foundation
of twelve colonies beyond the Apennines to match the number of
mother cities. These colonies held the whole of the country beyond the Po as far as the Alps, with the exception of the corner inhabited by the Veneti, who dwell round an inlet of the sea."[4]

We find that the twelve cities by which Livy says the Etruscans   3
settled Etruria, with the creation of annual magistrates over each
(called *lucumones*)[5] to govern the whole region, were as follows:
Luni, Pisa, Populonia, Volterra, Agillina, Fiesole, Rusellana,
Arezzo, Perugia, Chiusi, Faleria, and Volsinii. Of these only four
survive intact.

It is clear from Livy's report that the Etruscans were a most im-   4
pressive people, since the Romans took over from them the pur-
ple-bordered toga, robes of state, the decorative insignia of their
horses, equestrian finger rings, decorated togas and togas embroi-
dered with palm-leaf patterns, triumphal cars, ceremonial rods,
lictors, trumpets, and the curule chair.[6] Livy adds that the
Romans used to send their sons to Etruria for their education, as
later they were sent to Greece.[7] The greatest proof of Etruscan
power is that the Romans regarded the Etruscan wars with more
dread than the others they engaged in, and often appointed dicta-
tors to deal with them.

In 470 A.U.C. the Romans brought the Etruscans to heel, beat-   5
ing them in a great battle at Lake Vadimone.[8] Yet twice they tried
to rise up against the Roman people, first in the time of Hannibal
under the leadership of the Aretines. Of them Livy writes in Book
XXVIII that the consul Cornelius harried with judicial proceedings those in Etruria who were inclining towards Mago and showing a rebellious spirit.[9] They attempted another uprising at the
time of the Marsian (or Social) War. The rebellion involved

et Clusinorum multo sanguine atque urbium Arretii et Clusii vastatione sopita est.

6   Paruitque postmodum Etruria Romanis quietissime per annos circiter septingentos usque ad Arcadii et Honorii tempora, quando Romani imperii inclinatio inchoavit. Multas postmodum passa calamitates, quarum minores fuerunt quas Gothi intulerunt, a Longobardis vero crudeliter oppressa fuit. Eam, sicut libro *Historiarum* octavo ostendimus, principio adventus eorum in Italiam, supra ceteros omnes regiones afflixerunt adeo ut unicus eorum magistratus, castaldio Etruriae appellatus, gubernationi illius satisfacere potuerit.

7   Longobardis vero eiectis, cum Caroli Magni et filiorum temporibus Etruria sicut et aliae Italiae regiones respirare coepisset, eam Lodovicus Caroli filius cum Pascali Romano pontifice partitus est, ut Arretium, Volaterrae, Clusium, Florentia, Pistorium, Luca, Pisae, et Luna imperio, ceterae omnes pontifici Romano parerent. Postea vero quam reges, qui ex Caroli Magni stirpe erant, ab Italia sunt eiecti Berengariusque Italicensis imperator et Lotharius eius filius rex Italiam administrare coeperunt, maximas Italia atque horrendas incidit calamitates. In quarum una, ad annum salutis quadragesimum supra nongentesimum Iohanne X pontifice Romano, Hungari Etruriam omnem spoliaverunt, et mortales qui caedibus superfuerant utriusque sexus in Hungariam asportarunt. Aelius tamen Spartianus de eadem Etruria honoratius scribit, qui Hadrianum imperatorum dicit in Etruria praeturam gessisse. Sed iam ad nostrum revertamur ordinem.

8   Secus Macram amnem vetusta interiit Luna, inter capita Etruriae numerata, quae Eutychianum pontificem Romanum patre maximo genuit. Eius vero urbis desolationem, quae nunc est, diutissime antea inchoasse indicat Lucanus in primo his versibus:

Arezzo, Fiesole and Chiusi and was only put down with great bloodshed and the destruction of the cities of Arezzo and Chiusi.

Etruria was thenceforth peacefully subservient to Rome for 6 some seven hundred years, up to the time of Arcadius and Honorius, when the decline of the Roman Empire set in. After that she suffered many disasters — the lesser of them brought upon her by the Goths, while by the Lombards she was cruelly oppressed. As I mentioned in Book VIII of my *Histories*, when the Lombards first came into Italy they brought Etruria in particular so low that a single one of their magistrates, called the *castaldio* of Etruria, sufficed to govern her.[10]

But once the Lombards were expelled, and Tuscany and the 7 other regions of Italy had in the time of Charlemagne and his sons begun to take breath again, Charlemagne's son Louis divided up the region between himself and the Roman pontiff Paschal II: Arezzo, Volterra, Chiusi, Florence, Pistoia, Lucca, Pisa, and Luni were to submit to the Empire, all the rest to the pope. After the kings of the line of Charlemagne were expelled from Italy and Berengar, the emperor of Italy, and his son, King Lothar, began to rule the land,[11] she endured a string of terrible calamities. In the year 940, during the pontificate of John X, one of these saw the Hungarians ravage the whole of Tuscany and carry off all that survived the slaughter, male and female alike, to Hungary. Yet Aelius Spartianus is rather more complimentary when he writes that the emperor Hadrian had been provincial governor of this selfsame Etruria.[12] But let us return to our customary arrangement of the material.

Ancient Luni by the river Magra, once numbered among the 8 mother cities of Etruria, has perished. Luni bore the pontiff Eutychianus to an eminent father.[13] In Book I Lucan indicates in the following verses that the city's present desolation began a long, long time ago: "And so they decided, in the ancient manner, to summon Etruscan seers, of whom the eldest, Arruns, lived in the

'hoc propter placuit Tuscos de more vetusto acciri vates, quorum, qui maximus aevo, Arruns incoluit desertae moenia Lunae'. Indicatque Martialis poeta eius urbis regionem caseo abundasse his versibus: 'caseus Etruscae, signatus imagine Lunae, praestabit pueris prandia mille tuis'. Eius tamen urbis denominationem retinet regio Lunensis appellata, Genuensibus maiori ex parte subiecta.

9   Est ad Macrae dexteram supra Lunam Sarzana, cuius arcem Sarzanellum appellatam Thomas Fregosus Genuensis (vir sicut ostendimus illustris) et egregie communivit et intus lautissime ac splendidissime exaedificavit. *Idque oppidum novi nominis ingens per aetatem nostram nactum est ornamentum, quod te, Nicolae, genuit, praesentis temporis Romanum pontificem eius nominis quintum. Cuius vita successusque omnes poterunt posteros admonere virtutibus (praesertim doctrinae) incumbendum esse, quandoquidem acta apud celebris sanctimoniae cardinalem Sanctae Crucis, Nicolaum Albergatum Bononiensem, vita, et assidue litteris opera data, te nunc, nomine Thomam theologia et bonarum artium studiis celeberrimum, ad summi pontificatus apicem perduxit. Nec parvo est Sarzanae ornamento Philippus uterinus tibi germanus frater, quem Sanctae Susannae cardinalatus titulo insignisti.*[5] Sunt etiam item ad eandem Macrae[6] dexteram: Castrum Novum, Fossa Novi, Ortus Novus, Villafrancha, Torrens Bagnonus — cum oppido eius nominis, *Petri Noxetii, quo viro optimo atque humanissimo epistularum scriba secretario uteris, patria*[7] — Filatera, Malgratum, et in Apennini radicibus Pontremulum, nobile regionis oppidum.[8]

10   Sunt quoque interius hinc Fivizanum, Verucula et Gragnola. Inde Montionum, Charraria, Massa et aliquot minora castella in montibus olim violatorum,[9] Tiguliorum et Segaunorum ac Apuanorum, populorum olim Ligustinorum, appellatis.[10]

11   Qui montes, ab Apennino in litus Inferi Maris transverso ab oriente ad meridiem tractu, nunc Lunensis Carrariae montana di-

deserted city of Luna."[14] That the district of Luni was plentifully supplied with cheese is attested by the poet Martial in these lines: "Cheese, stamped with the seal of Etrurian Luna, will give your boys a thousand lunches."[15] Yet the territory called the Lunigiana preserves the city's name. Most of it is under the control of the Genoese.

On the right bank of the Magra above Luni is Sarzana, with its 9 citadel called Sarzanello. Tommaso Fregoso of Genoa (whom I have mentioned as a man of great distinction) made its defenses exceptionally strong and on the inside fine and luxurious.[16] *The town has in our time acquired a great new measure of renown in giving birth to you, Nicholas, reigning pontiff and the fifth of that name. Your life and achievements will prompt posterity to apply themselves to the virtues, especially the scholarly virtues. Already celebrated as Tommaso for your services to theology and liberal learning, the career you passed in the train of Niccolò Albergati (the Bolognese cardinal of Santa Croce and a man of signal holiness) and the constant labor expended on literature have carried you now to the very peak of the papacy. And your brother Filippo, dignified by you with the title of Cardinal of Santa Susanna, is no small ornament to Sarzana either.*[17] Also on the same right bank of the Magra are Castelnuovo di Garfagnano, Fosdinovo, Ortonovo, Villafranca in Lunigiana, the stream Bagnone, with a town of the same name *which is the home of Pietro da Noceto, that excellent and genial man who serves as your secretary and writer of papal letters,* Filattiera, Malgrate and Pontremoli, a well-known town of the region at the foot of the Apennines.

Further inland from here are Fivizzano, Verrucola, and 10 Gragnola; and then Monzone, Carrara, Massa, and a number of lesser castles in hills named for Ligurian peoples long ago dispossessed, the Tigulii, Segauni and Apuani.

These hills, which extend from the Apennine ridge in a south- 11 east slant to the shores of the Tyrrhenian, are today called the mountains of Carrara Lunigiana. In Book X Livy writes of them

cuntur. De hisque sic habet in decimo Livius: 'Sempronius a Pisis profectus in Apuanos Ligures, vastando vicos et castella eorum, aperuit saltum usque ad Meram[11] fluvium et Lunae portum. Hostes montem[12] antiquam sedem maiorum suorum, ceperunt et inde, superata locorum iniquitate, proelio deiecti sunt'.

12 Ex ipsis montibus fodinas habentibus celeberrimas, magna vis marmorum Romam olim portata est, adeo ut usque in praesens tempus columnae ibi et alia marmorum ingentia frusta cernantur, quae, post fractas Romani imperii vires derelicta, nullus, qui quaesiverit aut potuerit aut deterrente impendio asportare voluerit, est inventus, cum tamen minoris impendii et laboris marmora Pisas olim et nuper Florentiam et quandoque Romam Genuamque portata sint. Unde Iuvenalis, de marmoribus Ligusticis quae Romam portabantur, sic habet: 'nam si procubuit qui saxa Ligustica portat axis et eiectum[13] fudit super agmina montem'.[14] Dicitque Plinius albos Liguriae lapides serra faciliter secari.

13 Secundus in Etruria fluvius est Auxer[15] a quibusdam vetustis, sed a Livio Mera (ut supra apparet) appellatus, quem nunc Serclum dicunt. Cuique est remotius ad sinistram in maris litore Mutronum, arx vetustissimo in monumento aedificata, quam a Florentinis ad annum salutis sexagesimum quintum supra ducentesimum et millesimum ablatam Carolus, Siciliae rex, Lucensibus reddidit. Et tamen eam aetate nostra captam populus obtinet Florentinus. Intus Petra Sancta, et ad Auxeris ipsius ostium Virego.

14 Sed priusquam mediterranea et ad dexteram Auxeris ripam sita attingam, ad certiorem locorum indaginem oram Etruriae maritimam usque ad Tiberim describere libet. Quae quidem, sicut semper hactenus fuit, nunc quoque maiori ex parte silvosa est. Nam

as follows: "Sempronius set out from Pisa against the Apuani of Liguria, and after burning their villages and strongholds, opened up the pass leading to the river Mera[18] and the port of Luna. The enemy took up their position on a mountain where their ancestors had long been settled and though the approach was extremely difficult they were dislodged from it in battle."[19]

Great quantities of marble were once hauled to Rome out of these very hills, which were famous for their quarries. As a result, even today columns and other enormous blocks of marble can be seen there, abandoned after the might of the Roman Empire was shattered. No one has yet been found to acquire them, nor has anyone been able or willing to take them away, given the expense. Yet marble was once taken to Pisa at less effort and expense, and in more recent times to Florence, sometimes to Rome and Genoa too. Hence Juvenal writes on Ligurian marble being taken to Rome, "For if the axle with its load of Ligurian rocks collapses and pours the flying stone upon the throng."[20] And Pliny says that the white stone of Liguria is easily sawn.[21]

Some ancient authorities name the second river of Etruria the Auser, though Livy calls it the Mera (as we saw above [§11])[22] and it is nowadays called the Serchio. Some distance to the left of it, on the seashore, is Motrone di Versilia, a stronghold built on an ancient monument. It was taken from the Florentines by Charles of Anjou, king of Sicily, about the year 1265 and given back to the Lucchesi.[23] Yet the Florentine people have in our time captured it. Inland is Pietrasanta, and at the mouth of the Auser itself is Viareggio.

But for a clearer survey of the topography, I shall describe the coastline of Tuscany as far as the Tiber before I touch on the inland places and those on the right bank of the Auser. This coastal tract is today, as it has always been, for the most part wooded country. Flavius Eutropius in his *Life of the Emperor Aurelian* has this to say: "He decided to give away wine to the Roman people,

12

13

14

Flavius Eutropius in Aureliani imperatoris vita sic habet: 'statuerat vinum gratuitum Populo Romano dare ut, quemadmodum et panis et porcina gratuita praebentur, sic etiam vinum daretur. Quod perpetuum hac ratione constituerat facere: Etruriae per Aureliam usque ad Alpes maritimas ingentes agri sunt, hique fertiles et silvosi sunt. Statuerat itaque a dominis locorum incultorum (qui tamen vellent[16] gratis dare) emere, *atque ibi familias captivas constituere, vitibus montes conferre*,[17] atque ex eo vinum dare gratuitum'.

15   Prima post Auxerim sunt Arni ostia, a quibus paululum recedit Liburnum, Pisani portus munitissima arx. Apud quam in scopulo passus mille a continenti recedente fundata est turris pharea, nocturnum Tyrrheno mari navigantibus lumen quam remotissime praebens et Pisanum a longe portum ostendens. Arnum autem, recedentes tertio a mari miliario, Pisae pontibus iungunt superbisque aedificiis ornant. Eam urbem vetustam et gestarum rerum gloria claram ab Alpheis originem habuisse dicit Vergilius. Et Plinius Pisas inter Auxerim et Arnum amnes a Pelope et Territanis, Graeca gente, ortas asserit. Iustinus vero dicit Pisas in Liguribus Graecos auctores habere. Et Lucanus in primo: 'hinc Tyrrhena vado frangentes aequora Pisae'. Livius XXI: 'ea causa consuli fuit, cum Pisas navibus venisset, ad Padum festinandi'.

16   Pisae tertio Eugenio pontifice Romano ornatae fuerunt. Eam urbem, florentibus Romanorum rebus, nullum habuisse potentatum videmus. Postquam vero maritimae urbes Etruscae, hinc Luna inde Populonia, deletae fuerunt, quiescentibus per Caroli Magni et filiorum tempora Italiae rebus, Pisae multos habuerunt bello maritimo praestantissimos viros, quorum gesta in nostris *Historiis* celebrantur. Sed ab annis quadraginta postquam ea civitas Florentinis subiecta fuit, infrequens populo opibusque exinanita penitus est reddita.

so that wine might be given them for nothing, just as bread and pork were. And he resolved to make the scheme permanent with the following plan: along the Aurelian Way in Etruria, there were great stretches of fertile and wooded land right up to the Maritime Alps. He planned to buy uncultivated land from the owners (even though they would have been willing to give it for nothing), *and to settle the families of military prisoners on it. These mountainous tracts would be planted with vines* and the wine they produced given away."[24]

After the Auser come first the mouths of the Arno, and a little further on Livorno, a well-fortified stronghold which is the port of Pisa. Here a lighthouse has been set on a reef a mile from the mainland. It provides a light at a great distance to those sailing the Tyrrhenian sea at night and points the way to the harbor of Pisa from afar. Three miles from the sea, Pisa spans the Arno with her bridges and embellishes it with fine buildings. Vergil says that this ancient city with its famous history took its origin from the Alphæi.[25] Pliny tells us that Pisa was founded between the Auser and the Arno by Pelops and the Territani, a Greek people,[26] and Justin that Pisa in Liguria had Greek founders.[27] And Lucan in Book I: "On this side, Pisa, interrupting the stretches of the Tyrrhenian sea with her shoal."[28] Livy in Book XXI: "This was why the consul rushed on to the Po after he arrived with his ships at Pisa."[29]

Pisa was honored by giving birth to the Roman pontiff Eugenius III.[30] As long as Roman fortunes flourished, the city evidently had no real power. Yet following the destruction of the Etruscan coastal cities, Luni on one side and Populonia on the other, and while things were quiet in Italy during the time of Charlemagne and his sons, Pisa produced many men outstanding in naval warfare, whose exploits are celebrated in my *Histories*. But forty years ago the city was brought under Florentine control, and she has become thinly populated and quite drained of resources.

17   Liburno intus contigua sunt stagna eius oppidi nomine appellata. Deinde est Mons Niger. Succeditque eo in litore fluvius Cecinna nunc quoque, ut olim a Plinio, appellatus, cui ad sinistram ipsis in ostiis haerent vada Volaterrana a priscis appellata. Quod autem hic portus fuerit Voliensium[18] et Volaterrani cognomine Volienses appellati sint auctor est Plinius. Magna dehinc ad Umbronem fluvium, quem Plinius navigiorum capacem fuisse scribit, intercapedo habetur, in qua primum est in litore oppidum Sanctus Vincentius. Interiusque Vibona, item oppidum vetusti admodum nominis. Superiusque Subretum. Sinum deinde efficit mare, ad quem oppidum est Portus Barratus. Supraque Campilia. Maior deinde habetur sinus, ad quem est Plumbinum, novi nominis oppidum, quem locum Romanae ecclesiae rerum scriptores anno nunc trecentesimo Plumbinariam dixerunt. *Illustravit eius oppidi nomen proximo biennio Alphonsus Aragonum rex, cum diu terra marique obsessum et summis oppugnatum conatibus, post sestum quem assediabat mensem, a Rainaldo Ursino possessore Florentini populi impensa prudentiaque defensum obtinere nequivit.*[19] Ad partem Plumbino sinui adversam est portus Foresius, et in mediterraneis Scarlinum oppidum, in litore autem est Castrum Trove. Castilionum Piscariae dehinc habetur, litoreum paene castellum, ad paludis olim caenosae emissorium, *quod de Florentinis idem Alphonsus rex tertio ante anno vi expugnatum et postea, cum furto amisisset, per arma recuperatum nunc etiam tenet.*[20] Inde progressi lacum inveniunt Orbitelli, olim Aprilem dictum.

18   Postea Umbronis sunt fluvii ostia mediocres admittentia naves, apud quae Populonia fuit civitas vetustissima, de qua Livius, libro XXX: 'Claudium cos. profectum ab urbe inter portus Consanum Laurentinumque atrox vis tempestatis adorta Populoniam impulit.

Next to Livorno, inland, are lagoons named for the town, and   17
then Montenero. Following the coast, the river called Cecina by
Pliny (as it still is) comes next.[31] Just to the left of its mouth are
the shallows called the *Vada Volaterrana* by the ancients.[32] That this
was the harbor of Volterra, and that the Volterrans were called by
the name Volienses is again attested by Pliny.[33] From here there is
a great stretch to the river Ombrone (which Pliny says could
handle shipping),[34] along which the first coastal town is San
Vincenzo. Further inland there is Vibona, another town with an
ancient name. Suvereto is higher up. Then the sea forms a bay
where the town of Porto Baratti is situated. Above Baratti is
Campiglia Marittima. Then there is a larger bay, the site of the
modern Piombino, a place that the authors of the *History of the Roman Church* three hundred years ago called Plumbinaria.[35] *Alfonso,
king of the Aragonese, has made the name of this town famous in the last
two years. He besieged the place by land and sea, attacking it with all his
strength, but after six months of siege he was unable to take it, defended as
it was by its owner, Rinaldo Orsini, supported by the financial resources
and intelligence of the Florentines.* Opposite the bay of Piombino is
Portoferraio [on Elba], and in the interior we have Scarlino, while
on the shore is *Castrum Trove.* Castiglione della Pescaia comes
next, almost a castle on the shore, at the outlet of a once muddy
marsh, *a place the same King Alfonso took by force from the Florentines
three years ago, having recovered it by arms after it he had lost it by stealth,
and even now controls.*[36] Those who continue on from there will find
the Laguna di Orbetello, once called the Aprilis.[37]

After [Castiglione] there is the mouth of the river Ombrone,   18
which can take ships of middling size. This is the site of the ancient city of Populonia, of which Livy in Book XXX says: "Having left Rome, the consul Claudius was caught in a violent storm
between the ports of Cosa and Laurentum and driven into Populonia. He anchored there while the rest of the storm blew itself
out and then crossed to the island of Elba, and from Elba to

Inde, cum stetisset ibi dum reliquum aestatis exiret, Ilvam insulam, et ab Ilva Corsicam, a Corsica Sardiniam traiecit'. Et Vergilius: 'misit Populonia mater'. Hanc Niceta patricius Constantinopolitanus, dux navalis exercitus, regnante in Italia Bernardo Caroli Magni nepote, vi captam diripuit et igne ferroque funditus evertit, ut parva ipsius urbis vestigia nunc appareant.

19   Umbroni ad sinistram adiacet Grossetum civitas, ad dexteram vero Ischia primum, deinde Insula, superiusque Bonconventus, et paulo infra eius fluvii fontem Assianum. Deinceps maritimo in sinu Telamonis est portus (Telamotosa a Plinio appellatus), Senensis populi mercaturae satisfaciens. Inde Argentarius mons paene in insulam mari circumdatus, in quo est locus vetusti nominis Portus Herculis. Quem nullae nunc inhabitant gentes, cum tamen eo in monte et circa portum multa aedificiorum fundamenta cernantur. Post Montem Argentarium a mari paululum recedit Caput Alvei castellum, ad cuius fines Pissia labitur torrens, mutilatae in patrimonium Sancti Petri Etruriae finium limes. Pars enim Etruriae quam Matildis certe gloriosa (ut scriptores appellant) comitissa anno nunc tricesimo supra trecentesimum septimo Gregorio pontifici Romano in beati Petri patrimonium dono dedit, ad illum Pissiae torrentem hac in parte terminata fuit.

20   Sequitur fluvius Martha appellatus, lacu Vulsinensium nunc Bolsenae emissus, supra cuius ostia paulum a mari recedit Mons Altus castellum, vetusto in loco Graviscarum (ut appellat Vergilius, 'intempestarum', quod amnis propinquitas indicat) situm. Scribit vero Plinius apud Graviscas corallum gigni solitum, ut nunc quoque et gigni et expiscari constat. Minio inde habetur, cuius meminit Vergilius, eo item nunc nomine appellatus, iuxta quem tertio a mari miliario Cornetum est civitas, quam turrium

Corsica, from Corsica to Sardinia."[38] And Vergil wrote: "mother Populonia sent."[39] When Charlemagne's grandson Bernard was ruling in Italy, the admiral of the fleet, the Byzantine noble Nicetas, took Populonia by force of arms and utterly destroyed it with fire and sword, so that scant traces of the city itself can now be seen.

The city of Grosseto lies on the left bank of the Ombrone and 19 Istia d'Ombrone on the right, then Isola, above it Buonconvento, and a little below the source of the Ombrone at Asciano. Then on a bay of the coast is the port of Talamone (called Telamotosa by Pliny),[40] which serves the trading needs of the Sienese. After that, the peninsula of Monte Argentario surrounded by the sea, on which is Porto Ercole, so named in ancient times. No people now inhabit the place, though on the mountain and around the harbor extensive building foundations are to be seen. After Monte Argentario, the castle of Capalbio is set back a little from the sea. Along the town boundaries runs the Pescia stream, representing the border of Tuscany, here cut short in favor of the Patrimony of St. Peter. That is to say, the part of Tuscany which the "glorious" Countess Matilda (as authors rightly call her) gave to Pope Gregory VII for the Patrimony of St. Peter 337 years ago was bounded in this area by the stream of Pescia.[41]

A river known as the Marta comes next, which flows out of the 20 Lacus Vulsinensium, now the Lago di Bolsena. A little inland, above the mouth of the Marta, is Montalto di Castro, set on the ancient site of Graviscae ("unwholesome," as Vergil calls it— something borne out by its closeness to the river).[42] Pliny writes that coral grows at Graviscae,[43] and, as is well known, it still grows and is harvested there nowadays. Then comes the river Mignone, which Vergil mentions, still called by the same name now. And beside it, three miles from the sea, is the city of Corneto, whose numerous towers and proud walls proclaim its antiquity. I tend to think that this is in fact the city that the accounts of Ptolemy,

frequentia moeniumque superbia vetustissimam esse ostendunt. Id vero esse crediderim quod Ptolomaei, Plinii, Pomponii Melae descriptiones Castrum Novum appellant. Auctum vero esse traditur ruinis Tarquiniae, proximae olim urbis vetustae, ex qua Romanorum postremi reges, Tarquinii Priscus et Superbus originem duxere. Magnum aetate nostra ornamentum habuit ea civitas, malo terminatum fine, Iohannem Vitellensem Romanae ecclesiae cardinalem, qui in Hadriani mole, castello Sancti Angeli, captus interiit. Eius superest nepos litteris et prudentia ornatus, Bartholomeus, Cornetanus et Monteflasconensis episcopus. *Militat etiam Francisco Sfortiae Mediolanensium duci Antonellus Cornetanus, quem et dux ipse et commilitones affirmant omni hac in Sfortianorum equitum peditumque militia eum esse qui fortitudine audaciaque ceteros antecellat.*[21]

21   Abest a Corneto passuum milia decem portus celebris arcem habens munitissimam, cui Civitati Veteri nunc est appellatio. Nec dubito quin is fuerit Centumcellensis portus, mentio cuius apud veteres saepe habetur. Parvo enim spatio inde abest Centumcellensis olim[22] civitatis locus, quam Saraceni per tempora Bernardi regis Italiae, Caroli Magni nepotis, destruxerunt. Et postea reaedificatam nos ultimo habitatoribus anno nunc undevicesimo destitui vidimus. Fuitque is locus in quo Plinius nepos in *Epistulis* narrat Hadrianum imperatorem centum iudicibus ad audiendas, se praesente, causas publice institutis cellas totidem aedificasse deputatas, et in quo beatum Aurelium Augustinum libros *De trinitate* constat scripsisse. Civitatis vero Veteris portum praetergressi magna inveniunt vetusti aedificii fundamenta, in quibus Pyrgo appellatis parvum est sacellum, eoque in loco Pyrgos fuisse constat veteres a Vergilio appellatos. Et proximo in litore monasterium est Severae virgini dicatum, quod in arcem portumque proximis temporibus communitum est. Haud procul hinc mare influit Caeretanus am-

Pliny, and Pomponius Mela call Castrum Novum.[44] It is supposed to have been enlarged by the ruins of Tarquinia, a very old city once next to it. It was from this Tarquinia that the last Roman kings, Tarquinius Priscus and Tarquinius Superbus, took their origin. In our day Corneto had a figure of great distinction in Cardinal Giovanni Vitelleschi. He came to an unhappy end and died a prisoner in Hadrian's tomb, the Castel Sant'Angelo.[45] He is survived by his nephew, Bartolomeo, bishop of Corneto and Montefiascone, a man distinguished for learning and wisdom alike. *Antonello of Corneto, too, served in the forces of Francesco Sforza, Duke of Milan. The duke himself and his fellow soldiers affirm that of all the Sforza cavalry and infantry it was Antonello who excelled the rest in bravery and daring.*[46]

Ten miles from Corneto is a bustling harbor with a stout fortress today called Civitavecchia. This was undoubtedly the harbor of Centumcellae frequently referred to by the ancients. A short way away is the site of the former town of Centumcellae, destroyed by the Saracens in the time of Bernard, king of Italy, the grandson of Charlemagne. And though it was later rebuilt, I observed some nineteen years ago that it was finally devoid of inhabitants. This was the place where the emperor Hadrian had a hundred chambers built and assigned to a hundred judges appointed to hear lawsuits in public in the emperor's presence, according to the *Letters* of the younger Pliny.[47] Here too, it is believed, St. Augustine wrote his work *On the Trinity*.[48] Those who pass beyond the harbor of Civitavecchia will find substantial foundations of ancient buildings, and among those called "Pyrgo" is a small chapel. In this spot was evidently what Vergil referred to as "ancient Pyrgi."[49] Nearby on the shore is a monastery dedicated to the virgin Santa Severa, which has in recent times been built up into a fortress and port. Close by the river Ceretano flows into the sea, and inland along the river is what is now Cerveteri but which we know was once Caere, a town famous for the tradition that it pre-

21

nis, secus quem intus est Cervetere[23] nunc, quod fuit, ut scimus, Caere, servatorum (quo tempore Galli Senones urbem ceperunt) sacrorum memoria celebre oppidum. Cuius facti exemplar 'caerimoniis' vocabulum dedisse grammatici affirmant. De quo Livius in primo: 'inde Turnus Rutulique diffisi rebus ad florentes opes Etruscorum Mezentiumque eorum regem confugiunt, qui Caere, opulento tunc oppido, imperitabat'. Et Martialis coquus poeta scribit pernam fieri optimam apud Caeretanos sic: 'Caeretana mihi fiat vel Massa licebit'.

22   Et interius mille quadringentis passibus, sicut vult Plinius, ab oppido Caere distat locus Agillinae[24] urbis vetustissimae, quam inter capita Etruriae diximus numeratam fuisse. Estque nunc saxoso in tumulo parvis aedificiorum reliquiis notus. Sequitur pertenuis locus in paludibus, qui[25] Pergae olim appellatus,[26] nunc Palus dicitur, ab Ursinis possessus. Nec est quicquam aedificiorum aut ruinarum ultra quousque Romani portus a Claudio primum, dehinc a Traiano, aedificati reliquiae inveniuntur, certe maiores quam credere possit qui illas non inspexerit. De quibus nonnnulla in *Roma* diximus *instaurata*, et tamen quod inadvertentia ibi est omissum addere hic volumus: Portuensem urbem genuisse Formosum pontificem Romanum; et in ea omni palustri litoreaque insula, quam scissus supra Ostiam urbem secundo miliario Tiberis efficit, marmorum frusta, herbis rubisque et virgultis obsita ac alluvionibus semisepulta, passim paene contigua, videri; quae scabra et impolita a mercatoribus per felicia rei publicae et imperatorum tempora mari advecta quoscumque in[27] aedificii usus poterant dedolari. Et cum multitudo sit maxima (urbem, ut videtur, aedificatura), cernere est eorum partem tantae molis ut qui obeliscos ignoret Aegypto avectos[28] illa non credat potuisse navibus ferri. Litteras

served the ritual objects of Rome when the Senonian Gauls took the city; scholars assert that the example of that deed has given us the word *caerimoniae*.[50] In Book I Livy says of Caere, "Thereupon Turnus and the Rutulians, lacking confidence in their own resources, had recourse to the flourishing power of the Etruscans and Mezentius their king, who was ruling over Caere, a wealthy town in those days."[51] And the poet Martial the cook writes that excellent ham is produced at Caere: "Caeretan ham for me — or Massan will do."[52]

Further inland, less than a mile and a half from the town of   22
Caere, according to Pliny, is the site of the ancient city of Agillina,[53] which, as I said, was numbered among the principal cities of Etruria. It can be recognized now by the scant remains of buildings on a stony mound. Next comes a very small place in the marshes, once called Perga and now Palus ("The Marsh"), a property of the Orsini. Nor are there any buildings or ruins beyond it until one comes upon the remains of the harbor of Rome — first built by Claudius, afterwards by Trajan — which are a good deal more extensive than one who has not examined them might suppose. I said something about them in my *Roma instaurata*, yet I should add here what I inadvertently left out there, that the port city of Ostia gave birth to the Roman pontiff Formosus;[54] and all over the shore of the marshy island formed by a fork in the Tiber two miles upstream of Ostia, blocks of marble can be seen scattered about, almost side by side, choked by weeds, nettles, and shrubs and half buried by silt. Rough-hewn and unpolished, they were brought here by sea by traders in the prosperous days of the Republic and Empire, for whatever building use they could be cut and shaped to; and since they are there in enormous numbers (it seems a city could be built from them), some appear so massive that anyone unaware that obelisks were brought here from Egypt would scarcely believe they could have been transported by ship. Each block is inscribed on two sides with numerals: we know

unumquodque frustum numerales duobus in lateribus est inscriptum, quarum unis, docente Plinio, pondus lapidis, alteris, missorum a mercatore frustorum ordinem, significari novimus.

23 Ut autem unde supra digressi sumus revertamur: Auxer[29] fluvius, quem nunc Serclum vocant, primum habet ad dexteram oppidum Librafactam. Ad ortum vero suum in Apennino Grignanum, haud ignobile castellum. Et ad fluvii alveum, quousque ad mediterranea sit descensum, perpetua est vallis Carfagnana, castellis villisque plurimis habitata, maiorem cuius partem nunc obtinet marchio Ferrariensis. Ex his vero oppidis quae Auxeri descendendo ad dexteram adiacent, notiora sunt Castrum Novum et Barcha.

24 In mediterraneis vero Serclus Lucae urbis, Romanae coloniae, latera abluit, de qua Livius XXI: 'Hannibal in Ligures, Sempronius Lucam concessit'. Ostendimus vero in *Historiis* Narsetem eunuchum eam a Gothis possessam septem mensibus oppugnasse priusquam potiri potuerit. Luca urbs tertium Lucium pontificem Romanum genuit atque Alexandrum secundum (adversus quem Lombardi Cadolum Parmensem in idolum erexerant) genuit. Eam vero annus agitur quinquagesimus, cum malo suo sibi subegit Paulus gente Guinisia Lucae nobili genitus. Cumulaverat is triginta annis vim pecuniarum ingentem et filios procreaverat. Sed cum magno fastu ipse et filii adulescentes degunt beatique sibi et suis esse videntur, fortuna repente mutata, exemplar facti sunt multis quam nihil in rebus humanis solidum, nihil sit firmum. Capti enim et patria violenter abacti, primum cumulatas divitias, deinde vitam in carceribus amisere. Luca autem post Guinisiorum eiectionem, variis et multiplicibus agitata bellorum motibus, XX ferme annis magnas est passa calamitates, quae tamen Florentinum populum, eius ambientem dominium, pariter afflixerunt. Nam praeter alias ibi acceptas clades, eorum exercitus cui Guidantonius praeerat, Urbini comes, sicut in *Historiis* diffuse ostendimus, a Nicolao Piccinino superatus fususque est, quo in proelio quattuor

from Pliny that one set of markings indicates the weight of the stone, the other, the order in which the blocks were shipped by the trader.[55]

But to come back to the point from which we began to digress   23
before: the river Auser, now called the Serchio, has first on its right the town of Ripafratta. At its source in the Apennines it has Gragnana, an insignificant castle. And the course of the river as far as the interior lowlands is constantly accompanied by the valley of the Garfagnana with its many forts and estates, most of which is subject to the marquis of Ferrara. Castelnuovo and Barga are the most notable of the towns lying on the right bank of the Auser as it descends towards the sea.

The river Serchio in the interior washes the flanks of the city of   24
Lucca, a Roman colony about which Livy in Book XXI says: "Hannibal withdrew to Liguria, Sempronius to Lucca."[56] And I showed in my *Histories* that the eunuch Narses had Lucca, which the Goths controlled, under attack for seven months before he was able take possession of it.[57] Lucca gave birth to the Roman pontiff Lucius III, and to Alexander II also, against whom the Lombards put up Cadalus of Parma as antipope.[58] Paolo, one of the noble Lucchese family of the Guinigi, brought Lucca under his control some fifty years ago, to his cost. He had amassed a vast amount of money over thirty years, and he had fathered sons. But while he and his young sons lived with great haughtines and were a success in their own eyes and in those of their family, their fortunes suddenly changed without warning and they became for many an object lesson that nothing in human affairs is lasting, nothing constant. They were arrested and driven from the country by force, they lost their accumulated riches, and later, in prison, their lives.[59] But about twenty years after the expulsion of the Guinigi, Lucca was troubled by the various complicated upheavals that wars bring on and suffered many calamities, though in truth these afflicted Florence equally, the power encircling Lucca. In addi-

equitum, tria peditum milia, et ingentem machinarum bellicarum vim Florentinus amisit. Lucaque dudum honestis mercatoribus frequentata, Iampetro ornata est Graece et Latine eruditissimo et Victorini Feltrensis, praeceptoris sui, mores redolente.

25   Habet item ad dexteram Luca colles, in quibus est hinc castellum Verucula, inde Altus Passus, supra Lumenicus,[30] et ad fluvium Collodium, eiusdem nominis oppidum. Cui fluvio item adiacet Piscia oppidum, quod ad annum salutis LXX supra ducentesimum et millesimum Florentini Lucensesque (sicut Leonardus Arretinus scribit) destruxerunt. Et paulo inde abest Bugianum, superiusque est Ugianum. Qua vero Lucensis ager vergit in Florentinum, palus est Bentina in lacum a Florentinis conclusa, cui supereminet Mons Carolus oppidum. Et ubi is lacus in Arnum derivat, Bientina est castellum. Supremo autem in sinu amplae ac primariae totius Etruriae planitiei, Pistoria est civitas, in cuius agro Catilinae exercitum fuisse superatum multi ex vetustis scripsere. Haec (sicut Arretino placet) prima fuit Etruriae urbium quas populus Florentinus, tunc primum liber, ad annum salutis millesimum ducentesimum et quinquagesimum, sibi subegit; *fuitque Cypriani, in Romana curia litterarum apostolicarum abbreviatoris peritissimi, quem nuper amisimus, patria.*[31] Circumstantque eam oppida quattuor, Summanum, Seravallae, Victolinum, et, superius, Mons Catinus. Circumfluuntque amnes duo parvo distantes spatio, Stella et Umbro, qui secus Carmagnanum delapsi apud Montem Lupum oppidum in Arnum exonerantur. Visentiusque amnis deinceps ex Apennino defluens Prati, oppidi omnium Etruriae opulentissimi, moenia praeterfluit, *quod Geminiano, sacri palatii causarum auditore, viro optimo et iuris pontificii consultissimo cive ornatur.*[32] Supra Pratum

tion to other defeats suffered there, the Florentine army under Guidantonio, Count of Urbino, was beaten and put to flight by Niccolò Piccinino, as I showed in detail in my *Histories:* in that battle, Florence lost four thousand horse and three thousand infantry, and a huge quantity of war engines.[60] Lucca, long bustling with honest merchants, is graced by Gian Pietro da Lucca,[61] that great scholar of Greek and Latin and so reminiscent of the fine character of his teacher Vittorino da Feltre.

Lucca has hills on the right, among which is on this side the   25 castle of Verrucola, on that, Altopascio, above, Lumenico, and at the river Collodi, a town of the same name. Pescia lies along the river Collodi, too, a town that (as Leonardo Bruni writes) the Florentines and Lucchesi destroyed in A.D. 1270.[62] Buggiano is not far off from Pescia, and above Buggiano is Uzzano. Where the territory of the Lucchesi passes into that of the Florentines, there is the marsh Bientina that the Florentines have dammed into a reservoir, above which sits the town of Montecarlo. The castle of Bientina is found where this reservoir flows into the Arno. In the top corner of the large principal plain of Tuscany is the city of Pistoia, in whose territory Catiline's army was defeated, as we learn from many ancient writers. In Leonardo Bruni's account Pistoia was the first of the Tuscan cities that Florence — just free herself — brought under her control, in A.D. 1250. *It was the home town of Cipriano, an abbreviator of papal letters in the Roman curia, whom we recently lost.*[63] Around Pistoia are located Monsummano, Serravalle, Montevettolini, and, higher up, Montecatini. On either side of Pistoia, close to one another, are the two rivers, Stella and Ombrone, which glide down past Carmignano and discharge into the Arno at the town of Montelupo Fiorentino. Next the river Bisenzio flows down from the Apennines and passes by the walls of Prato, the wealthiest of all the towns of Tuscany, *which is adorned by its citizen Gemignano, auditor of the cases in the Sacred Palace, a fine man highly learned in canon law.*[64] Above Prato, there is the

est Mons Murlus oppidum, et Marina torrens qui[33] Calentianum oppidum praeterlabitur. Ultimusque ad Florentiae moenia Munio habetur amnis.

26   Florentiae urbis inclutae originem gestasque res abunde complexus est in historia sua clarissimus vir Leonardus Arretinus. Quod autem ad nos attinet: eius urbis origo refertur in Sullanorum militum (quibus is ager a Sulla distributus fuit) adventum et quia primas illi sedes ad Arni fluenta ceperunt,[34] 'Fluentiam' inde primo dictam volunt. Et quidem Plinius (apud quem primum eius loci mentio facta est) 'Fluentinos' dicit profluenti Arno appositos. Venerunt vero ii milites ad annum conditae urbis Romae sexcentesimum et septimum supra sexagesimum, unde initium Florentia habuisse videtur ante Christi Dei nostri adventum annis octoginta tribus aut circiter.

27   Multis ea civitas per Gothorum tempora incommodis agitata est. Nec tamen a Totila aut alio quopiam tunc aut alias umquam destructa fuit. Idque, quod de reaedificatione a Carolo Magno facta aliqui sentiunt, non probamus, cum Gesta Caroli ab Alcuino, eius praeceptore, scripta tantummodo dicant illum Romam euntem Florentiae Domenicum Pascha bis celebrasse. Servata vero est ab ingenti quod inciderat desolationis periculo unius civis, Farinatae Ubertini virtute. Cum Pisanis Senensibusque et aliis Etruscis in conventu apud Emporium habito Florentiam esse destruendam censentibus, Farinata, licet longo postliminio, in ipsam patriam reversus, eam dixit, quam non aedificasse⟨n⟩t, se vivo ab illis destrui non passurum. Itaque Florentia, acceptis vi et in se populariter traductis Faesulanis ad annum salutis quartum et vicesimum supra millesimum, plurimum opibus et gloria est aucta. Quo item anno Henricus primus imperator ecclesiam Sancti Miniatis ad muros Florentiae aedificavit.

28   Arsit vero Florentia duobus incendiis, parvo temporis spatio, ad annum salutis sextum et septuagesimum supra millesimum et centesimum. Et eo fere tempore primum per priores artium et vexilli-

town of Montemurlo, and the stream Marina which flows by the town of Calenzano. And last, at the walls of Florence, is the stream of the Mugnone.

The distinguished Leonardo Bruni of Arezzo has given a detailed account of the origin and history of the famous city of Florence in his *History*.[65] For our purposes, the city's origin can be traced back to the arrival of the veterans of Sulla's army in the territory that he had distributed among them. Because they first settled by the waters (*fluenta*) of the Arno, it is supposed the city was at first called Fluentia from that. And Pliny, in whom we find the first reference to the place, says the Fluentini were settled beside the flowing Arno. The veterans came in 667 A.U.C. and so Florence seems to have had her origin in about 83 B.C. 26

The city was troubled by many setbacks in the period of the Gothic invasions, yet she was never destroyed, by Totila or by anyone else, then or at any other time. I am not convinced by the writers who say that Charlemagne rebuilt the city, since the *Life of Charlemagne* by his teacher Alcuin says merely that Charlemagne observed Easter Sunday twice in Florence, on his way to Rome.[66] She did, however, run the risk of terrible destruction, from which she was saved by the valor of a single citizen, Farinata degli Uberti. At an assembly held at Empoli, the Pisans, Sienese, and other Tuscans urged that Florence should be destroyed; Farinata, who had returned to his fatherland after a long exile, declared that as long as he was alive, he would not let the city be destroyed by her enemies, who had not built her.[67] And so Florence, which had absorbed the inhabitants of Fiesole by force or by willing transfer in A.D. 1024, was very much enhanced in wealth and renown. In the same year, the emperor Henry I built the church of San Miniato by the city walls. 27

Florence burned down in two fires in a short space of time in the year 1176. And at about this time, the Priors of the Guilds and the Standard-Bearer of Justice first began to govern Florence, as 28

ferum iustitiae eodem quae nunc more gubernari coepit, fuitque
inter primos vexilliferos ex nobili gente Strozza unus. Basilica vero
insignis, quae per nostram aetatem curante Philippo Brunalicio,
nobilissimi ingenii Florentino, stupendi operis fornice est ornata
gloriosaeque Virgini dicata, anno salutis duodecies centeno et
nonagesimo quarto inchoata est. Et quarto abinde anno palatium
item superbissimum, quod inhabitant priores, aedificari coepit.
Quintoque postmodum anno productum est pomerium, et moenibus, quae nunc exstant, urbs est amplificata. Turris autem marmo-
rea, inter ceteras orbis campanarias speciosa, ad annum inde primum et tricesimum excitata. Per quae tempora civitas Florentina
duobus ornata est poetis, Dante Aldegherio et Francisco Petrarcha: e quibus hic, patre Florentino sed exsule apud Arretium natus, et Arquadae inter colles Euganeos mortuus ac sepultus est;
ille, Florentinis parentibus Florentiae natus, obiit Ravennae patria
exsul. Pauloque post Florentia Iotum habuit, pictorem celeberrimum Apelli aequiparandum.[35]

29 Habuit quoque Accursium, iurisconsultorum principem, qui
ius civile nunc exstans egregie interpretatus est. Famaque est, nullo
nobis confirmata auctore, Claudianum poetam fuisse Florentia
oriundum. Colutius vero Salutatus, etsi prius didicerit quam Ciceronianae imitatio eloquentiae sui saeculi adulescentibus nota esse
coepisset, et eloquens est habitus et multa scripsit prudentiam magis et doctrinam quam eloquentiam redolentia. Nicolaus Nicoli
aetate nostra, etsi nihil scripsit,[36] doctus tamen fuit et multis adulescentibus ut litteris operam darent opem attulit.

30 Ab his vero plus minus centum annis qui Francisci Petrarchae[37]
mortem et haec tempora intercedunt, mirabili felicitate Florentia
opes auxit.[38] Eius enim imperio aetate nostra Castrum Carum,
Mutiliana, Dovadula, Cassianum, Porticus, et alia castella in Romandiola, Pisae quoque ac Cortona, urbes vetustae, Burgumque
ad Sepulchrum, et regio Casentina in Etruria sunt subactae. Ab
ipsis vero centum annis superavit omnia Florentiae ornamenta

they do now. One of the Strozzi nobles was among the first Stan-
dard-Bearers. The famous cathedral was begun in the year 1294,
and in our time has been beautified with a dome, an astonishing
feat of engineering owed to the genius of the Florentine Filippo
Brunelleschi, and consecrated to the glorious Virgin. Four years
later building began on the similarly impressive Palace of the
Priors. Five years after that, the city limits were extended and
Florence was enlarged by its present walls. The marble campanile,
a beauty among the bell-towers of the world, was put up thirty-
one years later. At this time Florence was graced by two poets,
Dante Alighieri and Francesco Petrarca. Petrarca was born at
Arezzo of a Florentine father in exile, died and was buried at
Arquà in the Euganean hills; Dante was born in Florence of Flor-
entine parents, dying in exile at Ravenna. A little later Florence
had the famous painter Giotto, the equal of Apelles.[68]

Florence also bore Accursius, prince of legal scholars, who was   29
an outstanding interpreter of the civil law as it now is.[69] And there
is a tradition, not, I think, authenticated by any author, that the
poet Claudian was born at Florence.[70] Coluccio Salutati was considered eloquent, though he had been schooled before imitation of
Cicero's eloquence began to be known to the young men of his
age, and he wrote extensively, though leaving an impression more
of good sense and learning than of eloquence. In our day Niccolò
Niccoli, though he wrote nothing, was both learned and helpful to
many young men in applying themselves to study.[71]

Over the period from the death of Petrarch to the present,   30
roughly a century, Florence has been remarkably successful in augmenting her power. In our time Castrocaro, Modigliana, Dovadola, Casciana, Portici, and other castles in Romagnola, the ancient cities of Pisa and Cortona, and Borgo San Sansepolcro, and
the Casentino district of Tuscany have all come under her sway.
All the glories of Florence over these last hundred years have been

concilium in ea celebratum, in quo quartus Eugenius pontifex gloriosissimus Orientalis Ecclesiae cum Occidentali unionem, maximo diu quaesitam impendio, celebravit Iohanne Palaeologo imperatore Constantinopolitano et patriarchis,[39] archiepiscopis episcopisque, ac ingenti doctissimorum nobiliumque totius Graeciae virorum qui concilio interfuerant multitudine Romanae ecclesiae sumptibus in patriam reportatis. Armenii etiam, Aethiopes, Georgiani, et Iacobitae, Libyam Asiamque incolentes, Catholicae fidei documenta in eodem concilio ab Eugenio pontifice acceperunt.

31   Viris etiam nunc Florentia, ut olim semper, omni virtutum laude praestantissimis exornatur, Cosmo imprimis Mediceo,[40] quem omnes totius Europae cives opum affluentia superantem prudentia, humanitas, liberalitas, et (quod nos maxime ad eius laudes incitat) bonarum artium praesertim historiarum peritia celebrem reddunt. Cumulantque eius felicitatem Petrus et Iohannes, *et Carolus*,[41] nati paternae virtutis imitatores. Nec supprimenda sunt maxima quae Cosmus Florentiae urbi addidit ornamenta, monasterii enim Sancti Marci, admodum celebris, superbae atque ut aiunt insanae exstructiones ceterae, sed maxime bibliotheca alias omnes Italiae superans.[42] Praetereaque ad Sancti Laurentii fornices marmoreae columnae opusque id totum summi eius viri magnificentiam ostendunt. Quid quod privatae ipsius aedes[43] recens in Via Lata exstructae Romanorum olim principum et quidem primariorum operibus comparandae sunt? Quin ego ipse, qui Romam meis instauravi scriptis, affirmare non dubito nullius exstare privati aedificii principum in urbe Romana reliquias, quae maiorem illis aedibus prae se ferant operis magnificentiam.

32   Pallas etiam Strozza, clarissimus equestris ordinis Florentinus, opera studiis philosophiae assidue[44] Patavii impensa exilii incommoda prudentissime consolatur. Angelus quoque Acciaiolus, equestris ordinis, clarae gentis suae nobilitatem prudentia, inge-

eclipsed by the Council held there, when the illustrious pontiff Eugenius IV sanctioned the union—long sought and at great expense—of the Eastern and Western churches. The emperor of Constantinople John Palaeologus, the patriarchs,[72] archbishops, and bishops, and a great crowd of participants from the scholars and noblemen of the whole of Greece were taken back home at the expense of the Church of Rome. At this Council too, Armenians, Ethiopians, Georgians, and Jacobites, Christians dwelling in Libya and Asia, accepted from Pope Eugenius the teachings of the Catholic faith.[73]

As was customary in the past, so now Florence is favored with   31 men of distinction in every field, above all Cosimo de' Medici. Surpassing all the citizens of Europe in abundance of riches, he is celebrated for his wisdom, humanity, generosity and—something that particularly rouses our admiration—his profound intimacy with the liberal arts, history especially. His sons, Piero, Giovanni, *and Carlo*[74] crown his good fortune in replicating their father's virtues.[75] Nor must we pass over the greatest embellishment Cosimo has added to the city of Florence: the celebrated monastery of San Marco, in which among the other superb and, so to say, extravagant buildings, the library stands out as surpassing all others now in Italy. The marble columns for the arches of San Lorenzo, and indeed the work as a whole, demonstrate the great man's magnificence, and his private residence on the Via Larga, lately built, is surely equal to the works of Roman princes and potentates of long ago. I have myself *Restored Rome* in my writings, and I do not hesitate to say that in the city of Rome no remains of the private building of any prince boast work of greater magnificence than his residence.[76]

The famous Florentine knight Palla Strozzi wisely relieves the   32 hardships of exile in Padua with unremitting philosophical work. Agnolo Acciaiuoli, another knight, adorns his distinguished ancestry with his wisdom, liberal character, and literary study as much

nuis moribus et litterarum studiis non minus exornat quam ab ea
ipse decoratur. Andreas praeterea Floccus, apostolicus secretarius
canonicusque Florentinus, vir optimus, eloquentia et edito *De ma-*
gistratibus opere, ac Ianoctus Manectus, litterarum Graecarum
Latinarumque peritia atque eloquentia, et Baptista Albertus, nobili et ad multas artes bonas versatili ingenio, *Mathaeus quoque*
Palmerius, Eusebium Caesariensem et beatum Hieronymum in temp-
orum supputatione imitatus[45] patriam exornant. Decorat etiam urbem
Florentiam ingenio veterum laudibus respondente Donatellus
Heracleotae Zeuxi aequiparandus, ut vivos (iuxta Vergilii verba)
ducat de marmore vultus.

33   Secus Florentiam Faesulana urbs, vetusta et multorum scriptis
praesertim Salustii in *Bello Catilinario* et Livii illud idem scribentis
bellum, libro centesimo secundo, celebrata, interiit, vel (quod supra diximus) in Florentiam populo opibusque migravit. Oritur ex
montibus Faesulanis, qui ad orientem vergunt solem, Munio torrens, Florentina abluens moenia; secundum cuius alveum, sexto ab
urbe miliario, sacellum est, cui ea ratione inditum 'Ad Cruces' nomen fuisse opinor quod eo in loco sepulta fuerit moles illa cadave-
rum quae facta fuit in stupenda strage illa magnae partis ducento-
rum paene milium ex Radagasii Gothorum regis exercitu apud
Faesulas (sicut in *Historiis* ostendimus) interfectorum. Interque eos
montes et Apenninum vallis est amoenissima et vicis villisque
praesertim Mediceorum speciosissimis frequentata Mugellum appellata, quae Dinum habuit Mugellanum, iurisconsultorum superioris saeculi celeberrimum. Eam illabitur dividitque mediam Seva
fluvius ex Apennino oriundus. Primumque regionis Mugellanae
oppidum est via Bononiensi Scarparia Iacobo ornata, Angeli filio,
cuius, Graece Latineque doctissimi, exstat M. *Tullii Ciceronis vita* ex
Plutarcho in Latinitatem luculenter traducta. Deinceps habetur
Nicolaium dura Piccinini obsidione, cui fortiter restitit, nostris in
Historiis clarum. In[46] Sevam influit Ronta torrens, ad quem Via Fa-

as he is honored by it. That good man Andrea Fiocchi, apostolic secretary and canon of Florence, with his eloquence and the work he has published *On the Roman Magistrates* adds luster to his country, as do Giannozzo Manetti with his masterful eloquence in Greek and Latin letters, and Leon Battista Alberti with his noble and versatile intelligence in many good arts, *as well as Matteo Palmieri who imitates Eusebius of Caesarea and Saint Jerome in the study of historical chronology.*[77] Donatello, too, is another ornament of Florence.[78] With a talent equal to the excellence of the ancients, he is a match for Zeuxis of Heraclea, able (in Vergil's words) to "draw living expressions" from the marble.[79]

Beside Florence is the ancient city of Fiesole, celebrated by 33 many authors, in particular Sallust in the *Catilinarian War*, and Livy on the same war in Book CII.[80] It has now perished or rather, as I said above, it has migrated with its people and wealth to Florence. The Mugnone stream which washes the walls of Florence rises in the hills around Fiesole as they slope down to the east; six miles from Florence along its course is a chapel called Le Croci. I believe the name was given it because this was where a vast quantity of cadavers was buried following the stupendous slaughter of nearly two hundred thousand of the army of the Gothic king Radagaisus at Fiesole, as I showed in my *Histories*.[81] Between these hills and the Apennines there is a pretty valley called the Mugello, crowded with handsome villages and estates, particularly those of the Medici. From here hailed Dino da Mugello, a famous jurisconsult of the last century.[82] The river Sieve rises in the Apennines and flows down through the middle of the valley. The first town of the Mugello region on the road to Bologna is Scarperia, notable for its son Jacopo di Angelo, a fine scholar of Greek and Latin who made a splendid Latin translation of Plutarch's *Life of Cicero*.[83] Next comes *Nicolaium*, famous (in my *Histories*) for Piccinino's siege, which it resisted bravely.[84] The Ronta stream

ventina eiusdem nominis est vicus, et sub eo Sancti Laurentii Burgus.

34 Quintoque abinde miliario Sevam pariter illabitur Ducaria, a cuius torrente apud Gaudentium, Apennini vicum, oriundo, quicquid magno sinu complectitur Arnus amnis usque ad agri Arretini fines dicitur Casentinum, quam regionem montuosam ⟨a⟩ Populo Florentino proximis temporibus quaesitam fuisse ostendimus. Ubi vero Seva fluvius Arnum illabitur, est castellum moenibus munitum Pons ad Sevam dictus. Et Arnum quidem Florentia urbs ab eo divisa pontibus quatuor magni operis iungit. Sed quantum ad inchoatam attinet Florentini agri descriptionem: secundum Arni fluenta sub Florentia sunt castella Mons Lupus et Signia, quousque[47] navigia admittit Arnus. Supra Florentiam vero ad quintum decimum lapidem primum est ad Arni fluenta oppidum Incisa, cuius oppidi nomen originem habuisse coniector ab succiso obice saxeo cursum Arni solito remorari. Indicant namque quernarum trabium stipites maximi, quos defodientes agricolae inveniunt, vallem Arni superiorem, qua nullam habet nunc ager Florentinus vini optimi feraciorem, quantum profluenti Arno apposita planities ambit, ⟨ut⟩ qui attente leget initia XXII *Historiarum* Livii Patavini deprehendet, paludem fuisse, atque eam in qua 'ex verna primum intemperie variante calores frigoraque, aeger oculis Hannibal elephanto, qui unicus superfuerat, quo altius ab aqua exstaret vectus, vigiliis tamen et nocturno umore palustrique caelo gravante caput, altero captus est oculo'. Nam 'cum fama esset Flaminium consulem Arretium cum exercitu praevenisse', Hannibal ex hibernis movens (quae in Liguribus habuerat) Arretium contendebat.

35 Sunt autem Livii hac in parte verba: 'cum aliud longius ceterum commodius ostenderetur iter, propiorem viam per paludem petiit,

flows into the Sieve, where there is a village likewise named Ronta, on the road to Faenza, and under Ronta, Borgo San Lorenzo.

Five miles from Borgo S. Lorenzo, the Ducaria flows into the 34 Sieve. Whatever the river Arno embraces in its great arc from the Ducaria (which rises at the Apennine village of San Godenzo) right up to the borders of the territory of Arezzo is called the Casentino, a hilly region which, as we saw, was acquired in recent times by the Florentines. Where the river Sieve flows into the Arno, there is a walled stronghold called Pontassieve. The city of Florence spans the Arno, which divides it, with four substantial bridges. But to continue the survey of the territory of Florence: along the waters of the Arno below Florence are the castles of Montelupo Fiorentino and Signa, the latter the limit of shipping up the Arno. Up the Arno, fifteen miles from Florence, the first town is Incisa in Val d'Arno. I suppose the name originated in a stone breakwater designed to moderate the flow of the Arno which became undermined (*succiso*). Great blocks of oak trunks that farmers turn up as they dig the soil suggest that the upper Arno valley—now, as far as the floodplain of the Arno extends, the most productive of fine wine in the Florentine dominion—was once swampland. An attentive reader of the beginning of Book XXII of Livy's *History* will realize that that swamp—where Hannibal "whose eyes were affected by the changeable and inclement spring weather, rode upon the only surviving elephant so that he might be a little higher out of the water. Owing, however, to want of sleep and the night mists and the mud of the marshes, his head became affected and he lost the sight of one eye"[85]—was indeed this valley of the Arno. For "when he had word that the consul had anticipated him in reaching Arezzo," Hannibal left winter quarters, which he kept in Liguria, and rushed to Arezzo.[86]

Here are Livy's words on the matter: "Though another longer 35 but easier route was pointed out to him, Hannibal took the shorter way through the marshes of the Arno, which was at the

qua fluvius Arnus per eos dies solito magis inundaverat'. Et paulo
infra, exercitus incommoda et iumentorum hominumque stragem
quae fiebat describens, dicit 'per fluvii praealtas et profundas vora-
gines haustos paene duces. Et maxime omnium eos confecisse vigi-
lias per quatriduum iam et tres noctes toleratas, cum, omnia obti-
nentibus aquis, nil ubi in sicco fessa sternerent corpora inveniri
posset'. Iter igitur quod ab Liguribus Arretium ducturo longius
ostendebatur[48] per Lucensem, Pisanum, Volaterranum, et eius
quae nunc est Sena agros esse oportuisset, quod certe nullus regionis peritus dubitabit futurum fuisse, commodius; eo quo propiorem ingressus viam ad Arni fluenta ubi nunc est Florentia venit et
inde amnis Arni alveum apud nunc Incisam, vel paulo supra, est
ingressus, tamdiuque per paludem, qua fluvius Arnus per eos
dies solito magis inundaverat, est profectus quousque siccum, ubi
consisteret, primum in Arretino inveniret. Eam vero inundatio-
nem easque paludes non fuisse, sicut aliqui volunt, in ea planitie,
quam Pratum Signiamque et Florentiam intercedere videmus, ea
constat ratione: quod regionem illam, in qua Hannibal primum in
sicco constiterit, imprimis Italiae fertilem dicit Livius tunc fuisse
Etrusci campi, qui Faesulas inter Arretiumque iaceret.[49] Subiun-
gitque Livius: 'quoque pronior esset in vitia sua consul, irritare
eum atque agitare Poenus coepit. Et laeva relicto hoste Faesulas
petens, Etruriae agros praedatum profectus, quantum maximam
vastationem potest caedibus incendiisque consuli procul ostendit'.
Qui itaque, relicto hoste apud Arretium agente, ad laevam Faesulas petiit, vallem Arni superiorem profecto attigerat. Atque ut in
sicco consisteret, ea post tergum relicta, ulterius processerat.

36   Sed palus illa quo obduruerit modo ut aratrum pateretur cum
aliquando scire cupiverimus, confragosas apud Incisam oppidum

time in higher flood than usual."[87] And a little further on, describing the army's difficulties and the slaughter of pack animals and men that ensued, he says, "The deep, almost bottomless eddies of the river nearly swallowed up the guides. What distressed them most was want of sleep, from which they had been suffering for four days and three nights. Because everything was covered with water they could not find a dry spot on which to lay their exhausted bodies."[88] And so, though the route to Arezzo through Lucca, Pisa, Volterra and the territory of what is today Siena appeared to be longer to someone coming from Liguria, it ought to have been easier, as no one who knows the area will doubt that it would have been. So having taken the shorter route, he reached the waters of the Arno where Florence now is and then entered the course of the river at the present Incisa, or a little above it. And as the Arno was flooded more than usual at that time, he made his way through the swamp until he first found dry land to stand on in the territory of Arezzo. Now, this flooded area and these swamps were not in the plain that, as we saw, lies between Prato and Signa and Florence, as some have thought, for the following reason: Livy says that the region in which Hannibal first gained footing on dry land, the most fertile in Italy, was that portion of the Etruscan plain that lay between Fiesole and Arezzo.[89] And he adds: "By way of making him show these faults of character still more flagrantly, the Carthaginian prepared to irritate and annoy him. He left the enemy behind and marched to the left in the direction of Fiesole to plunder the plain of Etruria. He created as much a devastation as he possibly could and showed the consul in the distance scenes of fire and massacre."[90] If he left the enemy behind at Arezzo and made for Fiesole to his left, Hannibal had clearly reached the upper Arno valley. And to get to dry land he had to go further, leaving the valley behind him.

I have wondered from time to time how that swamp became 36 firm enough to take the plow. I observed that the banks of the

Arni ripas et saxorum fragmenta medio adhuc alveo haerentia cernentes, adapertum fuisse ⟨hunc alveum⟩ tenemus humano ingenio tumentem saxo, et repagulum aquae facientem fluminis fundum, labentibusque postea pro aequali amnis cursu aquis, quae residere et superiori in parte quaqua versum stagnare fuerant consuetae, exsiccatum limi humorem (quod alibi saepe contingit) campos feracissimos reliquisse.

37   Habet ea vallis, ad dexteram Arni post Incisam, Fichinum, quod oppidum Arretinus scribit a comite Guidone Novello exsulibusque Florentinis occupatum pace, per quam exsules in Florentiam reducti sunt, facta, fuisse a populo Florentino destructum. Habet quoque ea vallis Sanctum Iohannem, Montevargum, et Quaratam. ad sinistram vero, Castrum Franchum, Terram Novam, Laterinam, Pontenanum, e quibus Sanctum Iohannem et Castrum Franchum populus Florentinus, sexto et nonagesimo sexto supra millesimum et ducentesimum salutis anno, aedificavit; Terram Novam vero Poggii viri eloquentissimi et aliquot editis operibus clari patriam Guido Petramalensis, Arretinus episcopus, muro quem nunc habet cinxit.

38   In montibus autem altissimis, qui ad sinistram Arnum ibi tortuosissimum intercedunt, est Vallis Umbrosae monasterium. Sunt etiam aliquot regionis de qua diximus Casentinae oppida, quorum primaria habentur Romena, Burgus, et Puppium, a comitibus dudum habitata cognomine Guidis, Mutiliana oriundis quos proximis temporibus pepulit Populus Florentinus. Ad alteram vero Arni ripam et sub ipsius fonte est Porclanum, inferius Stia primum, dehinc Pratum Vetus, infra quod oppidum Arnus Corsolona augetur torrente secus Bibienam, *oppidum nobile.*[50] *In montibus vero ad sinistram est pulcherrima heremus Camaldulensis in qua beatus*

Arno at Incisa were bristling with rocks and some boulders are even now embedded in the middle of the channel. I believe that this channel full of rock was opened up by human ingenuity and that a barrier to the water made a bed for the river; as the water then flowed in that bed rather than in the regular channel of the river — it had before formed stagnant pools everywhere in the upper river — the mud dried out and left behind this extremely fertile land, as often happens elsewhere.

On the right bank of the Arno in the valley beyond Incisa lies 37 Figline. Leonardo Bruni writes that it was occupied by Count Guido Novello da Polenta and exiles from Florence, and that once peace had been made and the exiles brought back to Florence, it was destroyed by the Florentine people.[91] Further up the Valdarno, also on the right of the river, are San Giovanni, Montevarchi, and Quarata, and on the left, Castelfranco di Sopra, Terranuova, Laterina, Pontignano. Of these, the Florentines built San Giovanni and Castelfranco in the year 1296;[92] and Terranuova, the home of the eloquent Poggio, famous as the author of a number of works,[93] was given the walls she now has by Guido Tarlati da Pietramala, bishop of Arezzo.[94]

Set in the high hills that border the left of the Arno, at that 38 point very meandering, is the monastery of Vallombrosa. There are also several towns of the Casentino region that I mentioned above. The major ones are Castel di Romena, Borgo a Collina, and Poppi, long residences of the counts Guidi who came from Modigliana and were recently driven out by the Florentines. On the right bank of the Arno (and right beneath its source) is Porciano, and, lower down, Stia, then Pratovecchio, and below that town the stream Corsolona swells the Arno towards Bibbiena, *a fine town. In the mountains to the left is the lovely hermitage of Camaldoli, where the Blessed Romuald, founder of that order, did penitence. A little after that is the most holy mountain of La Verna, where Saint Francis received the stigmata from Our Lord.*[95] The Arno is fur-

Romualdus eiusdem ordinis inceptor paenitentiam egit. Paulo post Mons devotissimus Alvernae ubi Sanctus Franciscus a Domino nostro stigmata recepit.[51] Augetur etiam Larchiano torrente, qui ad dexteram habet Gellum et Choretium, parva oppida. Qua etiam Arnus se Arretium versus incurvat, est Castrum Novum. Si agrum Florentinum Arretino, Senensi, ac Pisano, et Volaterrano conterminum describere volumus, ad proximam vallem versus meridionalem plagam transeundum est, a Pesa fluvio appellatam. Cui fluvio, ad sinistram, proxima sunt ad ostium quo exoneratur in Arnum: Mons Lupus et supra Colina. Superius ipso sub fonte, Sambuca. Ad dexteram, Mons Iustus, Linarium, et Sanctus Donatus. Alius deinde sequitur fluvius Elsa appellatus, cui sunt ad sinistram: Emporium, Mons Rapolus, Mons Spertolus, Barberinum, Castellina; ad dexteramque Saminiatum, Gambassium, Florentinum, et Certaldum (Iohannis Boccatii, vulgaris potius quam Latinae eloquentiae fama clari, patria), et ad fontem Casulum. Augetur vero Elsa amnis torrente uno qui apud Staggiam oppidum delapsus, fertur ad Bonicium nobile oppidum. Et in ea insula quam Elsa fluvius torrensque praedictus efficiunt, Collis et Geminianum sunt oppida paucis Etruriae oppidis secunda. Est etiam Elsam inter et proximum qui Arnum illabitur torrentem Mons Topulus oppidum.

39   Sequiturque Era fluvius, apud quem hinc est Pons ad Eram oppidum proelio clarum, in quo cum Pisani Lucenses Florentinorum socios fudissent, superveniens Florentinorum exercitus, fortuna proelii conversa, Pisanos fudit, ex eisque ad tria milia cecidit. Pauloque superius Pecciolum, inde vero Calcinaria. Proximoque torrenti in Arnum defluenti hinc Pons Sachi oppidulum, inde est Balneum Aquarum, in quibus solis calentibus a sulphure aquis ranas gigni Plinius dicit. Ea in regione Pisani agri castella sunt alia Volaterranis contermina.

ther augmented by the stream Larchiano, which has on its right
bank the small towns of Gello Biscardo and Cerreto. Castelnuovo
is situated where the Arno bends around towards Arezzo. If we
want to survey the territory of Florence where it is bordered by
those of Arezzo, Siena, Pisa, and Volterra, we must pass over into
the southern reach of the next valley, which takes its name from
the river Pesa. On the left, the towns closest to the mouth of
the Pesa, where it discharges into the Arno, are Montelupo, and
Collina above that. Higher up, just beneath the source of the Pesa,
is Sambuca. On the right are Monte San Giusto, Linari, San
Donato. Another river follows called the Elsa, along whose left
bank are Empoli, Monterappoli, Montespertoli, Barberino Val
d'Elsa, Castellina; and on the right San Miniato, Gambassi, Castel
Fiorentino and Certaldo (the home of Giovanni Boccaccio, known
to fame for his eloquence in the vernacular rather than Latin),[96]
and, at the source of the Elsa, Casole d'Elsa. The Elsa is swollen
by a stream that tumbles down at the town of Staggia and proceeds to the fine town of Poggibonsi. On the island formed by the
Elsa and the stream just mentioned there are the towns of Colle di
Val d'Elsa and San Gimignano, second to few towns in Tuscany.
There is also the town of Montopoli between the Elsa and the
next stream that flows into the Arno.

Next comes the river Era, with Pontedera on this side of it.   39
The town is famous for the battle in which the Pisans first routed
the Lucchesi allies of the Florentines but the Florentine army then
appeared on the scene and, the balance of the battle tipping, swept
the Pisans from the field, about three thousand of them being
killed. Above Pontedera on the river is Peccioli, on the other side
Calcinaia. On this side of the next stream flowing down into the
Arno is the little town of Ponsacco, and on the far side Casciana
Terme, in whose hot sulphurous waters alone, Pliny says, frogs
grow.[97] In this part of the territory of Pisa there are other castles
bordering on the land of Volterra.

40 Superiusque arduis in montibus est Volaterra, de qua Livius in decimo: 'Scipioni hostes Etrusci ad Volaterras, structo agmine, occurrunt. Pugnatum maiore parte diei. Magna utrimque caede, nox incertis qua data victoria esset, intervenit'. Fuit Volaterra Persio satirico cive ornata; nunc Gasparis nostri patria, qui Graecas Latinasque litteras edoctus Bessarionis Niceni Graecorum cardinalis celeberrimi epistularum est scriba. Vetusta autem est haec civitas. Quam simul cum Arretio et Clusio a Tyrrhenis ante bellum Troianum eam fuisse conditam Leonardus Arretinus in Polybio edoctus affirmat, nosque supra docuimus inter capita Etruriae numeratam fuisse. Livius bellum civile Marii et Sullae describens libro LXXXVIII dicit: 'Volaterras, quod oppidum adhuc in armis erat, in deditionem accepit.' Auctorque est Plinius in callidis Volaterranorum aquis haud procul a mari sitis pisces gigni. Ea urbe casu ita potiti sunt Florentini ad annum salutis millesimum ducentesimum quinquagesimum, cum Volaterrani a Florentinis proelio, quod ad montis in quo sita est urbs radices committebatur, superati in urbem confugere eniterentur, insecutus eos miles Florentinus victor pari impetu cum victo ingressus urbem cepit.

41 Ab agri Volaterrani finibus regio incipit maritimae orae Etrusci pelagi, quam descripsimus, adiacens: quae, vastissima et populis pro ambitu infrequens, Senensi populo subdita est. In ea vero sunt (praeter superius enumerata): Massa civitas, Mallianumque et Paganicum. Dehinc ad sinistram Campagnaticum est arduo in colle situm, vinis ceterisque frugibus feracissimum, Petrioli quoque et alia balnea. Nam multa, quae nunc etiam frequentantur, agri Se-

Higher up in the rugged hills is Volterra, of which Livy in Book   40
X says: "The Etruscan enemy drew up their battle lines and threw
themselves against Scipio at Volterra. They fought for most of the
day. There were high casualties on either side, and when night
came on, uncertainty where victory lay."[98] Volterra has the distinction of having had the satirist Persius among her citizens, and is
now the home town of my friend Gaspare da Volterra, a scholar of
Greek and Latin and secretary of the celebrated Bessarion, the
Greek cardinal of Nicaea.[99] It is an ancient city. Leonardo Bruni
in his Polybius assures us that Volterra was founded by the Tyrrhenians before the Trojan War, at the same time as Arezzo and
Chiusi,[100] and I mentioned above that it was numbered among the
major cities of Etruria. Describing the civil war of Marius and
Sulla, Livy says in Book LXXXVIII: "He accepted the surrender of Volterra, a city still under arms."[101] Pliny maintains that
fish are born in the thermal waters of Volterra, situated not far
from the sea.[102] The Florentines gained control of Volterra in 1250
by chance in this way: the citizens of Volterra had been beaten by
the Florentines in a battle fought at the foot of the hill on which it
is set and were trying to fall back into their city, when the Florentine soldiery, quite as fired up in victory as the Volterrans in defeat, entered the city in pursuit of them and captured it.[103]

From the borders of Volterra begins the region adjacent to the   41
coastline (which I have already described) of the Tyrrhenian sea.
Huge and for its size sparsely populated, it is subject to the
Sienese. Apart from those noted above, it has the city of Massa
Marittima, Magliano, and Paganico. Beyond Paganico on the left
is Campagnatico, set on a steep hill with abundant vines and other
fruits, Petriolo, and other spa towns. We observe that many of the
baths in the Senese which are still frequented now were popular long ago. The poet Martial the cook writes to Oppianus: "Unless you bathe in the hot baths of Etruria, you'll die unbathed,
Oppianus."[104] High in the mountains to the right of Petriolo is

nensis balnea olim grata fuisse videmus. Martialis enim coquus ad Oppianum: 'Etruscis nisi thermulis laveris, illotus morieris, Oppiane'. Ad dexteram vero in montibus arduus est Mons Altinus, *quod oppidum Petro astrologo est ornamentum*.[52] Ea regio maritima superiori in parte vestigia habet urbis Rusellanae, quam diximus inter capita Etruriae numeratam esse, de qua Livius in decimo: 'M. Valerius Maximus dictator castra in agrum Rusellanum promovit. Eo et Etrusci hostes secuti: ubi, cum forte quodam loco male densatus agger pondere superstantium in fossam procubuisset atque, eo cum deos pandere viam fugae conclamassent, plures inermes quam armati evasere. Hoc proelio fractae iterum Etruscorum vires. Et pacto annuo stipendio et duum mensium frumento, induatiae biennii datae. Et infra: in Rusellanum agrum exercitus ductus. Ibi non agri tantum vastati sed oppidum etiam oppugnatum. Capta amplius duo milia hominum, minus duo milia[53] circa muros caesa. Et inferius: tres validissimae urbes Etruriae, Rusellae, Perusia, Arretium, pacem petiere'. Adiacetque Rusellarum loco Balnaeum cognomine Rusellarum.

42 Sena vero est interius, urbium Etruriae viribus opibusque nunc fecunda, quae et ipsa inter novas numerari potest, cum nullis in veterum monumentis reperiatur. Suntque qui affirment Carolum (cui Malleo fuit cognomentum) eam condidisse, et Caroli aetatem plus minus sexcentum et septuaginta abhinc annis abfuisse constat. Sed nuper Venetiis in Sancti Georgii de Alga celebri monasterio, quod gloriosus pontifex Eugenius, relicto primum saeculo, propria aedificavit paternae hereditatis pecunia, invenimus in libro litteris scripto pervetustis Iohannem Romanum pontificem nominis ordine duodevicesimum, acceptis de Perusina, Clusiensi, Arretina, Fesulana, Florentina, et Volaterrana diocesibus sex plebatibus, civitatem hanc aedificasse, quae ab ipso sex plebatuum numero Sena fuerit appellata. Habuit ea civitas tertium Alexandrum pontificem Romanum, qui a Federico Barbarosso agitatus

Montalcino, *a town adorned by Peter the astrologer.*[105] The upper
reaches of this coastal region have the remains of the city of
Rusellae, which as we said [§3] was numbered among the mother
cities of Etruria. Livy says of it in Book X: "The dictator M.
Valerius Maximus advanced his camp into the territory of Rusellae. And there the Etruscan enemy followed. In one part the
mound had been built up too loosely, and, owing to the weight of
those standing on it, crumbled down into the ditch, and many,
more non-combatants than soldiers, made their escape that way,
exclaiming that the gods had cleared the passage for their flight.
The might of the Etruscans was smashed a second time. After
they undertook to provide a year's pay for the army and a two
months' supply of corn, they were granted a two-year truce."[106]
And further on: "The army was led into the territory of Rusellae.
Not only were the fields laid waste there but the town was attacked as well. More than two thousand men were taken prisoner and under two thousand killed in the fighting around the
walls."[107] And further still: "Three mighty cities of Etruria, Rusellae, Perusia, and Aretium sued for peace."[108] Next to the site of
Rusellae is *Balnaeum Rusellarum.*

Siena is further inland, a Tuscan town of great power and   42
wealth but one which has to be accounted a modern city since it is
not found in any of the ancient accounts. There are those who
maintain that Charles Martel founded the city, and it is commonly
agreed that he lived some 670 years ago. But in the famous monastery of San Giorgio in Alga in Venice (built with money inherited
from his father by the illustrious pontiff Eugenius IV when he
first joined the religious life), I recently found in a book written in
an ancient hand that Pope John XVIII built the city from the rev-
enues of six parishes of the dioceses of Perugia, Chiusi, Arezzo,
Fiesole, Florence, and Volterra, and that it was called *Sena* precisely from the number of the parishes. This city bore Pope Alexander III, who was harried by Frederick Barbarossa and prevailed

quatuor adversum se erectos in idola adulterinos pontifices superavit. Magno autem decori Senarum urbi fuit celebratum in ea
concilium, in quo Gerardus Florentinus episcopus in secundum
Nicolaum pontificem Romanum creatus constitutionem fecit,
quae in decretis patrum exstat (distinctione tertia et vicesima)
pontifices Romanos eligendi cardinalium collegio et nemini praeterea ius esse. Eique concilio centum et triginta episcopi inter-
fuere.

43   Proelio etiam felicissime gesto clari facti sunt Senenses. Nam
cum Florentini Altinatibus foederatis opem laturi quarto a Senis
miliario via Arretina ad Arbiam fluvium consedissent, Senenses
auxiliaribus copiis Manfredi regis exsulibusque Florentinis immixti, facta eruptione, Florentinum exercitum fuderunt. Caesaque
sunt eo die Florentinorum tria millia et quatuor capta, ac curru,
qui ex more vexilla deferebat, cum ipsis vexillis Senas relato, tantus
Florentinos pavor incessit ut, urbe propemodum deserta, meliores
quique pars Bononiam pars Lucam commigraverint, exsulesque in
patriam sunt reversi.

44   Obiit proximo tempore Ugo Senensis, medicus et philosophus,
omnium sui saeculi, post functum vita Iacobum Forliviensem,
doctissimus et clarissimus habitus. Habuit etiam nuperrime Sena
illustre et micans sidus, sanctum Bernardinum, cuius reliquiae
apud Aquilam urbem veneranter conditae miraculis in dies magis
et magis coruscant, quamquam nescio quae maiora viri unius dici
aut scribi possint miracula operibus quae perpetuis triginta annis
in religione fecit. Eloquentissimus enim ac vehementissimus nec
minus efficax eloquiorum Dei suasor, in universa Italia a vitiis ad
virtutes mirabilem fecit animorum commutationem. Primusque

over the four false pontiffs who were raised up against him as antipopes.[109] It is one of Siena's great glories that the Council was held there in which Gerardo, bishop of Florence, later Pope Nicholas II, established the constitution (still in force among the canons of the church, distinction 23), to the effect that the right of electing the pontiff is reserved to the College of Cardinals and no other.[110] One hundred and thirty bishops took part in the Council.

The Sienese have the distinction of a glorious victory in battle. 43 Intending to bring help to their allies at Montalcino, the Florentines took up a position on the Arbia four miles from Siena on the road from Arezzo. The Sienese, strengthened by reinforcements from King Manfred and by Florentine exiles, broke out of the city and put the Florentine army to flight. Three thousand Florentines were killed, four thousand were taken prisoner, and when the *carroccio* (the cart which traditionally bore the Florentine battle standards) was captured and taken back to Siena with the standards themselves, such fear gripped the Florentines that with the city largely deserted, all the better sort fled Florence, some to Bologna, some to Lucca, and the Florentine exiles returned home.[111]

The physician and philosopher Ugo Benzi of Siena has recently 44 died. He was accounted the most learned and illustrious of all his contemporaries after the death of Giacomo della Torre da Forlì.[112] Very recently, too, Siena had a shining star in San Bernardino. His mortal remains, preserved at Aquila, glitter with miracles that multiply daily, though I cannot think that one could speak or write of any greater miracles of a single man than the holy works Bernardino performed continually over the course of thirty years. Supremely eloquent himself, he was so forceful and effective an advocate of the Divine Eloquence that he brought about a marvellous turning of hearts away from vice and towards virtue throughout all of Italy. And it was he who was the first to guide the order of St. Francis to that strict observance of its rule that is so wide-

omnium ordinem beati Francisci ad eam quae nunc tantopere viget observantiam regulae perduxit. Quo in divino opere eum summis adiuvit conatibus quartus Eugenius pontifex, omni in gerendo pontificatus munere sed imprimis augenda conservandaque religione praestantissimus. Nuncque Sena Silvio Aenea poesis laurea prius, deinde etiam episcopali mitra redimito, Franciscoque Patricio studiis eloquentiae deditissimo,[54] viris quoque plurimis iuris et philosophiae doctrina excultis ornatur.

45   Umbronem Senensis agri fluvium inter et Clanam paludem (sive fluvium Paliam, quem ea palus efficit), multa sunt montana ac campestria oppida, quae nullo (ut in superioribus factum est) ordine describi possunt. Est et Clusium, vetustissima urbs, cui olim Carmon Plinius dicit nomen fuisse. Fuit vero inter capita Etruriae primaria olim numerata, quam Gallorum Senonum bella et Porsennae ipsius regis historia claram imprimis reddunt. Ea nunc paene derelicta, urbi Senae subiecta est. Nec quicquam dubitamus quin populorum ceterarumque rerum reliquiis intereuntes olim Clusium et Rusellae urbem Senam dum conderetur a principio auxerint. Refert ex M. Varrone Plinius Porsennam regem exstruxisse sibi apud Clusium monumentum in quo mirabili opere labyrinthus fuit, cuius nullae Plinii temporibus exstabant reliquiae. Adiacent vero civitatis ipsius ruinae, episcopo etiam nunc ornatae, palustri fluvio Clanae[55] a Plinio, ut nunc, appellato. Ad superioremque eius partem, Senas versus, Politianum est nobile oppidum Florentinis subditum, amoenis in collibus situm. Hinc Turrita, deinde Lucinianum, *Bartolomaeo nunc Genuensi canonico viro doctissimo ornatum.*[56] Interius sunt Sanctus Quiricus, Corsignanum, Chiancanum et arduo in monte Radicofanum. Est ultimum ea in parte patrimonii beato Petro et Romanae ecclesiae a Mathildae co-

spread today. In this divine work Bernardino was given every assistance by the pontiff Eugenius IV, strenuous as he was in carrying out every duty of a pope and above all in propagating and preserving the faith.[113] Siena now is honored by Enea Silvio, crowned first with the poetic laurel and then by the bishop's mitre,[114] and by Francesco Patrizi's devotion to scholarship and eloquence,[115] and by a great many other men celebrated for their learning in the law and philosophy.

Between the river Ombrone in Sienese territory and the marsh-   45
lands of Chiana[116] (or the river Paglia, which is created by the marsh), there are many towns on hill and plain that do not lend themselves to description in any particular order (as was done in the case of the towns above). Among them is Chiusi, a very ancient city that Pliny says was once called Carmon.[117] It was once numbered among the first mother cities of Etruria, made famous in particular by the wars of the Senonian Gauls and the story of her king, Porsenna. Nearly abandoned now, the city is subject to Siena. There can be little doubt that Chiusi and Rusellae, both destined to perish at some point, contributed the remnants of their people and other goods to Siena at the beginning of its existence. Pliny tells us (from Varro) that king Porsenna had a mausoleum constructed for himself at Chiusi in which there was a wonderfully constructed labyrinth, no trace of which remained in Pliny's day.[118] The ruins of the city itself, which has the distinction of a bishopric even now, lie beside the marshy river called the Chiana by Pliny,[119] just as it is today. In its upper reaches towards Siena lies the fine town of Montepulciano, set among pretty hills and subject to the Florentines. After Montepulciano comes Torrita di Siena, then Lucignano, *adorned by Bartolomeo, now canon of Genoa, a man of great learning.*[120] Further inland are San Quírico, Corsignano, Chianciano, and on a steep hill Radicofani. Radicofani is the last castle in the part of her ancestral lands that the countess Matilda gave to St. Peter and the Church of Rome.[121]

mitissa dati castellum. Deinde ultra Clusium, Sarthianum est oppidum Alberto minorista, divinorum dogmatum praedicatore insigni, ornatissimum. Et post id, Cetona.

46   Fecit hactenus agrorum Florentini et Senensis describendorum necessitas ut illis conterminam urbem Arretium distulerimus. Ea civitas vetustissima inter prima Etruriae capita adnumerata est. Nam Livius, libro X, dicit legatos ad consulem venisse ex Arretio, Cortona, et Perusia, quae tunc principes civitatum Etruriae erant. Innuit vero Plinius Arretium in duas urbes fuisse divisam. Nam scribit: 'Arretini veteres, Arretini novi'. Causam rei huius eam videmus fuisse, de qua principio Etruriae diximus: cum, Hannibale Italiam premente, Etrusci ducibus Arretinis in rebellionem proclives viderentur (sicut in Livii habetur XVII), C. Terentius Varro obsides ab Arretinis senatorum filios accepit CXX. Romani enim tumultum in Etruria ab ipsis oriri verebantur. Et cum claves ac seras novas portis imposuisset, in Apuliam rediit. Postmodum bello Marsico (sive Sociali), cum Etrusci sese Marsis et Picentibus furoris socios adiunxissent, L. Sulla, qui ei bello finem imposuit, in Faesulanos Arretinosque desaevit adeo ut, Arretio civibus proscriptis exinanito, novam postea coloniam superinduxerit, unde novi et veteres fuerunt Arretini. Dicere enim solitus fuit Leonardus Arretinus se vidisse Arretii in ecclesia Sanctae Mariae ad Gradum lapidem litteris incisum vetustissimis[57] inscriptumque decretum Arretinorum veterum. Aucti tamen postea sunt opibus Arretini, eosque Livius in bello secundo Punico dicit iuvisse classem mirabili illa celeritate ab Africano paratam, multis variisque rebus construendis navibus et alendo militi opportunis. Viros Arretium habuit praestantissimos. Exstat namque in Macrobii *Saturnalibus* divi Augusti epistula, qua Maecenatem suum Arretii fuisse oriundum affirmat. Et Horatium videmus dicere Maecenatem ipsum regiam ab Etruscis originem duxisse. Cornelius vero

Then beyond Chiusi there is the town of Sarteano which is notable for the Franciscan friar Alberto da Sarteano,[122] a prominent preacher of divine truth. And after Sarteano there is Cetona.

The need to describe the territories of Florence and Siena has   46
caused us to put off our treatment of the city of Arezzo, which they border. This ancient city was one of the mother cities of Etruria. Livy says in Book X that emissaries came to the consul from Arretium, Cortona, and Perusium, which at that time were the chief Etruscan cities.[123] In fact, Pliny indicates that Arezzo had been divided in two when he speaks of "the old and the new Aretines."[124] We mentioned the reason for it at the beginning of our exposition of Tuscany: When Hannibal was pressing Italy hard and the Etruscans seemed to be inclining towards rebellion under Aretine leadership (as Livy says in Book XVII), C. Terentius Varro took 120 sons of senators from Arezzo as hostages, since the Romans feared they would stir up revolt in Etruria. And when he had imposed new keys and bolts on the gates of Arezzo, Varro returned to Apulia.[125] After the Marsian (or Social) War in which the Etruscans had joined the Marsians and Picentines as partners in their fury, Sulla, who had brought the war to an end, vented his rage on the people of of Fiesole and Arezzo to such an extent that proscription emptied Arezzo of her citizens and Sulla later planted a new colony there—whence the "old" and "new" Aretines. Leonardo Bruni used to say that he had seen in the church of S. Maria in Gradi in Arezzo a decree of the "old" Aretines carved in stone in very ancient letters.[126] Later Arezzo became wealthy and powerful, and Livy says that in the Second Punic War she helped the fleet that Scipio Africanus made ready with that remarkable speed of his with all manner of goods useful for building ships and provisioning armies.[127] Arezzo has had extraordinary men. A letter of the divine Augustus is preserved in Macrobius' *Saturnalia* in which the emperor asserts that his friend Maecenas was born in Arezzo.[128] And we find Horace

Nepos in *Attici Pomponii vita,* quod ad Arretii dignitatem facit, Atticum ipsum dicit praedium in Arretino possedisse, quod Caecilianum sit appellatum.

47 Longo postea elapso tempore Arretium ad annum salutis millesimum et decimum octavum Guidone ornatum fuit, celebri musico, et anno inde ducentesimo alterum Guidonem, episcopum ex Petramalensi familia, habuit civem et dominum, qui urbem ipsam muro cinxit quem nunc habet. Burgum quoque Sancti Sepulchri, Civitatem Castelli, Castilionem Arretinum, Terram Novam vallis Arni, et Civitellam (nunc ea de causa Episcopi appellatam) moenibus cingi communirique curavit. Insuper vias, quae ad omnes portarum Arretii exitus nunc cernuntur, dirigi, dilatari, et (ubi oportere visum est) sterni aut pontibus iungi fecit. Quin etiam eius fuit opus recta et spatiosa via, in qua ab Anglario in Burgum ad Sepulchrum ducente Nicolaum Piccininum ab ecclesiae copiis superatum fuisse ostendimus.[58] *Ex eadem Petramalensi familia Arretio dominanti fuere viri bellicosissimi Iannes Tedescus, Masius et Bartolomaeus equestris ordinis, Guillielmusque praesul ex nobilissima Ubertinorum familia Arretii dominus apud Campaldinum adversus Florentinos dimicans fortissime atque gloriosissime occubuit eiusque victoriae gratia scutum eius in Martis olim templo et nunc baptisterio etiam nunc appensum visitur.*[59] Aetate quoque nostra Arretina urbs decorata est viro eloquentissimo ac clarissimo Leonardo Arretino Caroloque Graecis et Latinis litteris eruditissimo, nunc populi Florentini cancellario; et Benedicto ac Francisco fratribus, iure consultissimis cognomine Accoltis, e quibus Franciscus non minus bonas artes et oratoriam ac omnem historiam quam leges excellenter edoctus est; ornata est etiam[60] Iohanne Tortellio, Romani pontificis[61] subdiacono et cubiculario Graecis ac Latinis litteris ac singulari humanitate praedito, cuius praeclarum *De orthographia* opus verba edocet selecta quibus e Graecia sumptis Latine utimur. Nec indignum ducent quod refe-

saying that Maecenas himself traced his lineage back to the Etruscan kings.[129] Cornelius Nepos in the *Life of Pomponius Atticus* says
that Atticus himself owned an estate called Caecilianum at Arezzo, something he regards as to the credit of the Aretines.[130]

Much later, in the year 1018, Arezzo was honored by the birth   47
of Guido d'Arezzo,[131] the famous musician, and two hundred
years after that the city had a second Guido, a bishop of the
Pietramala clan, as its citizen and master.[132] He encircled Arezzo
with the walls she has now, and saw to it that Borgo San Sepolcro,
Città di Castello, Castiglion Aretino,[133] Terranuova Valdarno, and
Civitella (now called after him Civitella del Vescovo) were walled
and fortified as well. In addition he had the roads now visible at
all the exits of the city gates aligned, broadened, and (where it
seemed necessary) paved or connected by bridges. The straight
broad road that leads to Borgo San Sepolcro from Anghiari was
also Guido's work, the road on which, as I have shown, Niccolò
Piccinino was defeated by the army of the Church.[134] *From the same
family of Pietramala, lords of Arezzo, came the warlike men Gianni
Tedesco, Maso and Bartolomeo, knights, and Bishop Guglielmino from the
most noble family of the Ubertini, the lord of Arezzo who fought so bravely
against the Florentines at Campaldino and fell gloriously. In memory of
that victory his shield may even now be seen hanging in the former temple
of Mars, now the Baptistery [of Florence].*[135] The city of Arezzo has
its ornaments in our time, too, in the eloquent and illustrious
Leonardo Bruni; Carlo Marsuppini, the present chancellor of the
Florentine Republic and very learned in Greek and Latin;[136] the
brothers Benedetto and Francesco Accolti, both jurisconsults,
though Francesco is no less highly accomplished in the liberal arts,
oratory, and the whole range of history than in the law;[137] and
Giovanni Tortelli, a pontifical subdeacon and chamberlain, rich in
Greek and Latin learning and of a singular humanity. His famous
work *On Orthography* explains the use of certain words in Latin
which derive from the Greek.[138] These many distinguished

remus tam multi praestantes viri Arretini Plinium scripsisse Arre-
tinos in Italia fictilium vasorum gloriam[62] obtinuisse, quod quidem
Martialis affirmat libro primo: 'sic Arretinae violant crystallina
testae'.

48   Cortona sequitur, urbium Etruriae vetustissima, quam Pelasgi
condidere, iisque pulsis, possedere Tyrrheni. Expugnavere autem
eam ac moenibus spoliavere Arretini, a quibus diu possessa fuit.
Aetate vero nostra Ladislaus, rex Neapolitanus, ipsam vendidit
Florentinis, in quorum subiectione perseverat; ea nunc Iacobo cive
iuris scientia claro et Perusinae urbis episcopo decorata est. Ad
eius urbis agri proximos fines lacus est Trasumenus, qui dicitur
Perusinus, acceptae per Flaminium consulem ab Hannibale cladis
memoria notissimus. Isque lacus in circuitu oppidis ornatur et cas-
tellis: Malborghetto (ad eam partem quae in Cortonam vergit),
Castilione Clusino, et Panicali Clanas[63] versus, deinde Monte
Pontighino, et, qua Perusiam a Florentina petitur, Passignano.
Trasumenum[que] autem et Clanas[64] inter oppidum est Castellum
Plebis. Sunt etiam in lacu tres insulae habitatae.

49   Succedit iis ordine Perusia urbs, vetustissima capitum et ipsa
Etruriae, sicut saepe supra diximus, olim primaria, quam Iustinus
ab Achaeis conditam fuisse dicit. Estque haec sola inter omnes
Italiae urbes felicitatem nacta penitus inauditam, quod eandem
paene status et rerum condicionem, quam ante conditam urbem
Romam et deinde Roma sub regibus, consulibus, imperatoribus et
tyrannis agente habuit, nunc retinet. Passa est tamen varias sed to-
lerandas agitationes. Nam Livius in nono: 'eodem anno, cum reliquiis Etruscorum ad Perusiam (quae et ipsa indutiarum fidem ru-

Aretines will not be offended if I mention that Pliny wrote that Arezzo had a reputation for her earthenware vessels,[139] which Martial likewise asserts in Book I: "So pots from Arezzo dishonor crystal glasses."[140]

Cortona comes next, the oldest city in Etruria. It was founded   48 by the Pelasgians and when they were expelled, taken over by the Tyrrhenians. The Aretines sacked it and deprived it of its walls, long remaining in possession of the city. In our time Ladislaus, the king of Naples, sold her to the Florentines and the city continues under their control. Jacopo, bishop of Perugia and a citizen distinguished for legal learning, now adorns the city. Near the borders of the city's territory is Lake Trasimene, also called the Lago di Perugia, well-known to history for the disaster suffered there by the consul Flaminius at the hands of Hannibal.[141] The shores of the lake are dotted with towns and castles: Borghetto (on the rim of the lake towards Cortona), Castiglione del Lago, and Panicale towards the Chiana, then *Mons Pontighinus*, and Passignano on the way to Perugia from Florence. Between Trasimene and the Chiana is the town of Città della Pieve. There are also three populated islands on the lake.[142]

The city of Perugia is next in order, the oldest of the Etruscan   49 mother cities, as I have often said above, and once the leader among them. Justin says it was founded by the Achaeans.[143] Among all the cities of Italy, Perugia has achieved a unique and unparalleled success in keeping now pretty much the same standing and substance that she enjoyed before the foundation of Rome and ever afterwards, while Rome passed under kings, consuls, emperors and tyrants. She has of course had various troubles, but manageable ones. Livy says in Book IX: "In the same year the consul Fabius fought a battle with the remnants of the Etruscans at Perugia (which had itself violated the terms of the truce). Victory was easy and decisive, and Fabius would have taken the city when he approached the walls had not Etruscan legates come out and

perat) Fabius cos., nec dubia nec difficili victoria dimicans, ipsum oppidum, cum ad moenia accessit, cepisset, ni legati dedentes urbem exissent'. Et libro decimo: 'nec in Etruria pax erat. Nam et Perusinis auctoribus post deductum a consule exercitum, rebellatum fuerat. Fabius quatuor milia quingentos Perusinorum occidit. Cepit ad mille septingentos quadraginta, qui redempti sunt singuli aeris CCCX milites; praeda alia omnis militi concessa. Et inferius: tres validissimae Etruriae urbes, Rusellana, Perusia, et Arretium, pacem petiere'. Quamvis autem per infaustissimi triumviratus tempora L. Antonium, M. Antonii fratrem, Octavius Caesar in Perusia obsederit, famemque raro alias similem auditam Antonii exercitus in ea clausus et Perusinus populus sustinuerit, captaque tum urbs ac diruta sit, eam tamen brevi instauratam moenibus portisque nunc exstantibus communivit idem Octavianus Augustus, a suoque cognomine Perusiam Augustam (sicut litterae cubitales portis incisae ostendunt) voluit appellari. De causis autem dirutionis sic habet Livius libro CXXV: 'L. Antonius cos., M. Antonii frater, Fulvia consulente, bellum Caesari Octavio intulit. Et receptis in partes suas populis, quorum agri veteranis Caesarianarum olim partium assignati erant (inter quos Perusinus erat) et M. Lepido, qui custodiae urbis Romae cum exercitu praeerat, fuso, hostiliter in urbem irruit. Libro autem CXXVI Livius sic sequitur: 'Caesar, annorum XXIII,[65] obsessum in oppido Perusia L. Antonium, conatum aliquando erumpere et repulsum fame, coegit in deditionem venire. Ipsique et omnibus militibus ignovit. Perusiam diruit'.

50   Baldus patrum nostrorum memoria in ea claruit, ac magis magisque eius nomen in dies claret, quin etiam Bartolo Saxoferratensi iurium civilis et pontificii obtinuit principatum. Viris nunc quoque pacis et belli artibus, sed imprimis docendo ac dicendi iure praestantissimis ea urbs abundat. Quorum primarios Ivonem, Io-

surrendered it."[144] And in Book IX: "Nor was there peace in Etruria. After the consul had withdrawn his army, there was an uprising led by the Perugians. Fabius slew 4500 of them and took 1740 prisoners, ransomed at 310 *asses* per head; the rest of the booty was given to the soldiers."[145] And further on: "Three mighty cities of Etruria, Rusellae, Perugia, and Arezzo, sued for peace."[146] In the time of that doomed triumvirate, Octavian besieged Lucius Antonius, Mark Antony's brother, in Perugia. Pent up inside, his army and the people of Perugia suffered almost unheard-of starvation before the city was captured and destroyed. And yet for all that Octavian soon repaired and strengthened the city with the walls and gates it now has, and had it renamed Perusia Augusta after himself, as the inscriptions on the city gates attest in letters eighteen inches high. On the reasons for the destruction of the city, Livy in Book CXXV has the following: "After consultation with Fulvia, the consul L. Antonius, the brother of M. Antonius, took the war to Octavian. He won over to his side the people whose lands had once been distributed to the veterans of Caesar's party, among them the Perugians. He routed Lepidus, who with his army had been put in charge of defending Rome, and stormed his way into the city."[147] And in Book CXXVI Livy continues the tale: "Aged twenty-three, Octavian besieged L. Antonius in Perugia and forced him to surrender— Antonius had tried a number of times to break out of the city but had been beaten back by hunger. Octavian pardoned Antonius and his army, but razed Perugia to the ground."[148]

In our fathers' day, Baldo degli Ubaldi won a great name in 50 Perugia, and indeed his renown gets greater day by day. He is regarded, along with Bartolo da Sassoferrato, as the doyen of civil and canon law.[149] The city is now full of men skilled in all the arts of peace and war, but most especially in the teaching and practice of law. Among them I know Ivone, *Giovanni Sparelli*,[150] Sallustio, Giovanni Petruccio and Benedetto Bargio to be leading figures.[151]

hannem Sparellium,[66] Salustium, Iohannem Petrucium et Benedictum Bargium novimus. *Alio autem in doctrinarum digniori genere virum nunc habet Perusia excellentem Angelum Minoristam inter nostri saeculi philosophos theologosque primarios numeratum.*[67] Ex his vero qui rei bellicae operam dedere, Biordus et Ceccolinus Michelocti primum, post eos Nicolaus, Franciscus, et Iacobus Piccinini, de quibus in Montono oppido simul cum Braccio dicemus,[68] fuere clarissimi. Nuncque Braccius Balionus incipit esse clarus.

51 Supra Perusiam a Tiberis ripa paulisper recedunt: Cisterna primum, dehinc Anglarium, quod, e regione Burgi ad Sepulchrum regionis Umbriae situm, viam habet ad illud rectissimam, in qua Nicolai Piccinini copias a quarti Eugenii pontificis gloriosissimi copiis fusas[69] fuisse in *Historiis* ostendimus. Distatque ab Anglario Tiberis ea via passuum tribus milibus, et superius ad Tiberis fontem est Cotulum, arx aerea.

52 Restat in Etruriae partibus regio quam beati Petri patrimonium diximus appellari. Supra Pissiam torrentem, ad quem eam in maritimis inchoare diximus, est Soana, oppidum septimo Gregorio pontifice Romano certe praestantissimo cive ornatum. Superiusque est oppidum Sancta Flora. Interiusque medium, id quod hinc Soanam inde Montem Alcinum et Radicofanum interiacet spatium, montes complent altissimi, Apennino paene (a quo plurimum distant) celsitudine comparandi, Monsamiata appellati. In quibus, diversa regione, aliquot sunt castella, sed praestantius est Sancti Philippi Balneum. Et proxime illos Vulsinensium montes inter lacum et Paliam amnem sunt: Porcenum, Aquapendens, Griptae, Sanctus Laurentius, Romanae ecclesiae oppida. Vulsinensium vero lacui adiacet oppidum Bulsena dictum, in ruinis aedifi-

In another, worthier branch of learning Perugia now boasts the excellent Franciscan friar Angelo, who is numbered among the principal philosophers and theologians of our time.[152] Of those who have practised the art of war, Biordo and Checcolino Michelotti in the first place, and after them Niccolò, Francesco, and Jacopo Piccinino (of whom, together with Braccio, we shall speak when we reach Montone) were all very well known.[153] Nowadays Braccio Baglioni is beginning to achieve fame on his own account.[154]

Above Perugia, back a little from the bank of the Tiber, are, 51 first, Cisterna, then Anghiari, set opposite Borgo San Sepolcro in the region of Umbria. Anghiari has a road that goes straight to Borgo San Sepolcro on which, as I showed in my *Histories*, the forces of the glorious pontiff Eugenius IV scattered the army of Niccolò Piccinino.[155] The Tiber is three miles from Anghiari on that road and, higher up, at the source of the Tiber, is the lofty stronghold of Cotolo.

There remains to be described the region of Tuscany which is 52 called, as was said above [§19], the "Patrimony of St. Peter." It begins, as I said, at the stream Pescia on the coast, above which is the town of Sovana, famous for her citizen, the illustrious Roman pontiff Gregory VII.[156] Higher up is the town of Santa Fiora. Further inland, high mountains fill the area that lies between Sovana on one side and Montalcino and Radicofani on the other. Nearly comparable in height to the Apennines, but a long way away, they are called Monte Amiata. Among them on the far side are a number of castles, most notably Bagni San Filippo. And near these mountains of the Volsinii, between Lago di Bolsena and the river Paglia, are Proceno, Acquapendente, Grotte di Castro, San Lorenzo, towns of the Church of Rome. The town called Bolsena lies beside the Lago di Bolsena: it was built on the ruins of the city of Volsinii, once numbered among the principal cities of Etruria. Of the city of Volsinii, Livy in Book X: "The other consul Postumius brought his army over into Etruria and first ravaged the territory

catum urbis Vulsinensium inter capita Etruriae olim numeratae. De qua Livius in decimo: 'consul alter Postumius, in Etruriam traducto exercitu, primum pervastaverat Vulsinensium agros. Deinde, cum egressis ad tuendos fines haud procul moenibus eorum depugnat, duo milia trecenti Etruscorum caesi'. Et infra idem Livius undecimo libro dicit eam, totius Etruriae potentissimam, permittente populo in libertatem restituto Romanis subactam, cum servi illam captis dominis occupassent. Scribitque Plinius nullum esse in Italia agrum feraciorem olea quam Vulsinensem, in quo sata primo anno fructificet. Inde ad dexteram haud longe abest castellum, Caput Montis, lacui imminens, cui propinqua est insula nunc a fratribus sancti Francisci habitata et in qua rex secundus Ostrogothorum A⟨ta⟩laricus Amalasiuntham genitricem suam, praestantissimam mulierem, occidi est passus. Et post id, Martha ad lacus emissorium, ubi fluvius eiusdem nominis incipit. Deinde[70] in mediterraneis est Castrum civitas, cavis rupibus adeo circumdata ut illam adeuntes speluncam potius quam civitatem ingredi suspicentur. Obiit nuper clarus civitatis illius civis Paulus, iure consultorum saeculi sui facile princeps. Castro proxime adiacet Tuscanella, oppidum ecclesiae opulentissimum. Dehinc arduo in colle Mons Faliscorum est, corrupte dictus Mons Flasconus.

53   Interiusque arduis item in collibus Paliae amni vicinis, civitates sunt: hinc Balneum Regium, inde Urbs Vetus, nomina quarum ante millesimum annum nullus ponit scriptor. Sed in *Historiis* asserit Arretinus Urbevetanos a Florentinis originem habuisse. Fuit vero Urbs Vetus nostra aetate infelicitate par Bononiae et Narniae civitatibus, quod inter cives Merculinae et Muffatae, uti appellant, factionum maxima in ea et crudelissima sanguinis effusio sicut et in illis commissa est. Ornatur autem ecclesia et palatio magnifici operis, quod Urbanus V pontifex Romanus ad annum salutis septimum et sexagesimum supra millesimum exstrui curavit. Magno

of Volsinii. The townsmen came out to defend their borders and a battle ensued not far from their walls; 2300 of the Etruscans were killed."[157] And later, in Book XI, he says that Volsinii, the most powerful city of Etruria, when their slaves had captured their masters and occupied the city, was subjugated to the Romans with the compliance of the [Volsinian] people, once they had been restored to liberty.[158] Pliny writes that no land in Italy is more productive of oil than Volsinii, where an olive tree yields fruit in its first year.[159] Not far to the right of Bolsena there is a castle, Capodimonte, overlooking the lake, and nearby an island on which Franciscan friars now live, where Athalarich, the king of the Ostrogoths, suffered his mother, the renowned Amalasuntha, to be murdered.[160] After Capodimonte comes Marta, at the outlet of the lake where the river of the same name begins. Then, further inland, is the town of Castro, so hemmed in by hollowed-out cliffs that visitors might well think they are entering a cave rather than a city. Its distinguished citizen Paolo di Castro died in recent times, by some way the foremost jurisconsult of his age.[161] Tuscania is close by, belonging to the Church and very wealthy. Finally, on a steep hill is the Mons Faliscorum, corrupted now to Montefiascone.

Further inland, likewise among high hills bordering the river 53 Paglia, are the towns of Bagnoregio on one side and Orvieto (*Urbs Vetus*, 'ancient city') on the other, though no writer records their names before A.D. 1000. But in his *Histories* Leonardo Bruni says that the Orvietans took their origin from the Florentines.[162] In our time Orvieto has suffered the unhappy fate of Bologna and Narni: in this city, as in those, much blood has been cruelly shed by the citizens of the so-called "Mercorini" and "Muffati" factions. The city is distinguished by its cathedral and by a magnificent palace whose construction was undertaken by Pope Urban V in the year 1067.[163] Restored at great expense, it was furnished with a citadel to prevent the citizens from harming each other, and the citadel

instauratum impendio ornatur et arce, ut enim obvietur ne cives in se ipsos saeviant; arx ibi aedificatur munitissima.[71] Eam urbem praeterlabitur Pallia fluvius, qui a Clanis paludibus (ut diximus) ortum ducens inter Ameriam et Ortam cadit in Tiberim.

54 Estque Orta ad Tiberis fluenta civitas vetusta, cuius nomen prius habet veterum scriptorum Plinius, nisi forte eam esse velimus de qua Vergilius: 'Ortanae classes'. Post eam secundum Tiberis ripam in via Flaminia pons invenitur, olim Tiberi ad viam Flaminiam a Caesare Augusto impositus nuncque, castello superimposito, dirutus. Continebat[72] vero stante Romana re ad eum pontem hinc inde maxima aedificia, quae ab Ocriculo ad ipsam urbem Romam ita continuabantur ut non vicus unus neque plures villae viderentur esse sed ipsam urbem usque ad Ocriculum protendi appareret.[73] Siquidem Ammianus Marcellinus, Constantis Caesaris, Constantino primo nati, adventum a Constantinopoli Romam libro sextodecimo describens, dicit ipsum duxisse in comitatu Hormisdam Persarum gentis architecturae peritissimum, iussisseque illi ut primaria quaeque dignioraque urbis Romae aedificia diligenter inspecta ordine sibi ostenderet. Et cum Ocriculum de itinere esset ventum, Persam, imperatore iubente, omnium colloquio destitutum ab Ocriculo Romam prius ingressum fuisse quam quo in loco Urbs inchoasset discernere ac intelligere noverit.

55 Post Tiberis pontem (ut diximus, dirutum), primum in via Flaminia Burghettus est, vicus Sancti Leonardi appellatus. Octavoque inde miliario eadem via est Civitas Castellana, altissimis insuperabilibusque rupibus adeo circumdata ut ad inexpugnabilem munitionem nullo indigeat muro. Eam vero nonnulli ex doctioribus

built there is extremely well-fortified.[164] The river Paglia, which rises in the marshlands of Chiana (as I mentioned [§45]) and feeds into the Tiber between Amelia and Orte, flows past the city of Orvieto.

Orte is an ancient city beside the waters of the Tiber. Pliny is   54 the first among the ancients to mention it by name, unless perhaps we should think it is the place from which Vergil's "Ortan levies" come.[165] Along the Tiber beyond Orte we find a bridge on the Via Flaminia, built over the river by Augustus, and now in ruins with a castle built on top.[166] While Rome endured, the road was lined by great buildings on either side of the bridge, and they continued without interruption from Otricoli[167] right down to Rome— giving the appearance not of a village nor even a series of estates but of the city itself stretching all the way to Otricoli. In fact Ammianus Marcellinus describes in Book XVI the arrival in Rome from Constantinople of the emperor Constans, the son of Constantine I. He says that the emperor brought with him in his retinue an architectural expert, a Persian named Hormisdas. Constans directed him to make a careful examination of all the important and impressive buildings of Rome and to show them to him one by one. When they reached Otricoli on the journey, Ammianius says, the emperor forbade anyone to converse with the Persian, and it was not until he entered Rome on the way from Otricoli that he was able to see the difference and realize where the city actually began.[168]

After the Tiber bridge (in ruins, as I mentioned), first on the   55 Via Flaminia comes Borghetto, also known as Borgo San Leo- nardo. Eight miles further down the Via Flaminia is Civita Castel- lana. The place is encircled by very high cliffs which cannot be climbed, so it has impregnable defenses without the need of walls. Various scholars have in our time proposed and ventilated the view that this was the site of the city of Veii, besieged by the Romans for a decade and later the place where Camillus spent his

aetatis nostrae opinantur praedicantque fuisse locum Veientanae urbis, decennio a Romanis obsessae et postea a Camillo felici in relegatione sua habitatae. Sed Tiberis primum, qui a Civitate Castellana tribus distat passuum milibus et Veiis proximus ac prope contiguus fuisse describitur, deinde Plinius erroris eos redarguunt. Dicit namque Plinius Tiberim intra sextum decimum lapidem dividere Veientanum agrum a Crustumino primum, dehinc a Fidenate, deinde Latium a Vaticano. Et Crustumium fuisse ubi nunc est Mons Rotundus, Fidenasque prope Romam secus Anienem in Umbriae descriptione ostendemus, quod quidem Francisci Fiani, poetae Romanarum historiarum peritissimi, auctoritas confirmat. Is enim Fiano oriundus, propinquo Tiberi castello, certissimis docuit coniecturis Veios fuisse apud Pontianum, castellum Tiberi item et Fiano propinquum.[74]

56 Veiorum urbis loco situque ostenso, rerum quas cum populo Romano illi gesserunt breviarium conficere libet. Fidena Veientum Etruscorum colonia trans Tiberim fuit inter Crustuminum Romanumque agrum. Fidenates facta in Romano agro praeda onustos, Romulus tanto impetu est insecutus ut simul cum fugientibus Fidenas ingressus sit. Veii, ut Fidenates ulciscerentur, agrum Romanum populati sunt. In eos Romulus legiones eduxit, paxque[75] inter utrosque composita. Post haec, rege Tullo Hostilio regnante, Fidenates, Romanis per Romuli pacem subditi, rebellarunt, Veientesque[76] opem tulerunt, Mettio Fufetio rege Albano in id bellum advocato, qui cum neutris fidem servasset, a Tullo in quatuor frusta laceratus est. Tullus victor Fidenas vendicavit, Albamque evertit. Tertium regibus exactis cum populo Romano Veientibus bellum

happy exile.[169] But in the first place the Tiber—which is three miles distant from Civita Castellana, while it is said to have been very close to and almost touching Veii—and then Pliny, expose their error: he says that in the space of sixteen miles the Tiber separates the territory of Veii from that of Crustumerium, and then from the territory of Fidenae, and then Latium from the Vatican.[170] I will show in my survey of Umbria [§25] that Crustumerium was where Monterotondo is now and that Fidenae was near Rome along the river Aniene. This is confirmed by the authority of Francesco da Fiano, a poet with an expert knowledge of Roman history:[171] born at Fiano (a castle near the Tiber), he has shown by convincing arguments that the site of Veii was at Ponzano Romano, a castle likewise close to the Tiber, and to Fiano.

Having established the location of Veii, a brief synopsis of the 56 Veientes' dealings with the Romans is in order. Fidenae was a colony of the Etruscans of Veii across the Tiber between the territories of Crustumerium and Rome. The Fidenates were weighed down with booty taken in Roman territory when Romulus chased them so forcefully that both pursued and pursuers entered Fidenae together. To avenge the Fidenates, Veii ravaged Roman territory. Romulus led his legions against them before a peace was arranged between the two parties. Subsequently, in the reign of King Tullus Hostilius, the Fidenates, who had been made subject to the Romans in accordance with the peace of Romulus, rose up against them with the support of Veii: Mettius Fufetius, the king of Alba Longa, had been summoned to help in the war, but since he behaved treacherously towards both sides, King Tullus had him torn in quarters.[172] The victorious Tullus recovered Fidenae and destroyed Alba Longa. After the expulsion of the kings there was a third war between Veii and the Romans. In the first engagement the Romans came off worst; beaten again in the second, the most ferocious of all, the Romans forced their soldiers to swear that

fuit, in quo prima pugna Romani fuerunt inferiores. Secunda vero omnium atrocissima superati, milites iurare coegerunt se, nisi victores, numquam redituros. Qua religione obstrictis animis, obstinatius quam ante pugnatum est, non sine utrorumque maxima occisione. Ceciderunt Cn. Manlius cos. et Q. Fabius, alterius consulis frater, capta Romana castra, sed mox, fortuna mutata, sunt recuperata, victique tunc Romani vicerunt. Quartum exinde fuit bellum, in quo trecentos Fabios cum quinque milibus servorum clientumque Veientes ad Cremeram interfecerunt. Quinto bello, Veientes L. Memmium cos. non procul item a Cremera castra habentem magno aggressi impetu repulsum fugatumque castris exuerunt. Moxque fugientes Romanos insecuti Ianiculum ceperunt, urbemque Romanam aliquot mensibus obsessam tenuerunt. Sexto demum bello, urbs Veientana decem annis a Romanis obsessa a Camilloque capta est, ubi tantum praedae fuit quantum antea Romani trecentis quinquaginta annis ex omnibus aliis victoriis habuerant. Universus populus Romanus tunc ad praedam in castra vocatus est. Fuitque tam gratus Romanis situs ut de Roma relinquenda Veiosque transferenda aliquando sit cogitatum et inter patres actum. Hinc est versus: 'Roma domus fiet. Veios migrate, Quirites'.

57   Sequitur ad Tiberim mons Soracte a priscis dictus, de quo Vergilius: 'hi Soractis habent arces',[77] et Plinius: 'ad Soractem Varro asserit fontem esse, cuius sit latitudo quatuor pedum, soleque oriente eum exundare ferventi similem. Avesque quae gustaverint iuxta mortuas iacere'. Quod quidem nos certius ea ratione credimus quia, cum vir summus Prosper Columna Romanae ecclesiae cardinalis nosque simul Antiatis urbis ruinas perlustraremus, silvas ibi vicinas (in quibus maximae sunt ruinae) ingressi, fonticulum offendimus, in cuius labris aviculae duae, post gustatam (ut apparebat) aquam, occubuerant. Soracti autem monti nunc nomen

they would never return home except as victors. With this solemn oath in mind, they fought more stubbornly than before, and vast slaughter ensued on both sides. The consul Cn. Manlius and the brother of the other consul, Q. Fabius, fell in battle. The Roman camp was captured, but it was soon recovered as their fortunes changed, and the conquered Romans then became the conquerors. Thereafter there was a fourth war, in which the Veientes destroyed three hundred of the Fabii clan, with five thousand of their slaves and clients, at the river Cremera.[173] In the fifth war, the Veientes made a massive assault on the consul L. Memmius, who was like-wise encamped not far from the Cremera. They drove him off, putting him to flight and stripping him of his camp. In their pur-suit of the routed Romans they captured the Janiculum, and for several months kept Rome under siege. Finally, in a sixth war, Veii was besieged by the Romans for ten years and taken by Camillus. There was as much booty there as the Romans had acquired from all their other victories over the past three hundred and fifty years. All the people of Rome were summoned to the camp to share the booty. The Romans were so taken with the site that they even once discussed (and debated in the senate) leaving Rome and moving to Veii. Hence the line: "Rome is about to become one great house. Move to Veii, citizens."[174]

Following Civita Castellana on the Tiber is the mountain the ancients called Soracte, on which Vergil says: "These men hold the heights of Soracte,"[175] and Pliny: "Varro says there is a spring on Soracte, four feet wide. When the sun comes up, the spring bubbles up as if it were boiling, and birds that have tasted of it lie dead nearby."[176] I find this all the more credible for something that happened when his eminence Prospero Cardinal Colonna[177] and I were surveying the ruins of the city of Antium together. Entering a nearby wood where there were extensive ruins, we found a little spring and at its edge two small birds which had apparently died from drinking the water. But Mount Soracte now has a new

est novum: Sancti Silvestri ab eius sancti pontificis Romani sacello, quod summo in cacumine aedificatum habet. Idemque obtinet Silvestri vocabulum ad radices eius montis Tiberi imminens oppidulum. Soracte autem per hiemem esse nivosum sic ostendit Horatius *Epistularum*[78] primo: 'vides ut alta stet nive candidum Soracte, neque iam sustineant onus silvae laborantes, geluque flumina constiterint acuto?'

58   Ulterius via Flaminia est Arianum *Pandulphi Sabelli patritii Romani facile omnium aetatis nostrae Romanorum praesertim nobilium saecularium eloquentissimi*[79] oppidum, quod, ab ara Iani olim dictum, in Theodorae Romanae nobilis mulieris praedio beati Gregorii temporibus aedificatum fuisse legimus. Ultra Arianum eadem Flaminia est Castrum Novum, et usque ad portam olim prius Flumentanam, dehinc Flaminiam, et nunc Populi dictam, nil aliud habet via Flaminia communitum. At post Ortam civitatem, intus sunt hinc Galliensium oppidum, Romano urbis Romae pontifice olim *et nunc Iohanne Gallesio grammatico et rhetore*[80] ornatum, inde Nepesum, civitas in Romanorum historiis crebro inventa, quam Livius XXVII[81] dicit fuisse unam ex duodecim coloniis, quae difficillimis rei publicae temporibus, Hannibale in Italia agente, militiam detractavere. Et libro XXVIIII[82] scribit eam cum aliis post sextum annum dedisse duplum.

59   Lacum Vulsinensium praetergressos campi excipiunt amplissimi, in quibus est Viterbium civitas parum vetusta, cuius parvi admodum castelli primum nomen ad annum hinc sexcentesimum erat Viturvium. Et e regione illius ad sextum lapidem ruinae exstant ingentes Faleriae urbis, quam diximus inter capita Etruriae numeratam fuisse. Eius a Camillo captae celebris est memoria,

name: Monte San Silvestro, from a chapel of that holy pontiff
built on the very summit. The little town at the foot of the mountain overlooking the Tiber has the same name, San Silvestro. Horace in the first book of *Odes* shows us that Soracte is covered in
winter snow: "Do you see how deep the snow stands on white
Soracte, and how the laboring trees can no longer bear their burden, how stiff the streams are with sharp ice?"[178]

Further along the Via Flaminia is Rignano Flaminio (Aria- 58
num), *a town belonging to the Roman patrician Pandolfo Savelli, easily
the most eloquent of the secular Roman nobles of our time*.[179] The town
was originally named for an altar of Janus (*ara Jani*). We read that
it was built on the estate of a Roman noblewoman Theodora in
the days of St. Gregory.[180] Beyond Rignano, likewise on the Via
Flaminia, is Castelnuovo di Porto. Beyond Castelnuovo, the Via
Flaminia has no fortified settlement until the present Porta del
Popolo of Rome, originally called the Porta Flumentana and later
the Porta Flaminia. Inland below Orte there are the towns of
Gallese on one side (once adorned by Romanus, pontiff of Rome,
and now by the grammarian and rhetor Iohannes Gallesius),[181] and Nepi
on the other. This town is frequently found in the history of
Rome. In Book XXVII Livy says it was one of the twelve colonies
that declined to furnish soldiers in a time of utmost difficulty for
the republic, when Hannibal was on the offensive in Italy.[182] And
in Book XXVIII he writes that after six years Nepi, along with
the others, doubled its military contribution.[183]

Those who pass beyond Lago di Bolsena come upon a broad 59
plain in which lies the not very old city of Viterbo, whose first
name six hundred years ago was that of the small castle of
Viturvium. Six miles from Viterbo as the crow flies are the extensive remains of the city of Faleria, which, as we saw, was numbered
among the chief cities of Etruria. The story of its capture by
Camillus is well known: how he had the treacherous Falerian
schoolmaster bound and flogged and dragged back to the city by

quod perfidum ille grammaticum vinctum verberatumque in urbem reduci curavit a pueris quos hosti prodere quaesivisset. Scribitque Plinius: 'in Falisco agro amnis aquam potatam candidas boves facere.' Et alibi: 'haud procul urbe Roma in Faliscorum agro,
familiae sunt paucae quae vocantur Hirpiae, quae, sacrificio annuo
quod fit ad montem Soracte Apollini, super ambustam ligni
struem ambulantes non amburuntur. Et ob id perpetuo senatus
consulto militiae omniumque aliorum munerum vacationem habent.'

60   Adiacet Viterbium monti, quem Ciminum fuisse appellatum
constat. Quod etiam nomen olim fuit subiecto ad alteram montis
partem lacui nunc Vici dicto. Quorum utriusque Vergilius sic meminit: 'et Cimini cum monte lacus'. De quo monte et rebus apud
eum apudque Sutrium gestis, sic habet Livius in nono: 'Sutrium
ab Etruscis obsidebatur. Flectit consul Fabius in clivos agmen.
Aspreta erant strata saxis. Non tulerunt impetum Etrusci, ver-
sisque signis, fuga effusi castra repetunt. Sed equites Romani praevecti[83] per obliqua campi, cum se fugientibus obtulissent, in silvam
Ciminam penetratum est. Romanus, multis milibus Etruscorum
caesis, duo de quadraginta signis militaribus captis, castris etiam
hostium cum praeda ingenti potitur. Silva erat Cimina magis tum
invia atque horrenda quam nuper fuere Germanici saltus. Nullus
ad eam diem, nec mercatorum quidem, abdita ea intrare aut ferre
quicquam praeter ducem ipsum audebat. Tum ex ducibus qui aderant, M. Fabius et ceteri.[84] Caesa aut capta eo die hostium milia ad
quadraginta'. Eodemque in monte, qua via olim fuit Cassia, castellum est Surianum, arcem habens omnium Italiae munitissimam,
quae diu a Brittonibus (etiam posteaquam eos Albricus Cunii

the boys whom he had sought to betray.[184] Pliny writes that "in Faliscan territory there are rivers whose waters turn oxen white when they drink it."[185] And elsewhere: "In the territory of the Falisci not far from Rome, a few families are found who are known by the name of Hirpi. These people perform a yearly sacrifice to Apollo on Mount Soracte, when they walk over a pile of burning wood without being scorched. On this account, they are always exempted from military service and from all other public duties by decree of the senate."[186]

Viterbo lies next to a mountain which is agreed to have been 60 called Mons Ciminus. This was once also the name of the lake at the foot of the other side of the mountain, now called Lago di Vico. Vergil mentions both in these words: "And the lake of Ciminus, with its mountain."[187] On Monte Cimino and its history and the history of Sutri, Livy has the following in Book IX: "The Etruscans were laying siege to Sutrium. The consul Fabius deflected his column on to the rising ground, which was rough and covered with stones. The Etruscans did not wait for the charge but faced about and made for their camp in disorderly flight. The Roman cavalry, however, galloping in a slanting direction across the plain, headed off the fugitives, who entered the Ciminian Forest. Many thousands of Etruscans were killed, thirty-eight standards were taken, and in the capture of the camp the Romans secured an immense amount of booty. The Ciminian forest was in those days more impenetrable and frightful than the German forests were recently found to be; not so much as a single trader had, up to that time, ventured into the forest's depths, or taken anything in, except for the Roman general. The generals then present included Marcus Fabius and others. About forty thousand of the enemy were killed or captured on that day."[188] On Monte Cimino, where the Via Cassia once ran, there is the castle of Soriano, its citadel the most heavily fortified in all Italy. For a long time the Bretons held it, even after Alberigo count of Cunio

comes Italia expulerat) possessa fuit. Nullaque itinera Romam perducentia aetate nostra aliquandiu tuta esse permiserunt, quousque Martini V pontificis Romani opera opibusque in potestatem ecclesiae arx ipsa pervenit.

61 Euntibusque ea via Romam obvium est oppidum nunc Vetralla, olim Forum Cassii dictum, quod indicat Sanctae Mariae ecclesia Vetrallae contigua, quae in Foro Cassii appellatur. Adiacent ad sinistram Sutrium versus colles castigatioresque monticuli, quibus dicitur Montaniola, quae est aliquot oppidulis habitata.[85] In quis duo sunt, quae Romanae ecclesiae integerrimam fidem Longobardorum temporibus servaverunt, Polimartium et Bleda, duobus Romanis pontificibus suis civibus, Sabiniano (cuius temporibus fames horrenda Italiam et urbem Romam vexavit) et Pascali primo ornata. Deinde est Sutrium civitas vetustissima, apud quam proelium illud ingens superius sumptum ex Livio commissum fuit, cui urbi in montibus adiacent[86] hinc Roncilionum, inde Crapalica. Et in via Cassia duodecimo a Sutrio miliario sunt Bachanae, vetusti nominis locus, qui, sicut nunc est, semper antea tabernis hospitatoriis deputatus fuit. Ex parvoque lacu Bachanas attingente, parvus oritur fluvius apud Valcham in Tiberim cadens, qui, licet aquis sit tenuis ac exilis, celebratum in historiis habet nomen. Est namque Cremera apud quem trecenti Fabii cum quinque milibus servorum a Veientibus (sicut supra diximus) ad internicionem caesi fuerunt.

62 Bachanis secundo miliario adiacet Campagnanum, Ursinorum oppidum. Supra Sutrium[87] ad dexteram quinto decimo miliario est lacus[88] Tarquiniae, nunc Anguillariae, ab oppido quod illi imminet dictus: ex quo familia fluxit (ut in Romanis nostrae aetatis vetusta) comitum Anguillariae appellata, e quibus Ursus, *cum Pandulpho Sabello*[89] urbis senator, Franciscum Petrarcham laurea[90] insignivit. Adiacentque lacui hinc Barbaranum, Romani huius tempo-

drove them out of Italy. Even in our day, for a while none of the roads leading to Rome was safe from these Bretons, until the stronghold itself passed into the hands of the Church thanks to Martin V's energy and resources.[189]

Traveling along the Via Cassia towards Rome we meet what is now the town of Vetralla, formerly known as Forum Cassii: the church of Santa Maria just outside Vetralla indicates as much, being called "S. Maria di Foro Cassio." Next to Vetralla, towards Sutri on the left, are hills and neat little mountains called Montagnola, which is settled by several villages. Among these there are two that maintained unbroken faith with the Church of Rome throughout the Lombard period, Polimarzo and Blera. The latter can boast two citizens who became pope, Sabinianus (in whose time a dreadful famine troubled Italy and the city of Rome) and Paschal I.[190] Then comes the ancient city of Sutri where that great battle (quoted from Livy above) was joined.[191] Next to Sutri in the hills are Ronciglione on one side and Capranica on the other. Twelve miles from Sutri on the Via Cassia is Baccano, a place with an ancient name that has always been, as it is now, given over to inns for travelers. A small river arises in the little lake that sits beside Baccano, flowing down into the Tiber at Valca. Slight and short of water as it is, its name is celebrated in history, for it is the river Cremera where (as I mentioned) three hundred Fabii and five thousand of their slaves were slaughtered by the men of Veii.[192]

Two miles from Baccano lies Campagnano di Roma, a town belonging to the Orsini. Fifteen miles to the right beyond Sutri is the Lacus Tarquiniae, now Lago di Anguillara, named for the town overlooking it. From here derive the family of the counts of Anguillara, an ancient one by the lights of present-day Romans; one of them, the Roman senator Orso, *with Pandolfo Savelli*[193] gave Petrarch the crown of laurel.[194] Near the lake are on one side Barbarano Romano, a town belonging to the Roman people of the

61

62

ris populi peculiare oppidum, inde Vicarellum et, Romam versus, Galeria Ursinorum.

63   Sunt quoque plurima, Sutrium, Ameriam, Nepesumque inter et Romam, castella in villis olim civium Romanorum aedificata, quae (et alia loca nihil vetustatis aut alicuius memorandae dignitatis habentia) duximus omittenda, praeter unum fama celeberrimum et aspectu penitus neglegendum. Nam ad Montem Rosulum, qui quatuor passuum milibus a Sutrio Nepesoque paene pariter abest, lacus est altam quidem aquarum profunditatem habens, circuitu vero brevis, quem, inspecta Livii descriptione, lacum esse coniicimus Vadimonis, apud quem superati a Romanis Etrusci ad annum urbis conditae quadringentesimum septuagesimum manum dedere et sese Romano populo publice permiserunt, sicut in Livii nono his verbis habetur: 'interea res in Etruria gestae ad Vadimonis lacum. Etrusci, lege sacrata coacto exercitu, cum vir virum legisset, tandem superati sunt. Illeque[91] primum dies fortuna vetere abundantes Etruscorum opes fregit. Caesum in acie quod roboris fuit. Castra eodem impetu capta direptaque'.

present, Vicarello on the other, and, towards Rome, Galeria degli Orsini.

There are also a good many castles built on the site of ancient 63 Roman estates between Sutri, Amelia, Nepi and Rome, which I have thought it best to omit, along with other sites that have nothing ancient or historically valuable about them, except for one celebrated in history but in appearance wholly unimpressive. At Monterosi, four miles from Sutri and almost as much from Nepi, there is a lake, small in size but very deep. Having looked at Livy's description, I believe it is Lake Vadimone.[195] This was where in 470 A.U.C. the Etruscans were beaten into surrender by the Romans and publicly subjected themselves to the Roman people. As Livy has it in Book IX: "Meanwhile an engagement took place at Lake Vadimone in Etruria. The Etruscans had assembled an army under sacred law, in which each man chose his comrade, but they were at length defeated. That day broke for the first time the power of the Etruscans after their long-continued and abundant prosperity. All their might was cut down on the field of battle, and their camp was taken and pillaged in the same assault."[196]

LIBER II

Regio tertia. Latina[1]

1 Finis Etruriae ad Tiberim nos perducens Romam ordine descri-
bendam offerebat. Sed cum id anno ante quarto tribus libris IV
Eugenio Romano pontifici celeberrimo inscriptis sub *Romae instau-
ratae* titulo effecerimus, urbem ipsam relinquentes, regionem in
qua est Latinam novo volumine describemus. Huius regionis vocabuli causam Vergilius in VIII ponit his versibus: 'primus ab aethe-
rio venit Saturnus Olympo, arma Iovis fugiens et regnis exsul
ademptis. Is genus indocile ac dispersum montibus altis composuit
legesque dedit. Latiumque vocari maluit, his quoniam latuisset tutus in oris.' Servius autem grammaticus, Vergilium in VII exponens, populos proprie Latinos appellatos dicit eos qui intererant
Albani montis viscerationi. Quos quidem Latinos tanto amore
Romanam gentem prosecutos fuisse videmus ut Livius libro
LXXII enumeratis Italiae populis qui Bello Sociali defecerunt a
Romanis, dicat auxilia Latini nominis et exterarum gentium missa
populo Romano.

2 Hanc autem regionem, aetatis nostrae ac superiorum aliquot
saeculorum morem (licet absurdum) secuti, Campaniam et Maritimam appellabimus. Et quidem Campaniam scimus dictam fuisse
a priscis regionem quae est circa Capuam, scimusque Latii appellationem a principio pauciora complexam fuisse iis quae[2] nunc
Campaniae et Maritimae vocabulo comprehenduntur. Sed contra
videmus Strabonem Cretensem, qui Tiberii Augusti temporibus
floruit, ponere in *Geographia* fines Latinorum maritimam regionem

BOOK II

Region 3. Lazio

The border of Tuscany taking us to the river Tiber, in the normal 1
course of things Rome would be the next to be described. But this
I did four years ago in my three books of *Rome Restored*, dedicated
to the illustrious pontiff Eugenius IV, and so I shall omit Rome
and describe the region of Lazio, in which it lies, in this new book.
The explanation of the region's name is given by Vergil in these
lines of *Aeneid* Book VIII: "Then Saturn from airy Olympus first
came down, in flight from the arms of Jove, exiled from his stolen
kingdom. The savage race scattered through the high hills he
made an ordered society, and gave them laws. He chose to call the
place Latium because he had hidden *(latuisset)* unharmed on these
shores."[1] The commentator Servius, explaining a passage in *Aeneid*
VII, tells us that the peoples properly called Latins were those
who took part in a communal sacrificial feast on the Alban
Mount.[2] It is apparent that those Latins had such a strong attach-
ment to Rome that Livy in Book LXXII lists the Italic peoples
who deserted her in the Social War and then says that the Latin
communities and foreigners sent auxiliaries to help the Romans.[3]

 I shall follow the usage of this and earlier times, illogical as it is, 2
and call the region 'Campania and Marittima.' We know that the
ancients called the territory around Capua *Campania*, and that
the name *Latium* from the outset embraced the rather few tracts
that are comprehended at present by the name Campania and
Marittima. On the other hand, we note that in his *Geographia*[4]
the Cretan Strabo (who flourished in the time of the emperor
Tiberius) locates the lands of the Latins in the coastal region that
extends from the Tiber mouth to the Gulf of Sitano (where the

ab ostiis Tiberinis ad Sitanum sinum, in quo fuit Sinuessa, urbs maritima, et in mediterraneis Aborigines, Rutilos, Volscos, Hernicos, Aequicolos, Marsos et eos qui proximum Marsis incolunt Apenninum usque ad veteris Campaniae terminos. Unde peritissimum hunc vetustatis scriptorem et simul Plinium (qui ab eo sumpsit) secuturi, eam Latinorum regionem nostrae nunc Campaniae et Maritimae cogimur applicare. Nec satis scio si in nostra Latina regione rebus praesentibus ita satis potero facere sicut Livii Patavini, Divi Augusti, Vergilii, Strabonis, et Plinii adiumento vetustissimis satisfaciam, quamquam non est eo in flore nunc quo priscis temporibus fuit, adeo ut per eius oppida Hadrianum imperatorem gloriosissimum, dictatorem, aedilem, et duumvirum[3] fuisse scribat Aelius Spartianus.

3   Ut ergo a maritimis incipiamus: Ostiam urbem condidit mare inter et Tiberim Ancus Marcius, quamquam Servius grammaticus, in Vergilii VII, dicit exitum Tiberis naturalem non esse, nisi circa Ostiam ubi primum Aeneas castra constituit — cum postea in agro Lavino castra fecerit ingentia, quorum vestigia suis temporibus viderentur. Describit vero eam Strabo importuosam propter alluviones Tiberis. Oportuisseque dicit tunc adhiberi scapharum copiam quae ministeriis servirent, et onera exciperent, ac rursus onerarent ut levatae naves facilius flumen attingerent. Ea enim tempestate Romanus portus non erat, quem postea Claudius fecit. Tiberiusque imperator tunc primum Antii portum, Strabonis temporibus inchoabat. Unde, haec legens scribensque, in eam venio considerationem, quae prudentes quosque debet attentos et vigiles reddere ut rebus humanis parum confidant, non potuisse scilicet imperatorum Romanorum, et quidem potentissimorum, profusionem opum et adhibitam diligentiam efficere quin Ostiae civitatis, Antiatisque et urbis et portus, ac Romani item portus opera paucioribus annis mille integra permanserint et quin eadem, quae prius fuerat, Ostiae annis iam quingentis manserit importuositas.

coastal city of Sinuessa was), while in the interior he places the aboriginals, the Rutuli, Volsci, Hernici, Aequicoli, Marsi and those who inhabit the Apennines next to the Marsi right up to the borders of old Campania.[5] And since I intend to follow Strabo, a writer well versed in antiquity, and Pliny too, who drew on him, I am obliged to attach the region of the Latins to our present-day Campania and Marittima. Nor am I confident that I shall be able to give satisfaction in the case of contemporary Lazio in the way that Livy, the emperor Augustus, Vergil, Strabo, and Pliny will help me to do justice to the region's antiquities. Lazio no longer flourishes as it did in ancient times, so much so that Aelius Spartianus could write that the renowned emperor Hadrian was dictator, aedile, and *duumvir* of the towns of the region.[6]

To begin with the coast, Ancus Marcius founded the city of 3 Ostia between the sea and the Tiber. Commenting on *Aeneid* VII, however, Servius says that the outlet of the Tiber was only natural around Ostia, where Aeneas first set up his camp, though he later founded a great encampment in the territory of Lavinium, traces of which were to be seen in Servius' time.[7] Strabo in fact describes Ostia as having no harbor because of the silting up of the Tiber. He says that they had to use a supply of lighters to service the boats, to take off cargoes and put them on again, so that with their loads lightened the ships might more easily reach the Tiber.[8] In those days there was no harbor at Rome, though Claudius later had one built. In Strabo's time Tiberius began work on a harbor at Anzio. Reading and writing this provokes in me the reflection — and it is something that should make every person of good sense wary of trusting too much in human capacities — that lavish expense and considerable effort on the part of emperors (very powerful emperors too) were not enough to keep the structures of the city of Ostia, the city and port of Anzio, or the harbor of Rome intact for as much as a thousand years; but, as in the days of old, Ostia still remains without a harbor after 500 years.

4   Primam calamitatem passa est Ostia Cinnae et Marii temporibus, cum scribat Livius libro LXXIX Cinnam et Marium quatuor exercitibus, ex quibus duo Q. Sertorio et duo Carboni dati sunt, urbem circumsedisse, Ostiam coloniam expugnasse ac crudeliter diripuisse. Habuitque aliquando Ostia ingentia aedificia, quorum nullum nunc exstat vestigium. Flavius Eutropius scribit Aurelianum Augustum coepisse fundare Ostiae forum nominis sui ad mare, in quo postea praetorium publicum fuit constitutum. Nec omittendum duximus eam optimos habuisse melones, ex quibus decem aliquando Clodium Albinum imperatorem unica cibatione inter multa alia comedisse scribit Iulius Capitolinus. Et quia aerem semper habuit ut in maritimis habitatoribus gravem, sacrosancta lege populi Romani vacationem militiae et publicorum munerum habuit, quam vacationem Livius XXVII scribit sub adventum Hasdrubalis in Italiam fuisse ad dies XXX suspensam ut plures milites res publica haberet. Urbem Ostiam, cum a Saracenis fuisset destructa, Leo IV pontifex Romanus instauratam Corsis replevit. Et tam[4] diu destructa ac derelicta mansit ut nihil sit reliquiarum praeter turrim quam celebris famae pontifex Romanus Martinus V in urbis Romae potius quam in ostiorum Tiberis et portus custodiam aedificari curavit.

5   Post Ostium Antium est, Romana colonia, de qua Livius in VIII: 'Antium nova colonia missa. Naves inde longae abductae interdictumque mare.' Et infra: 'naves Antiatum partim in navalia Romae subductae, partim incensae rostrisque earum suggestum in Foro exstructum adornari placuit, Rostraque id templum appellatum.' Eam urbem Strabo dicit ab Ostia distantem stadiis ducentis

Ostia suffered her first disaster in the time of Cinna and 4
Marius. Livy writes in Book LXXIX that they laid siege to Rome
with four armies (of which two were given to Q. Sertorius, and
two to Carbo), captured the colony at Ostia and cruelly sacked it.[9]
Ostia had at one time massive buildings, no trace of which remains now. Flavius Eutropius writes that the emperor Aurelian
began to build by the sea at Ostia a forum named after himself,
where later a municipal magistrates' court was established.[10] It is
worth mentioning that Ostia had excellent melons. According to
Julius Capitolinus the emperor Clodius Albinus sometimes devoured ten of them, among much else, at a single sitting.[11] Because
Ostia always had an atmosphere oppressive to its inhabitants (as
happens in coastal regions), she enjoyed by solemn law of the Roman People exemption from military service and civic responsibili-
ties. In Book XXVII Livy writes that the exemption was suspended for thirty days when Hasdrubal came to Italy, so that the
Republic might have more soldiers.[12] After Ostia was destroyed by
the Saracens, Pope Leo IV restored it and repopulated it with
Corsicans. So long has it remained ruined and derelict that no
trace of the city survives, except for the tower that the famous
pope Martin V had erected, to protect the city of Rome rather
than the mouth of the Tiber and the port of Ostia.[13]

Anzio comes next, a Roman colony of which Livy says in Book 5
VIII: "A new colony was planted at Anzio. The warships of the
Antiates were taken away and they were forbidden to take to the
sea."[14] And further on: "Some of the ships of the Antiates were
taken into the docks at Rome, others were burnt and their prows
(*rostra*) fastened on the front of a raised gallery which was constructed in the Forum, and which from this circumstance was
called the Rostra."[15] Strabo says that the city of Anzio was 260
stades[16] from Ostia and was built on a cliff in his time by the emperors Tiberius, Drusus, and Germanicus for their leisure and re-
lief from cares of state. Many very costly residences were built

sexaginta fuisse temporibus suis aedificatam super rupe ab imperatoribus Tiberio, Druso, et Germanico ad otium relaxationemque
laborum civilium, et additas fuisse aedes multas magnificentissimi
operis, cum antea Antiates praedae studium cum Tyrrhenis com-
mune haberent—quamvis Romanis subiecti essent. Unde Alexander Epirotas, et postea Demetrius successor, captivos praedones
remittentes Romanis dixerunt dono eis dare corpora propter illam
quam cum Graecis haberent cognationem, indignum tamen ducere viros ipsos et simul Italiae imperare et myoparones ad pirati-
cam emittere. Fuit autem in Antiatum foro Castoris et Pollucis
templum, quos servatores suos nominabant: haec a Strabone. Sed
Horatius uoluisse videtur Fortunam ab Antiatibus in primis fuisse
cultam, his versibus ad Fortunam scriptis: 'O Diva gratum quae
regis Antium, potens[5] vel imo tollere de gradu mortale corpus vel
superbos vertere funeribus triumphos.' Livius autem libro LXXX
scribit Cinnam et Marium expugnasse Antium. Et videmus Sue-
tonium ac alios scribere Neronem postea tam insanis molibus exstruxisse et portum et urbem Antiatum ut non modo aerarium sed
Romanum quoque imperium pecuniis exhauserit, effodiendisque
postea thesauris ita applicuisse animum ut mentitos per singula
mathematicos hariolosque nihilominus sectaretur. Habuitque
Antium (sicut supra de Ostia diximus) sacrosanctam a publicis
muneribus vacationem, quae pariter eodem tempore est suspensa.

6   Urbem vero Antiatum nunc esse nullam, sed in mari, in litore,
in nemoribus mirandas exstare ruinas vidimus. Neptunium autem,
oppidum in Antii vestigiorum angulo aedificatum, novam et iu-
cundam in re parva considerationem efficit. Mirarique soleo nullam eius rei, quam cum orbe condito originem habuisse oportuit,
fieri a Plinio mentionem: alitur eius oppidi populus non exiguus

there, whereas earlier the Antiates shared with the Tyrrhenians a common enthusiasm for piracy, even though they were Roman subjects. This is the reason that when they sent back to the Romans pirates they had captured, Alexander of Epirus and afterwards Demetrius his successor said that though they were handing over their persons in view of the kinship between the Greeks and the Romans, they took exception to the fact that the very men who were masters of Italy should be at the same time sending out galleys on pirate raids. The forum of Anzio had a temple of Castor and Pollux, whom the Antiates called their Saviors. Thus Strabo.[17] Yet in these lines addressed to her, Horace seems to have thought that Fortuna was the chief deity cultivated by the Antiates: "O goddess, you that rule over pleasant Anzio, with power to raise our mortal bodies from the lowliest estate or to turn proud triumphs into funerals."[18] In Book LXXX Livy writes that Cinna and Marius stormed Anzio.[19] Later we find Suetonius and others writing that Nero piled up such extravagant buildings at the port and city of Anzio that he drained not just the treasury but the whole Roman empire of cash. Thereafter he was so obsessed by turning up treasure that he would minutely interrogate fraudulent astrologers, and soothsayers likewise.[20] As was said of Ostia above [§4], Anzio too enjoyed solemn exemption from civic duties, which was equally suspended at the same time as Ostia's.

The city of Anzio no longer exists, but I have seen wonderful 6 ruins still there in the sea, on the beach, and in the woods. The town of Nettuno, however, built in a corner of the remains of Anzio, gives rise to a further agreeable reflection: a small matter, admittedly, but I am always surprised that Pliny makes no mention of it since it must have been around since the creation of the world. The quite substantial population of Nettuno provides for itself by fishing, fowling, and hunting, while the former territory of Anzio, which in those days was extremely fertile in wheat and wine, as Strabo indicates, is now covered by a strip of forest eigh-

piscatione, aucupio, et venatu, quod Antiatum olim ager (ut Strabo innuit), tunc segetis vinique feracissimus, nunc a Civita Indivina Prosperi Columnae cardinalis oppido in maris[6] litora duodeviginti miliarium[7] latitudine silvis obtegitur. Neque enim est haec Lavinia,[8] prima Aeneae urbs, cuius incolis postea ob Aeneae memoriam bello Latino Romani pepercerunt. Sicut Livius VIII libro sic scribit: 'Laviniis[9] civitas data sacraque sua reddita, cum eo ut aedes lucusque Sospitae Iunonis communis Laviniis cum populo Romano esset.' Quin potius Lanuvium[10] a quo Murenarum gens Romae praeclara fluxit quodque omnibus paene in vetustis Romanorum monumentis celebre habetur.[11]

7   Sed ad Neptunium. Mare saxosum, vel potius glareosum, pisces quidem multos atque optimos habet. Venationem vero amplissimae ut usquam silvae apris capreisque[12] abundantem praebent. Aucupium quoque duplex est, eiusque tempora sunt diversa. Nam, cum ad prima veris signa hirundines et simul cum ipsis coturnices (a sono vocis nunc 'qualeae' dictae) transmisso Mari Infero in Italiam redeunt, omnia Antiatum quondam litorum supercilia passuum quinque milibus Neptunienses contiguis retibus complent. Sedensque unusquisque in fundi proprii et magno pretio comparati loco ad particulam retium propriam venientes noctu coturnices fistula illicit. Et cum turmatim illae retibus intricentur, si aliqua de longissimo volatu fessa extra rete in sabulum ceciderit, eam auceps manu percipit. Fuisseque audivimus intra mensem unum, quo continuatur aucupium dies aliquot, in quorum singulis centum huiusmodi avicularum milia capta sint. De ipsis vero coturnicibus sic habet Plinius: 'Coturnices ante[13] semper adveniunt quam grues. Parva avis, et cum ad nos pervenit terrestris potius quam sublimis, advolat non sine periculo navigantium: cum ap-

teen miles wide all the way from Civita Indivina, Cardinal Prospero Colonna's town, to the seashore. Nor is this town Lavinia, Aeneas' first city, whose inhabitants the Romans spared in the Latin War in honor of his memory.[21] Of which Livy in Book VIII writes as follows: "the citizens of Lavinium received civic status and the restitution of their sacred things, with the proviso that the temple and grove of Juno Sospita should belong in common to the Roman people and the citizens living at Lavinium."[22] Lanuvium, instead, is the town from which came the distinguished Roman family of the Murenae. It is celebrated in nearly all the historical records of ancient Rome.[23]

But to return to Nettuno. The sea there has lots of rocks, or 7 rather gravel, and many excellent fish. Dense forests offer, as ever, good hunting of boar and deer. Fowling is of two sorts, depending on the time of year. At the first sign of spring, swallows and quail (now known as *quaglie* from their call) return together to Italy across the Tyrrhenian sea. The people of Nettuno then cover the whole shoreline of old Anzio with continuous netting for a space of five miles. Each man sits on his own patch of ground, purchased at great expense, and with a pipe lures the quail as they arrive at night on to his own bit of the nets. When they are entangled in the nets in large numbers, the fowler picks up any that fall on to the sand beyond the net, exhausted by the long flight. I have heard that in a single month when the fowling was carried over several days, 100,000 of these little birds may be caught every single day. These are the very quail of which Pliny says: "The quail always arrive before the cranes. It is a small bird, and when it has arrived, more generally keeps to the ground than flies aloft. Their flight is not without danger to mariners, for when they approach land they often smash into the sails of a ship, and that too always in the night, and the vessel often sinks. They will not fly when the south wind is blowing, as that wind is humid and apt to weigh them down. They like, however, to be borne along on the breeze,

propinquavere terris, quippe velis saepe incidunt, et hoc semper noctu, merguntque navigia. Austro non volant, humido scilicet et graviore vento, aura tamen vehi volunt propter pondus corporum viresque parvas.' Et infra: in Campania primum veris principio multiplicare conspiciuntur priusquam venisse sciantur. Aliud item in Antiate agro est aucupium per autumnum. Palumbes[14] cum mari transvolato Italiam relicturae sunt, aliquamdiu in nemoribus Antiatum commorantur. Quare peritissimi Neptunienses retia quam maxima in id aucupii magno parata impendio suspendunt. Exinde palumbes quascumque longo tractu viderint congregatas in arboribus considere, iactu lapidis et clamore territas, in aera volare compellunt. Dumque aves in magnum coactas numerum advolando, tensis retium insidiis viderint supereminere, contorta funda parvum lapidem, vel natura album vel gypso delinitum, maximo emittunt crepitu. Quo territae bombo palumbes, ut accipitres ('Chiluones' a Plinio appellatos), quibus nunc 'falchonibus' est nomen, quas in lapide bomboque fundae timent, declinando serventur, terrae quam possunt volatu rapidius appropinquant, sicque amentes in retia se praecipitant. De palumbis Plinius dicit eas quotannis advolare mari in Veliternum agrum, qui quidem ager Antiati continet. Et alibi scribit: 'post hirundines, sturnos, turdos abeunt palumbes, sed quonam incertum. Hirundines vero in propinqua abeunt apricos secutae[15] montium recessus.' Ex aucupio palumbarum Romanus nostri temporis populus nuptias et convivia maiori ex parte parat. Melioris namque saporis et nutrimenti hae parvae quam aliae sunt palumbes.[16]

8   In medio duarum quas descripsimus maritimarum urbium Ardeam ponit Strabo, Rutilorum olim habitationem, stadiis circiter septem a mari recedentem, et dicit prope eam fuisse Aphrodisium[17] ubi panagyrim Latini agerent. Idque Plinius appellat lucum Iovis[18] Indigetis, cui propinquus est amnis Numicus. Vergilius au-

the body being so light and their strength so limited."[24] And further on: they are observed to breed first in Campania in early spring, before it is realised they have arrived.[25] They also catch birds at Anzio in the autumn. After they have flown over the sea, wood pigeons gather for a while in the woods of Anzio as they prepare to leave Italy. The expert fowlers of Nettuno hang up huge nets specially made for this sort of fowling at great expense. When they see a great number of pigeons gathered together and roosting in the trees, they terrify them by throwing stones and shouting, and make them fly off. In their flight the birds are forced into a great flock. When the fowlers see them above the snares of the nets they have spread, they sling small stones at them (either naturally white or coated with gypsum) with a great shout. Terrified by the whirring noise, the pigeons try to save themselves by dodging the hawks (what Pliny called "Chilyones" and are now called falcons),[26] which in their terror they imagine in the whirring of the slingshots. Flying as quickly as they can, they come near to the ground and thus distracted hurtle into the nets. Pliny says that every year these pigeons fly over the sea to the territory of Velletri, a district which borders that of Anzio.[27] And he writes elsewhere: "The wood pigeons leave Italy after the swallows, starlings and thrushes, but whither is unclear.[28] The swallows go away to seek sunny mountain retreats in nearby countries."[29] Most of the present-day people of Rome catch wood pigeons for weddings and banquets, for these small birds are better in flavor and more nutritious than other cock pigeons.

Strabo locates Ardea, where the Rutili once dwelt, between the two coastal cities that I have described, about seven stades from the sea, and he says that Aphrodisium, where the Latins held their *panegyris*, was nearby.[30] Pliny calls it the sacred grove of Jupiter Indiges, close to which is the river Numicus.[31] Vergil in Book VII writes as follows: "To the city of bold Rutilus, Allecto the fury came, a city that Danaë is said to have founded for her Argive set-

8

tem libro septimo sic habet: 'audacis Rutili[19] ad muros, quam dicitur urbem Acrisioneis Danaë[20] fundasse colonis, praecipiti delata Noto. Locus Ardea quondam dictus avis et nunc magnum[21] manet Ardea nomen.' Et infra: 'quinque adeo, magna[22] positis incudibus, urbes tela novant: Atina potens, Tiburque superbum, Ardea, Crustumeri, et turrigerae Antemnae'.[23] Et Servius, Vergilii septimo, dicit: 'Hyginus, ab augurio avium, Ardeam. Et Ovidius, improprie ac fabulose, incensam ab Hannibale Ardeam et in hanc avem esse conversam.' Item Servius, eodem libro, verbum exponens 'Sacranae acies': 'dicunt quendam Corybantem venisse ad Italiam et tenuisse loca quae nunc Urbi vicina sunt, et ideo[24] populos Sacranos appellatos: nam sacrati sunt matri deorum Corybantes.[25] Alii Sacranas acies Ardeatum volunt, qui aliquando, cum pestilentia laborarent, ver sacrum voverunt: unde Sacrani sunt dicti.' Dicit Plinius Ardeam fuisse conditam a Danaë,[26] Persei matre. Fuitque Ardea una ex duodeviginti coloniis quae, dum Hannibal magis urgeret Romanos, militiam et collationem tributorum detractaverunt. Id vero oppidum, raro habitatum colono, nunc Iacobus Columna possidet, quod Leone Romano pontifice, sicut coniicio, nominis ordine secundo ornatum fuit. Numicus vero fluvius, quem Strabo dicit propinquum esse Ardeae, a Vergilio sic celebratur in septimo: 'et fontis vada[27] sacra Numici.' Et infra: 'fontis stagna Numici.' Super quo Servius: 'Ista iam ab incolis discuntur, quod ait "stagna" verum est. Nam Numicus ante ingens fluvius fuit in quo repertum est cadaver Aeneae et consecratum. Post, paulatim decrescens, in fontem redactus est, qui ipse sacratus est: Vestae enim libari non nisi de hoc fluvio licebat.'[28]

tlers when she had been carried to shore by the swift south
wind. The place was called Ardea by our forebears, and now
only the great name 'Ardea' remains."[32] And later he says: "Five
cities, no less, established mighty smithies and make new arms:
powerful Atina, proud Tibur, Ardea, Crustumerium and Amiternae crowned with towers."[33] Servius on *Aeneid* VII writes:
"Hyginus says that the name 'Ardea' comes from augury of birds.
And Ovid tells us, mistakenly and with a poet's licence, that
Hannibal burned Ardea and the city was transformed into that
bird."[34] Servius again, expounding a phrase "battle lines of the
Sacrani" in the same Book VII, says: "A corybant is said to have
come to Italy and to have occupied a region near where Rome now
is, and that is why the people were called 'Sacrani', the corybants
being 'sacred' to Cybele, mother of the gods. Others hold that the
Sacranae acies are the battle lines of the Ardeans, who when they
were suffering from plague sometimes made a spring sacrifice, *ver
sacrum*, and so were called 'Sacrani.'"[35] Pliny says that Ardea was
founded by Danaë, the mother of Perseus.[36] When Hannibal was
pressing the Romans hard, Ardea was one of the eighteen colonies
that declined to furnish them with soldiers and capital levies.[37]
The town is now the property of Jacopo Colonna and has a scant
farming population. It has the distinction of having produced the
Roman pontiff Leo—Leo II, as I surmise.[38] The river Numicus,
which Strabo says is near Ardea,[39] is celebrated by Vergil in Book
VII in these words: "The sacred waters of Numicus' spring,"[40] and
below: "And the pools of Numicus' spring."[41] On which Servius
writes: "We gather from the present inhabitants that the word
'pools' in Vergil is accurate. The Numicus used to be a mighty
river; Aeneas' corpse was found in it and he was deified there. The
river later shrank little by little and was reduced to a spring, which
itself was held sacred, for libations could be made to Vesta only
from this river."[42]

9   Post Antium est quinto miliario Astura Antonii Columnae arx
mari circumdata, prope quam Astures fuere vetustissimi, de quibus Vergilius: 'Astur equo fidens.' Ad quam parum feliciter divertit
M. Cicero Antonii gladios fugiens: evasurus tamen, si coeptam ibi
navigationem continuasset. Pari item infelicitate ad eandem Astu-
ram se de fuga contulit Conradinus Henrici filius, quem genitor
Fredericus secundus imperator, Siciliae rex, in carcere mori coegerat. Rex enim Petrus Arrago insulam Trinacriam, Constantiae
uxori suae hereditario iure avi sui Frederici superius dicti debitam,
armis ceperat. Conradinusque Carolum primum Andegavensem
ita posse Neapolitano regno pellere confisus (sicut illum Arrago
Trinacria expulerat), apud Beneventum infauste conflixerat.[29]
Unico sociatus comite, fugiens Asturae interceptus, ad Caro-
lumque perductus, tam detestando quam semper alias regibus et
praestantibus insueto principibus more exemploque securi publice
est percussus.

10   Deinceps est Circeius mons magna parte mari circumdatus, in
quo Circen fabulae perhibent habitasse. Habuit vero is mons Strabonis aetate urbem (ut dicit) parvam et Circes templum ac Mi-
nervae antra, dicitque monstrari consuevisse quandam Ulixis phia-
lem. Servius, in Vergilii septimo, super 'Circeae raduntur litora
terrae': 'Mons est, ante insula fuit. Paludibus enim a continenti se-
parabatur, quas exclusit limus[30] de Albanis montibus fluens, et dicebatur "Aeaeus"[31] ab errore transeuntium quo homines mutaban-
tur in feras.' De qua re beatus Aurelius Augustinus, dum *Dei
civitatem* aedificat, sic habet: 'Varro astruit[32] Circen socios Ulyxis
mutasse in bestias.' Et infra: 'Nam de mulieribus malis artibus im-

Five miles from Anzio is Torre Astura, the stronghold of Anto- 9
nio Colonna surrounded by the sea.[43] Nearby dwelt the Astures of
long ago, on whom Vergil writes: "Astyr, trusting in his horse."[44]
Here Cicero put in as he fled Antony's swords, unluckily for him;
had he there continued the voyage he had begun, he would have
escaped them.[45] Similar bad luck attended Conradin, son of
Henry (whose own father, the emperor Frederick II, king of Sicily,
made him die in prison), when he fled to Torre Astura. King
Pedro of Aragon had seized Sicily by force of arms on the grounds
that it belonged to his wife Costanza by hereditary right from her
grandfather, the Frederick mentioned above. Conradin, believing
that he could drive Charles I of Anjou out of the Kingdom of Naples in the same way that Pedro had expelled him from Sicily,
fought a disastrous battle at Benevento. Accompanied by a single
attendant he took to flight, but was intercepted at Astura and
brought before Charles, and then publicly beheaded in a manner
as abominable as it has been uncommon at other times and with
other kings and princes.[46]

Then comes Monte Circeo, largely surrounded by sea, where 10
the Circe of fable is supposed to have lived. In Strabo's time this
promontory had a small city (as he calls it) with a temple of Circe
and grottoes of Minerva. Strabo says that it was customary to
show visitors a sort of cup that had belonged to Ulysses.[47] Servius
says on the passage "they skirt the shores of Circe's realm" in
Aeneid VII: "The present mountain was formerly an island separated from the mainland by marshes, which mud flowing down
from the Alban Hills cut off, and it was called "Aeaeus" from the
wandering of those passing by, through which men would be
changed into wild animals."[48] On this matter, St. Augustine says
in the course of building his *City of God:* "Varro adds that Circe
changed the companions of Ulysses into beasts."[49] And below:
"Indeed, when I was in Italy, I myself used to hear of such cases
from one region of that country. It was said that females with

butis, et nos, dum essemus in Italia, audiebamus talia de quadam
regione illarum partium: mulieres imbutas his malis artibus in
caseo dare solere (quibus possent sive vellent) viatoribus unde in
iumenta verterentur necessariaque comportarent. Post quae per-
functa opera iterum ad se redirent. Nec tamen in eis mentem fieri
bestialem sed rationalem humanamque servari.' In hoc monte oppidum fuit quod et Circeium dictum est, Liviusque utrumque Cir-
ceios appellat. Sed nos in *Romanae ecclesiae gestis rebus*, praesertim
Gelasii secundi temporibus, ad annum salutis millesimum centesimum et vigesimum, saepe legimus in Circeio monte fuisse arcem
Circeiam, omnium quas Romana ecclesia ubique haberet munitissimam, quae afflictis Romanae ecclesiae rebus auxilio saepe fuit.
Nunc ad eius montis radices oppidum est Sanctae Felicitatis. Fluvium, qui proxime illabitur, Storacem Strabo, Plinius Nymphaeum vocat, super quo hi Formium fuisse dicunt oppidum.
Deinceps est perpetuum mare.

11   Et in mediterranea regione porrigitur campus Pontinus, quam
regionem totam vetustissimis et multis ante conditam Urbem
temporibus Ausones habitarunt, qui etiam Campanum habebant
agrum. Unde Italiam Ausoniam et Ausonium pelagus vocitatum
fuisse Strabo asserit. Post Ausones fuerunt Osci, quibus etiam
Campania erat communis. Et denique omnia fuerunt Latinorum
usque ad Sinuessam. Sed quicquid Strabo hic habeat, Plinius sic
dicit: 'Mirum est quod de hac re tradere hominum notitiae possumus. Theophrastus, qui primus externorum aliqua de Romanis diligentius scripsit (nam Theopompus, ante quem nemo mentionem
habuit, urbem tantummodo a Gallis captam dixit, Clitarchus[33] ab
eo proximus legationem tantum ad Alexandrum missam), hic iam
et plusquam fama Circeiorum insulae mensuram posuit stadia oc-

knowledge of these wicked arts would, when they wished and were able to do so, administer drugs on a piece of cheese to travelers, who were thereupon turned into beasts of burden and used to carry articles of all kinds, returning to their original form only when they had finished their tasks. Yet their minds did not become bestial, but were kept rational and human."[50] The mountain has a town which is also called Circeium, and Livy calls both promontory and town Circeii.[51] I have often seen mentioned in the *History of the Roman Church* (particularly in the time of Gelasius II, about the year 1120) a citadel of Circe on Monte Circeo. It was the most stoutly fortified of all the citadels of the Roman Church and often brought succour to the Church in time of trouble.[52] At the foot of the mountain there is now the town of S. Felice Circeo. The river which flows into the sea close to S. Felice, Strabo calls "Storax" and Pliny "Nymphaeus."[53] Above the river, Strabo and Pliny say, was the town of Formia, then the open sea.[54]

The region of the Pontine plain stretches inland. All of it was   11
inhabited in very ancient times, long before the founding of Rome, by the Ausonians, who also occupied Campania. This is why Italy was called Ausonia, and the Tyrrhenian sea the Ausonian, according to Strabo. After the Ausonians came the Oscans, and they too had a share in Campania. Later on the whole region as far as Sinuessa belonged to the Latins.[55] But whatever Strabo might have to say here, Pliny expresses himself as follows: "It is remarkable what we can add to the sum of human knowledge on this matter. Theophrastus, the first foreigner who treated of the affairs of Rome with any degree of accuracy (for Theopompus, before whose time no Greek writer made mention of Rome, only spoke of the capture of the city by the Gauls, and Clitarchus, the next after him, only of the Roman embassy to Alexander), Theophrastus, I say, following something more than mere rumor, gave the circuit of the island of Circeo as being eighty stadia in the work he wrote during the archonship of Nicodorus at Athens, the

tuaginta [milia], eo volumine quod scribit Nicodoro Atheniensium magistratu,[34] qui fuit urbis nostrae quadringentesimo quadragesimo anno. Quicquid vero terrarum est, praeter decem milia passuum ambitus, annexum insulae post eum annum accessit Italiae. Aliud miraculum: a Circeis palus Pontina est, quem locum XXIIII urbium fuisse Mucianus ter cos. prodidit. Deinde flumen Aufentum supra quod Terracina oppidum, Volscorum lingua Anxur dictum, ubi fuere Amyclae a serpentibus deletae.'

12   Repetii a Strabone Plinioque vetustissima, quae et ipsi a vetustissimis acceperunt. Livius vero, XLVI, scribit Pontinas paludes a Cornelio Cethego cos., cui ea provincia obvenerat, siccatas. Agrumque ex his factum, a campis Pontinis ad Terracinensem agrum stadia centum fuisse tradit[35] Strabo, cum nostri octo passuum milia nunc computent. Terracinae etiam nunc adiacet paludis Pontinae pars, quam paludem[36] faciunt amnes duo, e quibus maior Aufens appellatus, apud Terracinam olim via Appia Mare Inferum attingebat. Terracinam dicit Livius, cum fuisset a Romanis direpta, causam dedisse solutioni stipendii militaris: 'Fabius (quod maxime petebatur) ad Anxur oppugnandum sine ulla populatione accessit. Anxur fuit, quae Terracinae nunc sunt, urbs prona in paludes et ab ea parte oppugnationem ostendit. Circummissae quatuor cohortes cum C. Servilio Ahala, cum imminentem urbi collem cepissent, loco altiore (qua nullum erat praesidium) ingenti clamore ac tumultu moenia invasere. Pronuntiatum ne quis praeter armatos violaretur. Reliquam omnem multitudinem voluntariam exuit armis, quorum ad duo milia quingenti vivi capiuntur. A

440th year of our city [314 B.C.]. Whatever land, therefore, has
been annexed to that island beyond a circumference of about ten
miles, has been added to Italy after that year. Another wonderful
circumstance: near Monte Circeo are the Pontine Marshes, formerly the site, according to Mucianus, who was three times consul, of twenty-four cities. Next to this comes the river Uffente, on
which is the town of Terracina, called in the language of the Volsci
Anxur, the spot too where Amyclae stood, a town destroyed by
serpents."[56]

I have sought to retrieve from Strabo and from Pliny the very   12
earliest material, which they themselves had from the earliest
sources. In Book XLVI Livy writes that the Pontine Marshes were
drained by the consul Cornelius Cethegus, to whom the task had
been assigned.[57] And Strabo reports that the arable land created
from them stretched for a hundred stades from the Pontine plains
to the territory of Terracina, though the distance is reckoned nowadays to be eight miles.[58] Even now part of the Pontine Marsh ad-
joins Terracina (the marsh is formed by two rivers, the larger of
which, called the Uffente, formerly reached the Tyrrhenian sea at
Terracina on the Appian Way). Livy says that it was the plunder
of Terracina that first caused the Romans to pay their soldiers:
"Fabius marched to Anxur, which was the chief objective, without
losing time in devastating the country. Anxur (modern Terracina)
was a city that sloped down towards the marshes. Fabius made a
show of attacking the city on that side. Four cohorts were des-
patched with C. Servilius Ahala by a circuitous route to seize the
hill which overhung the town on the other side. After doing so
they made an attack amid loud shouts and uproar from their
higher position upon that part of the town where there was no de-
fence. An order was issued that none but those taken with arms
should be injured. On this Fabius disarmed the whole of the rest
of the population without resistance and prisoners to the number
of 2500 were taken alive. He would not allow his men to touch the

cetera praeda Fabius militem abstinuit. Postea, ubi venerunt tribuni, oppidum vetere fortuna opulentum tres exercitus diripuere. Cuius praedae gratia factum est ut stipendium miles tunc primum acciperet, cum ante id tempus de suo quisque munere eo functus esset.' Octavo autem libro Livius habet: 'Cohors una, cum haud procul Anxur esset, ad Lautulas saltu angusto inter mare et montes consedit.' Et Servius septimo Vergilii super verbo, 'Circeiumque iugum,' dicit: 'circa hunc tractum Campaniae colebatur puer Iuppiter, qui Anxurus dicebatur quasi *axiros*, id est sine novacula,[37] quod barbam numquam rasisset et colebatur etiam Iuno virgo quae Feronia dicebatur'.[38] Est autem fons iuxta Terracinam qui aliquando dictus est Anxur.' Et infra Servius: 'Haud longe a Terracina oppidum est Satura,[39] et eius cognominis fluvius Ufens (quem Vergilius significat angustum esse), qui inter valles serpens mare petat.' Suetonius Tranquillus in *Vita Tiberii imperatoris* scribit: 'iuxta Terracinam, in loco cui Praetorio nomen est, cenante eo, complura et ingentia saxa fortuitu superne delapsa sunt. Multisque amicorum et ministrorum elisis, praeter spem evasit.' *Terracinae etiam casu theatri viginti hominum milia per Tiberii imperatoris tempora interiisse scribit idem Tranquillus. Qui, inferius vitam Neronis scribens, dicit eum immanissimae insatiabilisque crudelitatis imperatorem optasse similem cladem suis quoque temporibus accidere, ut eius calamitatis memoria suum quoque imperium faceret posteris memorabile.*[40] Aelius Spartianus in *Vita Hadriani* dicit Palmam consularem virum Hadriani insidiatorem, Terracinae interfectum fuisse. Idemque Aelius scribit An-

other spoils of war. Then when the tribunes arrived, the three armies sacked the town, which owing to its long-continued prosperity contained great wealth. It was thanks to this booty that it came about that the Roman soldier was for the first time paid a wage. Previously, each man had served at his own expense."[59] In Book VIII, Livy has: "One cohort, which was stationed not far from Anxur, took up a position at Lautulae in a narrow pass between the mountains and the sea."[60] And Servius on the phrase "Circe's ridge" in Aeneid VII says: "Jupiter was raised as a boy around this part of Campania, and he was called 'Anxyrus' as though from *aneu xurou*, meaning 'without a razor,' because he had never shaved his beard; and the maiden Juno, called Feronian Juno, was also worshipped." There is a spring near Terracina formerly called 'Anxur.'"[61] And Servius, further on: "Not far from Terracina is the town of Satura and the river Ufens [Uffente] of that cognomen which supplies the second element of the town's name [Satura Ufens], and which Vergil says is narrow, and it winds its way through the valleys to the sea."[62] Suetonius, in his *Life of the Emperor Tiberius* writes: "In a place called Praetorium near Terracina, a great many large rocks fell by accident from the ceiling as the emperor dined. Though many of his friends and servants were crushed, he made an incredible escape."[63] *Suetonius also writes that in the time of the emperor Tiberius 20,000 souls perished in the collapse of an amphitheater at Terracina.*[64] *Later, writing of the life of Nero, he says that that monstrous and insatiably cruel emperor longed for a similar disaster to occur in his time so that the memory of the calamity might make his reign too seem remarkable to posterity.*[65] Aelius Spartianus in his *Life of Hadrian* says that it was at Terracina that Palma, a man of consular rank who had conspired against the emperor, was put to death.[66] The same Aelius writes that Antoninus Pius restored the harbor of Terracina.[67] And Livy in Book XXVI says that the colony of Anxur enjoyed irrevocable exemption from military levies, which was suspended at the time of Hasdrubal's advent in Italy.[68]

toni⟨n⟩um Pium instaurasse Terracinensem portum. Et Livius libro XXVI dicit Anxurinam coloniam habuisse sacrosanctam vacationem, quae adventu Hasdrubalis sit suspensa. Libro autem XXI dicit Minucium a Fabio Maximo dictatore missum ad firmandum saltum, qui sub Terracina imminet mari, ne Hannibal per viam Appiam in agrum Romanum iret praedatum. Lucanus autem, accessum Caesaris primum post leges ad Rubiconem transgressas describens, sic dicit: 'Et iam praecipites superaverat Anxuris arces et qua Pontinas via dividit uda paludes.' De Anxure sic habet Martialis coquus poeta, ad Faustinum: 'O nemus, o fontes, solidumque madentis harenae litus, et aequoreis splendidus Anxur aquis.' Et ad Frontinum: 'Anxuris aequorei placidos, Frontine, recessus.'

13   Servius grammaticus Vergilii versum libri IX *Aeneidos*, 'tacitis regnavit Amyclis,' exponens, sic habet: 'Inter Caietam et Terracinam oppidum est constitutum a Laconibus, qui comites Castoris et Pollucis fuerunt et ab Amyclis, provinciae Laconiae civitate. Hi secundum sectam Pythagoream a caede omnium animalium abstinuerunt adeo ut natos in vicinis paludibus serpentes occidere nollent—a quibus interempti sunt'. Aliter: 'cum frequenter nuntiaretur hostes adfuturos et inani terrore civitas quassaretur, lege caverunt ne quis hostes nuntiaret adfuturos. Postea, cum vere venirent hostes, nullo nuntiante, deleti sunt. Et sic Amyclae silentio periere, unde Vergilius appellavit eas tacitas et[41] Lucilius satiricus: "mihi necesse est loqui, nam scio Amyclas tacendo periisse".' Solum Terracinae dicit Strabo intus[42] attingere Formias, Minturnas,[43] et Sinuessam. Addiditque venientes a Brundisio Romam prope Terracinam attingere fossam plenam in multis locis palustri-

In Book XXI, Livy says that the dictator Fabius Maximus sent
Minucius ahead to secure the pass that overlooked the sea below
Terracina. This was to prevent Hannibal from using the Appian
Way to plunder the territory of Rome.[69] When he describes
Caesar's first arrival in Italy after he had ridden roughshod over
the law at the Rubicon, Lucan says: "And now he had passed over
the precipitous heights of Anxur and the point where the waterlogged road cuts through the Pontine Marshes."[70] On Anxur, the
poet Martial the cook has this to say to Faustinus: "Ah, wood and
fountains and the firm shore of moist sand, and Anxur gleaming
in her sea waters!"[71] And to Frontinus: "The calm retreat of
Anxur by the sea, Frontinus."[72]

The grammarian Servius, commenting on the verse "he ruled   13
over silent Amyclae"[73] in Book IX of the *Aeneid*, has this to say:
"The town was founded between Gaeta and Terracina by Spartans, who came as followers of Castor and Pollux from Amyclae, a
city of Laconia. As adherents of the sect of Pythagoras, they re-
frained from all slaughter of animals, to the extent that they were
unwilling to kill the snakes that bred in the marshes nearby, by
whom *they* were killed." An alternative explanation: "because the
arrival of an enemy was often announced and the city would trem-
ble with baseless dread, they forbade by law any report of an ap-
proaching enemy. But afterwards when an enemy really did appear
and no one reported it, they were destroyed. And so it was that
Amyclae perished in silence, whence Lucilius the satirist: 'I *had* to
speak, for I know that Amyclae perished by staying silent.'"[74]
Strabo says that the territory of Terracina reaches inland as far as
Formia, Minturno, and Sinuessa. And he adds that travelers from
Brindisi to Rome reach a canal near Terracina which is fed in
many places by marsh and river water. It lies beside the Appian
Way and is navigated mostly by night, sometimes by day; those
who take to it at night leave it in the morning. Next, he says,
comes Formia, a Spartan foundation, which was formerly called

bus et fluvialibus aquis, propinquam viae Appiae, et navigari nocte maxime, quandoque interdiu, eosque qui ad vesperam intrant mane egredi. Deinceps haberi Formias, Laconicum aedificium, quae antea 'Hormiae' diceba⟨n⟩tur — a bono portu, quem Lacones *euormon*[44] dicunt. Eam urbem amoenissimi situs, in qua Cicero Formianam habuit villam, Saraceni ad annum salutis octingentesimum quinquagesimum sextum destruxerunt, et tunc, Erasmi martyris reliquiis Caietam translatis, datus est Caietanae ecclesiae a Gregorio IV Romano pontifice primus episcopus. Servius tamen in VII dicit Iunonem virginem aliquando dictam fuisse 'Formiam': unde locus apud quem colebatur sit dictus. Livius in VIII: 'Formianis, quod per fines eorum tuta pacataque semper fuisset via, civitas sine suffragiis data.' Additque praedictis Strabo dehinc incipere sinum Gaietae sic a Laconibus nominatum, quod concava omnia 'Gaieta' illi appellant. Et tamen Strabo consentit Caietam scribere quosdam[45] a nutrice Aeneae fuisse dictam, sicut Vergilius, septimi principio: 'tu quoque litoribus nostris, Aeneia nutrix, aeternam moriens famam, Caieta, dedisti.' Sed licet Caietae sinus arxque celebris et pervetustae fuerint famae, ea tamen non fuit civitas priusquam Formias (ut supra ostendimus) destruxerunt Saraceni. Distat vero a Terracina arx (ut Strabo) et (ut nunc est) civitas Caieta stadiis centum, quae nunc viginti milia computantur. Portum Caieta eo in sinu habuit semper optimum, quem tamen Aelius Spartianus ab Antonino Pio magnis exstructionibus instauratum scribit. Et Faustinam eius uxorem scribit idem Aelius condiciones sibi et nauticas et gladiatorias Caietae elegisse.

14   Primaque est ea in via civitas Fundana decimo a Terracina miliario, de qua Livius libro VIII: 'Fundanis, quod per fines eorum tuta pacataque[46] semper fuisset via, civitas sine suffragio data.' Et infra: 'Fundanus Vitrubius[47] Bacchus, Privernis se ducem rebellio-

Hormiae from its "good anchorage," or *euormon* as the Spartans say.[75] Cicero had his Formian villa in this picturesque setting but the city was destroyed by the Saracens about the year 856. Thereafter the remains of the martyr Erasmus[76] were transferred to Gaeta, and Formia's first bishop was given to church of Gaeta by the Roman pontiff Gregory IV.[77] Servius on *Aeneid* VII, on the other hand, says that as a girl Juno was called 'Formia' and the place where she was worshiped was named after her.[78] Livy says in Book VIII: "Because they had always allowed free passage through their territory, the citizens of Formia were given Roman citizenship without the vote."[79] And Strabo adds to what he said above that the Gulf of Gaeta (so named by the Spartans because they call all hollow things *caieta*) began at Formia.[80] Yet Strabo allows that some writers say that Gaeta was named after Aeneas' nurse,[81] as Vergil says at the beginning of Book VII: "You too, Caieta, nurse of Aeneas, have brought in death eternal fame to our shores."[82] But though the bay and citadel of Gaeta were celebrated in remotest antiquity, the town itself did not exist before the Saracens destroyed Formia, as I showed above. The citadel of Gaeta (as in Strabo) and the present-day town of Gaeta are a hundred stades from Terracina, a distance nowadays reckoned as twenty miles. Gaeta has always had an excellent harbor on its bay, though Aelius Spartianus writes that Antoninus Pius made extensive restorations there.[83] Aelius also writes that Antoninus Pius's wife Faustina used to arrange liaisons with sailors and gladiators at Gaeta.[84]

The first town on the Appian Way is Fondi, ten miles from Terracina, on which Livy writes in Book VIII: "Because they had always allowed free passage through their territory, the citizens of Formia were given Roman citizenship without the vote."[85] And below: "Vitrubius Bacchus of Fondi offered himself to the people of Priverno as leader of their rebellion, and forced the Romans to dispatch the consul Lucius Papirius against them. The Privernates

14

nis exhibens, Romanos compulit ut Lucium Papirium cos. in eos
mitterent. Fusi Privernates. Plautius alter cos. in Fundanos duce-
bat. Ingredienti fines senatus Fundanus occurrit: negare se pro Vi-
trubio sectamque eius secutis precatum venisse, sed pro Fundano
populo, quem extra culpam belli esse ipse Vitrubius indicasset,
cum receptaculum fugae Privernum habuit, non patriam Fundos.
Cos. collaudatis Fundanis eis pepercit.' Fundanorum vina Martialis coquus innuit non esse talia quae inveteranda sint: 'Haec Fundana tulit felix autumnus opima. Expressit mustum[48] consul, et
ipse bibet.'

15   Euntibusque a Fundis Formias sinistrorsum est Villa oppidum,
a quo Galba imperator originem duxit. Dextrorsumque est lacus
Fundanus. Inde Itrum quinto miliario, quae civitas Lemurnarum
fuit, de qua Horatius: 'tandem defessi Lemurnarum venimus urbem.' Et altero item quinto, sed extra viam Appiam, est Caieta. Ea
autem decem milia passuum viam habent silicibus Romano veteri
modo stratam inter arduos celsosque montes — sed viti, olea, arbo-
rumque consitionibus amoenissimos. Et secundum litus marisque
undas a Terracina petitur turris Sancti Anastasii, deinde oppidum
Spelunca appellatum, ubi dicit Strabo speluncas patere ingentes,
quae habitationes magnas speciosasque exciperent. Post speluncas
in litore est Caieta, a qua nunc urbe ad Traiectum (sive Lirim) fluvium, nunc Gaurianum appellatum, milibus decem terra est omnium — non solum[49] Italiae, sed orbis totius — amoenissima, quod,
fontibus ibi scatentibus, aquae passim lucidissimae citrangulis
arantiisque (ut nostri citrea appellant)[50] consita interfluunt ir-

were put to flight. The other consul Plautius led his army against Fondi. As he was crossing their frontier, the senate of Fondi met him and explained that they had not come to intercede for Vitrubius and those who had belonged to his party, but for the people of Fondi. They pointed out that Vitrubius himself had cleared them of all responsibility by seeking shelter in Priverno and not in Fondi, though it was his own city. The consul commended the citizens of Fondi and granted them leniency."[86] Martial the cook suggests that the wines of Fondi are not the kind to need maturing: "The rich autumn of Opimius' consulship bore this wine of Fondi; the consul squeezed out the must, and he himself will drink it."[87]

Those heading leftwards from Fondi to Formia reach the town   15 of Villa, where the emperor Galba was born,[88] while to the right is the Lago di Fondi. Five miles further on is Itri, which was the city of the Lemurnae, of which Horace says: "At last, exhausted, we came to the city of the Lemurnae."[89] Another five miles from Itri, but off the Appian Way, is Gaeta. This ten-mile stretch of road is paved with flint in the old Roman fashion as it makes its way through high and rugged hill country—though with its vines, olives and stands of trees, the landscape is perfectly charming. Following the coast and seashore from Terracina one comes upon Torre Anastasia, then the town called Sperlonga, where, Strabo says, there are wide-open caverns of immense size which have been occupied by large and splendid residences.[90] After Sperlonga comes Gaeta on the shore: ten miles from the present town of Gaeta, at the river Traetto (or Liri), now called the Garigliano, is the most beautiful countryside, not just of Italy but in all the world, for the springs that bubble up there give bright clear water that flows all over land planted with lemons and oranges (as we Latins call the citrus-tree), irrigating it. The principal spring, only ten paces from its first emergence from the ground, turns a good number of mills that are dotted around about a pretty and well-

rigantque loca. Praecipuusque fons decimo post primam scatu-
riginem passu molas versat plurimas vico celebri pulcherrimoque
circumdatas. Per quae loca Scipionem Laeliumque conchas et umbilicos legisse Cicero indicat in secundo *De oratore:* 'Laelius et Scipio semper adinvicem rusticari tuncque mirabiliter repuerascere
erant soliti, cum rus ex urbe tamquam e vinculis evolassent, et ad
Caietam Laurentumque conchas et umbilicos legere consuevissent,
et ad omnem animi remissionem ludumque descenderent.'

16   Quo quidem in decem milium spatio Herculanea fuit via, omnium quas Romanum ubique habuit imperium amoenissima. De
qua Cicero oratione *In legem agrariam Rulli* secunda sic habet: 'acce-
dent salicta[51] ad Minturnas. Adiungitur et illa via vendibilis Herculanea multarum deliciarum et magnae pecuniae.' Suntque deinceps Castellonum oppidum et Honoratum villa, quam Honoratus,
Fundorum comes, speciosissimam aedificavit. In conspectu autem
speluncarum, quas ad Caietae sinum esse diximus, sunt propositae
in pelago insulae duae: Pandana[52] et Pontia, sicut Livius IX libro
dicit, colonia a Romanis deducta. Eas dicit Strabo parvas, sed
pulchre habitatas inter se parum, sed a continenti ducentis quinquaginta stadiis distare. Fuerunt vero hae insulae post Strabonis
tempora multorum martyrum et Christi confessorum exsilio deco-
ratae.

17   Sinum Caietanum tangit Caecubus mons vini praestantia celeber, et Caecubum,[53] civitas Fundorum, in via Appia. Haec autem
omnia loca boni vini copiam habere dicit Strabo. Et Plinius: 'Cae-
cubae vites in Pontinis paludibus madent.' Vestusta est autem
utraque civitas et suo quaeque ornata fuit Romano pontifice,
Caieta secundo Gelasio, Funda Sotere, patre Concordio.[54] Sed
iam limites attingimus nostrae huius Latinae regionis: Sinuessam
et Liris sive Gauriani ostia, et maritimam absolvimus oram. Et ta-

known village. In this neighborhood, Cicero tells us in Book II of *De oratore*, Scipio and Laelius gathered shells and cockles: "Scipio and Laelius would always go off into the country together and would become marvellously boyish again, once they had flown to the countryside from the city as if slipping their shackles. At Gaeta and Laurentum they used to gather seashells and cockles, and indulge themselves in all manner of diversions and mental relaxation."[91]

On this ten-mile stretch was the Herculanean Way, the 16 pleasantest of all the roads of the Roman Empire. In his second oration *Against the Agrarian Law of Rullus*, Cicero has this to say of it: "Add to these the osier beds of Minturno. Besides them, that very saleable road to Herculaneum, a road of many delights and of considerable value."[92] Next come the town of Castellone and then Castellonorato, which Onorato, count of Fondi, built in most impressive style.[93] Within sight of the caverns, which as I said are on the Bay of Gaeta, two islands are set in the sea, Ventotene and Ponza, the latter a colony planted by the Romans, as Livy says.[94] Strabo says that these islands, small but with a healthy population, are close to one another but 250 stades from the mainland.[95] After Strabo's time, these islands were honored by the exile of many martyrs and confessors of Christ.

The Caecuban Mount, famous for its excellent wine, touches 17 the Gulf of Gaeta, as does Caecubum, a town in the district of Fondi on the Appian Way. Strabo says that the whole region has an abundance of good wine.[96] And Pliny says: "Caecuban vines ripen in the Pontine Marshes."[97] Both of the cities there are ancient and each has been graced by a Roman pontiff, Gaeta by Gelasius II and Fondi by Soter, the son of Concordius.[98] Now we are coming to the border of our region of Lazio at Sinuessa and the mouth of the Liri (or Garigliano), and have finished our description of the sea coast. But before we return to the interior, we

men priusquam ad mediterraneam redeamus, ea docebimus quae Liris ad sinistram in regione Latina habet.

18   Supra Traiectum oppidum, tribus milibus passuum a mari distans, est Liri contiguum Speninum castellum. A quo distant octo milia passus Fractae, totidem a Ponte Corvo semotae, quod oppidum Fregellas fuisse ostendimus superius. Aliis item octo miliaribus abest Ceparanum nobile oppidum. Reliqua ad fontem Liris proximius[55] accedentia in Vestinorum Samnitiumque partibus dicentur. In mediterraneo autem Latinorum solo frequentes fuere urbes infinitaque paene oppida et castella, ex quibus auctor est Plinius quinquaginta tres populos sine vestigiis interiisse.[56]

19   Hac autem describenda mediterranea regione modum hactenus in aliis servatum a fluviorum ostiis fontibusque et discursu servare nequibimus.[57] Sed alium certius facturum satis, qui in nulla reperiatur alia Italiae regione, tenebimus: viis incedendo tribus, Appia, Latina, Tiburtina, quae inter se diversae ad Lirim amnem et Sinuessam Caietamque perducunt. Nec tamen certiore gradu ita per singulas pedem figere poterimus quin delabi et aberrare videamur — quod quidem necessitas faciet, cum viae alicubi dirutis pontibus aversae, alicubi[58] ut penitus ignorentur omnino sint perditae.

20   Igitur Roma nunc petentibus Terracinam iter, est primum duodecimo miliario Marinum, quod non absurde Marianam villam fuisse ut credam facit proxima L. Murenae villa semi etiam integra, et praedium Portium vulgo notum. Eademque Lucii Murenae villa, priscum nunc quoque retinens nomen, credere nos hactenus fecit aut Marinum (si ea non fuerat, ut diximus, Mariana villa) aut Zagarolum, novi nominis oppidum, sed, ut ruinae indicant, vetustum fuisse Lanuvium, ex quo vetustissimo et celebratissimi nominis municipio Urbi propinquo Murenas patricios et consulares viros originem duxisse Cicero in oratione *Pro L. Murena* affirmat.

shall mention the places on the left bank of the Liri in the region
of Lazio.

Three miles from the sea, above the town of Traetto, is the   18
castle of Spigno Saturnia beside the Liri, and eight miles from
Spigno is Fratte, a town some eight miles again distant from
Pontecorvo (that town, as we have shown, was once Fregellae). It
is a further eight miles inland to the well-known town of Ceprano.
(The remaining places closer to the source of the Liri will be discussed when we come to the territory of the Vestini and the
Samnites [§55].) In the interior of Lazio there were numerous cities and almost numberless towns and castles, from which, according to Pliny, fifty-three peoples have perished without trace.[99]

In describing this inland region, we shall not be able to adhere   19
to the plan used in other regions, orienting ourselves by the
mouths, sources and course of rivers. We shall adopt another
method (one suited to this region alone) which will meet our
needs better, by proceeding along three roads, the Appian, Latin,
and Tiburtine, which lead in different ways to the river Liri and to
Sinuessa and Gaeta. Nor will our path on these roads be so clear
as to avoid apparent slips and aberrations, inevitably so, since the
roads have sometimes been diverted when bridges were destroyed,
while at other points all trace of them has been lost and they cannot be recognized at all.

Present-day travelers from Rome to Terracina come first to a   20
place called Marino, twelve miles out: the villa of Lucius Murena
next to it, still fairly well preserved, and the estate commonly
known as Porzio, leads me to think that Marino may not improbably have been the villa of Marius. This villa of Murena, if it actually kept its ancient name, I have hitherto been led to believe
was either Marino (if it was not, as I said, the estate of Marius) or
Zagarolo—the name of the town is modern but its ruins indicate
that it was the ancient Lanuvium. Cicero in his speech *Pro Murena*
asserts that the patrician and consular Murenae had their origin in

Nuper autem in oppido quod corrupte 'Civita Indivina' appellatur, a Prospero Columna cardinale possesso, lapis repertus est litteris inscriptus maiusculis,[59] quae Lanuvium illud oppidum esse ostendunt.

21   A Marino autem octavo miliario sunt Velitrae, civitas vetusta, de qua Livius in octavo: 'In Veliternos veteres cives, quod toties rebellassent, graviter saevitum, et muri deiecti, et senatus inde abductus, iussique trans Tiberim habitare. In agrum senatorum coloni missi, quibus ascriptis speciem antiquae frequentiae Velitrae receperunt.' Estque ea civitas, cum aliter vetustate sua, tum ea ratione notissima, quod Octavii Caesaris Augusti progenitores inde originem habuere. Quintoque ab ea miliario ad sinistram distat vetustissimi nominis oppidum Cora, ab uno trium fratrum condita, quorum alius Tibur aedificavit, alius monti proximo Catillo cognomen dedit. De quo Vergilius in VII: 'Tum gemini fratres Tiburtia moenia linquunt, fratris Tiburti dictam cognomine gentem, Catillusque acerque Corax, Argiva iuventus.' Deinceps a Velitris recto itinere instituto est quarto decimo miliario oppidum Sarmineta. Et tertio absunt 'Aquae Foetidae,' ad quas palus incipit Terracinam usque (non minus nunc quam Strabonis aetate consueverit) navigabilis, quam locorum vicinitatem Martialis coquus poeta indicat his versibus: 'O nemus, o fontes, solidumque madentis harenae litus, et aequoreis splendidus Anxur aquis, et non unius spectator lectulus undae, qui videt hinc puppes fluminis inde maris.'

22   Ab hisque aquis quinque miliaribus distat Setia vetusti nominis oppidum arduo in colle situm, vini (ut refert Plinius) optimi ferax. Et Martialis coquus poeta: 'Pendula Pontinos quae spectat Setia campos exigua vetulos misit ab urbe cados.' Et alibi: 'Setinum do-

the very old and famous municipality of Lanuvium near Rome.[100] Recently, however, in a town owned by Cardinal Prospero Colonna and corruptly called "Civita Indivina," a stone inscribed in capital letters was found showing that *that* town is Lanuvium.[101]

Eight miles from Marino is the ancient city of Velletri. In Book VIII Livy says of it: "The Veliternians, who had been Roman citizens from ancient times, were in consequence of their numerous revolts severely dealt with; their walls were pulled down, their senate deported and ordered to live on the other side of the Tiber. Colonists were sent on to the land they had possessed, and their numbers made Velitrae look as populous as before."[102] The city is famous not only on account of its antiquity but for the fact that the forebears of Augustus originated there. Five miles to the left of Velletri is a town with the ancient name of Cori; it was founded by one of three brothers, of whom the second built Tivoli, and the third gave his name to Monte Catillo near Tivoli.[103] On whom Vergil in Book VII: "Then the twin brothers Catillus and fierce Corax, youth of Argos, leave behind the walls of Tivoli and the race named for their brother Tiburtus."[104] After that comes the town of Sermoneta, thirteen miles as the crow flies from Velletri. And three miles from Sermoneta are the Aquae Foetidae, "Stinking Waters," where the marshland begins, though navigable now, no less than it was in Strabo's day, all the way to Terracina. The neighborhood is mentioned by the poet Martial the cook in these lines: "Ah wood and fountains and the firm shore of moist sand, and Anxur gleaming in her sea waters, and the couch that gazes on double wave, seeing on one side river craft, on the other sea-going vessels!"[105]

Sezze, an ancient town set on a high hill, is five miles from Aquae Foetidae, and according to Pliny produces excellent wine.[106] And the poet Martial: "Sezze, that perched aloft looks down upon the Pontine flats, sent old jars from a tiny city."[107] And elsewhere: "Setine wine, masterly snows, cup hard on cup, when shall I drink

21

22

minaeque nives densique trientes, quando ego te, medico non prohibente, bibam?' Privernumque item vetustum, quinque a Setia distans, non ut olim campestre est sed arduum in collem mutatum, postquam Teutonica simul et Britonum rabie fuit destructum, Eius autem alumna fuit Camilla, quam virginem Vergilius miris effert laudibus: 'Volsca de gente Camilla.' Super quo verbo, Servius exponit eam fuisse Privernatem. Solidior vero et certior Privernatium laus fuit illa argutissima oratoris eorum ad senatum Romanum responsio: cum interrogatus qualis esset pax quam Privernates tantopere peterent, respondit perpetuam, si bona daretur, futuram. Fluvius ipsum praeterfluens oppidum dictus est olim Amasenus, de quo Vergilius in VII: 'Amasene pater,' *et in VIII:* '*ecce fugae medio summis Amasenus abundans spumabat ripis.*'[60] Circumstantque Privernum oppidula Maientia, arx Gorga, et arx Sicca. Somninum hinc quinque miliario est oppidum, quod sit arduo in colle situm pro Somnino dictum, a quo abest item quinque Terracina.

23   Hanc inter ubique montuosam et eam viam, quae primo secundum litus est descripta, habetur Appia, eiusque viae prima urbs ad sextum decimum ab Urbe est Alba, qua quidem in via multo maiora sunt aedificiorum monumentorumque et iactarum molium vestigia quam quisquam possit credere, qui omnia attente non viderit. Estque haec Alba cuius meminit Vergilius in primo: 'Albanique patres'. Nam tredecim fuerunt Albani reges de Aeneae et Laviniae gente. Et Livius scribit, Alba a Romanis destructa, Albanos in urbem receptos Caelium montem incoluisse. De cuius origine Vergilius in VIII: 'Ascanius clari condet cognominis Albam.' Eam urbem trecentis ante Romam annis conditam ultimo immunitam reddidit Henricus III, rex Germanicus. In parvo cuius angulo oppidulum nunc exstat a Sabellis civibus Romanis possessum, sicut et possident Sabellum, vetustissimi nominis nunc op-

you without a doctor's ban?"[108] Priverno, also ancient, is five miles from Sezze. It is not as formerly a town of the plains but was moved to a steep hillside after its destruction by the fury of Germans and Bretons.[109] Camilla was a child of Priverno, the maiden that Vergil praises to the skies as "Camilla of the Volscian race."[110] Servius *ad loc.* explains that she was from Priverno.[111] A more concrete and definite commendation of the Privernates came in the famous witticism of their ambassador to the Roman Senate: when asked what kind of peace it was that the Privernates were so keen to have, he replied, one that would last forever, provided the terms were good.[112] The river that flows past the town of Priverno was formerly called the Amasenus, whom Vergil addresses in Book VII as: "father Amasenus."[113] *And, in Book VIII: "while they were in mid-flight, behold, Amasenus in spate foamed to the top of his banks."*[114] Around Priverno are the little towns of Maenza, Roccagorga, and Roccasecca. Five miles from Priverno (and from Terracina too) is the town of Sonnino set on a steep hill named after the town.

This road is in the mountains all the way, and between it and 23 the road along the shore described earlier lies the Appian Way. The first city on the Appian Way is Alba, sixteen miles from Rome. Along the road, there are the remains of buildings and monuments and foundations of enormous structures, much more extensive than one might believe without an attentive examination. This is the Alba that Vergil mentions in Book I: "and the Senate of Alba."[115] There were thirteen Alban kings of the line of Aeneas and Lavinia. Livy writes that once Alba was destroyed by the Romans, the Albans were transferred to Rome and lived on the Caelian Hill.[116] On the origin of Alba, Vergil says in Book VIII: "Ascanius will found the famous town called Alba."[117] The city was founded 300 years before Rome but lately stripped of its defenses by the German king Henry III.[118] In a small corner of Alba there is now a village owned by the Roman Savelli. They also own the town of Castel Savelli, long celebrated in history, from

pidum, a quo Romanae nunc familiae nobili nomen fluxit. In eo Ludovicus cardinalis Aquileiensis, Romani pontificis camerarius, monasterium, quod Honorius III de gente Sabella aedificavit, paene funditus dirutum magna instauravit impensa adeo ut — sive monasterii sive villae inter ceteras Italiae amoenissimae rusticanas inibi habitationes habeat — ductus aquarum instauraverit et de- mortuae urbi aliquam oppidi faciem reddiderit.

24   Eademque in via Appia est proxima Albae sexto miliario Aricia olim civitas vetusta, de qua Livius, in VIII: 'Aritini eodem iure quo Lavinii in civitatem accepti.' Nunc vero penitus est derelicta, cuius marmora et cetera ornamenta Marini oppidi ecclesias deco- rarunt. *Estque Aricia una ex urbibus quinque quas facit Vergilius, in VII, ministrasse tela Aeneae, quo in loco appellat eam 'potentem', quia fuit praestans in regione civitas.*[61] Eam dicit Servius nactam esse nomen a morbis quos gigneret, quia vicina esset Pontinae paludi. Et alio loco dicit Ariciam a Vergilio appellari 'matrem' ut plauderet adula- returque Augusto, cuius mater fuerit Aricina. Nam Iulia Caesaris soror genuit Attiam ex Balbo in Aricia, et Attia ex Octavio genuit Octavianum. Sic enim habet Vergilius: 'ibat et Hippolyti proles[62] pulcherrima bello, Virbius insignem quem mater Aricia misit.' Est vero haec Hippolyti fabula ab Ovidio scripta. Nam Diana Hippo- lytum ab inferis revocatum misit Ariciam, quem nutriri[63] curavit ab Egeria nympha, Numae Pompilii amica, cuius monitis et consi- lio rem publicam administrare simulabat. Appellat itaque Vergilius Hippolytum 'Virbium,' id est, 'bis virum.' Nota est vetus historia: Etruscos, qui cum Arunte, regis Porsenae filio, ad oppugnandum Ariciam iverant, amisso duce redeuntes Romam amice et hospita- liter fuisse acceptos. Quibus fuit datus ad habitandum in urbe ce-

which the noble family now derives its name. The papal chamberlain Ludovico, Cardinal of Aquileia, restored at great expense the monastery that Honorius III (himself of the Savelli family) built in Alba after it had been almost completely destroyed. Whether it was to have a country retreat in a monastery or in a villa more splendid than any other in Italy, he went so far as to repair the water supply and restored to a dead city some semblance of a town.[119]

Six miles further on the Appian Way from Alba is Ariccia, an old town in bygone days, about which Livy says in Book VIII: "The men of Ariccia were given the same political rights as the Lavinii."[120] Ariccia is now utterly derelict, and its marble and other ornaments adorn the churches of the town of Marino. *Ariccia was one of the five cities that Vergil has supplying armor to Aeneas, in a passage of Book VII where he calls it "mighty," because it was the foremost city of the region.*[121] Servius says that it got its name from the sicknesses to which it gave rise from being near the Pontine Marshes.[122] Elsewhere Servius says that Vergil calls Ariccia "mother" to congratulate and flatter Augustus, since his mother was born there.[123] (Julia, Caesar's sister, bore Atia to Balbus in Ariccia, and Atia bore Octavian to Octavius.)[124] And thus Vergil has: "Hippolytus' handsome son Virbius rode out to war, sent for glory by his mother Aricia."[125] This version of the Hippolytus myth was related by Ovid.[126] Diana recalled Hippolytus from the underworld and sent him to Aricia. The goddess had taken care that he should be nursed by the nymph Egeria, the friend of Numa Pompilius, by whose advice and counsel Numa pretended to run the state. Vergil accordingly calls Hippolytus "Virbius," that is, "twice a man."[127] There is a well-known ancient tradition that the Etruscans had advanced under Aruns, son of Porsenna, to attack Aricia. When they lost their leader, the Etruscans returned to Rome, where they were kindly received and given hospitality. They were assigned a district to live in, a populous part of the city which was ever afterwards called "the Tuscan quarter."[128] On that account Porsenna in

24

leberrimo loco vicus semper postea 'Tuscus' appellatus. Quam ob
rem Porsena obsides in foedere habitos benigne remisit. Livius
libro LXXX scribit Cinnam et C. Marium expugnasse Ariciam
coloniam. Plinius vero dicit brassicam Aricinam altitudine non ex-
celsam reputari utilissimam, quia sub omnibus paene foliis fruc-
tificat cauliculis peculiaribus, cum Sabellanae brassicae folia dicat
fuisse in admiratione crispa. Eorumque crassitudinem extenuare
caulem sed dulcissimum ex omnibus perhiberi. Et Martialis poeta
Aricinos porros sic laudat: 'mittit praecipuos nemoralis Aricia
porros.'

25   Deinceps eadem via secus Storacem sive Nymphaeum amnem,
ubi olim fuit Forum Appii vetus oppidum, nunc est monasterium
Fossa Nova appellatum, quod, centum olim pluribusque monachis
habitari solitum postquam multis annis manserat derelictum,
quarti Eugenii pontificis religiosissimi opera adiumentoque Cister-
ciensium abbas anno ante quinto decem duodecimve monachis habitari curavit. Fundique civitas postmodum habetur, quae superius
descripta ab Honorato Caietano principe humanissimo posside-
tur.

26   Alia, quae nos ad Latinorum limites ducit, via est Latina, in
qua primum decimo ab Urbe miliario cernuntur vestigia Columnae oppidi, a quo clara Columnensium familia multis ante saeculis originem habuit et cognomen. Ibique Algidum incipit vetusti
et in historiis celebrati nominis silva, in cuius medio bifurcatum
est iter hoc nostrum: et hinc ad dexteram XIIII a Columna distat
Valmontonum, ubi Lavicos fuisse ad finem huius regionis ostendemus; inde ad sinistram minore spatio abest Gallicanum, quem locum Gabios fuisse coniicimus. Eo autem itinere in ipso Algidi
silvae ingressu Regillus est lacus, apud quem Aulus Postumius dictator prospere adversus Tarquinium Superbum patria eiectum et
Latinorum exercitum Romanis bellum inferentem[64] pugnavit. A

a friendly spirit returned the hostages he held under the treaty. Livy writes in Book LXXX that Cinna and Gaius Marius took the colony of Ariccia by storm.[129] Pliny says that the cabbage of Ariccia, though of no great height, is looked upon as the most useful of them all, for beneath nearly all of the leaves there are small sprouts peculiar to this variety, though he says that the leaves of the Sabine cabbage are wonderfully crisp—their thickness makes the stalk thin, but that stalk is said to surpass all others in sweetness.[130] And the poet Martial praises Ariccian leeks in these words: "Wooded Ariccia sends wonderful leeks."[131]

Next on the Appian Way, on the site of the ancient town of Forum Appii along the river Storax (or Nymphaeus), there is now a monastery called Fossanova.[132] Though it once housed a hundred monks or more, it remained for many years in a state of dereliction until five years ago the Cistercian abbot—with the help and support of that most devout pope Eugenius IV—saw to it that it was occupied by ten or twelve monks. A little further on is the city of Fondi which I described above [§§14, 16], a possession of the cultivated prince Onorato Caetani.

The second road, which takes us to the border of Lazio, is the Via Latina. On this road some ten miles outside Rome, we first see the remains of the town of Colonna, from where many centuries ago the famous Colonna family took their origin and their name. And there begins a forest with the ancient name of Algidus, much mentioned in history, in the middle of which our route bifurcates: on one side, to the right, lies Valmontone, fourteen miles from Colonna, which I shall show was the site of Labico at the edge of Lazio; on the other, to the left, not so far from Colonna, is Gallicano, which I believe was the ancient Gabii. At the very beginning of the forest of Algidus on that route is Lake Regillus, where the dictator Aulus Postumius fought a successful battle against Tarquinius Superbus (who had been thrown out of the city) and an army of Latins then making war on Rome.[133] Three

25

26

Gallicano autem (sive Gabiis) tertio distat Praeneste civitas, de qua inferius copiose dicemus. Et inde secundo absunt Cavae, Odoardi Columnae oppidum, et pariter secundo item miliario est Zinazanum. Quod oppidum, civitatulae cuipiam aedium ornatu, populi frequentia, et opum affluentia comparandum, a Martino quinto pontifice gloriosissimo, multisque Romanae ecclesiae cardinalibus, et simul a praestantibus Romanae curiae viris per aestatis caumata saepenumero inhabitatum est.

27 Abest a Zinazano decem passuum milibus Anagnia civitas in Hernicis vetustissima, de qua Vergilius: 'Hernica saxa colunt, quos dives Anagnia pascit.' Servius vero exponit Vergilium allusisse ad historiam: 'Nam Antonius, Fulvia Augusti sorore contempta, postquam duxit Cleopatram Aegypti reginam, eius monetam in Anagnia cudi iussit, unde dives est a Vergilio appellata.' Hernicos autem Servius Sabina lingua a saxosa patria dictos vult, quia *hernae* Sabini *saxum* dicerent. Livius in IX: 'P. Cornelius Arvina, M. Tremulus coss. concilium populorum omnium habentibus Anagninis in circo, quem Maritimum vocant, praeter Alatrinatem et Verulanum, omnes Hernici bellum Romanis indixerunt. Et infra: Marcius cos. omnem gentem Hernicam in deditionem accepit. Et inferius: Anagninis, quia arma Romanis intulerant, civitas sine suffragii latione data, concilia connubiaque adempta, et magistratibus praeter quam sacrorum curatione interdictum fuit.'

28 Anagnia civitas duobus Romanis pontificibus, tertio Innocentio et octavo Bonifacio civibus, decorata. Bonifaciusque vel ea ratione gloriosus pontifex fuit, quod annum Iubilaeum primus Romano-

miles from Gallicano (Gabii), is the city of Palestrina, of which we shall speak in detail below. Two miles from Palestrina is Rocca di Cave, a town of Odoardo Colonna,[134] and another two miles from Cave is Genazzano. In the splendor of its buildings, the liveliness of its populace, and its affluence, this little town can compare with any in Italy. The illustrious pontiff Martin V and many cardinals of the Roman Church, as well as the leading figures of the Curia, often made Genazzano their residence in the summer heat.[135]

Ten miles from Genazzano is the ancient city of Anagni, in the 27 territory of the Hernici. Vergil says of it: "Those that rich Anagnia nurtures dwell among the Hernican rocks."[136] Servius explains that Vergil was making an historical allusion: "When Antony had spurned Augustus' sister Fulvia and married Cleopatra, queen of Egypt, he ordered coinage to be struck at Anagni in her honor, which is why Vergil called the place "rich."[137] Servius thinks they were called Hernici in the Sabine tongue from their rocky land, the Sabines calling rock *hernae*.[138] Livy writes in Book IX: "In the consulship of P. Cornelius Arvina and Marcius Tremulus, the men of Anagni convened a council of all the tribes in what they call the 'Circus Maritimus,' and all the Hernicans, with the exception of the men of Aletrium and Verulae, declared war on Rome."[139] And below: "The consul Marcius accepted the surrender of the entire Hernican people."[140] And below that: "Because they had borne arms against the Roman people, the men of Anagni were given citizenship without the vote; they were deprived of their municipal self-government and the right of intermarriage with each other, and their magistrates were forbidden to exercise any functions except those connected with religion."[141]

The city of Anagni has been graced by two of her citizens who 28 became pope, Innocent III[142] and Boniface VIII. The great distinction of Boniface lay in the fact that he was the first Roman pontiff to hold a Jubilee year. The Jubilee being celebrated this year, the fourth, has attracted far greater throngs than all others

rum pontificum Romae instituit. Isque, qui quartus praesenti anno celebratur, Iubileus maiorem multo ceteris hucusque habuit populorum multitudinem, melius in dies ut videbatur processurus, nisi exardescere incipiens praesenti Iunio pestilentia et multos absumpsisset, et curiam abire suasisset, et populos ab adventu deterruisset. Inde vero fuit Bonifacius infelix, quod Sarram Columnensem capitali prosecutus odio Praeneste vetustissimam urbem, quam is Sarra paterna possederat successione, solo aequavit. Et duos ex ea familia cardinales dignitate privavit, quos Clemens V illico restituit. Et postmodum regem Franciae Bonifacius adeo irritavit ut, immissus adiutusque ab eo Sarra eundem pontificem in patria et domo paterna ceperit, Romamque captivum abduxerit, ubi nulla magis ratione alia diem male obiisse creditus est quam quia simplicem corde et sanctum virum Caelestinum quintum, qui pontificatu quo se per renuntiationem exuit illum ornaverat, in Fumonis carcere mori coegerat. Scribit Plinius Fucinum lacum, qui Marsorum appellatur, subterraneos habere cuniculos quibus aqua certo effluens⁶⁵ tempore amnem faciat. Et sive Plinii textus (ut saepe alibi) eo in loco corruptus sive aliter vitiatus et mutilatus est, non satis potuimus intellegere quo in loco fluvium ille oriri affirmet. Sed fontem esse scimus Anagniae Tophanum nomine, qui hieme, quando Fucinus glacie astringitur, siccus, vere postmodum, aestate, ac autumno ingentem evomit vim aquarum, quae Lirim amnem a Sancto Vito oriundum adaugent.

29   Est vero quinto ab Anagnia Ferentinum, Romana colonia olim et ipsa Hernicorum, de qua Livius libro tertio: 'progressus Tullius ad caput Ferentinum.' Et libro VII: 'Ferentinum urbem Hernicorum vi cepit. Et libro nono: 'Hernicorum tribus populis, Alatri-

up till now and seemed destined to become ever more successful, had the plague that began to flare up this June not carried off so many, and persuaded the Curia to leave, and discouraged pilgrims from coming to Rome.[143] Boniface was unlucky thereafter in pursuing Sciarra Colonna with unremitting hatred, razing to the ground the ancient city of Palestrina which Sciarra owned by ancestral inheritance. He also divested two Colonna cardinals of their office (though Clement V immediately restored them). Boniface subsequently so angered the king of France that the latter sent Sciarra against him and helped him to seize Boniface in his family home at Anagni and take him off to Rome as a prisoner, where he died. It was believed that Boniface came to this bad end chiefly because he had compelled Celestine V — a simple soul and a saintly man who had honored Boniface with the papacy that he himself resigned — to die in prison at Fumone.[144] Pliny writes that the Fucine Lake, also known as the Lake of the Marsians, has subterranean cavities through which water flows at regular intervals and creates a river.[145] It may be that Pliny's text has been corrupted at this point (as is often the case) or is otherwise faulty or mutilated, but I was not able to determine where he maintains that this river rises. But I do know a spring at Anagni called the Tufano, which is dry in winter when the Fucine Lake is frozen over, but later in the spring, summer, and autumn discharges a great quantity of water to swell the river Liri (which itself rises at San Vito).

Ferentino is five miles from Anagni, once a Roman colony and 29 another town of the Hernicans. In Book III Livy says of it: "Tullius arrived at the source of the river Ferentina."[146] And, in Book VII: "He stormed the Hernican city of Ferentino."[147] And in Book IX: "Three of the Hernican communities — Alatri, Veroli, and Ferentino — had their municipal independence restored to them as they preferred that to the Roman franchise."[148] And below: "The next place to be attacked was Ferentino, and

nati, Verulano, Ferentinati, suae leges, quia maluerunt quam civitatem Romanam, redditae'.[66] Item inferius: 'Ferentinum inde,
quamquam nihil quietis dabatur, tamen summa alacritate ductum.
Ceterum ibi plus laboris et periculi fuit, et defensa summa vi moenia sunt, et locus erat munimento naturaque tutus. Sed evicit omnia assuetus praedae miles. Ad tria milia hominum caesa. Praeda
militum fuit.' Suetonius autem Tranquillus scribit Othonis imperatoris, qui Galbae successit, maiores ortos fuisse oppido Ferentino, familia vetere honorata atque ex principibus Etruriae. A Ferentino quinto itidem est Frusinona, de qua Livius: 'Frusinates
tertia parte agri damnati, quod Hernicos ab eis sollicitatos compertum.' Fuitque duobus olim ornata Romanis pontificibus, Hormisda patre Iusto per consulatus Symmachi et Boethii tempora, et
Silverio eodem genito Hormisda, quem, Iustiniano primo imperatore, Theodatus rex Gothorum tertius per pecuniam ordinavit. A
Frusinonaque distat quindecim miliaribus Ceperanum, nostrae
huius regionis alter limes. Sed propinquo huic itinere sunt ad Zi-
nazani dexteram: Pallianum, Serronum, Pillium, Acutum, Trivi-
lianum, Collis Pardi, Anticulum, Verulae vetus oppidum, de quo
Livius, in IX: 'Verulanis suae leges, quia maluerunt quam civitatem Romanam, redditae. Connubiumque inter suos, quod aliquamdiu soli Hernicorum habuerant, permissum est.' Et Fumone
Caelestini pontificis Romani carcere et morte clarum. Deinceps
Alatrum, vetusti nominis civitas, cui simul cum Verulanis suae leges redditae a Romanis et connubium permissum. Hinc Babucum,
olim civitas apud Livium Bovillarum nomine nota, deinde Turri-
tium, Pofae, Vicus, Ripae, Porcilianum, Trevum, Felectinum.

though no rest was allowed the men, they marched there with high spirits. Here, however, they had more trouble and more risk. The position had been made as strong as possible by nature and by art, and the walls were defended with the utmost energy, but a soldiery habituated to plunder overcame all obstacles. As many as 3000 of the enemy were killed; the plunder was given to the troops."[149] Suetonius writes that the ancestors of the emperor Otho, who succeeded Galba, came from the town of Ferentino, his family being old and distinguished and descended from an Etruscan royal house.[150] Another five miles takes us to Frosinone. On Frosinone Livy writes: "The Frusinates were fined a third of their land when it was discovered they were behind the Hernican rebellion."[151] Frosinone had the distinction of producing two Roman pontiffs, Hormisdas, the son of Justus, in the time of the consulate of Symmachus and Boethius, and Silverius, the son of the same Hormisdas. (The king of the Goths Theodatus III bought Silverius' appointment as pope when Justinian I was emperor.)[152] Ceprano, the second border town of our region, is fourteen miles from Frosinone. But on the first stretch of the route to Frosinone, there are to the right of Genazzano the towns of Paliano, Serrone, Piglio, Acuto, Trivigliano, Collepardo, Anticoli in Campagna [now Fiuggi], and the ancient town of Veroli. On Veroli, Livy writes in Book IX: "The citizens of Veroli had their municipal independence restored to them as they preferred that to the Roman franchise, and the right of intermarriage with each other was granted them, a privilege which for a considerable period they were the only community among the Hernicans to enjoy."[153] Fumone is famous for the imprisonment and death there of Pope Celestine. Then comes Alatri, an ancient city whose citizens had their laws restored and the right of intermarriage granted by the Romans at the same time as those of Veroli. Next Bauco, formerly a town known by the name Bovillae in Livy, then Torrice, Pofi, Vico nel Lazio, Ripi, Porcigliano, Trevi nel Lazio, Filettino.[154]

30   Altera autem via, quam medio in Algido liquimus, primum est oppidum, olim Labici,[67] de quo Livius libro IV: 'et renuntiatum est novos hostes, Labicanos, consilia cum veteribus iungere. Labicos legati missi, cum responsa inde retulissent dubia, quibus nec tum bellum quidem parari nec diuturnam pacem fore appareret, Tusculanis negotium datum adverterent animos ne quid novi tumultus Labicis oriretur. Nuntiarunt legati Labicanos arma cepisse et cum Aequorum exercitu depopulatos agrum Tusculanum castra in Algido posuisse. Q. Sulpicius Priscus dictator, captis direptisque illorum castris, oppidum Labicos corona circumdatum scalis captum diripuit. Censuitque senatus frequentem coloniam Labicos deducendam. Coloni ab Urbe mille quingenti missi bina iugera acceperunt.' Id oppidum nunc dicitur Valmontone, quod proprio iure a nobili Comitum familia possessum, nuper magno privatum est decore, Lucido diacono cardinali studiorum humanitatis flagrantissimo. Sed eius frater Altus, vir doctus simul et prudens, Iohanne ornatus filio rei bellicae gloria apud Venetos florente, oppidi illius aliorumque quibus praesunt decus conservat. Fuitque Labicanum olim uvis copiosum optimis, ex quibus Clodium Albinum pondo viginti unica cibatione comedisse scribit Iulius Capitolinus.

31   Proximumque est Valmontoni Monsfortinus oppidum Stephani nostri familia nobili, quae oppidi cognomen habet, oriundi patria atque villa. Deinceps sunt Zanchatum, Gavignanum et Signia oppidum vetus, vinum, ut inquit Plinius, faciens Signinum, quod alvum maxime restringit. Hinc Martialis coquus poeta: 'Po-

The second branch of the road (which we left in the middle of   30
the forest of Algidus [§26]) has as its first town Labici, on which
Livy in Book IV writes as follows: "It was reported that a new enemy, the Labicans, was forming a coalition with their old foes. Envoys were sent to Labici. The reply they brought back was evasive;
it was evident that while there were no immediate preparations for
war, peace would not last long. The Tusculans were requested to
be on the watch for any fresh movement on the part of the
Labicans. Envoys came and reported that the Labicans had taken
up arms and in conjunction with the Aequi had ravaged the
Tusculan territory and fixed their camp on Algidus. Having seized
and destroyed their camp, the dictator Q. Sulpicius Priscus completely surrounded the town of Labici, took it with scaling ladders
and plundered it. The Senate decided that a body of colonists
should be settled at Labici. Fifteen hundred colonists were sent
from Rome, and each received two *iugera* of land."[155] The town of
Labici is now called Valmontone, which has recently lost its great
ornament in the Cardinal Deacon Lucido, a member of the Conti
family, who own the place in their own right. He was a fervent
supporter of humanist studies, but his brother Aldo, a man both
learned and wise, and Aldo's son Giovanni, who brings him credit
with the martial distinction he has achieved at Venice, ensure the
continuance of the glory of Valmontone and the other towns over
which they hold sway.[156] Labici once had an abundance of fine
grapes, of which Julius Capitolinus writes that Clodius Albinus
devoured twenty pounds at a single sitting.[157]

Next to Valmontone is Montefortino [now Artena], the town   31
of my friend Stefano, who was born on an estate in his home town
to the noble family named after it. Then there are Zancato,
Gavignano, and the ancient town of Segni. Pliny says it produces
the wine called Segnine, a very effective astringent for the stom-
ach.[158] The poet Martial says: "Will you drink Segnine wines, that
constricts loose bowels? Let your thirst be sparing, lest you re-

tabis liquidum Signina morantia ventrem? Ne nimium sitias,[68] sit tibi parca sitis.' Quae Signia Vitaliano pontifice Romano, patre Anastasio, ornata fuit. Ulteriusque sunt Scurcula, Merulum, Supinum, Patrica, Caecanum, et Castrum, ubi alius est nostrae Latinae regionis (nunc Campaniae) limes.

32   Tertia restat nobis per quam ad alios nostrae Latinae regionis limites itur, Tiburtina via a Tibure dicta, quam civitatem, sextodecimo ab Urbe distantem, multo ante Romam originem a Graecis habuisse vult Strabo, et Vergilius eam a Tiburto conditam facit, cuius frater Catillus nomen monti dederit propinquo. Fuitque Tibur una ex quinque civitatibus quas facit Vergilius Aeneae arma fabricasse, ubi Tibur appellat 'superbum.' Et Servius exponit: 'aut nobile aut quia aliquando Tiburtini a senatu responsum acceperunt quod essent "superbi."' Ubi etiam Vergilius in septimo dicit 'sub Albunea,' Servius exponit Albuneam altum esse fontem in Tiburtinis montibus ab aquae qualitatem quae in ipso fonte est, sic dictum. Et Plinius Tiburtinum lapidem non magis ab ipso vocabulo Romae trito, consternenda,[69] ornanda, conservandaque Roma, iuvisse dicit constare quam eum ad omnia fortem idoneumque fuisse. Horatius autem agrum Tiburtinum vitem amare sic indicat: 'Nullam, Vare, sacra vite prius severis arborem circa mite solum Tiburis et moenia Catili.' Sunt Tiburi propinquae ingentes admirandaeque ruinae, cum aliorum paene infinitorum magnificentissimi operis aedificiorum tum villae quam Hadrianus imperator exstruxit. De qua sic scribit Aelius Spartianus: 'Tiburtinam villam mire aedificavit ita ut in ea et provinciarum et locorum celeberrima nomina poneret.' De Tibure cetera ex Strabone paulo post cum de Praeneste ageret dicemus. Ea civitas Simplicium pontificem Romanum genuit, quam Fredericus primus imperator Ro-

press them too much."[159] The Roman pontiff Vitalianus, son of
Anastasius, was an ornament of Segni.[160] Beyond Segni there are
Sgurgola, Morolo, Supino, Patrica, Ceccano, and Castro dei
Volsci, where we again reach the border of our region of Lazio (or
Campania, as it now is).

A third road awaits us, the Tiburtine Way, named after Tivoli,   32
which takes us to the other borders of our region. Strabo maintains that the town of Tivoli, sixteen miles from Rome, had a
Greek origin well before the foundation of Rome,[161] and Vergil
has it founded by Tiburtus, whose brother Catillus gave his name
to the nearby mountain.[162] Tivoli was one of the five cities that
Vergil has fashioning armor for Aeneas, where he calls it
"proud."[163] Servius comments: "either because Tivoli was illustrious, or because the Tiburtines once received a response from the
Senate saying that they were 'haughty.'"[164] In the passage where
Vergil also says in Book VII, "under Albunea,"[165] Servius explains
that Albunea was a spring high in the Tiburtine mountains, so
called from the nature of the water in it.[166] Pliny says that it is
commonly thought that Travertine, the limestone of Tivoli, was
not so much useful for (in the well-worn Roman phrase) "paving,
adorning, and preserving Rome" as for being durable and adapt-
able to all purposes.[167] Horace indicates that the vine greatly favors
Tiburtine soil in these words: "Plant no tree, Varus, before the
holy vine in the mild soil round Tivoli and the walls of Catillus."[168]
There are huge and impressive ruins in the neighborhood of
Tivoli: apart from all the other sumptuous buildings, almost without number, there are the remains of the villa that the emperor
Hadrian constructed. Aelius Spartianus writes of it: "His villa at
Tibur was marvellously constructed, and he actually gave to parts
of it the names of provinces and places of the greatest renown."[169]
(We shall give other material from Strabo about Tibur a little later
when we treat of Praeneste.)[170] Tivoli bore the Roman pontiff
Simplicius,[171] and the German Roman emperor Frederick I rebuilt

manus Teutonicus, ab aliis Teutonicis aliquot annis prius spoliatam dirutamque, reaedificavit.

33   Supra eam civitatem sunt montes ardui et late diffusi, in quibus fortissimi olim habitaverunt Aequicoli, de quibus Vergilius, in septimo *Aeneidos*: 'horrida praecipue cui gens assuetaque multo venatu nemorum duris Aequicola glaebis. Armati terram exercent semperque recentes convectare libet praedas et vivere rapto.' Fuerunt vero ex primis Latinorum populis qui, Romana republica crescente, deleti sunt. Nam Livius libro nono: 'Populus Romanus bellum fieri Aequis iussit. Ad XL oppida, intra LX dies, omnia oppugnando ceperunt, quorum pleraque diruta atque incensa sunt, nomenque Aequorum prope ad internicionem deletum.' Primum ipsis in montibus ad Anienis sinistram est oppidum, amoenis Ursinorum Talliacoccii comitum domibus ornatum, Vicus Varronis appellatum. Superius Portella et Cantalupum oppidula. Deinde arduo in monte Rivus Frigidus, quo superato, alii item celsiores superandi sunt montes, Apennini iugis quantumlibet altis comparandi, quorum in summitate putei (ut fertur) plures. Sed, quos viderimus, duo exstant tam alte excisi defossique ut deiectum bilibre saxum non prius referat casus sui sonitum quam duo Vergiliani versus debita sint pausa pronuntiati. Quae quidem, perforatis succisisque et excavatis in imo montibus (sive a Marcio aedile sive a Claudio imperatore) perducendis Romam a lacu Fucino aquis, ne conclusus aer cursum aquae moraretur, spiracula fuerunt adhibita. Suetonius namque Tranquillus Claudium principem dicit triginta milia servorum[70] undecim annis emittendo lacu Fucino et aqua Romam perducenda tenuisse.

34   Supra Rivum Frigidum recta est Arceolum, secus quod planities incipit (ut in ea montium summitate) gratissima. In qua vetus

it after it had been sacked and destroyed some years earlier by other Germans.[172]

Above the town is a wide sweep of rugged mountains. There 33 once dwelt the hardy Aequicoli, of whom Vergil speaks in Book VII of the *Aeneid*: "the Aequicoli, an exceptionally rough people that constant hunting in the forests has inured to the harsh terrain. They plough the earth in armor and always delight in carrying off fresh spoils and living on plunder."[173] They were in fact among the first of the Latin peoples to be wiped out as the Roman Republic grew in strength. Livy says in Book IX: "The Roman people ordered war to be declared against the Aequi: within sixty days they stormed and captured all forty towns. Most of these were sacked and burnt, and the nation of the Aequi was almost exterminated."[174] To the left of the river Aniene in these mountains is first a town called Vicovaro, distinguished by the pleasant dwellings of the Orsini, counts of Tagliacozzo.[175] Higher up are the little towns of Portella and Cantalupo. Then there is Riofreddo on a steep hill, and once this hill is crossed there are other, even higher mountains to be surmounted, comparable to any peak of the Apennines. On the highest point there are a number of "shafts," as they are called. Two that I have examined still exist, sunk so deep that you could drop a heavy stone and recite two lines of Vergil without undue haste[176] before hearing it reach the bottom. A channel was cut through the base of the mountains, either by the aedile Marcius or the emperor Claudius, to carry water from the Fucine Lake to Rome, and the shafts were connected to it as vents so that trapped air might not stem the flow of water. Suetonius says that the emperor Claudius employed 30,000 slaves over eleven years on the job of draining the lake and getting the water to Rome.[177]

Directly above Riofreddo is Arsoli, and beside it begins a plain, 34 all the more welcome among these mountain heights. In the plain is the site of ancient Carsoli, of which Livy writes in Book X:

tissimi fuerunt Carseoli, de quibus Livius libro decimo scribit: 'eodem anno Carseolos colonia in agrum Aequicolorum deducta.' Et libro XXVII dicit eam fuisse unam duodeviginti coloniarum, quae, Hannibale in Italia agente, milites et pecuniam senatui dare recusaverunt. Deinceps sunt Cellae, Sculcula, et Peretum, unde in Talliacoccium est descensus. Quod novi nominis oppidum, sed populo divitiisque refertum, nuper maximum amisit ornamentum, Iohannem cardinalem Tarentinum philosophiae litterarumque sacrarum doctrina clarissimum.

35   Iamque ad Marsorum regionem est perventum, quam Hannibal (sicut Livius vigesimo secundo scribit) devastavit, et iterum revertens ab Urbe Roma (sicut Livii vigesimo sexto habetur) per eius agrum iter fecit. Eaque in regione interiit Valeria civitas, Bonifacii quarti pontificis Romani—quo hortante, Phocas imperator Pantheon Romae in omnium Christi martyrum basilicam permisit consecrari—patria. A qua civitate per Longobardorum tempora Marsorum nomen in Valeriam est conversum. Fuisse vero Marsos[71] oppidum a quo nomen regio accepit Plinius sic asserit: 'Gellianus auctor est lacu Fucino haustum Marsorum oppidum conditum a Marsya, duce Lydorum.' Et ea in regione Albam et Marrubiam urbes fuisse claras ex sequentibus apparebit. Vergilius libro VII: 'Quin et Marrubia venit de gente sacerdos.' Et Servius exponit: 'Medeam, quando, relictis Colchis, Iasonem secuta est, ad Italiam pervenisse et populos quosdam circa Fucinum ingentem lacum habitantes, *qui Marrubii appellabantur quasi circa mare habitantes*[72] propter paludis magnitudinem, docuisse remedia contra serpentes, quamquam alii Marrubios a rege dictos volunt. Hique populi Medeam "Angitiam" nominaverunt eo quod serpentes suis carminibus angeret.' Et Plinius: 'Simile et in Italia Marsorum genus durat, quos a Circae filio ortos tradunt et inde inesse eis vim

"That same year a colony was settled at Carsoli in the country of the Aequicoli."[178] And in Book XXVII he says that Carsoli was one of the eighteen colonies that declined to give the Senate soldiers and money during Hannibal's time in Italy.[179] Then there are Celle, Scurcola, and Pereto, from where you descend into Tagliacozzo. Though it is of recent foundation, the town is rich and populous. It recently lost its great ornament in Cardinal Giovanni, Archbishop of Tarento, a distinguished philosopher and theologian.[180]

We have now reached the land of the Marsians, to which, as 35 Livy relates in Book XXII, Hannibal laid waste,[181] marching through the territory a second time as he returned from Rome, as he says in Book XXVI.[182] The town of Valeria in this region has disappeared, the home of Pope Boniface IV at whose request the emperor Phocas had the Pantheon at Rome consecrated a basilica to all the martyrs of Christ.[183] The name of the town of Marsi was changed to Valeria in the time of the Lombards. Pliny in fact maintains that the region got its name from the town of the Marsi: "According to Gellianus, a town of the Marsi, founded by the Lydian captain Marsyas, was swallowed up by the the Fucine Lake."[184] From what follows, it is clear that the famous cities of Alba and Marruvium lay in that region. Vergil in Book VII writes: "Yes, and there came a priest from the race of the Marruvii."[185] And Servius comments: "When Medea left Colchis to follow Jason, she came to Italy and taught the peoples living around the great Fucine Lake (*who were called Marruvii as if living by the sea [mare],*[186] because of the size of the swamp) remedies against snakes — although others would have them called Marruvii after their king. The Marruvii called Medea 'Angitia' because her spells distressed the snakes."[187] And Pliny: "A similar people, the Marsi, linger on in Italy. They are said to descend from the son of Circe and so to have a certain natural power. Yet all men have a kind of innate poison against snakes. They say that snakes that are

171

naturalem eam. Et tamen omnibus hominibus contra serpentes inest venenum. Ferunt ictas saliva ut ferventis aquae contactu fugere, quod si in fauces penetraverit etiam mori — idque maxime humani ieiuni oris.' Quam opinionem serpentum in ea regione frequentium et peritiae incantationis Marsorum opinionem confirmat Iulius Capitolinus, ubi *Vitam* scribens *Heliogabali imperatoris*, dicit serpentes eum per Marsicae gentis incantationem collegisse, eosque subito ante lucem, ut solet populus ad ludos celebres convenire, effudisse, multosque afflictos morsu aut fuga allisos. Nec falsa aut fabulosa tenenda sunt ea, quae hic de serpentum incantatione sunt scripta. Propheta namque David, in Psalmo LVII, sic habet: 'Furor illis secundum similitudinem serpentis, sicut aspidis surdae obturantis aures suas, quae non exaudiet vocem incantantium, et venefici incantantis sapienter.' Et beatus Aurelius Augustinus in dicti Psalmi expositione sic scribit: 'Attende quid ibi dicatur ad similitudinem, quid moneatur ad prohibitionem. Ita ergo et hic data est quaedam similitudo de Marso, qui incantat ut educat aspidem de tenebrosa caverna. Utique in lucem vult educere. Illa autem amando tenebras suas, quibus se involutam occultat, dicitur quod cum exire noluerit, recusans tamen audire illas voces quibus se cogi sentit, allidit unam aurem terrae et de cauda obturat alteram. Atque ita voces illas quantum potest evitans, non exit ad incantantem.'

36   Livius, bellum scribens Italicum libro LXXII (quod, quia a Marsis inchoavit, dictum est Marsicum), inter populos qui Romanis rebellarunt enumerat Marrucinos et Marsos. Et libro LXXVI dicit Marsos a L. Cinna et Caecilio Pio[73] legatis superatos pacem petisse a Sulla. Bellumque hoc id felicitatis Romae urbi attulit, quod M. Cicero in eo militans abominatus est Romanorum civium crudelitates et ad litterarum studia se contulit: unde factum est ut Roma ingenium haberet quod sua magnitudine illi par esset.

spat on flee as if from scalding water, because if the saliva gets into their throats, they can actually die, especially if the saliva is from someone fasting."[188] Julius Capitolinus confirms the prevalence of snakes in the region and the skill of the Marsi in incantation. In his *Life of Heliogabalus*, he says that the emperor would collect snakes using Marsian spells and suddenly let them loose just before dawn, when the people were gathering in crowds for the games, and that many were bitten or crushed trying to get away.[189] These remarks on snake charming are not to be thought false or fictitious. The prophet David says in Psalm LVII: "Their madness is like the madness of a serpent, they are like the deaf adder that stops her ear, which will not hearken to the voice of charmers, charming never so wisely."[190] St. Augustine in his exposition of the psalm writes: "Note what is being said there as to the simile and the warning that is given by way of prohibition. This, then, is an analogy of a Marsian who casts a spell to entice an adder out of a dark cave. He means to lead her into the light at all costs. But she loves the shadows in which she wraps herself, and hides herself away. Being unwilling to come out and refusing to listen to the voice that she senses driving her on, it is said that she presses one ear to the earth and covers the other with her tail. Avoiding that voice as best she can, she does not come out to the snake-charmer."[191]

Writing on the Italic War (which, because it began with the Marsi, was called the Marsian War) in Book LXXII, Livy lists the Marrucini and Marsi among the peoples who rebelled against Rome.[192] And in Book LXXVI he says that the Marsi were defeated by the legates Lucius Cinna and Caecilius Pius and sought a peace with Sulla."[193] That war turned out well for the city of Rome in that while he was engaged in it, Cicero was repelled by the acts of cruelty perpetrated by the Romans and turned to literary studies:[194] and so it happened that Rome found a genius of a greatness equal to her own.

36

37   Abest a Talliacoccio Fucinus Marsorum lacus decimo miliaribus, et edito in colle Apenninum versus est Alba Marsorum, Romana colonia, sicut Livium diximus libro X scripsisse, qui et libro
XXVII eam fuisse dicit unam ex duodeviginti coloniis quae, Hannibalis temporum difficultate, militiam detractaverunt. Eamque
Strabo urbem (ut appellat) solam in Latina regione pro mediterranea scripsit, quam dicit excelso in monte sitam lacui Fucino imminere pelagi similitudinem magnitudine habenti, ex eoque lacu duc-
tos fuisse fontes Aquae Martiae, qua potaretur Roma. (Nosque in
Roma instaurata ostendimus Martium in sua aedilitate introduxisse
aquam eius nomine appellatam, quae quidem aqua supra omnes
alias introductas probabatur.) Et Plinius dicit Iuvencum amnem
supernatare Fucinum, qui Iuvencus Romam a Marcio sit perductus. Additque alibi Plinius in lacu Fucino piscem esse qui octenis
natet pennis, cum ceteri omnes ubique quaternis tantummodo na-
tent. Alba vero dicit Strabo, quia esset natura loci et munimento
arcis valida, saepe Romanos praesidii loco servandis in custodia
noxiis usos fuisse. Et nos in Livio invenimus libro LXI[74] Q. Fabium Maximum consulem, Pauli nepotem, adversus Allobrogas et
Bituitum Arvernorum regem feliciter pugnasse, ex Bituitique exercitu occisa CXX milia, ipsumque, cum ad satisfaciendum senatui
Romam profectus esset, Albam custodiendum fuisse missum.

38   Circumstant lacum Sancti Potiti,[75] Sancti Ionae castella, Pater-
numque, Transacum, Gaianum, Avecianum, et Mallianum oppida,
et Celanum quod comitatus titulo possidet Leonellus *Acclociamu-
rus*[76] bonarum artium litteris praesertim historiae deditissimus.
Suntque item ad Fucini et Celani oram Piscina, Veneris oppidum,
Viticula, Castrum Vetus, Gorgianum, ad quae oppida est nostrae
hac in parte Latinorum regionis limes.[77] Omissa vero sunt a nobis

Ten miles from Tagliacozzo is the Fucine Lake of the Marsi, 37
and on a high hill towards the Apennines is Alba of the Marsi, a
Roman colony, as we noted Livy saying in Book X.[195] Livy also
says in Book XXVII that Alba was one of eighteen colonies that
declined to make a military contribution in the troubled time of
Hannibal.[196] Strabo wrote that only this city (as he calls it) in
Lazio was like an inland city, being set, as he says, on a high hill
overlooking the Fucine Lake. The lake is so big as to seem like a
sea, and from it springs led to the Aqueduct of Marcius, which
supplied Rome with drinking water.[197] (In my *Rome Restored* I
showed that Marcius established the aqueduct named after him in
his aedileship, and indeed it was more highly thought of than all
the others.)[198] And Pliny says that the Giovenco, which Marcius
brought to Rome, flows on top of the surface of the Fucine
Lake.[199] Pliny adds elsewhere that there is a fish in the lake that
swims with eight fins, though all other fish everywhere swim with
only four.[200] Strabo says that the Romans often used Alba as a secure place to keep criminals in custody, because its natural setting
and fortified citadel made it impregnable.[201] I found in Livy, Book
XXII, that the consul Quintus Fabius Maximus, grandson of
Paulus, won a victory against the Allobroges and Bituitus, king of
the Arverni. One hundred and twenty thousand of Bituitus' men
were killed, and after the king himself had gone to Rome to make
amends to the Senate, he was sent to Alba and imprisoned.[202]

Around the lake stand the castles of S. Potito and Sta. Iona, 38
and the towns of Paterno, Trasacco, Gagliano, Avezzano, and
Magliano, and also Celano, which is the property of its count
Lionello *Acclozamora*, a devotee of good letters and of history in
particular.[203] Along the shore of Fucino and Celano there are also
Pescina, the town of Venere, Viticcio, Rocca Vecchia, Goriano,
towns that mark the limit of Lazio in this part of our region. I
have in fact omitted several castles and towns which do not lie in
the vicinity of the three roads mentioned above: in one and the

superius nulli praedictarum trium viarum propinqua aliquot castella et oppida: una tamen eademque in montium regione, Praeneste Tiburque inter et Vicum Varronis ac Zinazanum sita, Rocha Cavarum Capranica, quae praestantissimam Romae dedit familiam Capranicensem, in qua Paulus archiepiscopus, gravissimo Martini quinti pontificis Romani testimonio, maximae in suo saeculo prudentiae vir fuit. Et Dominicus cardinalis Sanctae Crucis, frater eius, multa civilis pontificiique iuris et studiorum humanitatis doctrina magnaque prudentia nunc claret, cum tamen Angelus Asculanus episcopus frater et Nicolaus protonotarius nepos eisdem doctrinis virtutibusque ornentur. Deinceps sunt oppida: Guadagnolum, Polium, Casa Corbola, Sanctus Gregorius, Rocha Liricis dicta. Sunt etiam his proxima oppida: Caecilianum, Sambuca, Sarracinescum, Rocha Mutiorum, Giranum, Ceretum, Anticulum, Rivate,[78] Afile, Civitella et Olibanum, clarissimae ac prudentissimae mulieris Suevae Albae Marsorum comitissae, ac Prosperi cardinalis Columnae et fratrum genetricis, deliciae. Post Olibanum sunt Piscianum et Sanctus Vitus oppidum,[79] fonte uno Liris (sive Gauriani), quem propinquum habet, clarum.

39   Estque superius celsis in montibus Sublacum (veluti Plinius appellat, Sublaquaeum), nobile oppidum, lacui eiusdem et tamen prisci nominis imminens. Redditque utrumque fama celebratum beati Benedicti non magis diutina conversatio ibi habita quam eius toto orbe notissimum ibi aedificatum magnifici operis monasterium. Cernitur vero in dextra Anienis ripa, ab ipso Sublaci lacu ad vicum usque Varronis, incisus saxeo in monte ductus aquarum, quae formis partim eo incisis modo, partim altum defossis, partim sublimi fornice muroque excitatis Romam quadragesimo miliario veniebant.

40   Sed in hac eadem Latinorum regione ad praedictorum declarationem: Romanis in conspectu esse dicit Strabo Tibur et Praenes-

same hill district, however, set between Palestrina, Tivoli, Vicovaro and Gennezano, is Rocca di Cave Capranica, which gave Rome the illustrious family of the Capranica. According to the weighty testimony of the Roman pontiff Martin V, the archbishop Paolo Capranica was the wisest man of his time. His brother Domenico, the Cardinal of Santa Croce, is now distinguished for his great wisdom and for his considerable learning in civil and canon law and in the liberal arts, while his brother Angelo Capranica, bishop of Ascoli, and their nephew the protonotary Niccolò are blessed with the same learning and virtue.[204] There follow the towns of Guadagnolo, Poli, Casa Corbuli, S. Gregorio da Sassola and Rocca Lerici. Next to these, there are the towns of Ciciliano, Sambuci, Saracinesco, *Rocha Mutiorum* [Rocca di Mezzo?], Gerano, Cerreto Laziale, Anticoli Corrado, Roiate, Affile, Civitella, and Olevano Romano — the favorite resort of that excellent and sagacious lady, Sveva, Countess of Alba dei Marsi, the mother of Cardinal Prospero Colonna and his brothers.[205] After Olevano come Pisoniano and San Vito Romano, a town notable for having nearby one source of the river Liri or Garigliano.

Higher up amid lofty mountains is Subiaco, or Sublaqueum as Pliny calls it,[206] a well-known town that overlooks a lake of the same ancient name. Both are famous not only for St. Benedict's lengthy sojourn at Subiaco but also for the magnificent monastery built there in his name, known throughout the world.[207] On the right bank of the Aniene one sees an aqueduct cut into the rock of the mountain and extending from the lake of Subiaco to Vicovaro: its channels are partly incised in this way, partly bored deep in the rock, at other points carried aloft on an arched wall, carrying the water that used to reach Rome forty miles away.

But to sum up what has been said about the region of Lazio: Strabo says that Tivoli, Palestrina, and Tuscolo can be all seen from Rome. Tivoli, he says, has a waterfall by the temple of Hercules which is created by the Aniene tumbling down from a great

39

40

te[80] et Tusculum. Et Tibur quidem, qua est Heracleum, habere cataractem, quem facit Anio decidens ex loco altissimo in profundam vallem et per lucos iuxta ipsam urbem ubi incipiat esse navigabilis. Inde digredi ad metalla lapidis Tiburtini et eius qui est in Gabiis, qui etiam dicitur rubeus,[81] unde plurima opera Romae fabricata sunt. De Praeneste dicit Vergilius, in septimo: 'Nec Praenestinae fundator defuit urbis, Caeculus.' Et Plinius dicit Praeneste dici quia arbor prinus multa sit in eo monte. Eam vero civitatem dicit Strabo habuisse insigne templum Fortunae a Sulla aedificatum, a quo petebatur oraculum. Additque Plinius simulacrum id Fortunae adeo fideliter fuisse inauratum ut crassissimae inaurationes dicerentur Praenestinae. Et alio loco de pavimentis tractans, dicit lithostrota acceptavere iam sub Sulla, parvulis certe crustis, quod in Fortunae delubro Praeneste coepit. Et ambas urbes Tibur et Praeneste Strabo dicit in eadem montana regione constitutas esse sed distare invicem stadia centum, et Praeneste distare ab urbe Roma etiam duplo sed Tibur minus. Dicique a quibusdam Graecas esse ambas, atque Praenestinam Polystephanum vocari prius. Qua in parte Strabonem crediderim divinasse, cum possit Praeneste nunc Polystephanum dici qua civitas est Stephani Columnae. Additque Strabo, quamquam utraque munito sit loco, positum[82] tamen munitiore Praenestum, quod urbis summitas montem habet excelsum et retro quidem a continenti montana regione dorsum elatum, quem non dubito esse montem in quo est munitissima arx Rocha Cavarum dicta. Dicit quoque idem praeter situs Praenesti munitionem occultas fossas undique foratas usque in campos esse, alias aquationis gratia, alias ob latentes invasiones, in quarum una obsessus Marius interiit. Livius libro LXXXVII scribit: 'Sulla C. Marium, exercitu eius fuso deletoque ad Sacri-

height into a deep valley and passing through the woods beside the city, where the river starts to be navigable. From there it flows past the quarries of Travertine and Gabian stone (also called redstone), of which many works of art at Rome are fashioned. Of Palestrina, Vergil says in Book VII: "Nor was Caeculus, Palestrina's founder, absent."[208] Pliny says that the city was called Praeneste because of the abundance of holm-oak on the hill.[209] Strabo says that the city had a remarkable temple to Fortune built by Sulla, where oracles were once sought.[210] Pliny adds that the statue of Fortune there had been so durably gilded that the thickest kind of goldleaf was called Palestrina leaf.[211] And elsewhere, dealing with floors, Pliny says that mosaics came into use as early as Sulla's time, with tiny cubes at least, a development which began in the temple of Fortune at Palestrina.[212] Strabo says that the two cities, Tivoli and Palestrina, are located in the same mountainous region but a hundred stades apart, and that the distance from Rome to Palestrina is twice that, but somewhat less to Tivoli. Some people say both cities are Greek, Strabo continues, and that Palestrina was formerly called Polystephanum.[213] And in this regard I rather think he foresaw the future, since Palestrina may well be called "Polystephanum" now as the city of Stefano Colonna.[214] Strabo adds that, though each is naturally well protected, Praeneste is the more so because its topmost point is a high mountain, and to the rear of the city is a neck of land higher than the main mountain range from which it projects.[215] I am sure that this must be the mountain with the heavily fortified stronghold called Rocca di Cave. Strabo also says that in addition to the natural strength of its position, Palestrina has secret passages bored through it from all sides as far as the plains — some for water-supply, others for secret attacks. In one of these Marius died while he was under siege.[216] Livy writes in Book LXXXVII: "Sulla laid siege to Marius at Palestrina after he had routed and destroyed his army at Sacriportus."[217] And in Book LXXXVIII: "He ordered the non-

portum, in oppido Praeneste obsedit.' Et libro LXXXVIII: 'Praenestinos inermes occidi iussit.' Quam crudelitatis maximae historiam Lucanus in II perstringit his verbis: 'Iam quot apud Sacri
cecidere cadavera Portum.' Et infra: 'Vidit Fortuna colonos Prae-
nestina suos cunctos simul ense recepto unius populum pereun-
tem tempore mortis'. Et item Livius infra: C. Marius Praeneste
obsessus a Lucretio Ofella Sullanarum partium, cum per cunicu-
lum caperet fugam et sentiret se evadere non posse, cum Thelesio
fugae suae comite, utrimque gladio concurrerunt et occisi sunt.'

41   Usi autem sunt libenter Romani principes eo secessu ad animi
curarumque relaxationem. Sed Aurelius Antoninus[83] imperator
optimus ibi parum fortunatus fuit: nam scribit Iulius Capitolinus
eum in secessu Praenestino agentem filium, nomine Verum Caesarem, septennem amisisse, quem non plus diebus quinque luxerit.
Et Plinius de metallis tractans sic habet: anno Urbis
CCCCCCLXXI, 'quod ex Capitolinae aedis incendio ceterisque
omnibus delubris Gaius, Marii filius, Praeneste detulerat, tredecim milia pondo auri, sub eo titulo in triumpho transtulit ⟨Sulla⟩
et argenti sex. Item ex reliqua omni victoria pridie transtulerat auri
pondo quindecim milia, argenti pondo centum quindecim milia.'
Prosequitur vero Livius libro XXIII Praenestinos milites miris
laudibus quod, cum apud Cannas infelicissime pugnatum esse
audissent, apud Casilinum divertentes in eo oppido obsidionem
omnium memorabilium durissimam fortissime pertulerunt. Unde
senatus consulto duplex stipendium et quinquennii vacationem
militiae habuerunt. Addit vero unum Strabo usu per aetatem nostram et saepius anteactis temporibus compertum: munitionem

combatant citizens of Palestrina to be killed."[218] This tale of terrible cruelty is touched on by Lucan in Book II: "How many corpses fell at Sacriportus, pray?"[219] And later: "The Fortune of Palestrina saw her settlers taken by the sword all together, a whole people slain as by a single death."[220] And Livy again, further on: "When Marius was besieged at Palestrina by Lucretius Ofella of the Sullan faction, he tried to escape through a tunnel but realized that he could not get away. He and Thelesius, his companion in flight, ran onto each other's drawn swords and were killed."[221]

The Roman emperors liked to retire to Palestrina to relax from 41 their cares. But the good emperor Marcus Aurelius had a great misfortune there, for Julius Capitolinus writes that while he was on holiday at Palestrina, he lost his seven-year-old son Verus Caesar, whom he mourned not more than five days.[222] In Pliny's discussion of metals, he writes as follows: "In 671 A.U.C., the gold that Marius' son Gaius had taken to Palestrina from the conflagration of the Capitoline temple and from all the other shrines amounted to 13,000 pounds, which with a placard above it to that effect was carried along in his triumphal procession by Sulla, along with 6000 pounds of silver. Sulla had likewise on the previous day carried in procession 15,000 pounds of gold and 115,000 pounds of silver as the proceeds of all his other victories."[223] In Book XXIII Livy praises the soldiers of Palestrina to the skies: when they heard of the disastrous battle at Cannae, they made for Casilinum and there endured with utmost bravery a terrible siege, a siege more remarkable than any other, in the light of which the Senate decreed that the men of Palestrina should be granted double pay and an exemption from further service for five years.[224] Strabo adds something discovered by experience in our own time, as it has been on many occasions in the past: that is, that good defenses, which in other cities are generally accounted a blessing, have often proved calamitous to the citizens of Palestrina on account of civil strife at Rome. Revolutionaries seek refuge there,

scilicet, quae aliis civitatibus conducere consueverit, Praenestinis saepe calamitati fuisse ob Romanorum seditiones. Defugere enim illuc eos qui tumultu sint usi, hisque expugnatis fieri ut etiam Praenestini urbem deserant, causa in eos translata. Quod enim supra est dictum: hac de qua Strabo dicit ratione factum videtur ut Sarrae Columnensis temporibus Praeneste fuerit desolatum. Et Ponceletti[84] ac Nicolai Fortebratii aliorumque Urbi infestorum receptione factum vidimus ut urbs obsessa captaque solo aequaretur.

42   Fluvium eius regionis Verrestim Strabo appellat. Et addit in ea montana regione ipsarum urbium aliud dorsum esse, quod inter tibias linquit Algidum. Et illud quidem dorsum esse excelsum usque ad montem Albanum. In quo dorso sit Tusculum sita urbs, non inepte fabricata. Romanae vero nascenti rei publicae haec urbs hinc infesta fuit, quod Mamilius[85] Tusculanus gener Tarquinio exsuli socero auxilium attulit, unde pugna ad Regillum originem habuit. Romanus autem populus Tusculis post rebelliones cum Latinis factas pepercit, sicut Livius in VIII scribit: 'Tusculanis servata civitas quam habebant, crimenque rebellionis a publica fraude in paucos auctores versum.' Et Plinius inter insignia fortunae variantis exempla ponit Lucium Furium Tusculanum: 'Is Tusculanorum Romanis rebellantium consul eodem quoque honore transfuga exornatus est a populo Romano, qui solus eodem anno quo fuerat hostis Romae triumphavit ex his quorum consul fuerat.'[86] Livius libro XXVI accessum Hannibalis ad urbem Romam describens dicit: 'per Anagninum agrum venit in Lavicanum, inde Algido Tusculanum petit. Nec receptus moenibus infra Tusculum dextrorsum Gabios descendit.' Addit vero superioribus Strabo: Tus-

and when they have been defeated it turns out that the blame is turned on the Praenestines and they too have to abandon the city.[225] This bears on what I said earlier, for Strabo's explanation seems to account for the destruction of Palestrina in the days of Sciarra Colonna. And we have seen it happen that the city was besieged, captured, and razed to the ground because she took in Ponceletto and Niccolò Fortebraccio and other enemies of Rome.[226]

Strabo calls the river that flows through this district the Verrestis.[227] He adds that in the mountainous area where these cities are found, there is another ridge which leaves Mt. Algidus with spurs on either side, and that this ridge is high as far as Mt. Alban. The well-built city of Tusculum is located on this ridge.[228] The city was an enemy of the early Roman Republic on account of Mamilius of Tusculum having brought help to his father-in-law Tarquinius Superbus when he was ejected from Rome; this was the genesis of the battle at Lake Regillus.[229] The Romans spared the Tusculans following the uprisings that they staged with the Latins, as Livy writes in Book VIII: "They were allowed to keep the civic rights they had before, and responsibility for the rebellion was removed from the people as a whole and fastened on a few individuals."[230] Pliny gives the case of Lucius Furius of Tusculum as a striking example of the vagaries of fortune: "The consul of the rebellious Tusculans, L. Furius, came over to the Romans and obtained from them the same honor. He is the only individual who, in the same year in which he had been its enemy, enjoyed the honour of a triumph in Rome, and that too, over the people whose consul he had previously been."[231] Describing the coming of Hannibal to Rome in Book XXVI, Livy says: "Hannibal came through the district of Anagni into the neighborhood of Labico. From there he made for Tusculum over Mt. Algidus, but was refused admittance, so he turned to the right below Tusculum towards Gabii."[232] Strabo adds to the account quoted above as fol-

42

culum ornari insitionibus circum atque aedificiis—et ad eam maxime partem quae est versus Romam. Tusculi namque collem dicit esse fecundum aquisque abundantem, et paulatim multis in locis in altum attolli, habereque regiam magnificentissimi apparatus, et continua esse loca, quae ad Albanum vergunt montem, eandem cum virtutem tum apparatum habentia. Deinceps campos esse, quorum alii ad Romam attingunt eiusque suburbia, alii ad mare.

43 Haec sumpsimus paene ad litteram ex Strabone de hac regione Columnensi familiae ante quadringentos annos (sicut nunc est) maiori ex parte subiecta. Et quidem apud Praeneste montes peritissime sunt descripti. Sed minora non ponit Strabo loca, qui Horatii Flacci poetae villam omisit illis in montibus sitam, loco quem Sancti Iohannis in Campo Horatii nunc appellant. Alia etiam a Strabone omittuntur, quae, si eo tempore non erant, scimus ante quingentos annos fuisse. Cavas enim a situ dictas cavae fossae, in qua sunt Odoardi Columnae nunc oppidum; temporibus Paschalis secundi Romani pontificis, sicut Pandulphus Hostiarius scriptor tradit, Petrus Columna possidebat hereditario iure sibi a patre relictum,[87] sicut etiam tunc Praeneste, Pillum et Pullanum, nunc dicta Pillium et Pallianum, alii ex ea familia possidebant. Quae autem de Tusculanae olim urbis collibus dicit, vera esse ostendunt etiam nunc monasterium Sanctae Mariae de Gripta Ferrata in villa Ciceronis Tusculana aedificatum et Marinum ac superiori edito in colle Rocha Papae, Prosperi Columnae cardinalis oppida. Circa quae duobus aut tribus a Tusculo miliaribus distantia agri fertilitatem et aquarum abundantiam videmus esse maximam. Regiae autem magnificentissimi (ut Strabo dicit) apparatus fundamenta esse non dubitamus, quae proximis pariter Griptae Ferratae et Marino locis fornices e manu factos cavernasque habere videmus oppidi unius populum in habitationem, et quidem commodam, admissuras.

lows: "Tusculum is graced by groves and villas on every side, particularly towards Rome, the hill on which it is situated being fertile and well watered. The hill rises gradually, to a considerable height in many places, and has a magnificently laid out royal estate. The places round about that stretch towards Mt. Alban are equally fertile and have the same style of buildings. Then, he says, come the plains, some extending to Rome and its suburbs, others to the sea."[233]

On this district, which has for the most part been subject to 43
the Colonna family for the last 400 years, just as it is today, I have taken my information from Strabo almost to the letter. Certainly he gives an expert description of the mountainous area around Palestrina, but he does not include sites of lesser importance and omits, for example, the villa of the poet Horace which is located in those hills, a place now called S. Giovanni in Campo Orazio. Strabo omits other places too that we know existed 500 years ago, if not in his time. Cave, for instance, which is named for its position in a deep hollow where today is a town possessed by Odoardo Colonna: in the time of Pope Paschal II,[234] Pietro Colonna owned it by ancestral inheritance from his father, as the writer Pandolfo the Ostiary tells us, just as others of the Colonna family used to own in those days Palestrina, *Pullum* and *Pullanum* (now Pugliano and Paliano) as well.[235] But what Strabo says of the hills of the former city of Tusculum is shown to be still true by the monastery of Santa Maria di Grottaferrata (built on Cicero's Tusculan estate), and Marino, and Rocca di Papa on its high hill, all towns of Cardinal Prospero Colonna. We can see the great fertility of the soil and abundance of water around these towns, situated two or three miles from Tusculum. I am sure the foundations of the magnificently laid out royal estate (as Strabo puts it [§41]) still exist, and we can observe in places adjacent to both Grottaferata and Marino its vaults and man-made caverns that could comfortably accommodate the populace of an entire town.

44   Est etiam Tusculo propinquum olim Lucullanum, Lucii Luculli villa, cui nunc dicitur Frascatum, ubi aquam Virginem, quae nunc unica Romam perducitur, inventam esse constat. Tusculanique, duce Rainone eorum tyranno, Frederici imperatoris Barbarossae appellati copiis coniuncti, populum Romanum clade maxima affecerunt, quae Cannensi cladi prope similis numero caesorum fuisse dicitur, adeo ut Roma postmodum caput numquam attollere potuerit. Unde factum est ut anno inde septimo Romanus populus ipsam urbem tanta animorum ferocia demolitus sit ut vix fundamentorum vestigia nunc appareant. Ea vero vetus et praeclara olim urbs, nunc solo titulo civitas, gentem Porciam inde oriundam et (quod est consequens) illustrissimos Catones habuit cives. Quae diu post pontificibus Romanis tribus, sexto Benedicto, qui primum Henricum regem Teutonicum coronavit, decimoque nono Iohanne illius germano, et septimo Benedicto utriusque nepote ornata fuit. Nec aliam habet aliquam pristinae felicitatis et gloriae partem praeterquam quod eam titulo episcopatus gubernat vir summus, Graece Latineque eruditissimus *et summa praeditus cum bonitate tum etiam humanitate,*[88] Bessarion Graecorum cardinalis Nicenus, Bononiae nunc et exarchatus Ravennatis Apostolicae Sedis legatus.

45   De campis, quos Strabo dicit aut ad Urbem aut ad mare pertinere, nimis verum esse videmus quod suburbiis tunc et villis habitatos nunc solis tectos ruinis et silvis proprie magis campos appellari posse constat. Cum autem Albam Strabo a principio nominaverit, proximam illi Ariciam omisit, quam nunc solo aequatam, tunc urbem in via Appia fuisse supra ostendimus. Est Albae Marinoque proximus Albanus lacus, emissorio cuius mirabili opere[89] facto (licet tenues) effluant aquae. Origo nunc habetur amnis, qui apud locum caedis apostoli Pauli labens paludem "Ad Aquas Salvias" appellatam efficit. Estque is lacus, de quo vates

Also near Tusculum is the former Lucullanum, the estate of   44
Lucius Lucullus.²³⁶ It is now known as Frascati, a place where it is
believed the Aqua Virgo originated: this aqueduct alone now goes
all the way to Rome.²³⁷ The citizens of Tusculum under their
leader, the tyrant Rainone, joined forces with the emperor Frederick Barbarossa and dealt the Roman people a great defeat: in the
number of slain it is said to have almost matched the disaster at
Cannae, so that Rome would never be able to raise its head
again.²³⁸ And so it came about that seven years later the Romans
demolished the city with such ferocity that scarcely a trace of its
foundations can now be seen. This ancient and famous former
city, now a township in name only, was the place of origin of the
Porcia clan and so had as its citizens the illustrious Catos.²³⁹ Long
afterwards Tusculum was graced by three Roman pontiffs: Benedict VI (who crowned the German king Henry I), his brother
John XIX, and their nephew Benedict VII.²⁴⁰ Nothing remains to
the city of her ancient prosperity and renown, save for its being
ruled by an excellent bishop, profoundly learned in Greek and
Latin, *a man of consummate goodness and humanity*, Bessarion, the
Greek cardinal of Nicaea, now Apostolic Legate to Bologna and
the Exarchate of Ravenna.²⁴¹

Of the fields that Strabo says extend to Rome or the sea, it is   45
plainly all too true that what was once built up with suburbs and
country villas is now covered only with ruins and woods and really
may be called with more justice "fields." At the outset Strabo mentioned Alba but he omitted the neighboring town of Ariccia,
which, though it is now razed to the ground, was then a city on
the Appian Way, as I mentioned above [§24]. The Lago di Albano
is close to Alba and Marino; its water is let out through an inge-
niously made drain, though the flow is meager. The lake is nowadays believed to be the source of the river that flows by the place
where the Apostle Paul was martyred and forms a marsh called Ad
Aquas Salvias.²⁴² We learn from Livy that this is the lake of which

Etruscus (sicut Livius refert) praedixit futurum ut, si emitteretur inde aqua, Romani Veiis potirentur.

46   Distat ab Albano Ariciaque pariter passus circiter quatuor[90] mille lacus, quem Suetonius Tranquillus Nemorensem appellat, ad quem dicit C. Caesarem villam inchoasse quam reliquerit imperfectam. Cuius quidem lacus aqua, mirabilis operis emissorio educta, Numicum amnem efficit, quem apud Ardeam in mare labi diximus. Ad eumque lacum est situm oppidum Nemus appellatum. Servius grammaticus in septimo Vergilii versus hos exponens, 'audiit et Triviae longe lacus,' dicit Nemus appellari lucum haud longe ab Aricia, in quo lacus est ubi speculum Dianae dicitur. Et Nemorensi item oppidum proxime adiacet Cynthianum, quod a Cynthia, quae et Trivia, nomen (licet nunc corruptum) habuit. Hunc vero lacum Dianae speculum a maioribus[91] appellatum, Romana re florente, eo fuisse dignum nomine nullus mirabitur, qui praesentis temporis amoenitatem eius inspexerit. Vallis enim concavae in circuitu bis mille passus complexo[92] hic lacus dimidium obtinet.[93] Pars reliqua, ubi C. Caesarem aedes diximus inchoasse, tunc (ut videtur) nemorosa fuit, a qua oppidum exstans Nemus appellatum est. Eaque nunc arboribus frugiferis adeo pulchre est consita ut nulli in Italia quantumvis cultissimo consitionibus loco cedat.

47   Quantum autem lacus ipse maioribus fuerit gratus magnum hoc tempore apparuit argumentum.[94] Prosper enim Columna, cardinalis patriciusque Romanus, cum Nemorense illud Cynthianumque castellum paterna possideat hereditate, piscatores[95] aliquando audivit Nemorenses dicere naves suo in lacu binas esse submersas, quae nec adeo putres sint ut laceratae funiculos de industria alligatos nec retia casu implicata tractae sequantur. Nec integrae suis ipsorum omnium incolarum viribus queant extrahi.

an Etruscan seer predicted that if its water was ever drained off, the Romans would gain possession of Veii.²⁴³

A lake which Suetonius calls the Lacus Nemorensis, or Lago di 46
Nemi, is about four miles away from both the Lago di Albano and Ariccia. He says that Caesar began to build a villa there which he left incomplete.²⁴⁴ The water of this lake is drawn off by an inge-nious drain and forms the Numicus, or Rio Torto, which as we said [§8] reaches the sea at Ardea. The town called Nemi lies on the lake. The grammarian Servius, commenting on the line of *Aeneid*, Book VII, "and Diana's lake heard it from afar,"²⁴⁵ says that there is a grove not far from Ariccia called *Nemus*, or "Wood," in which there is a lake called Diana's Mirror.²⁴⁶ The town of Cynthianum likewise lies beside the Lago di Nemi: it got its name from the goddess Cynthia (also known as Trivia), though the name has been corrupted.²⁴⁷ No one who has seen its present beauty will doubt that it lives up to the name "Diana's Mirror" given it by our forebears in the days of Rome's grandeur. The lake occupies half of a hollow depression which is two miles in circum-ference. The rest (where, as I mentioned, Julius Caesar made a start on his villa) was apparently wooded in those days, and the present town of Nemi takes its name from that fact. The district has splendid stands of fruit trees, so much so that its orchards yield to nowhere else in Italy, however well looked after it may be.

Strong evidence of how attractive this lake was to our forebears 47
has recently come to light.²⁴⁸ Prospero Colonna, the Roman cardi-nal and patrician who inherited from his ancestors the town of Nemi and the castle of Genzano, once heard the fishermen of Nemi saying that there were two ships sunk in the lake. They were not so rotten that they would be torn apart and come away when ropes were attached to them for the purpose, nor when they hap-pened to become tangled up in their nets. Neither could they be hauled out entire by the main strength of all the inhabitants to-gether. Devoted as he is to the liberal arts, especially history, and

Quare vir ipse, bonarum artium studiis et in primis historiae deditissimus nec minus vetustatis indagator curiosissimus, quid magnae naves parvo et altissimis undique circumdato montibus in lacu sibi voluerint noscere animum adiecit, nosterque Leo Baptista Albertus, geometra nostro tempore egregius, qui de re aedificatoria elegantissimos composuit libros, ad id operis est vocatus.

48   Hic vasa vinaria multos colligata in ordines ea ratione in lacu disposuit ut in ipsis, tamquam pontibus, hincinde starent machinae, quibus per harpagones ferreos grossioribus appensos rudentibus captam mordicus navem lignarii artis eius periti attraherent. Et a Genua urbe maritima mercede conducti aderant, piscibus quam hominibus similiores, nonnulli, quorum partes fuerunt in lacus profundiora natando descendere et quanta esset navis quamque integra sentire et demissos funibus harpagones in morsum capturamque applicare. Tandem capta ligataque ad proram navis, cum integra non sequeretur, fracta est, et eius particula trahentes harpagones est secuta. Quam spectaculo fuit omnibus Romanae curiae nobilioris ingenii viris. Eam vero hac ratione fabricatam fuisse apparet.

49   Navis tota lariceis[96] asseribus trium digitorum crassitudine compacta, bitumine extrinsecus delibuta fuit. Quod bitumen (ut etiam nunc apparet) croceum purpureumve contexuit continuitque velamen, et plumbeis desuper chartis superficies tota ab aquis imbribusque navem bitumenque defensura obtecta est. Quas quidem chartas claviculi, non (ut nunc assolet) ferrei sed aenei, frequentes infixi ita compresserant ut omnis humor perpetuo arceretur. Interior vero navis pars non ab imbribus magis et humore quam ab igne et ferro certissimam habuit defensionem. Nam cum argilla et creta quicquid ligneae soliditatis navem intus compegerat ad digiti unius crassitudinem tectum delibutumque esset, ferrum vehementi igne concoctum liquefactumque super infuderunt. Quo ad digiti unius et alicubi duorum crassitudinem sensim dilatato, tan-

being the painstaking antiquarian that he is, the cardinal accordingly applied himself to discovering why those great ships should
be found in a small lake completely surrounded by high mountains. My friend Leon Battista Alberti, the great mathematician of
our age and author of a graceful work on the art of building, was
summoned to help in the task.[249]

Leon Battista arranged wine barrels tied together in a number   48
of rows on the lake with the idea of setting up winches on either
side, as from a bridge. With these experienced carpenters could
use an iron hook suspended from especially thick ropes to catch
the ship and draw it up. Some workers—more like fish than
men—were hired from the seagoing city of Genoa. It was their job
to swim down into the deeper parts of the lake to find out how
much remained of the ship and in what state of preservation, and
to use the hooks let down on ropes to dig into the ship and grab
hold of it. Though the ship was at length gripped by the prow and
tied up with rope, it would not follow in one piece and fell apart, a
fragment of it coming up with the grapples. This fragment greatly
diverted all the fine minds of the Roman Curia gathered there. It
seems to have been constructed in the following fashion.

The ship was entirely made of larchwood, braced by beams   49
three inches thick and caulked on the outside with pitch. The
pitch was covered and protected by a coating of yellow or red material, as can be seen even now, and the entire surface was clad
with sheets of lead to protect the ship and the caulking from the
waves and rain. A mass of bronze nails (not iron as we use now)
was driven into the sheets of lead to seal them and permanently
keep out all moisture. The interior of the ship was just as well
protected against fire and iron missiles as against rain and damp.
When all the solid wood inside the ship had been coated and
caulked with an inch of clay and chalk, they poured over it molten
iron that had been heated in an intense fire. The metal gradually
spreading out an inch thick, in places two inches, the iron ship (so

tundem magnitudinis ferrea (ut ita dixerim) habuit navis quantum laricea prius habuerat. Et ferro insuper alia argillae ac cretae bitumatio (vel, ut olim in aedificiis appellabatur, 'complastratio') superinfusa est. Observatumque fuisse videmus ut, concocto liquefactoque ferro priusquam refrixisset, argilla cretaque[97] et ipsa eodem decoquenda calore superinducerentur quo et substrata et superius deducta argilla unum sicut etiam nunc sunt commixtum ex latericio et ferro bitumen efficerentur.

50   Dumque huic expiscandae navi omnis undique infudat multitudo, fistulae in fundo lacus inventae sunt plumbeae bicubitales longitudine, firmissima crassitudine, quas mutuo morsu ac compagine combasiantes in quantumvis maximam longitudinem producere licuit. Earum vero singulis elegantes insculptae sunt litterae, auctorem[98] ut coniicimus navis suum[99] Tiberium Caesarem Augustum indicantes. Censuitque Leo Baptista fontis copiosissimi lucidissimique ad Nemorense oppidum scatentis aquas nunc molas convolventes multo ipsarum fistularum ordine ad medium usque lacum fuisse perductas, quae aedibus inservirent amplissimis lautissimisque, quas navibus praedictis superimpositas fuisse tenemus. Pulchrum autem et paene mirum est videre clavos maiores aeneos, quibus cubitalibus navis constructa erat, ita integros, ita politos ut nuper a fabri ferrarii incudibus exisse videantur. *Quo inductus exemplo tu, Pater Beatissime Nicolae, impositam basilicarum urbis Romae tectis plumbeorum imbricum defensionem claviculis aeneis communisti.*[100]

51   Lucanus in tertio viam, sicut supra diximus, describens, qua C. Caesar primum post belli civilis initia Romam venit, infrascriptos ponit versus, qui ad Albani quoque montis descriptionem satisfacere poterunt. Constabitque Caesarem a Terracina supra Ariciam ad Cinthianum, inde ad montem Albanum, ubi nunc Castrum est

to say) became as big as the one of larch before it. On top of the iron they poured another coating (or "plastering," as it used to be called in building work) of clay and chalk. It was apparently their practice, once the iron had been liquified by boiling and before it had cooled, to lay the mixture of clay and chalk on top of the iron so that it might be baked by its heat. The layer underneath and the clay laid on top would then fuse together, just as today we make a sealant of brick and iron.

A great throng poured in from all about to watch the ship being   50
fished out of the water. Meanwhile, some lead pipes were found at the bottom of the lake, three feet long and very strong and thick, which could be combined, as they mated one another with interlocking parts, to any desired length. Elegant letters were inscribed on each of them to indicate, so I thought, that the emperor Tiberius was the creator of the ship. Leon Battista thought that the very plentiful and clear spring waters that bubble up in the town of Nemi, where they nowadays turn mill wheels, were brought all the way to the middle of the lake through a long series of these pipes, to be used in the very large and luxurious houses that were placed, I believe, on top of the ships mentioned above. It was a fine and wonderful sight to see the great eighteen-inch-long bronze nails used in the construction of the ship, so well-preserved and shiny that they seem to have just come from the blacksmith's anvil. *Prompted by the example, holy father Nicholas, you have reinforced the lead tiles that protect the church roofs of Rome with bronze rivets.*[250]

In Book III Lucan describes the road on which Caesar first   51
came to Rome after the outbreak of the Civil War (as mentioned above [§12]) in the following lines — which will also serve as our description of Mt. Alban. It will be clear from Lucan that Caesar came from Terracina to Genzano above Ariccia, and thence to Mt. Alban, where Castel Gandolfo now is, from whose heights he first saw Rome: "And now he had passed over the precipitous

Gandulfum, pervenisse, quo de excelso monte Romam primum
inspexit: 'iamque praecipites superaverat Anxuris arces, et qua
Pontinam via dividit uda paludem, qua sublime nemus, Scythicae
qua regna Dianae, quaque iter est Latiis ad summam fascibus
Albam; excelsa de rupe procul iam conspicit urbem.' Et dixit:
'tene, deum sedes, non ullo Marte coacti deseruere viri? Pro qua
pugnabitur urbe?' Ultima nunc reliqua est nobis in hac Latinorum
regione pars urbi Romae Tibur Anienemque versus propinqua, ostiis Tiberinis, unde incepimus, e regione adversa.

52   Et ut eo unde nuper digressi fuimus revertamur: Praenestini
montis radicibus Algido proximum est Laurentii Columnae oppidum, nunc Gallicanum, qui, ut diximus, olim Gabii fuerunt vetustissimi, quos Livius in primo dicit fraude Sexti Tarquinii filii cap-
tos a Tarquinio patre. Et Vergilius[101] in VII: 'quique arva Gabinae
Iunonis,' ubi Servius exponit: 'Gabios diu in agris moratos tandem
Gabios condidisse. Quam ob rem Vergilius dixit "arva" non moenia.' Alibi tamen Servius super verbo 'Nomentum et Gabios' dicit
ab Albanis regibus eas conditas[102] fuisse. Et paucis passuum milibus inde abest Anio fluvius, quem Vergilius dicit 'frigidumque
Anienem.' Habetque originem a Sublaco, de quo scribit Plinius:
'Anio, in monte Trebanorum ortus, lacus tres amoenitate nobiles,
qui nomen dedere Sublaqueo, defert in Tiberim.' Livius scribit Ca-
millum apud Anienem Gallos, Roma redempta, exeuntes truci-
dasse, ubi Manlius, torque detracto a Gallo,[103] Torquatus est appellatus. Is in via Tiburtina ponte iungitur marmoreo, maximis
tamen quae habere solitus fuit ornamentis paene spoliato, quem
nunc Mamolum appellant. Hunc vero pontem Mamaeam, Alexan-
dri Syri imperatoris Romani certe optimi genetricem, Christianam

heights of Anxur[251] and the point where the waterlogged road cuts through the Pontine Marshes, where there is a lofty grove, the realm of Scythian Diana, and where lies the road for Latin fasces to the height of Alba: from a high cliff Caesar now glimpses the city in the distance."[252] And he said: "Why, have men deserted you, seat of the gods, though not forced to by war? What sort of city will the fight be for?"[253] The last part of the region of Lazio now remaining to us is that near the city of Rome towards Tivoli and the Aniene, directly opposite the Tiber mouth, where we began.

To return to the point from which we digressed a while ago: at   52
the foot of the hill of Praeneste, close to Algidus, is a town in the possession of Lorenzo Colonna, now called Gallicano but once, as I said, the very ancient city of Gabii. Livy says in Book I that Tarquinius Superbus captured Gabii through a trick played by his son Sextus.[254] Also Vergil in *Aeneid* VII: "Those who hold the fields of Juno of Gabii,"[255] where Servius explains: "Having long dwelt in the fields, the Gabinians at last founded the town of Gabii. This is the reason that Vergil said 'fields' and not walls."[256] Elsewhere, though, Servius writes on the passage "Nomentum and Gabii" that these cities were founded by the kings of Alba.[257] A few miles from Gabii is the river Aniene, which Vergil calls "the chilly Anio."[258] The river originates at Subiaco. Pliny writes of it: "The Aniene takes its rise in the mountain of the Trebani and carries into the Tiber the waters of three lakes remarkable for their beauty, which have given Subiaco its name."[259] Livy writes that after Rome had been won back, Camillus slaughtered the retreating Gauls at the Aniene, in the place where Manlius got the name "Torquatus" for tearing a torque from the neck of a Gaul.[260] A marble bridge crosses the river on the Tiburtine Way, though it has been practically stripped of the very considerable decoration it used to have, and is now called Ponte Mammolo. I found in the history of the Roman Pontiff Gelasius II that the bridge was built

mulierem, aedificasse in Gelasii secundi pontificis Romani rebus gestis invenimus. Sed quis proxime[104] illi subiectum Numentanae viae pontem construxerit nobis incertum est, qui certiores sumus omnes tres Anieni superimpositos pontes a Romanis fuisse destructos quando, Urbe a Belisario instaurata, Totilae adventum pavidi exspectabant. Secundusque est viae Numentanae pons, et ipse licet integer, ornamentis quae maxima habuit spoliatus. Demum tertius in via Salaria exstat a Narsete eunucho duce praestantissimo, Ostrogothorum oppressore (sicut incisus illi marmore titulus indicat) aedificatus.

53 Ad proximaque Anienis ostia quibus in Tiberim fertur, sed ultra ipsum Anienem, in Umbria regione fuisse coniicimus Fidenas urbem vetustissimam. De qua Suetonius Tranquillus in *Vita Tiberii Caesaris:* 'Fidenis casu theatri viginti hominum milia interierunt.' Cui cladi similem Gaius[105] saevissimus imperator sui imperii temporibus optavit.[106] Plinius etiam dicit: 'in Fidenati agro iuxta Urbem ciconiae nec pullos nec nidum faciunt,' et alibi Romanos accepisse lapides ad structuram ex Fidenati agro circa Urbem optimos. Et supra diximus Tiberim dividere agrum Veientem a Fidenate, mox Latium a Vaticano. De hac Vergilius in VI: 'urbem Fidenam.' Et Livius libro IV scribit: Legatis Romanorum a Fidenatibus occisis, quia ob rem publicam occisi erant, statuae in rostris positae. Et post Fidenas in potestatem redactas eoque colonos missos, quibus occisis, Fidenates cum defecissent, a M. Aemilio dictatore victi et Fidenae captae ac desolatae sunt.

54 Facta est alicubi superioribus in locis mentio accessus Hannibalis a Capua, tunc a Romanis obsessa et triplici vallo circumdata, ad

by Mamaea, the mother of that good emperor Alexander Severus and a Christian.[261] It is unclear to me who built the next bridge, on the road from Rome to Mentana, but I am more confident that all three bridges over the Aniene were destroyed by the Romans as they nervously awaited Totila's arrival, after Rome had been restored by Belisarius.[262] There is a second bridge on the road to Mentana, and though it is in itself intact, it has been robbed of the extensive decoration it once had. Finally, there is a third bridge, on the Via Salaria, which was built by the valiant captain Narses the eunuch, destroyer of the Ostrogoths, as an inscription carved in the marble records.[263]

Near the mouth of the Aniene, where it enters the Tiber, but 53 beyond it in the region of Umbria, was where I reckon the ancient city of Fidenae was located. In the *Life of Tiberius* Suetonius writes of Fidenae: "In the collapse of an amphitheater at Fidenae, 20,000 perished."[264] The inhuman emperor Caligula prayed for a similar catastrophe to happen during his own reign.[265] Pliny also says: "In the territory of Fidenae near Rome, storks neither produce offspring nor do they nest."[266] In another place he remarks that the Romans got excellent stone for building from Fidenae near Rome.[267] I said above [Etruria §55] that the river Tiber separates the territories of Veii and Fidenae, and shortly thereafter it separates Lazio and the Vatican. Vergil in Book VI mentions "the city of Fidenae."[268] And Livy writes in Book IV that statues of the Roman envoys who had been killed by the Fidenates were erected on the Rostra, because they had been killed serving the republic. Fidenae was brought back under Roman control and colonists sent there, but when the Fidenates rebelled, they too were killed. They were conquered by the dictator Marcus Aemilius, and the town was taken and laid waste.[269]

I have already referred in various places to Hannibal's coming 54 to the walls of Rome from Capua, which the Romans had laid under siege and surrounded with a triple palisade. I mean accord-

urbis Romae moenia. Quare libet ordine viam repetere qua is venerit. Livius libro XXVI primum dicit Q. Fulvium Flaccum cos. iturum[107] Romam Hannibalem secutum via Appia et Setiam Lanuviumque praemisisse qui commeatus in via pararent exercitui suo. (Setiaque et Lanuvium notissimae sunt et supra a nobis descriptae.) Hannibalem vero dicit praeter Cales in agrum Sidicinum per Suessullam Allifanumque et Casinatem, Interamnam, ac Fregellas ad Lirim venisse, *quae loca partim in veteri Campania (nunc Terra Laboris dicta), partim in Samnitibus, a nobis infra sunt indicata.*[108] Hannibal postea, Liri transmisso, agrum praesentis Latinae regionis attigit.

55 Primo, Fregellanum, qui locus, licet fuerit in Samnitibus, tamen habuit agrum suum in regione Latina. Et nunc dicitur Pons Corvus. De quo Livius in sexto: 'Hannibal infestius perpopulato Fregellano agro propter incisos pontes.' Et in octavo: 'P. Plautio Proculo P. Cornelio Scapula coss., Fregellas colonia deducta.' Et infra: 'C. Poetilius dictator cum audisset arcem Fregellanam ab Samnitibus captam, omisso Boviano, ad Fregellas pergit. Unde, nocturna Samnitum fuga sine certamine receptis Fregellis praesidioque valido imposito, in Campaniam rediit.' Ornataque fuit Fregellana colonia M. Sextilio, quem Livius dicit respondisse pro duodeviginti coloniis quae milites prius denegatos et tributa dare promiserunt.

56 Sequiturque Livius in Hannibalis itinere. Post Frusinatem, Ferentinatem, et Anagninum, quae loca nunc, parva nominis mutatione facta, sunt notissima. Ex Anagnino autem in Labicanum venit, quem locum, maxima nominis mutatione facta, diximus Valmontonem nunc appellari. Dicit enim Livius peritissime Han-

ingly to trace the route he took in its proper order. In Book XXVI
Livy says in the first place that the consul Quintus Fulvius Flaccus
followed Hannibal, who was heading towards Rome, along the
Appian Way and that he sent men ahead to Sezze and Lanuvium
to arrange provisions for the army on its march.[270] Sezze and
Lanuvium are very well known, and I described them above.[271]
Livy says that Hannibal marched past Cales into Sidicine territory,
then by way of Suessa, Alife, and Cassino, Interamna and Fratte,
as far as the river Liri. *Some of these places are in old Campania, now
called the Terra di Lavoro, some in Samnite territory, and I have indicated
them below.* Afterwards, Hannibal crossed the Liri to arrive in the
modern region of Lazio.[272]

First, there is the territory of Fregellae, which though it was   55
Samnite, had its land in Lazio. It is now called Pontecorvo.[273] In
Book VI Livy writes: "Hannibal completely destroyed the territory of Fregellae in revenge for the destruction of the bridges."[274]
And in Book VIII: "A colony was established at Fregellae in the
consulship of Publius Plautius Proculus and Publius Cornelius
Scapula."[275] And below: "On learning that the citadel of Fregellae
had been captured by the Samnites, he raised the siege of
Bovianum and marched to Fregellae. The place was retaken without a fight, the Samnites having evacuated it in the night, and after leaving a strong garrison there, the dictator returned to Campania."[276] Marcus Sextilius gave luster to the colony at Fregellae;
according to Livy, he responded on behalf of the eighteen colonies
that promised to contribute the soldiers and tribute monies previously denied.[277]

Livy continues to follow Hannibal's path. He afterwards came   56
into the districts of Frusinum, Ferentinum and Anagnia, all of
them, with a slight change of name, well-known places now.[278]
From the district of Anagnia he entered that of the Labici, a place
which has undergone a considerable change of name, as I said
[§§26, 30], and is now called Valmontone. Livy says that Hanni-

nibalem, qui esset in Labicano agro, movisse Algido, quia oppidum illud (sicut nunc est) tunc etiam Algido proximum ac prope contiguum erat. Et pervenisse Tusculum ea scilicet via qua nunc a Valmontono Marinum silvis petitur. Et quia sequitur Livius Hannibalem: 'cum non esset Tusculi moenibus receptus, dextrorsum descendisse Gabios,' certissimum nobis facit, quod superiore diximus loco, Gabios fuisse quod nunc est oppidum Gallicanum. Quae autem fuerit Pupinia, quam post Gabios accesserit, ignoramus: quod plurimas ea regio habet oppidorum villarumque ruinas a nemine habitatas, prisca quarum nomina nullus novit. Sed iam, magno circuitu ab ostiis Tiberinis secundum Maris Inferi litus ad Lirim (sive Gaurianum) et inde per Marsos et mediterranea ad Anienem facto, ad Tiberim est reditum. Quo in circuitu omnis regio olim Latina (sive, ut nunc dicitur Latium, Campania et Maritima) est conclusa.

bal, who was in the territory of the Labicani, moved adroitly over Mt. Algidus,[279] for Labico was then, as it is now, close to and almost touching the mountain. He then reached Tusculum, doubtless by the same road which today leads through the forest from Valmontone to Marino. And because Livy follows Hannibal's route with "when Hannibal was refused admission by the Tusculans, he turned down to the right towards to Gabii," I am quite sure that, as I said above, Gabii was what is now the town of Gallicano.[280] What the Pupinia was to which Hannibal proceeded after Gabii, I do not know.[281] The region has a great many remains of towns and estates where no one lives and whose ancient names no one knows. We have now completed the great circuit from the Tiber mouth on the shore of the Tyrrhenian Sea to the river Liri (or Garigliano), and from there through the territory of the Marsi and the places inland to the river Aniene, and so back to the Tiber. With that circuit the whole region of Lazio (or Campania and Marittima, as Latium is now called) is concluded.

LIBER III

Quarta regio. Umbria sive Ducatus Spoletanus[1]

1　Prolixiores fuisse videmur describenda Latina regione tertia quam aliarum habenda ratio postulabat, et tamen multo pauciora quam oportuit (certe quam voluissemus) in illa diximus, quae frequentata a Livio, Vergilio, et aliis vetustissimis scriptoribus loca plura habeat ceteris Italiae regionibus. Sed cum plus iacturae in ea quam in ceterarum aliqua sit factum adeo ut nulla incultior populisque infrequentior manserit, brevitatem nostram abinveniendi ea quae non exstent impossibilitate consolemur. Ad quartamque regionem transeamus: eam prisci dixere Umbriam, nostri ducatum appellant Spoletanum. Idque ducatus nomen primo ab exarchis Italiae sedem Ravennae tenentibus (sicut in *Historiis* ostendimus) inditum eam habuit vim ut a militari consuetudine tractum; dignitatem nunc referat quae post regiam est suprema.

2　Quantis vero olim polluerint viribus Umbri hinc maxime apparet, quod Livius in IX scribit: Umbri se urbem Romam oppugnaturos minati fuerunt.[2] Quam latos autem fines haec regio olim habuit hinc maxime constat, quod Plinius dicit sextam regionem Umbriam complexam agrumque[3] Gallicum circa Ariminum, et eam Galliae Umbrorum gentem Italiae antiquissimam existimari, trecentaque eorum oppida a Tuscis, *quando Etruriam ceperunt*,[4] debellata fuisse. Sabinos etiam videmus fuisse in Umbris comprehensos et Umbriam ad Superum usque nunc Adriaticum mare pertinuisse[5] hinc constat, quod Trogus Pompeius et magis aperte Plinius dicunt interiisse in Umbris Spinam, urbem Delphicis opi-

BOOK III

Region 4. Umbria, or the Duchy of Spoleto

It may seem that I have been rather more prolix in the description 1
of the third region, Lazio, than was warranted by the treatment
accorded the others, yet I said much less about it than I should
have—less, certainly, than I wanted—bearing in mind that Lazio
has more sites touched on by Livy, Vergil, and the other ancient
authors than the rest of the Italian regions. But since Lazio has
suffered more losses than any of the other regions, so much so
that none is more desolate or depopulated, let us console ourselves
for our brevity with the thought that you cannot discover what
does not exist. So let us proceed to the fourth region: in ancient
times people spoke of Umbria, but we call it the Duchy of
Spoleto. The term "duchy" was first applied to the region by the
exarchs who had their seat at Ravenna (as I showed in my *Histories*).[1] It originally had the force of a title taken from military usage; today it conveys a rank second only to royal authority.

How powerful the ancient Umbrians once were emerges most 2
clearly from what Livy writes in Book IX: The Umbrians threat-
ened to attack Rome.[2] How far the region extended may be gathered from Pliny's saying that his sixth region included Umbria and
the territory of the Gauls around Rimini, that the Gallic race of
the Umbrians was thought to be the most ancient in Italy, and
that thirty of their towns were conquered by the Etruscans *when
they took over Etruria*.[3] We also learn that the Sabines were included
among the Umbrians, and it is clear that Umbria reached as far as
the Upper Sea (now the Adriatic) from the fact that Trogus and,
more explicitly, Pliny say that Spina ceased to exist among the
Umbrians (it was a city built by Diomedes and famous for its trea-

bus claram,[6] a Diomede aedificatam, quae ostio Padi sibi proximo dedit Spineticum nomen. Et Ravennam, cui proxima fuerit Spina cuiusque ruinis ipsa sit aedificata, Sabinorum oppidum fuisse Valerius Martialis coquus poeta sic docet: 'Mollis in aequorea quae crevit spina Ravenna; non erit incultis gratior asparagis.'[7] Nos itaque, cum Umbriae fines lati nimis fuerint, huius nostrae regionis—quam consuetudinis inveteratae necessitas ducatum Spoletanum appellare coegit—fines constituemus:[8] Apenninum a Tiberis fonte superius in Etruria indicato usque ad Anienis fluvii etiam apud Urbem notissimi sinistram ripam et Tiberim quousque eum Anio illabitur.

3   Prima ex Apennino ad sinistram Tiberis partem descendentibus obvia sunt oppida Pratolinum et Mons Dolius. Exinde unico a Tiberi milliario abest oppidum Sancti Sepulcri Burgus appellatum, moenibus arcubusque[9] quatuor munitissimum, quas Guido de Petramala, episcopus et dominus Arretinus, superiori saeculo exstruxit. Nullum vetustatis signum eo in loco esse inspeximus, et tamen C. Plinii nepotis epistulam legentes, in qua villam suam ad radices Apennini et prope Tiberim amnem describit, theatralem (sicut ipse dicit) montium in circuitu positorum aspectum hoc in loco esse deprehendimus, ut in eius villae ruinis prima dicti oppidi fundamenta fuisse iacta credamus. Ornatur autem nunc id oppidum Malatesta Cataneo iure consultissimo, quem non magis Camertinorum cui praeest ecclesia quam vitae integritas sanctimoniaque conspicuum reddunt. Infra ⟨ad⟩ Tiberim est Tifernum, Civitas Castelli dicta, quae nunc cive ornatur praestantissimo Nicolao Vitellio equestris ordinis, quem studia humanitatis et mores ingenui apud quartum Eugenium pontificem praestantissimum imbibiti clarum reddunt. Ab hac urbe Plinius maior[10] in *Naturali historia* dicit Tiberim ratibus Romam usque navigabilem fuisse. Incipit eo in loco Tiberis longius[11] ab Apennino recedere ut quanto magis urbi Romae appropinquat,[12] eo maior nostrae huius

sures at Delphi, giving its name to a nearby mouth of the river Po).[4] And the poet Martial the cook tells us that Ravenna, adjacent to Spina, which was built on its ruins, was a Sabine town: "The soft thorn-bush that grew in watery Ravenna will not be more pleasant than wild asparagus."[5] Since the borders of Umbria were overly broad, I shall define the limits of our region — the force of inveterate custom obliges me to call it the Duchy of Spoleto — as follows: the Apennines from the source of the Tiber (already mentioned above in Tuscany [§51]) to the left bank of the well-known river Aniene near Rome, and the Tiber to the point where the Aniene flows into it.

As you come down from the Apennines along the left side of 3 the Tiber, you are first presented with the towns of Pratolino and Montedoglio. Then, a mile from the Tiber, is the town called Borgo Sansepolcro, strongly fortified with the walls and four city gates which the bishop and lord of Arezzo, Guido da Pietramala, erected in the last century:[6] I did not notice any trace of antiquity in the place, and yet from reading the letter of Pliny the Elder's nephew in which he describes his villa close to the Tiber at the foot of the Apennines, I could see the shape of a theatre in the hills encircling it, just as in Pliny's account, leading me to believe that Borgo's first foundations were laid in the ruins of Pliny's country estate.[7] Borgo Sansepolcro is now graced by the jurisconsult Malatesta Cattaneo, distinguished as much for his pious and honourable way of life as for his episcopal dignity at Camerino. Below Borgo on the Tiber is Tifernum, or Città di Castello, presently blessed with her citizen Niccolò Vitelli, a knight notable for his accomplishments in the liberal arts and the noble character that he absorbed at the court of the illustrious pontiff Eugenius IV.[8] The elder Pliny says in the *Natural History* that the Tiber could be navigated by raft all the way from Città di Castello to Rome.[9] At this point the Tiber begins to leave the Apennines behind, so that the closer we approach Rome, the

regionis latitudo[13] ⟨inter⟩ amnem ipsum montemque intercedat. Distatque a Tiferno viginti passuum milibus Eugubium civitas ad Apennini radices sita, quae vetusta Romanae ecclesiae iuris a Frederico gubernatur comite Montis Feretri, quem rei militari cum gloria deditum litterae et prudentia plurimum ornant. Supra Eugubium castella sunt Brancha, deinde Schigia, quo tramite facillimus est per viam olim Flaminiam Apennini in Romandiolam transitus.

4　　Et a Schigia secundum Apennini latera hanc ingredienti provinciam obvium fit Costaciarium, Eugubini agri oppidum, deinceps est Sigillum Perusinorum: inter quae duo oppida fluvius oritur Chiesius, qui inter Eugubinos Assisinatesque montes delapsus fertur sub Cannaria oppido in proximum amnem Tinium,[14] sive ut nunc dicitur Topinum. Post Sigillum est Fossatum arduo in Apennini colle castellum. Et quarto inde milliario est Vallidum, cui Gualdum dicunt, quod oppidum in civitatis a Longobardis subiecto in campo excisae locum fuit aedificatum. Parvusque torrens a Vallido brevi cursu labitur in Chiasium,[15] per cuius amnis alveum venientibus Ancona Picenique regione ex Fabrianoque traicientibus Apenninum per Fossatum Vallidumque iter est Perusiam. Et medio itinere Casa Castalda oppidum arduo in colle Chiasio imminet. Deinceps in Planellum vicum campis adiacentem via continuatur quousque ad Patullorum sive Vallis Cippi sive Sancti Johannis vicum pontibus Tiberis transmittitur.

5　　Post Vallidum recedere ab Apennino oppida incipiunt, primaque est Nuceria civitas vetusto cognomine Alphatenia, de qua Livius *in IX*: 'Decius[16] consul profectus ad Nuceriam Alphateniam oppugnando ad deditionem subegit.' Estque ad Tinium amnem (nunc Topinum) posita, secundum cuius alveum ingentes cernun-

broader the Umbrian plain between the mountains and river. Twenty miles from Città di Castello is the town of Gubbio, located at the foot of the Apennines: long under the sway of the Roman Church, the town is governed by Federigo Count of Montefeltro—his profession is military glory but his greatest distinction lies in his learning and wisdom.[10] Beyond Gubbio are the castles of Branca and then Scheggia, the easiest path over the Apennines into Romagna along the former Flaminian Way.

As you enter Umbria from Scheggia along the flanks of the 4 Apennines, you come upon Costacciaro, a town in the territory of Gubbio, and following that Sigillo di Perugia: between the two rises the river Chiascio, which comes down through the hills of Gubbio and Assisi and past the town of Cannara into the nearby river Tinia, or Topino as it is now called. Beyond Sigillo is the castle of Fossato di Vico, high on an Apennine hill. Four miles from Fossato is Vallidum, now known as Gualdo Tadino; Gualdo was built in place of a town, sited on the plain below, which the Lombards destroyed. A small stream flows from Gualdo which after a short while joins the Chiascio. The course of the Chiascio is the way to Perugia for those coming from Ancona and the region of Picenum, and crossing the Apennines from Fabriano via Fossato and Gualdo. Midway along this route, Casa Castalda looks down on the river Chiascio from a high hill. The road then continues to the village of Pianello in the plain, until it is carried across the Tiber by bridges at the villages of Ponte Pattoli, Ponte Valleceppi and Ponte S. Giovanni.

After Gualdo the towns begin to leave the Apennines behind, 5 and the first city one comes to is Nocera Umbra (in ancient times called Nuceria Alphatenia),[11] of which Livy *in Book IX* says: "*Decius* the consul set out for Nuceria Alphatenia, attacked it and forced its surrender."[12] Nocera is located on the river Tinia (the present Topino), along whose course great substructures for supporting the old Flaminian Way can be seen. Twelve miles along

tur moles sternenda via olim Flaminia iactae. Iturque illac duodecimo milliario Fulgineum, per quam is amnis defluit civitatem, quae suffecta fuit Foro Flaminii, vetustae urbi a Longobardis propinquo in loco ad annum nunc septingentesimum funditus excisae. Fuisse tamen legimus vetustis temporibus alios in Umbris Fulginates ab hoc loco remotissimos, qui apud Tudertinos habitasse videntur, eosque crediderim ad hanc inhabitandam urbem novam populariter commigrasse. Ornata vero fuit Fulginei civitas patrum nostrorum memoria Gentili, medico sui saeculi celeberrimo. Est apud Fulgineum[17] planities totius Umbriae amplissima pariter et amoenissima, in qua sunt quinto ad Fulginei dexteram milliario Pellium, ut appellat Plinius, et, ut nunc dicitur, Spellum,[18] vetusti nominis oppidum. Pari paene spatio Assisia arduo in colle sita, civitas vetustissima passuum tria milia a Chiasio recedens, seraphicoque Francisco, cuius servat reliquias, cive et eius templo omnium Italiae aedificii magnificentia celeberrimo ornatissima. Quam Propertius poeta Axim appellat, *innuitque construendo eius urbis muro consilium attulisse*[19] his versibus: 'Scandentisque Axis consurgit vertice murus, murus ab ingenio notior ille tuo.'

6   Tinius sive Topinus amnis cum ad Cannariam oppidum Chiesio iunctus est, suum amittit nomen. Et deinde Chiasius appellatus, Bettonio oppido a libertate diu servata insigni ad sinistram relicto, apud Torsanum oppidum labitur in Tiberim, nec ullo Tiberis praeter Narem Anienemque maiore augetur fluvio. Ad alteram vero Chiasii partem multa sunt Perusini agri oppida, e quibus Fracta Tiberi est contigua. Et interius est Montonum, Braccio rei bellicae praestantissimo duce illustratum, a quo Braccianorum sectam factionemque habuimus, in qua magnae per aetatem nostram celebritatis fuerunt Nicolaus Piccininus et postea Franciscus filius fuitque pariter Nicolaus Braccio ex Stella sorore nepos. Supersunt

the Flaminian Way from Nocera you come to the city of Foligno, through which the Topino flows. It took the place of Forum Flaminii, an ancient city nearby that was completely destroyed by the Lombards 700 years ago. Yet I have read that in antiquity there were other Umbrian 'Folignati' a long way from here, who seem to have lived in the territory of Todi, and I imagine they migrated as a people to occupy the new city. The city of Foligno was adorned in our fathers' time by Gentile da Foligno, the most famous physician of his day.[13] Around Foligno spreads a plain, at once the largest and the most attractive in all Umbria. On the plain five miles to the right of Foligno is the ancient town of Pellium, as Pliny calls it,[14] or Spello, as it is called now. Almost the same distance away is Assisi, a very old city set on a steep hill three miles from the river Chiascio. Assisi's chief adornments are her citizen the seraphic St. Francis (whose mortal remains are kept there) and his basilica, the most celebrated in all Italy for the grandeur of the architecture.[15] The poet Propertius calls the city Axis, *and he indicates that he advised on the construction of the city's walls*[16] in these lines: "the wall of Assisi rising on its hilltop rears up, that wall made more famous by your genius."[17]

The Tinia (or Topino) loses its name when the river joins the   6 Chiascio at the town of Cannara. Now called the Chiascio, it leaves behind it on the left the town of Bettona, illustrious for its long-preserved liberty, and flows into the Tiber at the town of Torgiano; apart from the Nera and the Aniene, it is the largest tributary of the Tiber. There are many towns in the territory of Perugia on the other side of the Chiascio, one of which, Fratta, lies beside the Tiber.[18] Further inland is Montone, made famous by its outstanding general Braccio Fortebraccio. His followers give us the name of the faction known as "Bracciani", among whom Niccolò Piccinino and later his son Francesco won great fame in our day, as did Braccio's nephew Niccolò, the son of his sister Stella. There are also the sons of Braccio and Niccolò Piccinino,

etiam Carolus Braccii et Jacobus Nicolai Piccinini filii, quorum ille aliquas, hic magnas in Venetorum exercitu copias ducunt, maximo exinde[20] pressi onere quod paternae virtutis et potentiae eorum uterque exemplar ad imitationem propositum habeat.

7 Supra Fulgineum ad sinistram arduo in colle, qui tamen longe Apennino abest, Trivium est. Cuius oppidi et situs et nomen faciunt ut credam hunc esse locum de quo scribit Servius, in expositione Vergilii, super verbo 'oliviferaeque Mutuscae.' Dicit enim: 'Haec Trevia postea dicta est, quam modo Trebulam dicunt.' De qua Martialis coquus poeta: 'humida qua gelidas submittit Trebula valles et viridis Cancri mensibus alget ager.' Et quidem hoc Trivium est nunc valde oliviferum et in Sabinorum vetustis finibus situm, sicut Mutuscas fuisse scribit Vergilius. E regione autem Trivii amoeno in colle Falcum est oppidum, haudquaquam vetusti nominis sed populo frequentatum. Ad collisque illius radices in via olim Flaminia est Mevania, de qua Livius in IX: 'Decius cos. magnis itineribus ad Mevaniam, ubi tum copiae Umbrorum erant, perrexit.' Fuitque id oppidum cive ornatum Propertio Aurelio Nauta, qui de seipso scribit ad Tullum *libro Monobiblo vel, ut Nonio Marcello placet,*[21] libro primo *Elegiarum:* 'proxima supposito contingens Umbria campo me genuit terris fertilis uberibus.' Idemque in *Elegiarum* quarto: 'Umbria te notis antiqua Penatibus edit—mentior an patriae tangitur ora tuae?—qua nebulosa cavo irrorat Mevania campo et lacus aestivis intepet Umber aquis. Scandentisque Axis,' et cetera. Postquam vero Propertii testimonium de seipso attulimus, alium Umbriae poetam dare volumus, ignotae nobis (sicut et ipsi Propertio fuit) patriae. Nam in eodem *Elegiarum* IV, sic dicit: 'ut nostris tumefacta superbiat Umbria libris, Umbria Ro-

Carlo and Jacopo, still alive today, of whom the former commands some Venetian forces, the latter very large ones; both of them feel the great responsibility of living up to the example of their fathers' bravery and ability.[19]

Beyond Foligno to the left is Trevi on its steep hill (but a long way from the Apennines). The position and name of the town lead me to think that it is the place of which Servius writes in his commentary on Vergil's phrase "olive-bearing Mutusca." He says: "This was later called Trevia, which we know now as Trebula."[20] On which the poet Martial writes: "Where damp Trebula dips her chilly vales and the green land shivers through the months of the Crab."[21] Trevi is in fact a great olive-producing district today and located within the ancient borders of the Sabines, just as Mutusca was, according to Vergil.[22] Facing Trevi on a pretty hill is Montefalco, by no means an old town but very populous. At the foot of that hill on the former Flaminian Way is Bevagna, of which Livy says in Book IX: "The consul Decius proceeded by forced marches to Bevagna, where the Umbrian forces were stationed at the time."[23] The town is given luster by her citizen Propertius, who writes about himself to Tullus in *his book Monobiblos, or as Nonius Marcellus would have it,*[24] his *Elegies:*[25] "There I was born in fertile Umbria with its rich earth, where it borders on Perugia and lies below it in the plain."[26] And again in Book IV of the *Elegies:* "Ancient Umbria gave birth to you at a noble hearth — am I lying, or do I touch on the area of your home? — where misty Bevagna sheds her dew over the low-lying fields and the waters of the Umbrian Lake become warm in summer, Assisi rising, etc."[27] Since I have mentioned Propertius' autobiographical statements, I should like to give Umbria another poet, whose home town is as unknown to me as it was to Propertius himself. In the same Book IV of the *Elegies,* he writes: "so that swollen with pride, Umbria might plume herself on my books, Umbria, the land of the Roman Callimachus."[28] *And Lucan in Book I writes: "And where Bevagna*

mani patria Callimachi.' *Et Lucanus in primo: 'est qui, tauriferis qua se Mevania campis explicat, audaces ruere in certamina turmas'.*[22]

8   Planitiei item, quam hoc in loco amplissimam esse diximus post Trevium, imminet Spoletium. Quam civitatem Livius libro XX coloniam a Romanis deductam fuisse scribit. Et libro XXII Hannibalem dicit post Trasumeni pugnam recto itinere per Umbriam usque ad Spoletium pervenisse. Inde cum, populato[23] agro, urbem adorsus esset expugnare, cum magna caede suorum repulsum, coniectantem ex unius coloniae haud prospere tentatae viribus quanta moles Romanae urbis esset, in agrum Picenum convertisse exercitum. Et libro XXIV idem Livius prodigia unius tempestatis enumerans, narrat Spoleti tunc ex muliere virum factum. Eusebius autem dicit Melissum Spoletanum grammaticum insignem Spoleti natum fuisse. Martialisque poeta vinum laudans Spoletinum sic dicit: 'De Spoletinis, quae sunt cariosa, lagonis[24] malueris quam si musta Falerna bibas.' Et nos *Historiarum* XII ostendimus Theodericum regem primum Gothorum Spoleti amplissimas aedificasse aedes, et alios, qui successerunt, Gothos destruxisse Spoletium moenibus eversis, quae Narses eunuchus refici curavit.[25] Ea civitas, ubi stante Romanae rei publicae felicitate theatrum fuit, arcem habet omnium Italiae munitissimam, et *quam aedificiorum pulchritudine nuperrime tu, pater sancte V Nicolae Pontifex Romane, Caesare Lucensi levire tuo, viro optimo ac praestantissimo curante,*[26] *ornatissimam reddidisti.*[27]

9   Nuceriae civitati et praeterlabenti Tinio sive Topino amni ac Fulgineo, Trevio, et Spoletio adiacent atque imminent colles montesque altissimi, pluribus tamen vallibus torrentibusque inter se divisi, ut ab amplissima quam descripsimus planitie Spoletana valle appellata ad Apenninum magna sit spatia[28] castellis, oppidis, civitatibus, vicis, et villis etiam vetusti nominis habitata, quae altera

spreads herself amid the fields that bear bulls, one bngs word that bold
squadrons of horse hasten to the fray."[29]

Spoleto too overlooks the plain, here, below Trevi, at its broad-   8
est, as I said. Livy writes in Book XX that a colony was sent out
to Spoleto by the Romans.[30] And in Book XXII he says that after
the battle of Trasimene, Hannibal reached Spoleto by marching
straight through Umbria; after laying waste to the countryside,
he attempted to storm Spoleto but was beaten back with great
slaughter on his side. Surmising from the strength of a single colony unsuccessfully assaulted how great an effort would be needed
to take Rome, he turned his army aside and made for Picenum.[31]
In Book XXIV Livy again catalogues the prodigies of a single
season and recounts how a woman at Spoleto was turned into
a man.[32] Eusebius says that Melissus Spoletanus, the famous
scholar, was born at Spoleto.[33] And the poet Martial has this to
say in praise of the wine of Spoleto: "You would prefer crusted
wines from Spoletine flagons to drinking Falernian must."[34] I
mentioned in Book XII of my *Histories* that the king of the Goths,
Theodoric I, built a vast palace at Spoleto, and that other Goths
who succeeded him tore down the walls and destroyed the city,
which Narses the eunuch took pains to restore.[35] Spoleto has the
strongest fortress in Italy, built where there was a theater in the
days of Rome's prosperity, and very recently embellished *by you,*
Holy Father Nicholas, with the beautiful buildings overseen by your
brother-in-law Cesare of Lucca, that excellent and distinguished man.[36]

Beside and overlooking Nocera Umbra and the river Tinia (or   9
Topino) flowing by it, and also Foligno, Trevi, and Spoleto, is a
chain of high hills and mountains — not continuous, however, but
separated from one another by numerous valleys and streams.
There is a great swath of country here, stretching from the broad
plain of the Valle Spoletana, just described, to the Apennines. It is
filled with castles, towns, cities, villages and estates, some even of
ancient foundation: one might almost call it another region — but

paene regio sed montuosissima possit appellari. Primum his in
montibus supra Fulgineum est Caput Aquae, castellum dictum a
scaturiente ibi celeberrimo fonte, qui fons amnem efficit brevi
cursu Tinium adaugentem. Supra est Collis Floridus, castellum
item lacui adiacens parum amplo et castelli ipsius nomine appellato, quem parvulus rivulus prope Fulgineum exonerat in Topinum. Imminentque undique lacui montes altissimi, in quibus
Sanctae Anatoliae notius est oppidum Camertinis subiectum. Et
per Collem Floridum iter est[29] ad arctissima Apennini claustra,
Seravallis appellata, per quae Camerinum petitur, civitas vetustissima in Piceno a nobis post hac describenda. Quamquam Seravallis prima domus tectum habet, cuius anterior pars in Umbros, in
Picentes posterior, aquam pluviam demittit.

10   Subest colli in quo Trivium esse diximus perlucidus fons, tan-
tam subito evomens aquam ut intra stadii unius cursum efficiat
fluvium, qui infra Fulgineum labitur in Topinum. Est vero is amnis Clitumnus, de quo Vergilius in *Georgicis*: 'hinc albi, Clitumne,
greges et maxima tauri victima saepe tuo perfusi flumine sacro Romanos ad templa deum duxere triumphos.' Quod vero Vergilius
supradictis in versibus innuit, Plinius diffuse scribit: eam oram
tauros gignere omnium Italiae maximos, in quis[30] plurimi sint albi.
Unde Silius Italicus in IV: *'Mevano Varenus, arat cui divitis uber
campi Fulginia, et patulis Clitumnus in arvis candentes gelido perfundit
flumine tauros.'*[31] Et Lucanus in primo[32] ostendit Mevaniam, secus
quam Clitumnus labitur in Topinum, esse in campis tauriferis. Et
Propertius item post superius ab eo scripta de Mevania addit: 'et
pecus et niveos abluit unda boves.' Trivium inter et Spoletium[33]
multa sunt Spoletinorum castella; quousque montes arduos pene-

a very, very mountainous one. First in these mountains above Foligno is the castle of Capodacqua, named for the famous spring which rises there and forms a river that soon feeds into the Topino. Above Capodacqua is Colfiorito, another castle, beside a lake of no great extent named after it, from which a small stream flows into the Topino near Foligno. The lake is overlooked on all sides by high mountains; the most notable town in the mountains is Esanatoglia, subject to Camerino. To get to Camerino, one travels by way of Colfiorito through a very narrow Apennine pass called Serravalle. Camerino is an ancient city of Picenum, which we shall describe in the next book, though the first house of Serravalle has a roof from the front of which rainwater runs off into Umbria, from its back into Picenum.

Beneath the hill where Trevi stands (described above), there is a 10 clear spring from which so much water wells up of a sudden that within the course of a stade it creates a river, which flows into the Topino below Foligno. This river is the Clitumnus, of which Vergil in the *Georgics* says: "Hence come your bulls, Clitumnus, the snow-white herd and noblest of victims, which, bathed in your sacred stream, have many a time led Roman triumphs to the temples of the gods."[37] What Vergil hints at in the verses quoted above, Pliny says more expansively: that district produces the biggest bulls in Italy, most of them white.[38] And so Silius Italicus in Book IV *writes: "Varenus from Bevagna, for whom Foligno plows the rich soil of her lush plain, and Clitumnus amid its spreading fields washes bulls white with its icy stream."*[39] And Lucan in Book I mentions that Bevagna, past which Clitumnus flows into the Topino, is set in "the fields that bear bulls."[40] And Propertius likewise, after the passage on Bevagna quoted above,[41] says: "Clitumnus bathes in his waters the flock and the snow-white oxen."[42] Between Trevi and Spoleto there are many castles of the Spoletans. Those who penetrate the high mountains come upon the town of Cerreto di Spoleto and the town of Ponte, which lies below it. The former is

trantes Ceretum et subiectum illi Pontem oppida inveniunt. Quorum primum infamis quaestus populo frequentatur, quod omnem paene Europam illi peragrantes, diversis ad fallendos homines suae miseriae famisque[34] religiosi alicuius instituti praetensis coloribus, stipem mendicando petunt et divitias inde multas accumulant. Et eo usque gentis illius processit infamia ut, quemadmodum a Gnathone adulatores 'Gnathonici,' sic ab hac gente importuni inverecundique petitores 'Ceretani' ubique per Italiam vocitentur. Quae ignominia ne Italos paene omnes per Europam et alios ducatus Spoletani incolas per Italiam inquinet, publico Romani pontificis edicto inhibitum est Ceretanis ne ultra mensem iniussu praetorum domo absint.

11   Pontani vero licet a Cereto originem ducant, aliquot viros per aetatem nostram doctissimos habuerunt, inter quos Ludovicus iure consultorum consultissimus fuit. Et ex eadem cognatione ac professione, Paulus Romae consistorialis advocatus celeber habetur.[35] Magnae etiam indolis praedictae succrescit Pontanae gentis[36] adulescens Jovianus,[37] qui iambico versu et scribendis elegiis assiduo deditus studio Propertii et Callimachi contribulium, aut vicini Ovidii, aut[38] quem magis imitatur, Catulli Veronensis, laudibus responsurus videtur. Pontem, oppidum a ponte dictum Narem ibi prope fluvium iungente, praetergressi ad sextum milliarium, inveniunt Cassiam, novi nominis oppidum sed populo frequens ac libertate conspicuum, quod fluvius attingit Cornus,[39] apud altissimum regionis montem (qui et ipse Cornus[40] appellatur) oriundus et in Narem fluvium apud Tripontium castellum defluens. Cuius castelli iurisdictionis possessionisque causa, Nursini Spoletinique crudelissima inter se proximis temporibus proelia commiserunt, in quibus capti superatique concertatoris sanguini et vitae nullus pepercit.

12   Septimo a Cassia milliario arduos inter montes, vallibus tamen cum amplis tum etiam amoenis distinctos, est Nursia urbs vetusta,

populated by people with a disreputable trade. They travel over
pretty much all of Europe dressed in the various habits of religious
orders so as to trick men into thinking them hungry and poverty-
stricken, seeking a living by begging and getting considerable
wealth from doing so. Their evil reputation has reached the point
where importunate and shameless beggars all over Italy are called
"Cerretani" after them, just as flatterers are known as
"Gnathonici" from Terence's Gnatho.[43] So that this shame should
not reflect on Italians throughout Europe or on other inhabitants
of the Duchy of Spoleto within Italy, a papal edict was issued forbidding the Cerretani to be away from their homes for more than
a month without permission of the civic authorities.

Though the citizens of Ponte originally came from Cerreto, 11
they have had several learned men in our time, among them
Lodovico Pontano, most learned of jurisconsults.[44] Of the same
family and same profession, the consistorial advocate Paolo da
Ponte is held in high regard at Rome.[45] Gioviano of the same
Pontano family, a young man of great natural ability, is now coming into his own: utterly dedicated as he is to the writing of iambic
and elegiac verse, he seems destined to match the glory of his
countrymen Propertius and Callimachus, or of Ovid, whom he resembles, or of Catullus of Verona, his chief model.[46] Passing six
miles beyond Ponte—a town called after the bridge crossing the
nearby Nera—the traveler comes upon Cascia, a recent foundation, but populous and notable for its independence. The town is
grazed by the river Corno, which rises in the region's highest
mountain (also called Corno), and flows down to join the Nera at
the castle of Triponzo. In recent times Norcia and Spoleto have
engaged in savage warfare for the control and possession of
Triponzo: neither blood nor life was spared the fighters taken after
defeat in battle by any opponent.

Seven miles from Cascia among high mountains (though they 12
are penetrated by substantial and attractive valleys) is the ancient

quam Livius, libro XXX, dicit dedisse milites Publio Scipioni armanda classe quam in Africam duxit. Parvusque illius moenia attingens torrentulus[41] medio inter Cassiam et Narem tractu illabitur Cornum[42] amnem. Vetustum vero et a scriptoribus celebratum est Nursiae nomen, quod quidem oppidum nunc libertate sed in primis alumno Benedicto monachorum patre[43] clarissimum. Priorem tempore Benedicto summum genuit virum, Quintum Sertorium, nulli Romanorum ducum virtute secundum. Servius grammaticus in Vergilii expositione, ubi verba sunt, 'quos frigida misit Nursia,' sic dicit: 'civitas frigida re vera, aut certe venenosa, nocens, nam ubique in contionibus suis Gracchi Nursinos sceleratos appellaverunt.' Servius vero videtur situm eius oppidi ignorasse: namque poeta excellentissimus, qui omnia et in primis historiam ac Italiae regiones peritius nosset quam Servius, 'frigidam' dixit Nursiam, non quia sceleratos cum sceleratis Gracchis Nursinos iudicaverit esse, sed quia altissimis frigidissimisque Nursia montibus cingeretur. Quod enim ipsa res docet:[44] Nursia gignit viros, quorum qui inferioris videntur esse condicionis, non magis perite et industrie aratrum et ligones, sive subulam et forfices, quam rei publicae, ad quem sedent, clavum tractare noverunt. Et digniori in civium coetu multos vidimus — plures audivimus — litteris ornatissimos, qualem habet aetas nostra Benedictum Reguardatum, qui, originem (sicut et nomen) referens in beati Benedicti progeniem, vir est non magis philosophiae et medicinae,[45] quibus claret artibus, quam prudentia et consilio excellens. Nursinum agrum[46] multas gignere rapas Martialis sic indicat: 'Nursinas poteris parcius esse rapas.'

13   Est supra Cassiam decimo milliario Connexa[47] novi nominis oppidum sed populo (ut in montuosis) frequentissimum. Et haec

city of Norcia. In Book XXX, Livy says it contributed soldiers to Publius Scipio when the fleet that he took to Africa had to be outfitted.[47] A little stream touches the walls of Norcia and flows into the river Corno from the area lying between Cascia and the Nera. Norcia is indeed an ancient town and much celebrated by writers: it is now noted for its independence, but above all for its son Benedict, the father of monasticism.[48] Before Benedict, Nursia bore the great Quintus Sertorius, second to none of Rome's generals in point of courage.[49] In his comment on Vergil's words "whom chill Nursia sent,"[50] the grammarian Servius says: "The city really is chilly, or at all events poisonous or harmful, for in their speeches the Gracchi constantly refer to the Norcians as 'criminals.'"[51] But Servius seems not to have known the actual situation of Nursia, for that finest of poets had more profound knowledge of everything than Servius, and in particular of the history and regions of Italy. When he called the city chilly, it was not because he reckoned the Norcians criminals along with the criminal Gracchi but because Norcia is encircled by very high and very chilly mountains. Actual experience shows us that Norcia bears men who, even if they appear to be of lowly estate, know how to steer their ship of state with no less assurance and skill than they apply to working with plows and mattocks, the cobbler's awl or the shepherd's shears. Among the better class of citizens, I have known many (and know more by repute) who had great literary accomplishments, such as in our day Benedetto Reguardati. His origins, as well as his name, go back to the family of St. Benedict himself, and he is as outstanding for his wisdom and good sense as for the arts of philosophy and medicine that have made him famous.[52] Martial informs us that the territory of Nursia produces an abundance of turnips in these words: "You'll be able to eat the Norcian turnips more sparingly."[53]

Ten miles beyond Cascia is Gonessa,[54] not an old town but, for a mountain settlement, full of people. These towns are in the

13

quidem in ea montium parte quae Spoletium e regione respicit. Citra Narem Vissium est, vetusti nominis oppidum viginti passuum milibus a Cereto et sub ipsis paene Apennini iugis remotum.[48] Vissii moenia abluit Nar fluvius, de quo Vergilius: 'sulphurea Nar albus aqua,' *ortum suum superiori in Apennini iugo habens. Estque*[49] amnis ipsius origo ea ratione memorabilis, quam sicut a maioribus tradi videmus et vis ipsa verbi significat: fons geminus fluvium inchoans ex duobus manat orificiis narium animalis cuiuspiam speciem in saxosi montis capite imitantibus. Ad hanc Naris ripam descendentes cum Ceretum Pontumque oppida praetergressi sunt, Schizinum inveniunt, oppidum sex a Spoletio miliaribus semotum, ubi sublicius pons Narem iungens iter Spoletio ad Montem Leonem oppidum Cassiamque et Leonessam ac ad castella circiter octo monasterii Ferentili praebet. Et inferius Narem quoque iungit pons lapideus ad oppidum Haronem, infra quod oppidum fluvius Nar Velini amnis lacusque casu mirabili adaugetur. Is amnis Velinus in Apennino binos habet fontes, primum remotiusque apud oppidum Civitatem Regalem appellatum, et alterum apud Interdochum oppidum.

14   Delapsusque ad civitatem Reatinam Velinus eam intersecat paene mediam, de qua Livius libro XXVI[50] adventum Hannibalis ad urbem Romam describens, Coelium dicit scriptorem iter ab Reate et Cutiliis ordiri. Ea civitas (sicut recte opinari videor) Vespasianum genuit, et Titum ac Domitianum filios, imperatores Romanos — quandoquidem vicus Phennae, a quo ipsi duxere originem, non solum in Reatino agro sed Reati propinquus[51] est. Dicit tamen Suetonius, a quo haec sumpsimus, Phennae vicum modicum in Samnio esse — sicut iure optimo Reatina civitas est ponenda, quae Thomam nunc habet Morronum eloquentia et singulari memoria praeditum. Progressus parvo ab Reate spatio Velinus amnis e multis rivulis et fontibus, quorum unum 'Neptumni' appellatum dicit Plinius, alio atque alio exoriri Velinum facit lacum,

stretch of mountains directly facing Spoleto. This side of the Nera is Visso, an ancient town some twenty miles distant from Cerreto and practically under the peaks of the Apennines. The Nera, *which originates high up in the Apennines*,[55] flows past the walls of Visso. Vergil writes of it: "The river Nar, white with its sulfurous waters."[56] The source of the Nera is noteworthy for a reason passed down to us by our forebears but apparent in the word itself: the double spring from which the river begins flows out of two orifices which have the appearance of the nostrils [*nares*] of some animal on the rocky mountain top. Following the bank of the Nera down past Cerreto and Ponte, one comes upon the town of Scheggino, six miles from Spoleto, where a pile bridge spanning the Nera provides a route from Spoleto to the towns of Monteleone, Cascia, and Leonessa, and to the eight or so castles of the monastery of Ferentillo. Below Scheggino, a stone bridge at the town of Arrone also spans the Nera, and below Arrone, it is augmented by the marvelous waterfall of the river (and lake) Velino.[57] The Velino has two sources in the Apennines: the first and more remote at the town called Cittareale, the other at the town of Antrodoco.

Descending to the city of Rieti, the river Velino passes more or less through the middle of it. In his description of Hannibal's advance on Rome, Livy mentions in Book XXVI that the historian Coelius has Hannibal's journey starting from Rieti and Contigliano.[58] I believe I am right in saying that Rieti bore the Roman emperors Vespasian and his sons Titus and Domitian, in that the village of Phenna, where those emperors originated, is not only in the territory of Rieti but close to the city. Yet Suetonius (from whom I have taken this) says that the little village of Phenna is in Samnium,[59] where indeed Rieti should properly be placed. Rieti now boasts Tommaso Morroni, a man blessed with eloquence and an extraordinary memory.[60] Not far in its course out of Rieti, the river Velino causes the formation of Lake Velino from a succession of rivulets and springs, one of which Pliny says

nunc a Pede Luci, propinquo oppido, vocitatum. Prius vero quam in lacum tot colligantur aquae, paludes efficiunt, in quibus tantummodo scripsit in *Admirandis* Cicero ungulas iumentorum indurari. In eo autem lacu Italiae umbilicum esse M. Varronem scripsisse refert Plinius.

15   Decidit autem eo ex lacu in Narem idem fluvius alta rupe, in quo exitu saxum crescere dicit Plinius. Sonitumque facit eius[52] in Narem amnem casus, qui decimo exauditur milliario. Cum tamen eundem ob casum fumus ascendat perpetuus, aerem in sublime obnubilans et spumans cum in fundum cadit aqua, scintillas exsilire facit, quae apud Interamniam sexto distantem milliario conspiciuntur. Vergilius in VII: 'Est locus Hesperiae medio, sub montibus altis, nobilis et fama multis memoratus in oris, Amsancti valles. Densis hunc frondibus atrum urget utrumque latus nemoris, medioque fragosis dat sonitum saxis et toto vertice torrens. Hic specus horrendum et saevi spiracula Ditis monstrantur, ruptoque ingens Acheronte vorago pestiferas aperit fauces, et cetera.' Servius sic exponit: 'Hunc locum Italiae umbilicum[53] cosmographi dicunt. Est autem in latere Campaniae et Apuliae iuxta Venusium, ubi Hirpini sunt, et habet aquas sulphureas, ideo graviores, quia ambitur silvis. Ideo ibi dicitur aditus infernorum, quod gravis odor iuxta accedentes necat, adeo ut victimae circa hunc locum non immolarentur sed odore perirent ad aquam applicatae: hoc erat genus litationis. Sciendum est tamen Varronem enumerare quot loca in Italia sunt huiusmodi. Unde Donatus dicit Lucaniae[54] esse, qui describitur locus a poeta, circa fluvium qui Calor vocatur. Quod ideo non procedit, quia [cum] ait "Italiae medio." "Sub montibus

was called Neptumni,[61] a lake now known as Lago di Piediluco from the neighboring town. Before all these waters coalesce into a lake, they form swamps in which alone the hooves of animals harden, as Cicero wrote in his *Marvels*.[62] Pliny says that Marcus Varro located the navel of Italy at the lake.[63]

The same river comes out of the lake and falls from a high cliff 15 into the Nera. Pliny says stone forms where the water escapes.[64] The crash of the Velino into the Nera makes a noise that can be heard ten miles away. Yet though spray is constantly thrown up by the cascading river, making the air on high dense with clouds and foaming up when it falls back into the depths as water, it throws out bolts of light that can be seen at Terni six miles away. Vergil writes in Book VII: "There is a place beneath high mountains in the middle of Hesperia, renowned and heard of in many lands, the Vale of Amsanctus. Flanks of forest, dark with dense leaves, close in on either side, and in its midst a broken torrent utters a roar with its rocks and whirling eddies. Here are disclosed an awful cavern and the vents of savage Dis, and where Acheron bursts forth, a vast abyss that opens jaws of death, etc."[65] Servius has this explanation: "Geographers say that this place is the navel of Italy. It is on the border of Campania and Apulia, near Venosa,[66] where the Hirpini live,[67] and it has sulfurous waters, the more oppressive because it is surrounded by forest. They say there is an entrance to the underworld there, because a suffocating stench kills those who come near to it, so much so that sacrificial animals in the vicinity were not slaughtered but perished of the stench when they come into contact with the water: this was a kind of soothsaying. One should realize, however, that Varro catalogues all the places in Italy that have this quality. On that basis Donatus says the poet is describing a place in Lucania by a river named Calore. But that cannot be right, because Vergil says 'in the middle of Italy.' And 'Under high hills:' this doesn't square with the facts either, unless you take it to refer to the whole of Italy, so that it would mean 'the

altis": hoc, nisi ad totam Italiam referas, non procedit, ut[55] sit, [non] "est in vallibus Italiae montuosae." Nam in hoc loco montes penitus non sunt.' Servius autem, cuius sunt praedicta verba, non minus a me quam Donatus ab eo reprehendi potest, quia iuxta Venusium non est Italiae medium, sed in hoc lacu Velino — sicut a Marco Varrone habetur. Et licet Venusii locus nobilis sit et habeat circa valles 'sanctas', scilicet fertiles, tamen non habet mirabilem fertilitatem quam hic habuit Velinus, quando a principio fuit exsiccatus. Nam ipse idem Servius, verba Vergilii alio in loco exponens, 'Rosea rura Velini,' dicit: 'lacus iuxta agrum, qui Rosulanus vocatur', *unde etiam Rosa dicitur totus ager qui a Reate ad Velinum pertinet lacum.*[56] 'Varro tamen dicit lacum hunc a quodam consule in Narem fluvium derivatum. Post quod tanta est consecuta fertilitas ut perticae longitudinem altitudo superaret herbarum. Quin etiam per diem quantum demptum esset, tantum per noctem crescebat.' Unde Plinius libro VIII: 'Caesar Vopiscus cum causam apud censores ageret, campos Rosiae dixit Italiae sumen esse, in quibus perticas pridie desectum gramen operiret.' Dicitur ergo notanter Vergilium significasse hanc soli fertilitatem per verbum 'Amsancti,' quod ipse Servius exponit: 'omni ex parte sancti.' Et cum cetera congruant, medium Italiae, altitudo montium, casus fluvii, et lacus, qui speciem prae se ferat spiraculorum saevi Ditis, hunc Velini casum in Narem locum esse Italiae medio a Vergilio descriptum ostendunt.

16   Interamnia est prima in ordine superiore post Spoletum, civitas vetusta, quam Livius libro XXVII dicit unam fuisse ex coloniis Romanis duodeviginti, quae difficillimis per Hannibalis praesentiam Romani populi rebus militiam et collationem tributorum detractaverunt. Cuius prata dicit Plinius quater in anno irrigua secari

place is in a vale of mountainous Italy,' for there, at the river Calore, there are no mountains at all."[68] But I must criticize Servius, whose words these are, no less than he criticized Donatus, because the middle of Italy is not around Venosa but in this lake Velino, exactly as Varro has it. And though Venosa is "renowned" as a place, and though it does have around it "sacred" valleys (that is, fertile), yet it does not have the marvelous fertility that Velino had, being from the outset reclaimed land. For Servius himself, expounding Vergil's words elsewhere, "the Rosean country of Velino,"[69] has this to say: "The lake beside the territory called Ager Rosulanus." *Whence the whole territory stretching from Rieti to lake Velinus is called Rosa.*[70] "But Varro says that some consul drained the lake off into the river Nera. This brought about such fertility that grass would grow taller than a ten-foot perch. In fact, as much would grow back by night as had been cut down in the day."[71] And so Pliny in Book VIII: "When he was pleading a case before the censors, Caesar Vopiscus said that the fields of Rosea — where grass cut back the previous day would cover poles on the next — were the udder of Italy."[72] Therefore Servius speaks with authority when he says that by the name *Amsanctus* Vergil was indicating the fertility of the soil. Servius himself explains it as "sacred in every part."[73] And because all the other elements correspond — the middle of Italy, the lofty mountains, the waterfall, and the lake (which presents the appearance of "the vents of savage Dis") — they show that this descent of the river Velino into the Nera was the place in the middle of Italy that Vergil describes.

In the order used above, Terni comes next after Spoleto, an ancient city that Livy in Book XXVII says was one of eighteen colonies that, at a time of the greatest difficulty for the Roman people owing to the presence of Hannibal, declined contributions of soldiers and money.[74] Pliny says that the meadows of Terni were harvested four times a year when watered, three times when not[75] — something which the proximity of the river Nar apparently brings

16

et non irrigua ter, quod Naris illam circumeuntis vicinitas efficere videtur. Ornatur ea civitas Johanne Macincollo, Camerae Apostolicae Auditore, legum ac bonarum artium studiis decorato.

17   Prius vero quam ad Naris fluenta ulterius prosequamur, omissa[57] secundum Tiberim repetamus. Postquam amnis Chiasius in Tiberim est delapsus, primum adiacet haud procul Tiberi oppidum Diruta, populo frequentatum. Deinde Ameria civitas vetustissima. Nam M. Cato,[58] sicut refert Plinius, eam ante Persei[59] bellum annis nongentis sexaginta[60] quatuor conditam prodidit. Vergilius in *Bucolicis:* 'Amerina retinacula.' Et Servius exponit: 'virgas quibus vites ligantur, quae virgae abundant circa Ameriam.' Fuitque Roscio olim ornata cive, quem Marcus Cicero parricidii accusatum contra Sullae dominantis potentiam defendit. Patrem enim Roscii, hominem locupletem et bonum, sed magis quam par esset erga filium inclementem, clam occiderunt quidam, filiusque per occasionem discordiarum quasi paternae caedis auctor ab iisdem interfectoribus accusabatur. Praeda ad Chrysogonum quendam Lucii Sullae satellitem redibat. Nemine itaque ob Sullae metum audente defensionem suscipere, innocentem bonumque adulescentem defendit Cicero, qui in Sullano exercitu militaverat. Fuitque postea Roscius tantae in histrionia excellentiae ut Cicero et ceteri florentissimae illius aetatis viri recitantem sedulo audirent. Qui adeo doctus fuit ut librum scripserit, in quo histrioniam eloquentiae comparavit. Interius est Tudertum, civitas vetusta, sive, ut Plinius appellat, Tuder, tertio Martino pontifice Romano cive ornata, cui multa subsunt oppida et castella Tiberis ripas et colles montesque adiacentes complentia — sed minime digna quae describendo singillatim[61] prosequamur.

18   Proxime vero illis atque etiam Interamniae, nisi medius interesset Nar, est Sanctus Geminus, praestans in regione oppidum.

about as it flows around the city. Terni is ornamented by the Auditor of the Apostolic Chamber, Giovanni Mazzancolli, noted for his study of law and the liberal arts.[76]

Now before we pursue the course of the Nera further, we should return to those places along the Tiber that were left out. After the river Chiascio joins the Tiber, the first place we come to is the bustling town of Deruta, not far from the Tiber. Then comes the very ancient city of Amelia — Pliny tells us that Marcus Cato stated that it was founded 974 years before the war with Perseus.[77] Vergil mentions "ties from Amelia" in the *Georgics*,[78] and Servius explains: "Wicker strips for tying up vines, branches that are abundant around Amelia."[79] Amelia could once boast of her citizen Roscius, whom Cicero defended on a charge of murdering his father against the power of Sulla, then at its height.[80] Certain persons secretly killed Roscius' father, a wealthy and good man, but harder on his son than he should have been. The murderers took the opportunity of the family quarrels to accuse the son of being responsible for his father's death. The proceeds of the murder would have accrued to Lucius Sulla's henchman, one Chrysogonus. No one else daring to mount a defense of Roscius for fear of Sulla,[81] Cicero — who had been a soldier in Sulla's army — defended the blameless and virtuous young man. Roscius later attained such pre-eminence in the actor's craft that Cicero and the other men of that brilliant age would listen rapt to his recitals. He was so accomplished that he wrote a book comparing the actor's art to oratory.[82] Further inland is the ancient city of Todi (Tudertum, or as Pliny calls it, Tuder),[83] graced by her citizen, the Roman pontiff Martin III.[84] Beneath Todi are many towns and castles that occupy the Tiber banks and the adjacent hills and mountains, but not worth pursuing with detailed individual treatment.

Close to these towns, and, were it not for the river Nera in the way, to Terni too, is Sangemini, a prominent Umbrian town. Terni

17

18

Estque ab Interamnia sexto milliario a Narnia, arduo in colle sita, a profluenti Nare dicta, quam Livius et Plinius Nequinum[62] fuisse dictam affirmant, et quae una fuit coloniarum quae, Hannibale Italiam premente, militiam et collationem tributorum detractarunt. In eius agro dicit Plinius scripsisse in *Admirandis* Ciceronem terram esse, ex qua siccitate lutum fiat, imbre pulvis. De Narnia Martialis sic dicit: 'Narnia sulphureo quam gurgite candidus amnis circuit, ancipiti vix adeunda iugo.' Haec pontem habuit superbissimi operis nunc dirutum, de quo Martialis: 'Sed iam parce mihi nec abutere, Narnia, Quinto: perpetuo liceat sic tibi ponte frui.' Ea civitas vetustissima, civili divisione alias aetate nostra sed magis magisque proximo tempore lacerata, horrendas suorum mortes vidit; Gattamelatam autem genuit, clarissimum belli ductorem. Et nunc Berardum habet Spoletinum episcopum, civilis et pontificii iuris excellentia celeberrimum. Septimo inde milliario in via item Flaminia est Ocriculum vetusti nominis oppidum, ultra quod Sabinae regionis fines Tiberim attingunt. Livius in IX: 'Ocriculani sponsione in amicitiam accepti'. Et in XXII dicit Fabium dictatorem via Flaminia profectum obviam consuli exercituique, cum ad Tiberim circa Ocriculum conspexisset agmen, viatorem misisse qui nuntiaret ut sine lictoribus ad dictatorem veniret.

19   Igitur a Velino lacu repetentes omnem ex veteri Umbria nobis reliquam regionem, ea quae ipsum Velinum et Reatinam urbem, Tiberim, Anienem flumina ad lacum Marsorum interiacent explicemus. Maximus autem is est montium et camporum globus,

is six miles from Narni, the latter set high on a hill and named for
the river Nar which flows past it; according to Livy and Pliny it
was formerly known as Nequinum.[85] Narnia was one of those colonies which declined to contribute soldiers and money when Hannibal was threatening Italy.[86] Pliny says that Cicero wrote in his
Marvels that there was land in the district of Narnia where mud
formed in time of drought, and dust when it rained.[87] Martial has
this to say of the place: "Narnia, circled by your river white with
sulfurous flood, hard of access on your double ridge."[88] Narnia had
a bridge of splendid workmanship, now in ruins, on which Martial
writes: "But come now, spare me, Narnia, and don't overdo it with
my friend Quintus: so may it be yours to enjoy your bridge for
ever."[89] This very ancient city (which produced Gattamelata, the
famous general)[90] has been torn apart by civil unrest at various
points in modern times but has of late seen ever more of her citizens meet a terrible end. She now claims Berardo Eroli, the
bishop of Spoleto, much celebrated for his mastery of civil and
canon law.[91] Seven miles from Narni, also on the Via Flaminia, is
the town of Otricoli, an ancient foundation, beyond which the
Sabine territory reaches the Tiber. Livy writes in Book IX: "The
Otricolans entered into an undertaking with Rome and were ad-
mitted to her friendship."[92] And in Book XXII he says that the
dictator Fabius set out along the Via Flaminia to meet the consul
and his army, and when he caught sight of the column in the
neighborhood of Otricoli by the Tiber, he sent an orderly to in-
form the consul that he should report to the dictator without
lictors.[93]

And so as we return from Lake Velino to the remaining portion 19
of old Umbria, let us give an account of those lands lying between
Velino and the city of Rieti and the rivers Tiber and Aniene, as far
as the Lake of the Marsians [i.e., the Fucine Lake]. This consti-
tutes a great mass of mountains and plains of which not even the
inhabitants have an adequate knowledge. There were many places

quem nec incolae satis norunt, et in quo multa fuerunt prisci vocabuli loca quae praesentibus conferri nequeunt, tum quia interierunt quaedam, tum quia incomprehensibilis mutatio in aliis est
facta. Erant autem olim haec omnia Sabinae loca regionis omnium
Italiae vetustissimae. Nam videmus Vergilium dicere ante inditum
nomen Italiae Oenotros illam coluisse. Et Oenotriam fuisse constat Sabinorum tractum, quod docet Servius, in VII, super verbo
'Oenotria tellus.' Romanos etiam originem habuisse a Sabinis per
'raptum mulierum' constat. Unde est quod dicit Vergilius: 'in parte
est data Roma Sabinis.' 'Et factum inter Romulum et Titum Tatium foedus per quod recepti sunt in urbem Sabini, ea lege ut in
omnibus essent cives Romani, nisi in ferendis suffragiis. Nam magistratus non creabant.' Dicimus ergo fuisse in Sabinorum montibus, qui nunc Reate inter et Sabinam praesentis temporis regionem altissimi cernuntur: 'Tetricae horrentis rupes, Montemque
Severum,' et Casperiam ac Forulos civitates. Fuerunt etiam 'Arcades, genus a Pallante profectum, qui regem Evandrum comites
sunt secuti', et Himella fluvius.

20   His generatim dictis, notiora particulariter explicemus. Primum est a Velini in Narem casu Sabinos nostri temporis petentibus Colles Scipionis, oppidum populo frequentatum, deinde
Mons Bonus et Teranum castella fluviolo propinqua, qui, nunc
nomine carens, Himella fuit ex montibus oriundus, quos Vergilius
supra docuit casui Velini in Narem imminere, et inter Ocriculum
ac Mallianum cadens in Tiberim. Ab ipso autem Imelae ortu apud
Pedelucum oppidum montes incipiunt, qui sinistra civitate Reatina perpetuo in meridiem tractu continui semperque crescentes
et quam longissime ab Apennino recedentes Aequicolorum olim,

there with an ancient name that cannot be matched with the present-day places, not only because some have ceased to exist but also because in other cases a bewildering transformation of the name has taken place. All these places belonged once to the Sabine territory, the most ancient in Italy. We note that Vergil says that the Oenotrians dwelt in Italy before it even had a name.[94] It is commonly accepted that Oenotria was a "Sabine region," as Servius tells us in commenting on the words "the land of Oenotria" in *Aeneid* Book VII.[95] It is also agreed that the Romans had their origin in "the rape of the Sabine women."[96] Hence Vergil's saying, "Rome was shared with the Sabines."[97] "An agreement was reached between Romulus and Titus Tatius by which the Sabines were welcomed into the city of Rome, on condition that they would be Roman citizens in all respects but the franchise, for they would not elect magistrates."[98] And so I say that Oenotria was a region in the mountains of the Sabines, now seen at their highest between Rieti and the present-day Sabine region: "Tetrica's rugged cliffs and Mons Severus," and the cities of Casperia and Foruli.[99] There were Arcadians too, "a race sprung from Pallas, companions and followers of King Evander,"[100] and the river Imelle.[101]

Having made these general observations, let us explain the more notable features of the Sabine land. A traveler making his way into the modern Sabine country from the fall of the Velino into the Nera first encounters the populous town of Collescipoli. Then come the castles of Montebuono and Tarano near a little river which, though lacking a name now, was the Imelle; as we learned from Vergil above, the Imelle rises in the mountains that overlook the fall of the Velino into the Nera and flows down into the Tiber between Otrícoli and Magliano Sabina. From the very source of the river Imelle at Lago di Piediluco, a mountain range rises and continues ever southward, with the city of Rieti on the left, growing in height and leaving the Apennines far behind as it hugs the mountains of Tagliacozzo (formerly the mountains of the

20

nunc Taliacotii, montibus proxime adhaerent Tiburque feruntur. Quos quidem montes, si vetustiora quaerimus, Arcades incoluerunt, et 'Tetricae horrentis rupes' Monsque olim Severus Mons Sancti Johannis nunc, et Mons Niger dicuntur. Supraque eos dextrorsum est oppidulum[63] Caput Farfari, dictum quod eo in loco Farfarus amnis habet[64] originem, qui fama notissimus Sabinam regionem praesentis temporis mediam dividit. Imelae autem sinistrorsum est propinquum villae nunc oppidum Vacuna appellatum, cuius meminit Horatius ad Aristium: 'Haec tibi dictabam post fanum putre Vacunae.' Acronque exponit Vacunam apud Sabinos plurimum cultam. Eam quidam Minervam, alii Dianam putaverunt, nonnulli Venerem. Sed 'Varro *Rerum Divinarum* primo, Victoriam esse ait, quod ea maxime hi gaudent, qui sapientiae vacant.' Imelae vero dextrorsum imminet Mallianum, civili cultu habitatum et primarium hoc tempore regionis Sabinae oppidum.

21 Post arduum montem, in quo Mallianum est, descendentes in Sabinae mediterranea vallem inveniunt, ut in montuosa regione, amplam, in qua Imelae fluvio proxima est Sanctae Mariae Sanctique Euthymi ecclesia, Sabinae regionis episcopium. Cui dextrorsum adiacet oppidum Turres, pro Curibus vetustissimis, Numae Pompilii patria, appellatum. Beatus enim Gregorius in *Registro* scribit Gratioso episcopo Nomentano:[65] 'Curam gubernationemque Sancti Euthymi ecclesiae Curium in Sabinorum territorio constitutae tibi providimus committendam.' Nomentum namque regioni Sabinae ad hanc urbi Romae conterminam partem continet. Quam urbem Seneca, *Epistula* quinta supra centesimam, dicit aerem habere insalubrem, unde nunc penitus derelicta est. Martialis autem coquus poeta cum villam ibi possederit, eam saepenumero laudat: 'Nomentana meum tibi dat vindemia Bacchum. Si te Quintus emat, commodiora bibas.' Et de rosa tractans, sic habet:

Aequicoli) and carries on to Tivoli. To go back to the remote past, these mountains were inhabited by the Arcadians, and "Tetrica's rugged cliffs" and the former Mons Severus are now called Monte S. Giovanni and Montenero respectively. Above these to the right there is the village of Castelnuovo di Farfa, so called because the famous river Farfa originates there, thereafter running through the middle of the present-day Sabine country. To the left of the river Imelle is a town now called Vacone, near the villa that Horace mentions to Aristius: "I'm writing this letter behind Vacuna's crumbling temple."[102] Acron explains that the goddess Vacuna was much venerated by the Sabines. She has been variously identified as Minerva, Diana, or Venus. But Varro "in Book I of his *Human and Divine Antiquities* says that she is Victory, because those with time for philosophy specially rejoice in her."[103] Magliano Sabina— a very civilised place and now the most important town of the Sabine region—overlooks the river Imelle to the right.

Descending into the interior of the Sabine country beyond the steep hill on which Magliano is set, you find a valley—spacious for a valley in the mountains. Here there is the church of Santa Maria and Sant'Eutimio, the cathedral of the Sabine region, beside the river Imelle: next to it on the right lies the town of Torri, called after the ancient Cures, the home of Numa Pompilius. St. Gregory in his *Correspondence* writes to Gratiosus, the bishop of Mentana: "We have provided that you should be entrusted with the care and governance of the church of St. Euthymius of Cures in the Sabine territory."[104] (Mentana is adjacent to the Sabine region, the part where it borders on Rome.) In *Letter* 105, Seneca says that the air of the city is unhealthy, which is why it is now completely abandoned.[105] The poet Martial the cook, however, praises the villa he owned at Mentana again and again: "A Mentanan vintage provides you with this wine of mine. Should Quintus buy you, you will drink better."[106] And in discussing roses he writes as follows: "Whether you were born in Paestum's fields or in Tibur's, whether

21

'Seu tu Paestanis[66] genita es, seu Tiburis arvis, seu rubuit tellus Tuscula flore tuo, seu Praenestino te villica legit in horto, seu modo Campani gloria ruris eras: pulchrior ut nostro videare corona Sabino, de Nomentano te putet esse meo.' Nomentumque cive ornatum fuit praestanti Crescentio, qui dignitatem consularem Eugenii III et quinti decimi Johannis pontificum Romanorum temporibus, omnium ultimus resumere ac aliquamdiu retinere est ausus. Habuitque pro arce Hadriani molem ab ipso postea Castrum Crescentii appellatam.

22 Supra Cures sinistrorsum in montibus sunt castella: Stronconum,[67] Mons Calvus, et Sanctus Petrus. Inferius ad dexteram, Cotanellum, Rocha Antiqua et aspera, secus quam torrens labitur Calentinus brevi cursu in Tiberim cadens. Cotanellum etiam et Rocham Antiquam supereminent colles ardui, ultra quos Buccinianum est oppidum, et superius oppidum Sancti Petri. Inter Calentinum etiam et Mallianum oppidum sunt castella: Collis Vetus, Stemiliana, Furanum, Gabinianum. Transmissoque Calentino, castellum est in colle Poggium Mirtetum, cui torrentulus adiacet Rivus Solis dictus. Videturque is esse quem Horatius, in primo *Epistularum*, sic describit: 'Me quoties reficit gelidus Digentia rivus, quem Mandela bibit, rugosus frigore pagus, quid sentire putas, quid credis, amice, precari?' Et Acron exponit: 'Mandela pagus in Sabinis, ubi rivus Digentia.' Supraque eius rivi fontem dextrorsum est Montopolis oppidum, publicam cuius aream innatum ferrei coloris obdurumque sternit saxum. Dedit vero Montopolis magnum huius saeculi Sabinis ornamentum, Petrum Odum, qui grammaticus Romae celeber Nasonianam Flaccianamque simul in omni carminum genere facultatem facilitatemque est nactus.

23 Sequitur ad Tiberim Farfari amnis ostium, fuitque is fluvius priscis temporibus Farfar et Fabaris appellatus. Nam Servius dicit

Tusculum's soil blushed with your bloom, or a bailiff's wife picked you in her garden at Praeneste, or you were lately the glory of Campania's countryside: to make you a more beautiful garland in my friend Sabinus's eyes, let him think you come from my place at Mentana."[107] Mentana was distinguished by her famous citizen Crescentius, who was the last to dare to revive the office of consul, and hold on to it for some time, in the days of the Roman pontiffs Eugenius III and John XV. He used the Castel S. Angelo as his fortress, later called the "Fort of Crescentius" after him.[108]

Above Torri in the hills to the left are the castles of Stroncone, 22 Calvi dell'Umbria, and San Pietro. Beneath Torri to the right are Cottanello and Roccantica ("antique", indeed, and rugged too), beside which flows the Calentino stream, which after a short while joins the Tiber. Steep hills tower above Cottanello and Roccantica, and beyond them is the town of Bocchignano, and above it Castel San Pietro. Between the Calentino and the town of Magliano are the castles of Collevecchio, Stimigliano, Forano, and Gavignano Sabino. Crossing the Calentino, one comes to a castle on a hill, Poggio Mirteto, which has a little stream next to it called the Rio Sole. This would seem to be the stream that Horace describes in *Epistles* I in the following manner: "Every time I regain my health in the icy Digentia — the stream drunk by Mandela, that village wrinkled with cold — what, my friend, do you suppose I feel? what do you imagine I pray for?"[109] Acron comments: "Mandela is a village in the Sabine country where the stream Digentia is."[110] Beyond the source of the stream, on the right, is the town of Montopoli, its piazza paved with a hard natural stone the color of iron. Montopoli has produced one of the great glories of our time in Pietro Odo, a famous scholar in Rome who displays the power and ease of an Ovid or a Horace in poetry of every kind.[111]

The mouth of the Farfa follows at the Tiber, a river that was 23 called "Farfar" or "Fabaris" in antiquity — Servius tells us that the river was also called "Farfarus" as it passed through the Sabine

Fabarim esse fluvium qui per Sabinos transiens et Farfarus dicitur; unde Plautus: 'dissipabo te tamquam folia Farfari'; Ovidius vero: 'et amoenae Farfaris undae', prout certe nunc etiam sunt amoenissimae. Longissimo enim tractu postquam Farfarus montes reliquit, per plana labitur culta opacis undique tectus arboribus. Qua quidem in amoenissima planitie, monasterium ipsi fluvio dextrorsum imminet amplissimum Farfense appellatum, castella ad decem possidens, quorum primum, Fara dictum, colli impositum est monasterio imminenti. Et illi dextrorsum adiacet oppidum Poggium Curesii,[68] a Curesio amne subtus delabente vocatum, quem quidem fluvium Alliam prisco nomine dictum fuisse constat. Farfensi etiam monasterio dextrorsum imminet Nerula, oppidum nobile. Superius sunt Scandrilia, Tophia, Mons Sanctae Mariae, Fraxum, Poggium Donadeum, Salixanum, Poggium *Sancti Laurentii, et in supremis*[69] Poggium Maiani.

24 Haec vero vallis quam Farfarus efficit, tam multis habitatam castellis, illa esse videtur in qua Horatius villam habuit. Montes enim, quos a Pedeluco Tibur usque continuari ostendimus, hac sola valle interrumpuntur. Horatius ad Quintum: 'scribetur tibi forma loquaciter et situs agri. Continui montes, ni dissocientur opaca valle, sed ut veniens dextrum latus aspiciat sol, laevum discedens curru fugiente vaporet, temperiem laudes. Quid, si rubicunda benigni corna vepres et pruna ferant, et quercus et ilex multa fruge pecus, multa dominum iuvet umbra?' Scribit etiam Horatius in primo *Carminum, ut videtur*[70] de eodem, sic: 'Velox amoenum saepe Lucretilem mutat Lycaeo Faunus et igneam defendit aestatem capellis usque meis pluviosque ventos.' Et Acron exponit Lucretilem esse montem in Sabinis. Ex eaque villa vinum fuit vile, sicut in frigidis locis nasci videmus, quod Horatius Maecenati misit cum his versibus: 'Vile potabis modicis Sabinum cantharis, Graeca quod ego ipse testa conditum levi, datus in theatro cum tibi plausus.' Erat etiam in huius villae agro silva, de qua Horatius *Carminum* item primo *sic*[71] scribit: 'Namque me silva lupus

country.[112] So Plautus: "I shall scatter you like the leaves of Far-far," and Ovid: "And Farfar's pleasant waves,"[113] — and they cer-tainly are very pleasant even now, for after a long passage through the mountains the Farfa leaves them behind and glides through cultivated plains, sheltered on all sides by shady trees. In this at-tractive valley, a very large monastery called the Abbazia di Farfa overlooks the river on the right.[114] It owns some ten castles, the first of them, called Fara in Sabina, set on a hill above the monas-tery. To the right, the town of Poggio Corese lies next to Fara, named after the river Corese that flows beneath it: it is thought that the original name of the river was the Allia.[115] The well-known town of Nerola is above Abbazia di Farfa on the right. Higher up are Scandriglia, Toffia, Monte Santa Maria, Frasso Sabino, Poggio Nativo, Salisano, Poggio *San Lorenzo, and highest of all, Poggio*[116] Maiano.

This valley that the Farfa creates, so full of castles, seems to be 24 the one where Horace had his farm. For the hills — which stretch from Piediluco to Tivoli, as I said — are broken only by this valley. Horace writes to Quinctius: "I shall write you a chatty account of the nature and site of my place: there are hills one after another, save where interrupted by a shady valley, so that the sun in its morning approach looks on the right side and warms the left as it speeds away in its flying car — you'd praise its mildness. What would you say if you knew that my bushes grow lots of red cornels and plums, that the oak and ilex delight the herd with plenty of acorns, and the owner with plenty of shade?"[117] Horace again writes, *apparently* about the same place, in *Odes* I: "Quick Faunus often exchanges Lycaeus for charming Lucretilis and protects my goats from the fiery summer heat and the rainy winds."[118] Acron comments that Lucretilis is a mountain in the Sabine country.[119] The farm produced an inferior wine, as we know happens in cold locations. Horace sent some of it to Maecenas with these verses: "You'll drink cheap Sabine wine from modest cups: I bottled and

in Sabina, dum meam canto Lalagen et ultra terminum curis vagor expeditus, fugit inermem.' Fuitque Horatio tam grata haec villa ut *Carminum* tertio scribat: 'Cur valle permutem Sabina divitias operosiores?' Et infra eiusdem villae fontem sic laudat: 'O fons Bandusiae splendidior vitro, dulci digne mero, non sine floribus cras donaberis haedo.' Et infra: 'Te flagrans atrox hora Caniculae nescit tangere, tu frigus amabile fessis vomere tauris praebes et pecori vago. Fies nobilium tu quoque fontium, me dicente cavis impositam ilicem saxis, unde loquaces lymphae desiliunt tuae,' ut non sit mirandum si Horatius, ad hanc veniens villam, fidem amico fefellit, sicut his versibus: 'Quinque dies tibi pollicitus me rure futurum, Sextilem totum mendax desideror.'

25   Sequuntur ad Tiberim fluvii Curesii sive Alliae ostia, ubi Sabinae regionis olim finis erat et Crustumii[72] incipiebant. Quorum populorum locorumque appellationem Plinius scribit sexto decimo ab urbe Roma milliario post Sabinos inchoasse et Veientes ab ipsis Crustuminis[73] e regione positis *Tiberi*[74] fuisse divisos. Unde Mons Rotundus Ursinae, Palumbaria Sabellae familiarum urbis Romae patriciarum, oppida ut in regione opulentissima, in Crustumeriis adnumeranda erunt. Allia vero fluvius est de quo Vergilius: 'Quosque secans infaustum interfluit, Allia, nomen.' Et

sealed it in a Greek jar myself on the day you received the theater's applause."[120] There was also a wood on Horace's land, and he writes of it, again in *Odes* I, *as follows:* "While I was singing of my Lalage and wandering without a care in the Sabine woods beyond the bounds of my estate, a wolf fled from me, unarmed though I was."[121] Horace was so fond of his estate that he could write in *Odes* III: "Why should I change my Sabine valley for the heavier burden of wealth?"[122] Further on he praises a spring of the same villa, in these words: "Spring of Bandusia, brighter than crystal, deserving of sweet wine and our garlands, tomorrow we'll honor you with a kid."[123] And below: "The implacable hour of the blazing dog-star cannot touch you; you offer your lovely coolness to bullocks weary of the plow, and to wandering flocks. And you too will become one of the famous fountains, as I write of the oak planted over the hollowed rocks where your clear babbling waters run down."[124] It is no surprise that when he went to his villa Horace broke his promise to his friend, as he relates in these lines: "Though I promised you that I would be off in the country just five days, false to my word, I am absent this whole month of August."[125]

Next comes the debouchment of the river Corese (or Allia) 25 into the Tiber, where the Sabine region once ended and the territory of Crustumium began. Pliny writes that the name Crustumium, as applied to people and places, began beyond the Sabine country sixteen miles from Rome, and that the territory of Veii was separated from that of Crustumium directly opposite it *by the Tiber.*[126] The towns of Monterotondo and Palombara Sabina, which belong to the noble Roman families of the Orsini and Savelli respectively, are therefore to be accounted part of Crustumerium, as being the wealthiest towns in the area. The river Allia is in the region of Crustumerium, on which Vergil writes: "and those whom Allia, unlucky name, flows between and divides."[127] Servius comments: "The Allia is a river not far from

Servius exponit: 'Allia fluvius haud longe ab Urbe est, iuxta quem Galli, Brenno duce, XV Kalendas Augusti, deleto Romanorum exercitu, postridie deleverunt Urbem'. Quam historiam Livius in VI diffuse narrat: unde dies illa Alliensis dicta prae ceteris omnibus nefasta semper est habita. Fidenae dehinc describendae inter Montem Rotundum Anienemque et Tiberim fuerunt, de quibus in Latina regione et in Etruria Veios describentes, quorum colonia erant, abunde diximus. Ornata fuit Sabina regio Landone Romano pontifice, cuius patriam ignoramus. Postquam ager Sabinus Crustuminusque[75] cum fluvio Allia Monteque Rotundo post tergum est relictus, Anio fluvius tertio a Roma milliario fertur in Tiberim.

Regio quinta. Picenum sive Marchia Anconitana[1]

1 Sed iam perventum est ad fines omnes ducatus Spoletini, Anioque fluvius nos traxerat ad loca in Latinorum partibus a Strabone Plinioque enumerata. Quare pedem referentes ad propinquam conterminamque regionem transeamus, quae olim Picenum dicta, nunc est Marchia Anconitana, cum tamen aliquando prius fuerit appellata Marchia Firmana. Nam in gestis rebus septimi Gregorii Romani pontificis in concilio Lateranensi legimus Robertum Guiscardum, quia Marchiam occupasset Firmanam fuisse excommunicatum. Piceni fines sunt: a septentrione, Apenninus (ipsum[2] a ducatu Spoletano, ut ostendimus, dividens); et ab oriente, praesertim hiemali, fluvius olim Isaurus, nunc Folia dictus; a meridie, Superum Mare prius; dehinc fluvius Troentus Asculum praeterlabens.

2 Livius libro XXII Hannibalis progressus describens, post inflictam ad lacum Trasumenum populo Romano cladem, dicit eum venisse in agrum Picenum, non copia solum omnis generis frugum

Rome beside which the Gauls under Brennus crushed the Roman
army on the 18th of July, and destroyed Rome itself the following
day."[128] Livy gives an extended account of this in Book VI:[129] why
that day, called the *Dies Alliensis*, was always held to be more ill-
omened than any other.[130] Fidenae would be next to be surveyed,
between Monterotondo, the Aniene and the Tiber, but we have
spoken of it in detail in regions Lazio and Tuscany when we described Veii, whose colony it was. The Roman pontiff Lando,
whose birthplace I do not know, was an ornament of the Sabine
region.[131] The Anio joins the Tiber three miles from Rome after
leaving behind the Sabine and Crustumine regions and the Allia
and Monterotondo.

Region 5. Piceno, or the March of Ancona

We have now been to all the borders of the Duchy of Spoleto, and   1
the river Aniene previously took us to the places in Lazio mentioned by Strabo and Pliny. So let us go back and cross into the
adjoining region, formerly called Picenum and now the March of
Ancona. In the past, though, it was also sometimes called the
March of Fermo—in the life of Pope Gregory VII we read that
Robert Guiscard was excommunicated at the Lateran Council for
seizing the March of Fermo.[1] The borders of Picenum are, to the
north, the Apennine mountains, which as I said divide it from the
Duchy of Spoleto; to the east (more particularly the north-east),
the river formerly called the Isauro, now the Foglia; to the south,
the Adriatic; finally, the river Tronto, which passes through
Ascoli.[2]

In Book XXII Livy describes the stages of Hannibal's march   2
on Rome after the disaster inflicted on the Romans at Lake
Trasimene, and says that he came into Picenum, a territory not

abundantem sed refertum praeda. Et Plinius scribit Picentes quondam uberrimae multitudinis trecenta sexaginta milia in rei publicae deditionem venere a Sabinis orti. Cum vero Socialis Belli incentores aut primi Marsis incentoribus socii fuissent, in eos a Romanis crudeliter est saevitum. Livius libro XXIII: 'C. Terentio procos. negotium datum ut in Piceno agro conquisitionem militum haberet.' Et libro XXVII Claudii Neronis cos. ad Livium Salinatorem cos. adversus Hasdrubalem ituri describens iter, eum dicit flexisse in Picenum. Martialis coquus poeta attribuit rerum trium proprietatem[3] Piceno his versibus: 'Haec, quae Picenis venit subducta trapetis, inchoat atque eadem[4] finit oliva dapes'; et alibi: 'Picentina Ceres niveo sic nectare crescit ut levis accepta[5] spongia turget aqua'; item alibi: 'Filia Picenae venio Lucanica porcae: pultibus hinc niveis grata corona datur.'

3   Libet vero ab orientali parte Piceni sive Marchiae Anconitanae descriptionem incipere. Isaurus amnis, Folia nunc dictus, ex Apennino ad Cotulum arcem ortum habens, Pisauri civitatis vetustae moenia attingit, ubi portum sed tenuem raro maioribus navigiis apertum facit. Eam civitatem, quae[6] penes Isaurum sit nomen nacta,[7] a Romanis conditam fuisse constat. Livius enim libro XXXIX eam a Romanis simul cum Mutina et Parma coloniam deductam scribit. Scribit Eusebius *De temporibus*, Accium, tragoediarum scriptorem, natum parentibus libertinis, Pisaurum inter colonos fuisse deductum et fundum Accianum fuisse iuxta Pisaurum, credimusque fuisse ubi nunc corrupte dicitur Farnazanum. Pisaurum urbem nos a Totila destructam a Belisarioque instaura-

only well supplied with all sorts of produce but stuffed full of plunder.[3] Pliny writes that Picenum was once remarkable for the density of its population: three hundred and sixty thousand of the Picenes (who were descended from the Sabines) took the oath of loyalty to the Roman Republic.[4] Because they were behind the Social War, or rather were the earliest partners of those who did start it, the Marsi, the Romans took savage reprisals on them.[5] Livy says in Book XXIII: "The proconsul C. Terentius was commissioned to raise a force in the territory of Picenum."[6] And in Book XXVII Livy describes the route that the consul Claudius Nero planned to take to join his colleague Livius Salinator against Hasdrubal, and says that he turned aside in the direction of Picenum.[7] In the following lines, the poet Martial the cook says that Picenum has three specialties: "These olives, fresh from the presses of Picenum, begin meals and also finish them;"[8] and elsewhere: "Picene bread grows bigger with its white nectar, as a light sponge swells when it's soaked;"[9] and elsewhere again: "I come, a Lucanian sausage, daughter of a Picene sow: hence is given a welcome garnish to white porridge."[10]

I should like to begin the description of Picenum (or the March 3 of Ancona) in the east. The river Isauro, now called the Foglia, has its source at the fortress of Cutolo in the Apennines, and descends to the walls of the ancient city of Pesaro, where it forms a harbor, not very extensive and one that seldom receives larger vessels. The city took its name from the Isauro and is known to have been founded by Romans: Livy writes in Book XXXIX that it was settled as a colony by the Romans at the same time as Modena and Parma.[11] Eusebius writes in his *Chronicle* that the tragedian Accius (the son of freedmen) was among the colonists sent out to Pesaro, and that the estate called the Accianum was near the city — I believe at the spot now corruptly named Farnazzano.[12] I mentioned in my *Histories* that Pesaro was destroyed by Totila and rebuilt by Belisarius.[13] In the last century the city had the out-

tam in *Historiis* ostendimus. Quae superiori saeculo principem nacta est praestantem, Malatestam Pandulphi filium, litteris moribusque ornatissimum, qui natos tres et unicam filiam inter rarissimas clarissimasque numerandam mulierem genuit, Paulam, Mantuanorum praesentis temporis principum genetricem.

4   Primum supra Pisaurum ad Isauri sive Foliae sinistram ripam oppidum est Mons Abbatis, e regione cuius oppidi Idaspis torrens Isauro iungitur, quod poeta Lucanus novit ubi dicit: 'et iunctus Idaspis Isauro.' Suntque multa inter Idaspim et Isaurum Pisaurensis et Urbinatis agrorum[8] oppida, e quibus Mons Fabrorum notius habetur. Editissimo autem inter flumina ipsa monte Urbinum est vetusti nominis civitas, cuius inter veteres primum meminit Cornelius Tacitus Vitelliano[9] bello. Et Plinius dicit: 'Urbinates cognomine Metaurenses.' Nosque in quinto *Historiarum* ostendimus Belisarium, quia fons in civitate per aestatis caumata aruerat, civitate ipsa per incolarum deditionem fuisse potitum. Fuit ea urbs diu a Montis Feretri comitibus pro Romana ecclesia gubernata, ut nunc quoque a Frederico gubernatur,[10] cui supra diximus Eugubium esse subditum. Habet vero nunc ipsa civitas Seraphinum Stacolum, iuris et bonarum artium doctrina ornatissimum, consistorialem in Romana Curia advocatum.

5   Supra Pisaurum ad sinistrum oppida sunt quam plura, sed ex his notiora Mons Barocius et Nuvolaria, inter quae torrens labitur Argilla nomen a limo quem altum et tenacem habet nacta, Fani Fortunae moenia attingens. Quae maritima civitas et ipsa Romanos habuit conditores; a Totilaque sicut Pisaurum destructa fuit et a Belisario instaurata.

6   Sunt tertio a Fano Fortunae millario Metauri fluminis ostia. Ad dextram cuius partem intus est Forum Sempronii civitas vetusta,

standing Malatesta di Pandolfo Malatesta as its prince, distinguished for his learning and character alike. He had three sons,
and a single daughter who must be counted among the rarest and
most brilliant of women, Paola Malatesta, the mother of the present princes of Mantua.[14]

The first town beyond Pesaro, on the left bank of the Isauro (or 4
Foglia), is Montelabbate, opposite which the stream Apsa joins the
Isauro, as Lucan knew when he said: "And the Idaspis, joined to
the Isaurus."[15] There are many towns in the territories of Pesaro
and Urbino between the Apsa and Isauro, of which Montefabbri is
the best known. Set on a very high hill between these same rivers
is Urbino, an ancient foundation which Tacitus is the first among
the ancients to mention, in his account of the war with Vitellius.[16]
Pliny speaks of "the men of Urbino, called Metaurenses."[17] In
Book V of my *Histories*, I related how Belisarius gained possession
of Urbino when its citizens surrendered because the water supply
had dried up in the heat of summer.[18] The city has long been governed by the counts of Montefeltro on behalf of the Roman
Church, and is now governed by the same Count Federigo that is
lord of Gubbio, as I mentioned before.[19] The city now boasts
Serafino Staccolo da Urbino, a Consistorial Advocate in the Roman Curia, distinguished by his learning in law and the liberal
arts.[20]

To the left beyond Pesaro there are a great many towns, the 5
better known being Mombaroccio and Novilara; between them
flows the stream Arzilla, which gets its name from its deep and
clinging muddy sediments.[21] It reaches the walls of Fano, a city on
the coast also founded by the Romans; like Pesaro, it was destroyed by Totila and rebuilt by Belisarius.

The mouth of the river Metauro is three miles from Fano. In- 6
land on the right bank of of the Metauro is the ancient town of
Fossombrone, overlooking the Flaminian Way. This too Federigo
da Montefeltro governs on behalf of the Church.[22] The Metauro

viae imminens Flaminiae, quam Fredericus idem Feretranus pro
Romana ecclesia nunc gubernat. Est vero is Metaurus amnis 'velox'
a Lucano appellatus, clade Hasdrubalis et Livii Salinatoris Clau-
diique Neronis consulum Romanorum victoria libro Livii XXVII
copiose narrata[11] clarus. Eum ad sinistram tertio supra Forum
Sempronii milliario fluvius illabitur Candianus. Sinistra in cuius
ripa, viae Flaminiae, quam Augustus Octavianus ab urbe Roma
Ariminum usque stravit, pars visitur mirabili et sumptuosissimo
opere facta, quod durissimo e saxo[12] mons quingentis excisus in
longitudinem passibus, iter praebuit curribus, et ne subiectus amnis rapidum currens viae corroderet fundamenta, murus ab aquis
in summam viam quadrato lapide pluribus locis in sublime excita-
tus illam sustentat. Sed maiori opera impensaque saxum siliceam
habens duritiem, ducentis, ut teneo, passibus longitudine et octo
altitudine perforatum, curribus item factum est pervium, cui a
forma actuque Forulo est appellatio: docetque titulus litteris cubitalibus in fronte excisus T. Vespasianum—et non Octavianum
Augustum, qui viam straverat Flaminiam—id Foruli opus fieri cu-
rasse.

7   Sed Candianus torrente auctus uno ad dexteram habet Aquala-
neam vicum tabernis hospitatoriis frequentatum, et paulo ultra habet Montem Falconem. Supra vero ad sinistram Callii civitatis
moenia abluit Candianus, et superius est Candianum oppidum ab
eo fluvio appellatum—quod tamen ex Luceolis, oppidi vetusti,
propinquo loco, qua ex via Flaminia Eugubium est iter, a Longobardis excisi, ruinis aedificatum fuisse non dubito. Estque Luceolis
locus ad quem libro *Historiarum* septimo ostendimus Narsetem eunuchum castra habuisse, quando mors ei Totilae fuit nuntiata. Et
libro IX diximus Eleutherium, Italiae exarchum ab Heraclio imperatore constitutum, quia usus perfidia ad imperium aspiraret, ab
exercitu Ravennate apud Luceolim interfectum.

was called "swift" by the poet Lucan,[23] and is famous for Hasdrubal's disaster and the victory of the consuls Livius Salinator
and Claudius Nero over him, which Livy recounts in detail in
Book XXVII.[24] Three miles above Fossombrone, the river Candigliano joins the Metauro on its left-hand side. On the left bank
of the Candigliano, a stretch of the Via Flaminia can be seen, the
road which Augustus built from Rome to Rimini. The workmanship is extraordinary and no expense was spared — the exceptionally hard stone of the mountain was cut away for half a mile to
provide a carriageway, and to stop the swift current of the river below it eating away the foundations, it is supported by a wall of
squared stone, in many places carried high up from water level to
the road surface. But even more work and expense went on making a tunnel through rock hard as flint — to a length, I believe, of
two hundred feet and a height of eight feet — to allow carts to pass
through, which from its form and function was called Furlo.[25] An
inscription at the entrance in letters eighteen inches high indicates
that it was Vespasian who had the work at Furlo done, and not
Augustus, the builder of the Flaminian Way.[26]

At a junction with a stream the Candigliano has on its right   7
bank the village of Acqualagna, crowded with inns, and a little
further on Montefalcone. Above Montefalcone on the left, the
Candigliano brushes the walls of the town of Cagli, and higher up
there is Cantiano, a town named for the river. Yet I am sure that
Cantiano was built on the ruins of the ancient town of nearby
Luceolis (destroyed by the Lombards), where there is a route from
the Via Flaminia to Gubbio. I showed in Book VII of the *Histories*
that Luceolis is where Narses the eunuch was encamped when
he got word of Totila's death.[27] And in Book IX I said that
Eleutherius, who had been made exarch of Italy by the emperor
Heraclius I, was killed by the army of Ravenna at Luceolis for as-
piring to become emperor himself by treacherous means.[28]

8   Supra Forum Sempronii plus minus octavo passuum milliario, Metaurus amnis Firmiani moenia abluit, oppidi Urbinatium, iuxta quod Mons est Hasdrubalis nomen habens. Quod eum ducem ibi superatum fuisse et constans in regione fama est et nos, Livii Patavini libris attente lectis, certissima deprehendimus coniectura. Interius vero ad Metauri superiora progredientes planitiem inveniunt speciosissimam, in qua primum est oppidum a Metauro paene in insulam circumdatum, quod Guilielmus, Durandi Carnotensis decanus, pontificii iuris consultissimus *Speculi*que singularis doctrinae libri auctor, cum Martini IV pontificis Romani nuntius et Romandiolae thesaurarius esset, a fundamentis aedificavit et a suo nomine Castrum Durantis appellavit. Quinto inde miliario est Sancti Angeli in Vado oppidum mercatoribus frequentatum. Et proxime Apenninum Mercatellum, superiusque Amola, castellum ad Apennini tramitem positum, qua in Etruriam a Romandiola difficili ascensu itur. Hanc regionem a Frederico Feretrano possessam, quae Massa Trabaria appellatur, Romanam ecclesiam, cuius iuris est, sic vocasse constat, quia ex ipsis Apennini iugis immensae magnitudinis abiegnae trabes Romam in aedium basilicarumque structuram portari consueverint, sicuti etiam nunc portantur. Unde videtur hac ratione Plinium non absurde scripsisse quod supra retulimus: Tiberim amnem a Tiferno huic Apennino loco propinquanti fuisse Romam ratibus navigabilem, uti certe nunc est, quando imbribus adeo intumuit ut clausurae eius cogendis ad molendina aquis ubique in alveo iactae, omnino prohibere nequeant. Sunt etiam in montibus qui, Metaurum inter et Isaurum ac Apenninum, Massae imminent Trabariae, Carola[13] oppidum et minora aliquot castella: Raspagata, Miraldella, Sorbedullum, Sanctus Martinus, Brasticaria, Belforte Campus, Turris

About eight miles above Fossombrone, the river Metauro   8
reaches the walls of Fermignano, a town belonging to Urbino, and
there is a mountain close by called Monte Asdrubaldo.[29] Persistent
local lore holds that the general Hasdrubal was beaten there, and
my own careful reading of the books of Livy has corroborated it.
Those who press on into the upper reaches of the Metauro come
across a very attractive plain, the first town on which forms a peninsula almost entirely surrounded by the Metauro. It was built
from the foundations and named Casteldurante after himself by
the Dean of Chartres, Guillaume Durand, a canon law expert
and author of an unusually learned book called the *Mirror*, at a
time when he was the nuncio of Martin IV and treasurer of
Romagna.[30] Five miles from Casteldurante is the town of S.
Angelo in Vado, much frequented by merchants. Mercatello sopra
Metauro is next to the Apennines, and higher up, is Lamoli, a castle positioned at the Apeninne pass where one makes the hard
climb from Romagna into Tuscany. Federigo da Montefeltro[31] controls this region, which is called Massa Trabaria. It is said that it
was so named by the Roman Church (which maintains legal jurisdiction over it) because it was the custom — and still is — to bring
huge fir timbers [*trabes*] from these Apennine mountains to Rome
for building palaces and churches. On this basis it seems reasonable enough for Pliny to write what we reported above, that the
Tiber was navigable by raft from Città di Castello, which ap-
proaches this spot in the Apennines, to Rome. And indeed it is
even now at times when the river is so swollen with rain that the
sluices placed along its course to channel water to the mills quite
fail to hold it back. In the mountains that overlook Massa Trabaria between the rivers Metauro and Foglia and the Apennines,
there are also the town of Carola and several lesser castles:
Raspagatti, Miraldella, Sorbetolo, S. Martino in Selvanera, Casa
Bruscara, Belforte all'Isauro, Torre dei Fossati, Paganico, Pirlo —
the remains of the once mighty dominion of the Ubaldini, and

Fossati, Paganicum, Perlum, potentis olim Ubaldinorum dominii reliquiae, quas Octavianus possidet Ubaldinus patre genitus Bernardino, cuius adulescentis egregie docti humanitas et modestia gravitate condiuntur prudentiaque senili, ut alterum in ipso exspectemus Iohannem Accionis proavum, qui patrum nostrorum memoria virorum sui saeculi arma tractantium facile princeps et tamen prudentissimus gravissimusque[14] est habitus.

9 Post Metaurum fluvium in Adriatici litore sequitur Cesanus torrens, ad cuius sinistram intus est Mondofum, et inde Mondavium, et supra Sanctus Laurentius, oppidum Ugone ornatum, domino familiae Montis Vetuli, qui vita et moribus dignitatem magis decorat abbatialem quam ab ea decus accipiant. Et interius ad Cesani fontem Pergula oppidum, quod nuper habuit Angelum rei bellicae gloria clarum. Misa fluvius post torrentem Cesanum primus mare illabitur ad Senae, nunc Senogalliae, moenia, urbis vetustissimae a Gallis quondam Senonibus habitatae, qui Urbe capta, direpta, incensa ac auro redempta, postmodum a Romanis, duce Camillo, ad internecionem fuerunt caesi. Et nunc solo aequata, in cuius superbissimorum olim moenium ambitu arces sunt[15] pertenues duae, quae a Sigismundo Malatesta, cum Fano Fortunae ac Arimino, pro Romana ecclesia gubernantur. Sunt vero multa interius circa Misam amnem oppida et castella, e quibus notiora Mons Novus, Mons Bodii, Corinaltum, et Rocha Contrata, cuius nomen saepe in aetatis nostrae historiis invenitur.

10 Et paulo superius augetur Misa Sentino amne ad Saxiferrati moenia delabente, cuius oppidi nomen saepe per ora virum volitare facit Bartolus iure consultorum superioris saeculi excellentissimus. Habet vero nunc id oppidum Alexandrum theologia ac philosophia et Nicolaum Perottum eloquentia ornatissimos. Sentinus

now under the control of Ottaviano, the son of Bernardino. The humanity and modesty of this exceptionally learned youth are tempered by the authority and wisdom of an older man, so that we may hope to see in him another Giovanni di Azzo. His great-grandfather was in our fathers' day regarded as far and away the leading soldier of his time, yet a man of great sense and authority.[32]

Next after the Metauro on the Adriatic coast comes the river 9 Cesano, on whose left, inland, is Mondolfo, and then Mondavio, and further on, S. Lorenzo in Campo, a town to which Ugone, head of the family of Montevecchio, adds luster. His life and character glorify his position as abbot, rather than his office shedding glory on him.[33] Further inland, at the source of the river Cesano, is the town of Pergola, which could recently boast the famous soldier Angelo della Pergola.[34] After the Cesano, the river Misa first reaches the sea at the walls of Sena (nowadays Senigallia), an ancient city once inhabited by the Senonian Gauls. (The Senones captured, plundered, and burned Rome and ransomed it for gold, but were subsequently slaughtered by the Romans under Camillus to the point of extinction.)[35] Senigallia has now been leveled, but in the circuit of her once proud walls there are two small forts, governed for the Roman Church—along with Fano and Rimini— by Sigismondo Malatesta.[36] Further inland along the Misa, there are many towns and castles, of which the better known are Montenova, Montalboddo, Corinaldo, and Rocca Contrata, whose name is often found in the histories of our times.

A little higher up, the Misa is joined by the Sentino, a stream 10 that flows down to the walls of Sassoferrato; the name of the town is often on men's lips, thanks to Bartolo da Sassoferrato, the most outstanding jurisconsult of the previous century.[37] The town now numbers among its citizens Alessandro da Sassoferrato, distinguished in theology and philosophy, and Niccolò Perotti, distinguished for his eloquence.[38] The Sentino retains its ancient name,

amnis vetustum retinet nomen, secus quem secundo supra Saxumferratum stadio Sentina urbs fuit vetusta, in cuius agro Livius libro X proelium scribit praeclarum fuisse gestum, in quo, Fabio Maximo Decioque coss., ab Umbris, Etruscis, Gallis, et Samnitibus cum Romanis pugnatum est. Et Decius filius, genitoris Decii exemplo, devotis[16] hostium telis obrutus interiit. Romanique victoria potiti, peditum quadraginta milia trecentos triginta, equitum sex milia de hostibus interfecerunt. 'Samnitiumque[17] agmen cum fuga prolapsi per agrum Paelignum fugerent, circumventum a Paelignis est. Ex milibus quinque ad mille caesi.' Estque id proelium in quo, 'cum structae acies undique starent, cerva fugiens lupum e montibus exacta per campum inter duas acies discurrit. Inde divisae ferae: cerva ad Gallos, lupus ad Romanos cursum deflexit. Lupo data est inter ordines via. Cervam Galli confixere.[18] Tum ex antesignanis[19] Romanus miles: "Illac fuga," inquit, "hinc victor Martius lupus, integer et intactus, gentis nos Martiae et conditoris nostri admonuit."' Ex Sentinae urbis a Longobardis destructae ruinis, Saxum Ferratum et pariter sexto abinde milliario Fabrianum oppida fuerunt a principio inchoata. Ortum vero habet Sentinus in Apennino ad tramitem unde Fossatum, Umbriae oppidum, est accessus.

11   Post Senogalliam prima inveniuntur in litore Esis fluvius sive Esini ostia, ad quae arx est munitissima Anconitanorum praesidio custodita. Intus ad Esim est eius nominis civitas et ipsa vetus, et interius ac sub primis Apennini collibus frequens opificibus Fabrianum. Quod nobilissimum totius Piceni sive Marchiae oppi-

and beside it, a quarter of a mile above Sassoferrato, was the ancient city of Sentinum. In the territory of Sentinum, Livy writes in Book X, there was a famous battle during the consulship of Fabius Maximus and Decius, in which the Umbrians, Etruscans, Gauls, and Samnites all fought against Romans. Decius, the son of Decius, died following his father's example, overwhelmed by the enemy missiles that he had cursed.[39] The victory went to the Romans, who killed 40,330 of the enemy infantry and 6,000 horsemen.[40] "The routed remains of the Samnite army attempted to escape through Paelignian territory, but were intercepted by the native troops, and out of 5000 as many as 1000 were killed."[41] And this is the battle in which, "while the two armies were standing ready to engage, a hind driven by a wolf from the mountains ran down into the open space between the two lines with the wolf in pursuit. Here they each took a different direction, the hind ran to the Gauls, the wolf to the Romans. Way was made for the wolf between the ranks; the Gauls speared the hind. On this a Roman soldier in the front rank exclaimed: 'On that side, rout; on this the victorious wolf, whole and unhurt, a creature sacred to Mars, reminds us of our Founder and that we too are of the race of Mars.'"[42] After destruction by the Lombards, the ruins of the city of Sentinum served to give a start to both Sassoferrato and the town of Fabriano six miles away. The Sentino river has its source in the Apennines at the pass which leads to the Umbrian town of Fossato di Vico.

After Senigallia we come first to the mouth of the river Esino 11 or Esis on the Adriatic coast, where a very strongly defended fortress has been garrisoned to protect Ancona.[43] Inland on the Esino is the city of Jesi, taking its name from the river, and itself old. Further inland, under the Apennine foothill is Fabriano with its many craftsmen. This is the best-known town in all Picenum (or the March of Ancona), built from the ruins of the ancient city of Sentinum some six miles away. It numbered among its citizens the

dum, Sentinae urbis vetustae ibi ad sex milia passuum vicinae excidio aedificatum, aetate nostra Gentilem habuit pictorem sui saeculi celeberrimum. In eoque[20] familia nobilis Clavellensium, viri simul pueri et infantes, e quibus Baptista litteris ornabatur, civium conspiratione, dum sacris in basilica interessent, ad internecionem sunt caesi. Fortunatum vero est praesenti anno, sicut et proximo fuit, Fabrianum Romanae curiae[21] eo ductae praesentia, unde multas divitias maxima cum dignitate accumulat.[22] Tulitque ipsius oppidi sors ut adulterini pontificis reliquiae pestiferi dogmatis in eo fuerint punitae, quod quidem memorabile facinus non ab re censuimus referendum.

12   Cum Iohannes XXII pontifex Romanus Ludovici Bavari adulterini imperatoris importunitati ac insolentiae constanter resisteret, veniens Romam ipse Bavarus quendam Petrum Colutii de Corbario Reatinae dioecesis Minorum ordinis in antipapam profanari curavit. Qui miser factae de se electioni cum esset assensus, anticardinales creavit et, complicibus in vesania impietateque sua coactis, pro viribus est conatus scindere Dei ecclesiae unitatem. Et tamen interim Iohanna Matthaei filia de Corbario repetiit in iudicio eundem maritum suum, qui secum annis quinque priusquam ad fratres Minores inhabilis confugisset, matrimonialiter fuerat copulatus. Fuitque per episcopum, servato iuris ordine, in Petrum sententia redintegrandi matrimonii promulgata. Sed cum Petrus ipse, in idolum profanatus, a Bonifacio comite Pisano captus et ad Romanum pontificem Avinionem perductus esset, diem in carceris paedore obiit.

13   Nec tamen semper postea defuerunt illius vesaniae sectatores, 'Fraticelli de opinione' vulgariter appellati, asserentes nec Iohannem XXII nec quempiam illius successorem iure et ordine creatum esse pontificem. Quod malum adeo diffusum est ut in multis

most celebrated painter of our time, Gentile da Fabriano.[44] Here
the noble family of the Chiavelli was wiped out — men, boys and
infants alike (among them Battista Chiavelli, an accomplished
man of letters) — butchered in a conspiracy of the townsmen while
they took part in a service in the cathedral.[45] Fabriano had the
good fortune this year, as it did last year, of having the Roman
Curia settle there, an opportunity to make a lot of money as well
as enjoy the prestige of its presence. It was also the lot of this town
to witness the punishment of the last followers of a damnable heresy promulgated by a false pope; it is not, I think, inappropriate to
recall this memorable wickedness here.

Pope John XXII stoutly resisted the aggressive arrogance of the   12
false emperor Louis of Bavaria, and so Louis himself went to
Rome and arranged for a certain Pietro di Coluccio of Corvaro, a
Franciscan of the diocese of Rieti, to be consecrated — or rather
desecrated — antipope. The poor wretch assented to his election
and appointed anti-cardinals. With these accomplices of his crazy
blasphemy, he tried with all his might to rend the unity of God's
Church. But in the meantime one Giovanna di Matteo of Corvaro
claimed in court that Pietro was her husband, and that they had
slept together as man and wife for five years — ill suited to the role
though he was — before he had taken refuge with the Franciscans.
After due legal process, a bishop published an order against Pietro
that the marriage should be reinstated. But Pietro himself, having
been blasphemously set up as an idol, was seized by Bonifacio,
Count of Pisa, and taken to the pope of Rome at Avignon, where
he died in a filthy prison.[46]

Not that adherents of Pietro's lunacy were ever in short supply   13
thereafter. Known as the "*soi-disant* Fraticelli" they maintained that
neither John XXII nor any of his successors had been lawfully and
by due process created pope.[47] This wickedness is so widespread
that in many of the great cities of Italy and throughout Greece (especially in what remains of Athens), many are still found who are

magnisque Italiae civitatibus atque per oram Graeciae, praesertim in Athenarum urbis reliquiis, multi hactenus sint inventi Romanis pontificibus eam ob fatuitatem animis et conventiculis clam initis adversantes—quamquam magis luxus et libidinis sequi oblectamenta videntur quam iuris pontificii quaerere fundamenta. Nam praeter stupra et adulteria, quae passim unusquisque abditis in locis et ad hoc occulte paratis committunt, aliud publicis eorum caeremoniis tale fit scelus. Vocatae et de industria seductae speciosiores quaeque—vel viduae, vel virgines, vel matronae—cum in antra noctu convenerint, sacerdotes et clerici eius sectae eodem in antro clausi divinas quidem laudes ad fidem a simplicibus comparandam ex ritu Christiano legunt, cantitant,[23] immurmurant. Quibus nocte, ut aiunt, media finitis, sacerdos eorum maior alta admonet voce binos debere, masculum et feminam, sancto spiritu invocato, in complexum carnalemque copulam commisceri. Inde luminibus ilico exstinctis, proximam sibi quisque aut manu captam aut etiam de industria observatam mulierem sibi prosternit. Si vero ex huiusmodi coitu conceperit mulier, infans genitus ad conventiculum illud in speluncam delatus per singulorum manus traditur tam diu totiensque baiulandus quousque animam exhalaverit. Isque in cuius manibus exspiravit maximus pontifex divino, ut aiunt, spiritu creatus habetur. Et cum alter item ex tam multis vitiatis mulieribus offertur foetus, eum sacerdotes illi collegialiter congregati prunis assant. Collectumque inde pulverem in vasculum mittentes, vinum superfundunt, quo novicios et exsecrabilibus huiusmodi initiandos sacris epotant. A quo combibendi modo crudelis haec superstitio, vasculi quo fit vocabulo, 'barilottum' appellata est. Retulit nobis religiosissimus et certe sanctus vir Iohannes Capistra-

opposed to the Roman pontiffs because of this foolishness, both in their hearts and in covens that they form in secret — though they appear to be more interested in pursuing lust and debauchery than enquiring into the fundamentals of canon law. Quite apart from fornication and adultery (which every one of them practices indiscriminately in secluded spots furtively equipped for the purpose), another such abomination is perpetrated in their public ceremonies. All the more attractive women — widows, virgins, or wives — are summoned and purposely led aside as they assemble at night in grottoes. Shut up in the same cave, the priests and clerics of the sect read, chant and intone praises of the Lord from Christian ritual in a way calculated to elicit the credulity of the simple-minded. When these devotions are finished at midnight, so they say, the priest tells them in a loud voice that couples (a man and a woman) must invoke the Holy Spirit and mingle with one another in carnal embrace and copulation. The lights are at once put out and every man lays down the woman closest to him, either groping for her or having previously kept an eye on her for the purpose. If a woman conceives as a result of intercourse of this kind, the newborn infant is brought to the coven in the cave. All of them then pass the child from hand to hand so long and so often that eventually it gives up the ghost. And he in whose hands the infant expired is held to be their high priest, chosen, as they put it, by the Holy Spirit. If another offspring of so many fallen women is similarly presented, the priests assemble as a college and roast it over live coals. They gather the ashes, put them in a small container, and pour wine over them, from which their novices and those being initiated into these unspeakable rites are given to drink. From the custom of communal drinking, this cruel ritual is called the *barilotto*, after the container they use. The pious and saintly Giovanni da Capistrano, who was appointed by the pope to prosecute these heretics, told me that a wicked young woman freely confessed to him that she had given birth to an infant in consequence

neus, huic persequendae hominum sectae a summo pontifice prae-
fectus: scelestissimam mulierculam sponte sibi fassam fuisse, cum
eo ex diabolico coitu peperisset infantem, genitum laeto animo
laetioreque fronte in cistella de industria ornatissima[24] ad speluncam detulisse, praefatam se munus afferre pretiosissimum; ean-
demque parentem non modo siccis oculis sed hilari animo eiulan-
tem miserandumque vociferantem assari filium inspexisse. Eam
itaque crudelissimam haeresim cum Fabriani nuper degens pontifex accuratius persequitur,[25] convicti ad duodecim et, resipiscere
pertinaciter recusantes, igne, ut erant meriti, sunt consumpti.

14   Est vero ad Esis fluvii dexteram sub ipsis Apennini iugis, qua
Vallidum Umbriae oppidum petitur, locus fratrum Seraphici Francisci Heremita dictus, quo viso, ut inquit poeta Ovidius, potes dicere 'numen inest.' Aedificiis — certe quantum religiosis viris sat sit
ea in locorum asperitate — tam commode instructus ut alia eiusdem ordinis Italiae urbium loca amoenitate superet. Servaturque
picta in eo tabula Gentilis Fabrianensis, opus ceteris quas viderimus praeferenda. Habet Esis fluvius ad dexteram intus Serram oppidum Sancti Quirici appellatum, quingentis passibus ab ipso
amne et arduo in colle semotum. Et aversa a Fabriano regione Ma-
thelica, oppidum non ignobile, cuius nomen in Picentibus ponit
Plinius, sexto abest milliario, iuxta quod labitur torrens brevi
cursu in Esim et ipse cadens. Secundum litus post Esis ostia, promunturium Cuneri[26] incipit, Mons Anconae dictus. Quod quidem
promunturium tam propinquum est Apennino ut aliqui montem
ipsum ibi opinati sint scripserintque finiri. Unde ostendit Plinius
eo in loco Italiam se flectere et ad aversam huius cubiti partem
concavum esse lunatum ac maximum, quod a Pistoria incipiens
per Casentinum Burgumque ad Sepulcrum tamquam primo cornu
procedens, theatralem[27] sinum apud Fossatum Validumque, et
postea alterum cornu ad Nursiam Cassiamque habeat.

of such diabolical coupling. She had taken the child—which had a happy disposition and was even happier in appearance—to the cave in an elaborately decorated chest, having told them in advance she was bringing them a precious gift; not merely without tears but in a very cheerful fame of mind, the mother looked on as her son was roasted alive, wailing and crying piteously. When the pope on his recent sojourn in Fabriano investigated this most cruel heresy more closely, about a dozen were found guilty, and when they stubbornly refused to return to their senses, they were burned at the stake, as indeed they deserved.

On the right bank of the Esino, under the very peaks of the 14 Apennines on the way to the Umbrian town of Gualdo Tadino, there is a house of the Franciscan friars called Valleremita. If you saw it, you would say with the poet Ovid: "There a deity indwells."[48] The buildings are so well laid out—certainly enough for the needs of religious in that rugged locale—that it is more attractive than any Franciscan house in the towns of Italy. An altarpiece painted by Gentile da Fabriano is kept there, a work I prefer to any other I have seen.[49] Further inland, the Esino has on its right the town of Serra S. Quirico, set back on a steep hill half a mile from the river. In the opposite direction from Fabriano, six miles away, is the well-known town of Matelica (a name placed by Pliny among the Picenes),[50] beside a stream that shortly flows into the Esino. Along the Adriatic shore beyond the mouth of the Esino, the promontory of Conero begins, called the Mount of Ancona. The promontory is so close to the Apennines that some have believed and stated in writing that the mountains come to an end there. This is why Pliny describes Italy as turning back on itself at this point, and in the part facing the "elbow," he says, there is a great crescent-shaped hollow that begins at Pistoia and proceeds through the Casentino to Borgo Sansepolcro at the tip of its first horn, has its theater-like inlet at Fossato di Vico and Gualdo Tadino, and then the second horn ending at Norcia and Cascia.[51]

15 Sub promunturio qua vergit in mare est Ancona, ab ipsa litoris et Italiae se flectentis curvitate dicta. Cuius vetustae urbis et a Doricis Graecis, Siciliae accolis,[28] aedificatae portum Traianus imperator, quod exstantes tituli etiam nunc ostendunt, insigni opere et tutissimum navibus et ornatissimum exstruxit. Ostendimus *Historiarum* quarto Anconam urbem dum Conon, Iustiniani imperatoris partium dux, male defensat,[29] Gothos suburbium, quod nunc mare inter et montem urbe inclusum est, igni ferroque vastasse. Et libro VII diximus Narsetis Eunuchi duces cum triginta navibus quadraginta septem Gothorum naves profligasse, et Anconam obsidione durissima tunc levatam fuisse. Undecimoque docuimus libro Saracenos temporibus Lotharii imperatoris et Sergii papae, qui dictus fuerat 'Os Porci', Auserensi urbe in Dalmatis eversa, navibusque Venetorum ceteis tribus[30] in Tergestino sinu captis incensisque, Anconam quoque captam ac spoliatam incendisse. Qua in expeditione Saraceni dissensionibus freti, quibus cum fratribus agitabatur Lotharius imperator, post incensam desolatamque Anconam quicquid urbium et locorum usque Idruntum ea habet ora maritima spoliarunt. Civibus ea civitas gravibus et honestis, in primis mercaturae deditis, sed maxime omnium servatae dudum libertatis gloria decoratur. Habetque nunc Franciscum Scalamontem et Nicolaum, iure consultos bonarum litterarum studiis ornatos, cum nuper amiserit Ciriacum, qui monumenta investigando vetustissima mortuos, ut dicere erat solitus, vivorum memoriae restituebat.

16 Primus post Cunericum[31] promunturium est amnis Musio, quem ad ostia Aspidum vocant. Tertioque ab eo amne milliario et paulo supra mare vetustissima interiit urbs Humana, et parvo abinde spatio adhaeret mari ipso in promunturio Siriolum oppi-

Below the promontory, where it reaches the sea, is Ancona, 15
named precisely for the curvature of the shore as Italy turns in on
itself. This ancient city was built by Dorian Greeks who dwelt in
Sicily.[52] Its harbor was made by the emperor Trajan, as surviving
inscriptions show even now; it is a remarkable piece of work, very
safe for ships and elaborately constructed.[53] In Book IV of my *Histories* I showed that while Conon, the leader of the emperor Justinian's forces, was putting up a poor defense of Ancona, the Goths
laid waste to the suburbs (which are now enclosed by the city between the mountains and the sea) with fire and the sword.[54] In
Book VII I said that captains of the eunuch Narses with thirty
ships put to flight forty-seven ships of the Goths, and so lifted the
terrible siege of the city.[55] And in Book XI I recorded how in the
days of the emperor Lothair and Pope Sergius (known as "Pig's
Snout"), the Saracens after destroying the Dalmatian town of
Cherso and seizing and burning three Venetian merchant vessels
in the Gulf of Trieste, also captured and sacked Ancona before
putting it to the torch.[56] On this same expedition, the Saracens,
after burning down and laying waste to Ancona, plundered all the
cities and places of the coast as far as Otranto, relying on the quarrels that had arisen between Lothair and his brothers. Ancona is
notable for her serious and honest citizens, who are principally devoted to trade, but above all for her long-preserved liberty. Among
the citizens nowadays are the jurisconsults Niccolò and Francesco
Scalamonti, distinguished for their literary attainments.[57] But she
has recently lost Cyriac of Ancona, who by his investigation of ancient monuments restored the dead to the memory of the living, as
he used to put it.[58]

First after the promontory of Conero comes the river Musone, 16
at its mouth known as the Aspio. Three miles from the Musone
and a little away from the sea, the ancient city of Numana has disappeared;[59] the town of Sirolo sits on the sea a short way from
Numana on the promontory itself. On the other side of the prom-

dum. Ad alteram vero promunturii partem in mediterranea versam primum est Castrum Ficardum. Interius decimo ab Ancona milliario est Auximum civitas vetustissima, cuius ardui montis, in quo est sita, radices Musio attingit. Haec urbs in multis locis, praesertim in *Belli civilis* C. Caesaris commentariis et nostris *Ostrogothorum historiis*, invenitur celebris. Eam enim ostendimus duram pertulisse et longam obsidionem priusquam in Belisarii potestatem deveniret ea maxima causa, quod Gothi illam valido praesidio defensabant. Superius item XII milliario sub Apennini collibus est Cingulum oppidum a Labieno aedificatum, cuius item celsum, sicut Auximi, montem Musio circuit, paulo superius ortum habens. Sed medio inter Auximum Cingulumque spatio est Staphilum, haud ignobile Piceni oppidum, superiusque ad dexteram inter colles Apennino proximos est Lapirus vetusti nominis castellum.

17   Attingit vero in mediterraneis mari propinquioribus Musio Recanetum civitatem, quae Ricinetum principio appellata est. Cum enim Gothi Eliam Ricinam civitatem campestrem ab Elio Pertinace Romano imperatore aedificatam, cuius Maceratae propinqua cernuntur fundamenta, demoliti essent, eius incolae in oblongum istud dorsum demigrantes Recanetum civitatem, sumpto nomine a prima parum mutato, aedificarunt: idque decreta Ricinatum marmoribus incisa, quae apud Maceratam sunt, nonnulla ex parte ostendunt. Ea civitas magnum ex patria nostra Forlivio habet[32] ornamentum, Nicolaum Asteum Recanatensem et Maceratensem episcopum nobisque affinem et, sacris et[33] philosophiae ac medicinae litteris, quibus adulescens operam dedit, egregie eruditum. Recanetum inter et Adriaticum mare paululum a Musione recedit celeberrimum totius Italiae, ut in aperto immunitoque vico, sacellum gloriosae Virginis Mariae in Laureto appellatum, quo in loco preces supplicantium genitricis suae intercessione exaudiri a Deo illud maximum certissimumque est argumentum, quod eorum, qui votis emissis exauditi fuerint, ex auro, argento, cera, pannis,

ontory, facing inland, is first Castelfidardo. Further inland, ten miles from Ancona, is the ancient city of Osimo, set on a high hill whose foot is skirted by the Musone. This city is well-known and often encountered in literature, especially in Caesar's commentaries on the *Civil War*[60] and in my own *History of the Ostrogoths*; I described how the city endured a long hard siege before passing into the control of Belisarius, primarily because the Goths had a strong garrison to defend the city.[61] Twelve miles further on from Osimo, Cingoli lies under the Apennines. The town was built by Labienus on a high hill,[62] and is encircled, just as at Osimo, by the Musone, which has its source a little higher up. Midway between Osimo and Cingoli is Staffolo, a not undistinguished Picene town, and higher up to the right among the Apennine foothills is Apiro, a castle of ancient foundation.

In the interior but closer to the sea, the river Musone passes the city of Recanati, originally called Ricinetum. The Goths destroyed Helvia Ricina, a city on the plains built by the Roman emperor Helvius Pertinax, whose foundations can still be seen close to Macerata. Helvia's citizens then migrated to that long ridge and built the city of Recanati, its name being taken from the former city with a slight change, as is shown in some part by decrees of the people of Recanati inscribed in marble preserved at Macerata.[63] Recanati's great ornament comes from my home Forlì and is related to me: Niccolò dall'Aste, bishop of Recanati and Macerata,[64] an outstanding scholar of sacred letters and of the medicine and philosophy which he studied in youth. Between Recanati and the Adriatic, set back a little from the Musone, is a shrine called the Chapel of the Glorious Virgin Mary of Loreto — the most famous in Italy of those in open, undefended villages. It provides the most striking evidence that God listens to the prayers of suppliants through intercession of His Mother — those whose prayers have been answered have hung up votive offerings of gold and silver, wax and pieces of cloth, garments of linen and wool,

17

veste linea laneaque appensa donaria, magno licenda pretio basilicamque omnem paene complentia, episcopus in Dei Virginisque gloriam intacta conservat.

18   Potentia amnis sequitur, ad cuius ostium vetusta interiit eiusdem nominis urbs inter primas Picentum aliquando numerata. Is amnis ex Apennino supra Matelicam et quasi e regione Nuceriae Alfateniae oriundus habet intus ad dexteram et sub primis Apennini collibus bis mille passuum distans Monticulum oppidum. Ad sinistram vero inferius Montem Sanctum, egregium in Picentibus oppidum. Superius vero et ad primos Apennini colles Potentia praeterlabitur Sanctum Severinum, nobile sed novum oppidum ad ruinas aedificatum Septempedae, oppidi vetustissimi a Longobardis solo aequati. Asinus inde torrens perexiguus mare illabitur, cui superius adiacet Sancta Maria in Cassiano oppidum ad dexteram, et intus ad sinistram paulum a mari recedit Civitas Nova, nobile oppidum. Et sexto ab Asino torrente milliario absunt Chienti amnis ostia, cui intus ad dexteram adiacet Mons Causarius[34] oppidum. Pauloque remotius Morrum, et tertio abinde milliario superius Macerata civitas novi nominis, quae et ipsa, sicut Recanetum, ab Eliae Picenae excidio initium habuit. Quintoque inde milliario superius est Mons Ulmi, oppidum non ignobile, quod Franciscus Sfortia, quo tempore primum Eugenio IV pontifici Romano hostis esse coepit, diripiendum militi concessit. Inde est Arantia, Varanensium villa. Superius item ad Chientum amnem est Tollentinum vetus oppidum, quod populo frequens beato confessore Nicolao ornatur: cuius relationis in numerum sanctorum apostolicas litteras ego, IV Eugenii pontificis Romani secretarius, confeci. Habuit vero Tollentinum per aetatem nostram Nicolaum Marrucium Tollentinatem inter primarios rei militaris duces adnumeratum. Habetque nunc Franciscum Philelphum litterarum

which though they would fetch a high price and nearly fill the entire basilica, the bishop keeps untouched for the glory of God and the Virgin.

The river Potenza follows, at whose mouth an ancient city of 18 the same name, once numbered among the principal cities of Picenum, has disappeared. This river rises in the Apennines above Matelica almost opposite Nocera Umbra.[65] About two miles inland it has on its right the town of Montecchio, under the first hills of the Apennines. To the left and lower down, there is the notable Picene town of Montesanto.[66] Higher up and in the foothills of the Apennines, the river Potenza flows by San Severino Marche, a fine town but of recent foundation, having been built on the ruins of the ancient Septempeda, which was leveled by the Lombards. The very small stream of the Asola then flows into the sea; higher up along the Asola is the town of Montecassiano on the right, and inland on the left, slightly set back from the sea, the well-known town of Civitanova. Six miles from the Asola is the mouth of the river Chienti, along which lies Montecosaro, inland on the right. And a little further off from the mouth of the Chienti is Morrovalle, and three miles from there, higher up, is Macerata, a recent foundation that, like Recanati, had its origin in the destruction of Helvia Ricina. And five miles after that, higher up again, is the not unimportant town of Montolmo, which Francesco Sforza gave over to his soldiers to plunder when he first turned against the Roman pontiff Eugenius IV.[67] Then there is Castello della Rancia, an estate of the da Varano family. Further on again is the ancient and populous town of Tolentino on the river Chienti, whose great adornment is the blessed confessor Nicholas of Tolentino. As secretary to Eugenius IV, it was I that prepared the papal letters to enrol him in the catalogue of saints.[68] In our time Tolentino had Niccolò Mauruzzi da Tolentino, who was reckoned one of the foremost captains of war,[69] and she still has Francesco Filelfo, famous for his mastery of Greek and Latin

Graecarum Latinarumque doctrina[35] ac editorum operum fama notissimum. Qui Tollentinum dicit Graecam fuisse coloniam, quod nomen ipsum significet — cum *tholon* significet 'rotundum', *enteino* autem 'intendo', quasi rotundum sit oppidum et intensum, sicut ipsius forma demonstrat. Estque paulo extra portam Tollentini, qua itur ad mare Adriaticum, locus nomine *gerousia*: id est 'senatus', quod *geron* Graeci 'senem' dicant.

19   Supra Tollentinum tertio milliario est Belforte oppidum. Ubi vero Chientus fontes in Apennino habet, Seravallis est, et castellum et vicus, quo tramite Camerinum ex Umbria adiri ostendimus. Est[36] ad sinistram superius Camerinum civitas vetustissima, ad quam Livius libro IX Fabii Maximi fratrem, quando motus Etruscorum iverat exploratum, pervenisse et multa exceptum comitate scribit. Et libro X dicit Camertes dedisse P. Scipioni, armanda classe quam duxit in Africam, cohortem unam sexcentorum militum armatorum. Haec urbs dudum fuit in Picentibus, sicut et nunc est, populi frequentia opibusque primaria, viditque proximis annis similem Fabrianensi nobilium Varanensium caedem. Sed nunc a duobus ex eadem Varanensium gente adulescentibus, Rudolpho et Iulio, litteris virtutibusque ornatis gubernata quiescit. Influit Chientum amnem supra Tollentinum torrens Fiastra, ex Apennino proxime fontes Naris Umbrorum amnis oriundus, cui in ipsis Apennini iugis adiacet Fiastrum, inde appellatum castellum. Et qua torrens ipse in Chientum labitur, est Caldarola oppidum non exile. Ad Chienti[37] sinistram intus est Sancti Elpidii oppidum. Superiusque Sancti Iusti castellum, quod torrens Laetus cognomine Vivus attingit, et in Chientum brevi cursu labitur.

20   Itemque superius ad primos Apennini colles Sancti Genesii est oppidum haud ignobile, cui interius Sernana adhaeret. Interque ea

and for the remarkable works he has published.[70] Filelfo says that Tolentino was a Greek colony, as the name of the town indicates: *tholon* in Greek meaning "rounded," and *enteino*, "I extend," so suggesting that the shape of the town is round and elongated, as indeed it is. Just outside the city gate on the way to the Adriatic there is a place called *Gerusia*, that is, the "Senate" or Council of Elders, because the Greeks call an old man *geros*.

The town of Belforte del Chienti is three miles beyond Tolentino. At the source of the Chienti in the Apennines there is Serravalle, both a castle and a village, which, as I mentioned, gives access to Camerino from Umbria.[71] Beyond Serravalle on the left is the ancient city of Camerino, where Fabius Maximus' brother Marcus Fabius was received with great warmth, as Livy writes in Book IX, when he went there to look into the Etruscan uprising.[72] In Book X Livy says that Camerino contributed a cohort of six hundred infantry to Publius Scipio when the fleet that he took to Africa had to be fitted out.[73] Camerino has long been, and still is, the leading city of Picenum in terms of population and wealth; in recent years it has seen the slaughter of the noble family of Varano, similar to what took place at Fabriano.[74] But now the city has found peace under the governance of two young men of the same da Varano family, Rodolfo and Giulio, distinguished in letters and virtue alike. Above Tolentino, the Fiastra flows into the Chienti, a stream that rises in the Apennines close to the source of the Umbrian river Nera; beside it in the Apennine hills lies the castle of Fiastra, named for the stream. Where the Fiastra joins the Chienti is Caldarola, a town of some consequence. Inland to the left of the Chienti is the town of Sant'Elpidio. The castle of Monte San Giusto is higher up, and the stream called Ete Vivo flows by shortly before it joins the Chienti.[75]

Further up, in the foothills of the Apennines, is the not undistinguished town of San Ginesio, to which Sarnano is attached further inland. And between these two towns is the plain of Pieca,

19

20

duo oppida planities Plicae est, apud quam Laetusvivus torrens originem habet. Ad eumque torrentem quinto infra Sernanum[38] milliario Urbs est Salvia, vetus nomen et pariter multae vetustatis ingentes aedificiorum ruinas habens, inter quas certum est tria fuisse theatra. Nec satis invenimus quo tempore aut a quo ea urbs fuerit condita. Paucis etiam in locis praeterquam in Plinio et nostra *Gothorum historia* illius nomen apud vetustos invenitur. Nunc quidem reliquiarum, et quidem ingentium, loco derelicto, exstat in earum angulo oppidum Urbisaliae, corruptum a vetusto tenens nomen. Sunt etiam tertio infra Urbis Salviae vestigia milliario ad Laetivivi torrentis undas ingentis monasterii Claravallensis ruinae.

21   At in litore prima sequuntur amnis nunc Tennae, olim Tigniae, ostia, cui amni haud longe ad dexteram adiacet oppidum, nunc Sancta Maria in Georgio appellatum, inter primaria Marchiae adnumeratum. Quae urbs olim fuit Tignium, de qua in *Commentariis* C. Caesaris sic habetur: 'Interea certior factus Tignium Thermum[39] praetorem cohortibus quinque tenere, oppidum munire, omniumque esse Tigniorum optimam erga se voluntatem, Curionem cum tribus cohortibus, quas Pisauri et Arimini habebat, mittit, cuius adventu cognito diffisus civium voluntate Thermus[40] cohortes ex urbe educit et profugit. Milites in itinere ab eo discedunt ac domum revertuntur. Curio summa omnium voluntate Tignium recepit.' Et citra ultraque Tennam multa sunt ibi propinqua agri Firmani oppida et castella, sed primum superius ad Tennam est Mons Sancti Martini, et tertio supra milliario est Penna. Post haec quarto milliario ad primos Apennini colles est Amandula, et ipsum inter primaria Piceni oppida numeratum. Ad sinistramque Tennae in Apennino est Mons Fortinus, nobile oppidum, supra quod in Apennini iugo Tenna fluvius fontem habet. Inferiusque ad

where the Ete Vivo rises. On this stream five miles below Sarnano
is the ancient foundation of Urbs Salvia with its vast ruined buildings of like antiquity, among which there were certainly three the-
aters. But I cannot establish precisely when or by whom Urbs Salvia was founded — the place is named by the ancients in few places
other than Pliny (and in my *History of the Goths*).[76] Though the site
of these extensive ruins has been abandoned, there is still the town
of Urbisaglia in a corner of them, preserving a corrupt form of the
old name. Three miles below the remains of Urbs Salvia, beside
the stream of the Ete Vivo, there are the ruins of the great
Cistercian abbey of Chiaravalle di Fiastra.

But to return to the coast: first follows the mouth of the river 21
now called the Tenna, formerly the Tignia, on the right bank of
which a short distance away lies the town now called Montegiorgio, which is numbered among the foremost towns of the
March of Ancona: this was once the city of Tignium, on which
we have the following passage in Caesar's *Civil War*: "Meanwhile
Caesar had been informed that the praetor Thermus was holding
Tignium with five cohorts and was fortifying the town, all the inhabitants of which were very well disposed towards him, so he
sent Curio there with the three cohorts he had at Pesaro and
Rimini.[77] When Thermus learned of his arrival, uncertain of the
goodwill of the citizens, he led his cohorts out of the city and took
to flight. During the march his soldiers deserted him and went
home. Curio took over Tignium to general approbation."[78] Close
to Montegiorgio on both sides of the river Tenna there are many
towns and castles of the territory of Fermo. First, higher up on
the Tenna, is Monte S. Martino, and three miles beyond, Penna
S. Giovanni. Four miles beyond Penna in the foothills of the
Apennines is Amandola, also reckoned to be one of the main
towns of Picenum. On the left bank of the Tenna in the Apennines is the well-known town of Montefortino, above which the
river rises on an Apennine height. Further down on the same left

ostia eadem sinistra castellum est Portus Firmanus appellatum, cum tamen mare et fluvius, nedum faciant ibi portum, sed vix tolerabilem navibus praebeant mansionem.

22   Intusque tertio milliario est civitas Firmana, Romanorum colonia ex duodeviginti quae difficillimis secundi belli Punici temporibus primo detrectarunt militiam et tributorum collationem,[41] postea in senatus et populi Romani potestatem se permiserunt. Neque vero fuit tunc Firmum intra hunc murorum ambitum quem nunc habet, et quo illam circumdedit superiore saeculo Iohannes Aulegius Vicecomes rei bellicae ductorum sui temporis praestantissimus, cum tamen saxeo in tumulo qui moenibus includitur oppidum fuerit pervetustum,[42] cui Castello Firmano erat appellatio. Cernunturque in saxo cubitales litterae, divi nescio cuius Augusti titulo incisae. Fuit pridem eo in tumulo arx munitione et ornatu inter primas Italiae numerata, quam, deturbato ac armis pulso quarti Eugenii Romani pontificis Francisco Sfortia, populus Firmanus muro et omni munitione simulque ornatu spoliavit.

23   Absunt a Firmano portu quinque miliaribus torrentis Laetimortui ostia, ad quae magni aedificii vestigia cernuntur. Estque fama nullius quod sciam vetusti litteris confirmata Picenum ibi fuisse urbem, a qua provinciam nomen autumant nactam esse. Is torrens paulo supra Petriclum[43] inter et Belmontem oppida ortum habet. Eundemque torrentem inter et proximum Asonem fluvium est Mons Rubianus oppidum, et superius ad Asonis dexteram intus sunt Servilianum, post Sancta Victoria, superiusque Mons Falco oppida. Et superius item summo in Apennino Mons Monachus non ignobile oppidum sub Asonis fluvii fonte situm. Ad Asonis sinistram litori fluvioque adhaeret Pedasum castellum. Supraque est Mons Florae, superius oppidum Mons Novem dictum,

bank, at the mouth of the Tenna, is the castle of Porto San Giorgio, though the sea and the river do not actually form a harbor there and barely afford the ships anchorage.

Three miles inland is the city of Fermo, one of the eighteen Roman colonies which at a time of the greatest difficulty in the Second Punic War at first declined to contribute soldiers and money, but later submitted to the authority of the Senate and People of Rome.[79] But ancient Firmum was by no means within the present ring of walls, which were erected in the last century by Giovanni Visconti da Oleggio, the foremost captain of war of his time.[80] There was nevertheless a very ancient settlement called Castellum Firmanum built on a rocky knoll within the present defenses. Letters eighteen inches high can be seen cut in the stone with an inscription to some deified emperor. That knoll formerly had a fortress which for its defenses and embellishments was accounted one of the best in Italy; when the arms of Pope Eugenius routed Francesco Sforza and drove him out, the people of Fermo tore down the walls of the fort and stripped it of all its defenses and ornament.

Five miles from Porto San Giorgio is the mouth of the stream Ete Morto, where the remains of vast buildings can be seen. It is rumored, without confirmation in any ancient source, so far as I know, that this was the site of the city of Picenum, whence it is supposed the region got its name. The Ete Morto has its source a little higher up, between the towns of Petritoli and Belmonte Piceno. Between the Ete Morto and the next river, the Aso, is the town of Monterubbiano. Inland and higher up, on the right bank of the Aso, are the towns of Servigliano, then Santa Vittoria in Matenano, and Montefalcone Appennino higher up. And higher still, on the roof of the Apennines, is the not inconsiderable town of Montemonaco, situated below the source of the river Aso. On the left bank of the Aso, the castle of Pedaso clings to both shore and river: beyond that is Montefiore dell'Aso, and above Monte-

quod a novem nobilibus fuit[44] aedificatum. Inde habetur Mons Altus, et Forcae, et superius oppidum Communalia Asculana appellatum.

24   Illabitur post haec mare torrens perexiguus, ad cuius ostia est Morcinum castellum. Interiusque Ripatransonum, quod oppidum loci natura muroque munitissimum nulli Picentum populo divitiis concedit. Et tamen dum pellendo provincia Francisco Sfortia bellum geritur, id oppidum Sfortiani diripuere. Supra est Cossignanum nobile oppidum. Superius, Castignanum. Superius item in mediterraneis tertio milliario a Cossignano est Aufida, nobile munitissimumque natura loci oppidum. Altissimis vero in montibus, qui praedictis oppidis e regione respondent, summo in Apennino est Mons Sanctae Mariae in Gallo oppidum. Cui ipso in Apennino propinqua est caverna ingens Sibyllae vulgo appellata, et paulo superius est lacus ille in Nursinorum agri Apennino quem vano ferunt mendacio piscium loco daemonibus scatere. Ea tamen duorum locorum fama multos diebus nostris, et plures superioribus, ut audivimus, saeculis, pellexit necromantia delectatos aut noscendarum rerum mirandarum avidos ut arduos illos montes magno vanoque labore conscenderent. Distant in litore ab Asonis fluvii ostio Griptae oppidum octo, a Griptisque Sanctus Benedictus item oppidum duobus milibus passuum. Quae maritima regio omnium Italiae praeter Surrentinam Caietanamque amoenissima, mali citrei quod nostri[45] 'arantium' vocant feracissima, vitibus item arboribusque et oleis est consita. Et tribus a Sancto Benedicto milibus distat arx Asculanus Portus appellata, quae ostiis Troenti fluminis ad custodiam est apposita, ubi fines sunt litorei nostrae regionis Piceni sive Marchiae Anconitanae.

25   Est primum intus ad Troenti dexteram oppidum Mons Brandonus, cive nunc uno felicissimum fratre Iacobo ordinis Sancti Fran-

fiore a town called Montedinove from having been founded by nine noblemen. Then come Montalto di Marche, and Force, and higher up, a town called Comunanza.

After these, a very small stream flows into the sea, at its mouth the castle of Morcino. Further inland is Ripatransone: well defended by the lie of the land and its own walls, it is a town second to none in Picenum for wealth, though while the war to expel Francesco Sforza from the province was going on, it was sacked by the Sforza troops. Above Ripatransone is the notable town of Cossignano, and above Cossignano is Castignano. Higher up in these inland regions, three miles from Cossignano, is the well-known town of Offida, well protected by its location. In the high hills of the Apennine uplands, directly opposite these towns just mentioned, lies the town of Monte Santa Maria in Gallo. Near this town, in the Apennines themselves, is a huge cavern commonly called the Cave of the Sibyl, and a little higher up, that lake in the Norcian Apennines which is quite falsely said to teem with demons instead of fish.[81] Yet the repute of the two places has driven many in our day (and many more in earlier centuries, as I heard) to climb these daunting hills with great effort, but all in vain, captivated by sorcery or eager to acquaint themselves with marvels. On the coast eight miles from the mouth of the river Aso is the town of Grottammare, and two miles from Grottammare is San Benedetto del Tronto. This maritime district, the most attractive in Italy except for Sorrento and Gaeta, is very productive of citrus fruit which we call "oranges." It is also thickly sown with vines, orchards and olives. Three miles from San Benedetto is the fortress called Porto d'Ascoli, set there to guard the mouth of the river Tronto, which forms the border on the coast of our present region of Picenum, or March of Ancona.

Inland, the first town on the right-hand bank of the Tronto is Monteprandone, now blessed with one of her citizens, the Franciscan friar Giacomo della Marca. The most fiery and eloquent

cisci de Marchia appellato, quem ardentissimum pariter et elo-
quentissimum verbi divini praeconem vitam ducere in terris
angelicam constans fama consentit adeo ut nullus dubitet, quod
multi vidisse affirmant, eum, ut est, vivum miraculis coruscare.
Tribus ab hoc oppido et totidem milibus a Ripatransonum abest
Aquaviva oppidum, ex quo duces Adriae provinciae Aprutinae originem duxere. Secundum hanc Troenti dexteram ipso in Apennino est Arquata oppidum nobile, quod Nursini pontificum Romanorum concessione in aliena obtinent regione. Superius quinto
milliario pariter ad Troenti dexteram est Accumulum nobile oppidum. Et item superius sub Troenti fonte est Amatrix oppidum ut
in montanis egregium, quod fortassis propinqua in regione, cum
ultra fontem et ad Troenti sinistram sit, adnumerari debuit.

26   Difficilis vero est montium huiusmodi et sitorum in ipsis locorum descriptio, quod saltuosissima sunt et rivis altisque rupibus
quandoque ita dividuntur ut nec pictura sit, nec elocutio, quae plenam illorum notitiam dare possit. Hinc unum dictis addere libet,
quod suo loco commode nequivimus explicare: ea in Apennini
parte, in qua superius oppidum Arquatam esse diximus, ipse
Apenninus se ipsum superans arduum facit grumum qui Nursinos
a Picentibus dirimit, appellaturque Mons Victor quod ceteros regionis montes altitudine vincat. Ad cuius orientale latus est lacus
ille daemonibus infamis, ad aliudque latus in meridiem versum
duo ipsius colles altissimi. Et paulisper in profundo inter se divisi
Furculas faciunt Prestae appellatas, inter quas Troentus labitur et
mox, ab ipsis Furculis per arctam et tamquam manufactam decur-
rens fossam, Arquatae moenia attingit. Ultra atque etiam infra
Amatricem medio in Apennino fluvius oritur nomine Castellanus,

preacher of the word of God, universal report has him leading the life of an angel on earth, so much so that no one doubts (and many affirm they have seen it) that he glitters with miracles even in life, as he is still.[82] Three miles from Monteprandone (and the same distance from Ripatransone) is the little town of Acquaviva Picena, where the dukes of Atri in the province of Abruzzo originated. Along the right bank of the Tronto in the middle of the Apennines is the well-known town of Arquata del Tronto, which the citizens of Norcia hold by papal dispensation, although it is in a different region from theirs. Five miles higher up, still on the right-hand side of the Tronto, is the notable town of Accumoli. And higher still, below the source of the Tronto, is Amatrice, a fine town for one in the mountains — it should perhaps be included in the next region, since it is beyond the source of the Tronto and to the left of it.

It is difficult to give a description of mountain country of this 26 sort and the places located in it: the wooded valleys are so broken up by streams and rocky cliffs that no picture or narrative could give a full account of them. So I should like to add something to what I said which I couldn't easily explain in its proper place: in the stretch of the Apennines where Arquata is located (as I said above), the very mountains rise above themselves to form a steep peak that separates Norcia from Picenum. It is called Monte Vettore [Mount Victor] as surpassing in height the other peaks of the region. On its eastern flank, there is that lake notorious for its demons, and on the other side, towards the south, it has two very high peaks. As they draw apart slightly from one another, they form a pass in the valley called the Forca di Presta. The Tronto flows through it, and in a short while runs down from the Forca di Presta along a narrow and (it almost seems) man-made channel to reach the walls of Arquata del Tronto. Beyond and below Amatrice a river called the Castellano rises in the middle of the Apennines. It carries on down to the walls of Ascoli Piceno not far

qui parvo cursu ad moenia Asculi defertur. Et parvo inde spatio cadit in Troentum, ut hinc Castellanus iste, Troentus inde Asculi moenia circumluant.

27   Ea civitas vetustissima aliquando Picentum primaria fuit. Et Livius cum libro LXXII dixisset Italicos populos Bello Sociali defecisse, primos ponit Picentes. Postea libro LXXVI dicit Asculum a Pompeio Strabone captum, quo in proelio cum terra tremuisset, Strabo Tellurem aede promissa placavit. Et tamen post caedem incendiaque commissa urbem evertit, quia Asculani initio belli missos ad se legatos interfecerant. Asculum viros saepe habuit praestantissimos: Titum Betutium Barrum oratorem, quem Cicero in *Bruto* ceteris suae aetatis oratoribus externis praefert; Ventidium Bassum ducem Romanum, qui primus Parthos attigit, in quem militare illud laedorium fuit dictum: 'qui mulos fricabat, factus est consul.' Habuit etiam Nicolaum III pontificem Romanum, Ciccumque excellentiorem mathematicum quam vulgarem poetam.

away, and then after a short space joins the Tronto, so that on one side the walls of Ascoli are skirted by the Castellano, on the other by the Tronto.

Ancient Ascoli was at one time the chief city of Picenum. 27 When Livy in Book LXXII speaks of the defection of the Italian tribes in the Social War, he puts the Picentes first.[83] Later, in Book LXXVI, he says that Pompeius Strabo captured Ascoli. When in the course of the battle there was an earthquake, Strabo appeased the earth goddess Tellus with the promise of a temple; and yet after slaughtering the citizens and setting fire to the city, Strabo destroyed it because at the beginning of the war the Ascolans had murdered the legates that had been sent to them.[84] Ascoli has had many outstanding citizens: the orator Titus Betutius Barrus, whom Cicero in the *Brutus* prefers to the other non-Roman orators of his era;[85] the Roman general Ventidius Bassus, who first got to the Parthians: it was Ventidius who was the butt of that abusive slur of the soldiers: "He used to rub down mules, and now he's consul."[86] Ascoli also gave birth to the Roman pontiff Nicholas III, and to Cecco d'Ascoli, better as an astrologer than as a vernacular poet.[87]

LIBER IV

Regio sexta. Romandiola sive Flaminia[1]

1 Sed iam finis adest Piceni seu Marchiae Anconitanae; deinceps
Flaminiam sive Romandiolam adeamus. *Viro autem hanc regionem
ex nostro instituto commendaturi, cuius peritia nostros emendet corrigatque
errores, talem accipere cogimur qui simul nos ipsamque ab invidis tueatur,
quod defuturos non dubitamus qui nos in patriae nostrae regione pulcherri-
mis referta particulis veritatem modumque contendant excedere. Tibi ergo,
insignis Malatesta Novelle, dicata erit Romandiola, ut, cum bonarum artium studiis aeque ac militia apprime delectatus historiam omnium saeculorum inter primos aetatis nostrae excellenter teneas, provinciam, in qua generis tui clarissima gens Malatesta diutissime floruit, emendatam et me,
eius parcissimum laudatorem, tua gravitate doctrinaque tuearis.*[2] Flaminiae quantum ad hanc spectat regionem vocabulum ante fini-
tum secundum bellum Punicum nusquam reperitur. Nam Flaminium vetus oppidum iuxta Tiberim et Soracte montem fuit, de
quo Vergilius in VII: 'hi Soractis habent arces Flaminiaque arva.'
Et Flaminia dicta est via quam Octavius Augustus ab urbe Roma,
vel potius a Circo Flaminio, sicut in *Roma instaurata* docuimus,
Ariminum usque stravit. Per totum vero secundum bellum Punicum, sicut et belli primi Punici temporibus factum erat, hanc regionem Livius Patavinus, quantum ad Romanos spectabat, solo
Arimini verbo appellat. Nam libro XXIV sic dicit: praetori Sem-
pronio provincia Ariminum obvenit, cum reliqua omnia Padum
versus Apenninum et Alpes partim Boios partim Galliam diceret
Cisalpinam.

BOOK IV

Region 6. Romagna, or Flaminia

Now we have come to the end of Picenum (or the March of 1
Ancona): let us proceed next to Flaminia (or Romagna). *Since in*
accordance with our plan we are to dedicate this region to a man whose ex-
pertise may emend and correct our errors, we are compelled to take some-
one who may simultaneously protect us and this Region from the envious.
We have no doubt that there will be no lack of persons who will contend
that we are exceeding truth and the mean in this Region which is our
homeland, filled as it is with the most beautiful details. So Romagna shall
be dedicated to you, the famous Malatesta Novello, since, as someone who
delights equally in the study of the liberal arts and military affairs, you have
an excellent grasp of the history of all ages, equal to best of our time, and so
can make free from errors this Province, in which your most famous
Malatesta clan has flourished for so long, and can protect me, who have
been most sparing in its praise, by your authority and learning.[1] You will
not find the word Flaminia applied to this region before the end of
the Second Punic war, for old Flaminium was a town beside the
Tiber and Mt. Soracte, of which Vergil says in *Aeneid* VII: "These
hold the heights of Soracte and the Flaminian fields."[2] "Flaminian"
was also the name given to the road that Augustus constructed
from Rome (more precisely, from the Circus Flaminius, as I
showed in *Roma Instaurata*)[3] to Rimini. As far as the Romans were
concerned, Livy calls the region only "Rimini" throughout the
Second Punic War, just as he had done in the First Punic War. In
Book XXIV he says that the province of Rimini was assigned to
the praetor Sempronius;[4] all the rest he refers to as the Po (towards the Apennines) or (towards the Alps) partly the Boii, partly
Gallia Cisalpina.

2   Similiter[3] dicimus de Aemilia, quae et ipsa in Romandiola est comprehensa. Livius autem libro XXXIX[4] scribit M. Aemilium cos., Liguribus subactis, viam a Placentia productam Flaminiae coniunxisse, ut certum sit viam a Foro Cornelii usque Placentiam inde Aemiliam appellatam. Et infra innuit Livius Q. Flaminium[5] fratrem, qui ut meretrici Placentinae placeret, Gallum securi percussit, quando Bacchanalia Romae sublata sunt, viam stravisse quam Flaminiam appellarit. Habueruntque fines Flaminia ab Isauro ad Vatrenum Fori Cornelii nunc Imolae amnem, et Aemilia inde ad Trebiam, Placentiae urbis fluvium, quam longitudinem et nunc habet Ravennatis ecclesiae exarchatus, cuius tota provincia id Romandiolae nomen olim obtinuit.

3   Quod quidem nomen ostendimus in *Historiis* Carolum Magnum et primum Adrianum pontificem Romanum post oppressos dominioque privatos Longobardos ea maxime causa indidisse, quod toto Longobardorum tempore Ravenna cum propinquis aliquot civitatibus et oppidis Romano populo fidem constantissime servasset. Sed nos, consuetudini adhaerentes iam inveteratae, fines Romandiolae intra Isaurum sive Foliam et Scultentinam sive Panarium amnes Apenninumque montem ac mare Adriaticum Padusamque paludem citra Padum, et ultra illum quicquid ager Ferrariensis ad Veronensium Patavinorumque paludes et ultima usque Padi ostia, Fornaces appellata, mare inter Adriaticum et Padum habet, constituemus.

4   Ad dexteram Isauri amnis ripam, primum habet Romandiola oppidum Poccium, deinde Montem Lurum, *proelio memorabile quo Picininum a Francisco Sfortia insigni clade superatum fuisse in Historiis ostendimus,*[6] inter Isaurum et proximum torrentem Crustumium, de quo Lucanus: 'Crustumiumque rapax,' sive, ut nunc appellant, Concham. Focaria est promontorium quatuor habitatum oppidis: Granariolo, Castro Medio, Gabitiis, Florentiola, vinetisque ac oli-

We likewise speak of Emilia, which is itself included within 2
Romagna. In Book XXXIX, Livy writes that after he had conquered the Ligurians, the consul M. Aemilius built a road from
Piacenza to join up with the Flaminian Way,[5] so it is clear that
the road from Imola to Piacenza was called the Via Aemilia after
him. Further on, Livy mentions that Marcus Flaminius' brother
Quintus (who when the Bacchic rites were taken to Rome, beheaded a Gaul to please a courtesan of Piacenza) built a road
which he named the Flaminian Way.[6] The boundaries of Flaminia
were defined as the land from the Foglia to the river Santerno at
Forum Cornelii (nowadays Imola), while Emilia went from the
Santerno to the Trebbia, the river of the city of Piacenza. This is
the present extent of the exarchate of the church of Ravenna,
whose entire territory acquired in the past the name "Romagna."

In my *Histories*, I showed that after the Lombards were defeated 3
and deprived of power, Charlemagne and Pope Hadrian I gave the
name Romagna to this region, in particular because throughout
the period of Lombard dominance, Ravenna and its neighboring
towns and cities had kept unbroken faith with Rome.[7] But I shall
keep to the usage, now long established, of defining Romagna as
lying between the rivers Isauro (the modern Foglia) and Scultenna
(modern Panaro) and bordered by the Apennines, the Adriatic
and the marshland of Padusa south of the Po, and beyond that,
the territory of Ferrara up to the marshes of Verona and Padua
and as far as the last mouth of the Po (called the Fornaci) between
the Adriatic and the river.

On the right-hand bank of the Foglia, the first town in Ro- 4
magna is Pozzo Alto, and then Monteluro, *memorable for the battle
where, as we show in the History, Piccinino was overcome in a great disaster by Francesco Sforza.*[8] It is between the Foglia and the next
stream, the Crustumium (or Conca as they now call it), of which
Lucan says: "raging Crustumium."[9] Focara is a promontory with
fine plantations of vineyards and olive groves, on which sit four

vetis egregie consitum. Superiusque sunt oppida: Tumba, Planum Montis, Mons Calvus, Pes Campi, Saxum Corbarium et Macerata Montis Feretri.

5   Sub Focaria Ariminum versus Catholica vicus, ad quem absorptum mari oppidum Concham eminentes aquis muri turresque per aequoris tranquillitatem ostendunt. Interius est Gradaria, Sigismundi Pandulfi villa, superbis aedificiis amoenisque consitionibus et amplissimis vinetis ornata, ad sinistram sita Conchae amnis, a quo submersum oppidum nomen habuit. Suntque superius: Sanctus Iohannes in Maregnano, *Sanctus Ioannes in Insula, Mons Vetularum,*[7] Mondainum, Saludetium, Mons Gridolfus, Meletum, Mons Florum, Gemmanam, *Ceretum Gilonum,* Tauletum, *Auditor, Sanctus Iohannes Auditori,* Planum Castelli, *Ripa Massana, Vallis Avelanae, Rivus Petrosus. Inferius* Castrum Novum, Mons Tavelii, *Fossa, Ripalta, Vallis Teveri, Castellina, Chiarignanum, Macerata, Montis Feretri,* Certaldum, Petri Turchi viri doctissimi patria, *Corbetulum,* Planum Iohannis (Francisci Nobilis et strenui a litterisque non abhorrentis viri patria), Planum Meleti, *Lovanum, Cauletum, Petra Caula, Mons Sanctae Mariae,* Petra Rubia, Carpegnum, a quo nomen accepit mons arduus amplissimusque, pascua praebens per aestatem animalibus uberrima. Qui quidem mons, Arimino sive, ut nunc dicitur, Maricla fluvio ab Apennino divisus, omnium Italiae Apenninum non contingentium montium est maximus. Subest item illi Castellatia. Dehinc sequuntur[8] Mons Cerognonus, *Mons Boago* et monasterium Sextini, apud quod multa exstant vetustatis monumenta.

6   Ad Conchae vero dexteram: *Misanum, Metianum,* Sanctus Clemens, *Sanctus Andreas in Patrignano, Besanigum,* Agellum, *Castrum Reale,* Corianum, *Mons Tauri, Passianum, Sanctus Savinus, Castrum Crucis, Mons Columbus,* Mons Scutulus, ubi haec scribimus, Albaretum, Gypsum, Tumba Gaiaeni, Mons Zardinus, Saxum, Mons Grimannus, *Mons Latianus,* Mons Taxorum, Mons Copiolus. *Est et torrens, Rivus Pellagi appellatus.*[9] Et mari[10] in Via Flaminia et prope

towns: Granarola, Casteldimezzo, Gabicce, and Fiorenzuola. Further inland are the towns of Tomba,[10] Pian di Castello, Montecalvo in Foglia, Piedicampo, Sassocorvaro, and Macerata Feltria.

Below Focara towards Rimini is the village of Cattolica. At 5 Cattolica, when the sea is smooth, walls and towers rise out of the water to reveal the town of Conca, which was swallowed up by the sea. Further inland is Gradara, an estate of Sigismondo Pandolfo Malatesta which is adorned with splendid buildings, pleasant farmland and extensive vineyards; it is located to the left of the river Conca, from which the submerged town got its name.[11] Higher up there are the towns of S. Giovanni in Marignano, *S. Giovanni Isola, Montevettolino*,[12] Mondaino, Saludecio, Montegridolfo, Meleto, Montefiore Conca, Gemmano, *Ceretum Gilonum*, Talacchio, *Auditore, S. Giovanni Auditore*, Piandicastello, *Ripamassana, Valle Avellana, Ripapetrosa. Lower down*: Castelnuovo, Monte Altavellio, *Fossa, Ripalta, Valle di Teva, Castellina, Chiarignano, Macerata, Montefeltro*, Certalto (home of the learned Pietro Turchi),[13] *Corbetolo*, Pian San Giovanni (home of Francesco de' Nobili, a man of action but no stranger to letters), Pian di Meleto, *Lovanum, Cauletum, Petra Caula, Monte S. Maria*, Pietrarubbia, Carpegna (which gives its name to the large, steep mountain that provides animals with good summer pasture). Monte Carpegna, which is separated from the Apennines by the river Ariminum (or the Marecchia, as it is now called), is the greatest of the mountains of Italy not touching the Apennine chain. At the foot of the mountain is Castellaccio. Then comes Monte Cerignone, *Mons Boago* and the convent of Sestino, where there are many ancient remains.

On the north bank of the Conca, there are *Misano, Metianum*, 6 S. Clemente, *S. Andrea in Patrignano, Besanigo*, Agello, *Castelleale*, Coriano, *Monte Tauro*, Passano, *S. Savino*, Croce, *Monte Colombo*, Monte Scudo (where I am writing this), Albareto, Gesso, Saiano, Monte Giardino, Sassofeltrio, Montegrimano, *Montelicciano*, Montetassi, Montecopiolo. *There is also a stream called Rio Pellagi*.[14]

mare imminet Sanctae Trinitatis ecclesia. Suntque ad eius torrentis dextram oppida et castella in Arimini sive Mariclae amnis sinistram vergentia: *Sancta Maria in Cereto, Ceresolum, Molationum,* Seravallae, *Sanctus Martinus in Vinco, Faitanum,* Veruculum, Sanctus Marinus, sub arduo cuius monte torrens ipse ortum habet. Superiusque in Montis Feretri regione: *Corpaloum, Firentinum, Vallis,* Mons Magius, Petra Acutula, *Lonzanum, Mons Fretavus, Petra Mauri, Castrum Novum,* Toranum, Sanctus Leo, episcopi sedes, Scaulinum Antiquum, Soane, Penna Biliorum, Maiolum, Ciconiaria, Montironum, *Martianum, Sanctus Sixtus, Vilianum, Turricella,* Mercatum Ranchi.

7 Succedit ordine Ariminum, vetusti clarique nominis colonia Romanorum, simul cum Benevento, sicut Livius XIIII libro scribit, deducta anno quod ex Eusebio computavimus ante Iesu Christi Domini nativitatem ducentesimo octuagesimo secundo. Ea civitas duram a Vitigite, Gothorum rege, pertulit obsidionem, Iohanne Vitaliani partium Iustiniani Imperatoris, sicut in *Historiis* ostendimus, illam viriliter defensante. Et nunc Sigismundo Pandulfo Malatestae clarissimo rei militaris duci vicariatus ecclesiae titulo est subiecta.[11] Eiusque latera irrigat eiusdem nominis fluvius Maricla nunc dictus. Scribit Livius libro XXI: 'L. Sempronium cos., compositis Siciliae rebus, decem navibus oram Italiae[12] legentem Ariminum pervenisse. Inde cum exercitu suo profectum ad Trebiam amnem.' Et libro CIX dicit belli civilis Caesaris et Pompei initio Curionem tribunum plebis pervenisse Ariminum, quam historiam Hirtius in *Commentariis* et Lucanus poeta diffuse narrant, ut eam prolixius a nobis scribi oportere non iudicemus. Et beatus Hieronymus, ecclesiae doctor, scribit concilium aetate sua et cui ipse interfuerit Arimini celebratum fuisse, quod postea patres[13] reprobaverint et gesta in eo censuerint esse nulla.

8 Eam civitatem suburbiumque coniungit pons nunc solus integer ex veteribus quattuor quos Octavius Augustus, Flaminia via ab

The church of the Holy Trinity on the Flaminian Way overlooks the sea nearby. On the right bank of this stream, there are towns and castles that slope down towards the left bank of the river Ariminum (or Marecchia): *S. Maria in Cerreto, Ceresolum, Molationum,* Serravalle, *S. Martino in Vinco, Falciano,* Verucchio, and San Marino, beneath whose high hill the Rio Pellagi rises. And further up, in the region of Montefeltro, there are *Corpaloum, Fiorentino, Valle,* Montemaggio, Pietracuta, *Lonzano, Montefotogno, Pietramaura, Castelnuovo,* Torrano, S. Leo (the seat of a bishop), Scavolino, Soanne, Pennabilli, Maiolo, Cicognaia, Montirone, *Martianum, Sestino, Viliano, Torricella,* the market town of Ranco.

Next in order comes Rimini, an ancient and famous Roman 7 colony which was founded (as Livy tells us in Book XIV)[15] at the same time as Benevento in 282 b.c., as I compute from Eusebius.[16] As I showed in my *Histories,* it endured a hard siege at the hands of Witigis, the king of the Goths, Johannes the nephew of Vitalianus making a spirited defense of it on behalf of the emperor Justinian.[17] Rimini is now subject to the famous military leader Sigismondo Pandolfo Malatesta as vicar of the Church.[18] Its flanks are washed by a river of the same name, now called the Marecchia. In Book XXI, Livy writes: "Once things were settled in Sicily, the consul L. Sempronius sailed along the coast with ten ships and reached Rimini. From there he marched with his army to the Trebbia."[19] And in Book CIX he says that at the beginning of the civil war between Caesar and Pompey, the tribune Curio came to Rimini.[20] Both Hirtius in his *Commentarii* and the poet Lucan relate the matter in detail, so that I do not think I need treat it at any great length.[21] The Doctor of the Church St. Jerome writes that in his day a council was held at Rimini, which he himself attended, though the Church Fathers afterwards repudiated it and nullified its acts.[22]

A bridge across the Marecchia links Rimini to its suburbs; it is 8 the only one to survive whole of the four ancient bridges (apart

urbe Roma Ariminum silicibus strata, praeter minorum pontium turbam maximo exstruxit opere atque impendio. Qui enim est ad Tiberim, Milvius nomine, a Marco Scauro, sicut Ammianus Marcellinus refert, constructus; multa quae ab Octavio accepit ornamenta omnino amisit. Et qui Tiberim item sub Ocriculo iungebat, parte una succisus, in arcis fundamenta concessit; is vero qui sub Narnia Narem amplectebatur fluvium, multis ut videtur saeculis vel succisum vel collapsum vetustate fornicem medium amisit.

9 Ornata fuit Ariminensis civitas superioribus saeculis Mastino Pandulfo et Galeotto ex Malatesta gente, principibus omni virtute ornatis. Ortique eodem Galeotto Carolus Malatesta, princeps fortissimus atque doctissimus, quem in *Historiis* Marco Catoni superiori similem fuisse diximus, et Pandulfus, qui Brixiae et Bergami *et Cremonae*[14] dominium multis obtinuit annis, *Sigismundi Pandulphi ac tuus genitor,*[15] inter aetatis nostrae principes primarii sunt habiti, cum tamen nulla ratione eis fuerit virtute inferior Malatesta tertius frater: claram vero dulcemque sui memoriam saeculo nostro reliquit Galeottus Robertus, qui licet paternae hereditatis urbes oppidaque amplum in Italia principatum iustissime simul et prudentissime administravit, res tamen mundanas tanta elevati in aeternae salutis desideria spiritus munditia et puritate contempsit ut postquam adulescens in caelum, unde venerat, restitutus carnis sarcina est exutus, beatitudinis famam signaque in terris reliquerit.

10 Ariminum nunc habet *Robertum Valturrem, bonarum artium studiis ornatum,*[16] Petrum *quoque* et Iacobum Perleones, fratres, Latinis et Graecis litteris apprime eruditos.

11 Ad sinistram Mariclae intus est, ut diximus, Verruculum, prima Malatestarum patria, Maiolumque, Bilium, ad fontemque in Apennino Castrum Ilicis. Est etiam, ut diximus, in exesi montis

from a mass of smaller ones) that Augustus built at great labor and expense when he paved the Flaminian Way in stone from Rome to Rimini. The Milvian Bridge, so called, on the Tiber was built by Marcus Scaurus, as Ammianus Marcellinus tells us:[23] it has entirely lost the extensive decoration given it by Augustus. The bridge that likewise spanned the Tiber below Otricoli has in part collapsed and been made into the foundations of a fort. And the bridge which crossed the Nera below Narni has lost its middle arch, having apparently been undermined over many generations or simply collapsed with the passage of time.

In earlier centuries Rimini was ornamented by Mastino, Pandolfo, and Galeotto of the Malatesta family, princes endowed with every virtue. Galeotto's sons Carlo (a prince both courageous and learned that I compared to Cato the Elder in my *Histories*),[24] and Pandolfo (who has held sway over Brescia and Bergamo *and Cremona*[25] for many years), *your father and that of Sigismondo Pandolfo,*[26] are reckoned to be first among the princes of our era. But the third Malatesta brother was surely not their inferior in virtue. Our age has been left vivid and affectionate memories of Galeotto Roberto. He governed the ample Italian realm of towns and cities that he inherited from his forebears with equal justice and wisdom, yet he despised the things of this world with such refinement and purity of spirit (elevated as it was by a longing for eternal salvation) that when, still young, he put off the burden of the flesh and was restored to the heaven whence he had come, he left behind him on earth the repute and tokens of saintliness.[27]

Rimini now has *Roberto Valturio, impressive for his studies in the liberal arts, and also*[28] the brothers Pietro and Jacopo Perleone, great scholars of Greek and Latin literature.[29]

Inland on the south bank of the Marecchia is Verucchio (as I said), the original home of the Malatesta, and Maiolo, Billi, and, at the source of the river in the Apennines, Casteldelci. And as I said, there is on the peak of a cavernous hill the town of San Ma-

cacumine Sanmarinum oppidum, olim Acer Mons dictum, per-
petuae libertatis gloria clarum. Ulterius via Flaminia est Sancta
Iustina vicus, et supra primis in collibus Sanctus Archangelus nobile oppidum. Et in via item Flaminia Savignanum oppidum intersecat Plusa vetusti nominis fluvius, qui sub Belaere castello mare
influit Adriaticum. Inde habetur parvus torrens Butrius, cui supra
viam Flaminiam adiacet Longianum, vite oleaque in circuitu perpulchre consitum.

12   Sequitur magni quondam nominis torrens perexiguus Rubicon,
Cisalpinae Galliae et Italiae arva disterminare solitus. Eum nunc
Pissatellum qui sub Flaminia via, Rubiconem vero qui supra acco-
lunt, vocant. Quem olim, stante et integra re publica Romana, lege
prohibitum fuit ne quispiam armatus illum iniussu magistratuum
transgrederetur. Eaque lex, loco mota in quo ab initio fuit posita,
marmore litteris incisa elegantissimis etiam nunc visitur, quam li-
buit hic ponere: 'Iussu mandatuve populi Romani consultum: imperator, miles, tiro, commilito armate, quisquis es, manipulariaeve
centurio turmaeve legionariae, hic sistito. Vexillum sinito, nec citra
hunc amnem Rubiconem signa ductum commeatumve traducito.
Si quis huius iussionis ergo ierit feceritve, adiudicatus esto hostis
populi Romani ac si contra patriam arma tulerit penatesque e
sacris penetralibus asportaverit. S.P.Q.R. SANCTIO PLEBI-
SCITI SENATUSVE CONSULTA.' Notiora sunt quae de
huius amnis et legis transgressione C. Iulii Caesaris scripta sunt a
multis quam ut ea a nobis hic scribi oportere iudicemus, satisque
fuerit et locum et legem indicasse.

rino, formerly called Agromonte and famous for the independence
that it has never lost. Further along the Flaminian Way is the
village of Santa Giustina, and above it in the foothills the well-
known town of Santarcangelo di Romagna. Also along the Flaminian Way, the ancient river Uso intersects the town of Savi-
gnano before flowing into the Adriatic below the castle of Bellaria.
Then comes the little stream Budrio, beside which, inland from
the Flaminian Way, lies the town of Longiano, encircled by pretty
plantations of grapes and olives.

A tiny stream follows that was once very famous, the Rubicon, 12
the traditional boundary between the lands of Cisalpine Gaul
and Italy. Those who live below the Flaminian Way call it the
Pisciatello, and those above it, the Rubicone. As long as the Roman republic stood inviolate, it was forbidden by law for anyone to
cross the Rubicon in arms without permission of the magistrates.
The law, which has been moved from the place where it was originally, can still be seen inscribed in marble in graceful lettering, and
I take the opportunity to set it down here: "Resolved by order and
mandate of the Roman People: commander, private, recruit, comrade in arms — whether you be of a company or a century, of a cavalry squadron or legion, here you must stop: you shall leave your
ensign be: nor shall you lead your standards, military command or
supplies across this river Rubicon. If anyone in the light of this law
shall have gone or acted contrary to its provisions, let him be ad-
judged an enemy of the Roman People, as if he had borne arms
against his country and had carried away the Penates from their
holy sanctuaries. The Senate and the People of Rome. This is the
sanction of the Plebiscite and these are the Decrees of the Senate."[30] The numerous accounts of Caesar's crossing of the river —
and of the statute — are too well known for me to need to recount
them here. Let it suffice to have indicated both the place and the
law.

13   Incipit vero hic secundum vetustos Gallia Cisalpina, de qua M.
Cicero in *Philippicis*: 'Nec vero de virtute, constantia, gravitate
Galliae taceri potest. Est enim ille flos Italiae, illud firmamentum
imperii Romani, illud ornamentum dignitatis.' Et Plinius: 'In hoc
tractu interiere Boi, quorum tribus CXII fuisse auctor est Cato.
Item Senones, qui ceperant Romam.'

14   Qua Rubicon torrens influit Adriaticum, portus est Cesenas,
parva admittens navigia. Intus supra Flaminiam sunt amoeni et fe-
racis agri Ariminensis castella, quorum primarium est Runchfrid-
dum. Ultra Cesenatem portum litori propinqua est Cervia civitas,
rarissimo habitata colono salinas faciente, quam Malatesta Novel-
lus Cesenae princeps praestantissimus in arctiorem restrictam or-
bem[17] muro nuper valido communivit. Et quinto abinde miliario
absunt Sapis fluvii ostia.

15   Adiacetque ei fluvio intus in via Flaminia civitas Cesena vetus
habens nomen, quae praedicti Malatestae Novelli, litteris praesertim historia ornatissimi, administratione nunc gaudet, et a quo
ornatur bibliotheca melioribus Italiae aequiparanda, cum tamen
hospitale idem in urbe sumptuosissimum aedificet ac ponte lapi-
deo et quidem insigni Sapim fluvium ad viam Flaminiam iunxerit
moenibusque illam novis alicubi communiat. Est vero nunc pluris
facienda quam innuerit[18] Marcus Cicero, cum in ultima ad Lentulum epistula, significare volens quendam Romanum civem parvi
faciendum esse, dicit non satis dignum esse cui Cesena aut taber-
nolae fuerint committendae. Plinius autem Cicerone posterior,
vina docens Italiae optima, connumerat Caesenaticum. Ea civitas
cum civilibus dissidiis tumultuaretur, ad annum salutis tricesimum
octavum supra millesimum tricentesimum a Britonibus, Romanae
ecclesiae fidem servare simulantibus, direpta fuit.

16   Superius ad Sapis fluenta intus est Emporium Sarracenum vicus, et paulo supra ad Apennini radices Sassina, vetustissima civi-

This is where Cisalpine Gaul begins, according to the ancients. 13
In the *Philippics*, Cicero says of it: "Nor is it possible to pass over
in silence the bravery, firmness and dignity of Gaul: she is the
flower of Italy, the bedrock of Roman rule, the chief ornament of
Roman prestige."[31] And Pliny: "In this area the Boii perished, who
had one hundred and twelve tribes according to Cato. Likewise
the Senonian Gauls, who seized Rome."[32]

Where the Rubicon flows into the Adriatic is Cesenatico, the 14
harbor of Cesena, which can take smaller vessels. Inland above
the Flaminian Way are the castles of the attractive and fertile
Riminese territory, Roncofreddo foremost among them. Beyond
Cesenatico is Cervia next to the coast, inhabited by a few peasants
who work the salt-flats. The excellent lord of Cesena, Malatesta
Novello, has recently fortified Cervia with strong walls, drawing it
into a smaller compass. Five miles from the town is the mouth of
the river Savio.

Inland along the Savio on the Via Flaminia lies the ancient city 15
of Cesena. It now rejoices in the rule of Malatesta Novello, a
prince notable for his literary attainments, especially in history;
and he is constructing a library that will rival the best in Italy,[33]
though he is also building in the city an exceedingly well-ap-
pointed hospital, and has carried the Flaminian Way over the river
Savio with a fine stone bridge, and is fortifying the city elsewhere
with new walls. Cesena is now a place of more consequence than
Cicero suggested when, in his last letter to Lentulus, he wanted to
represent a certain Roman citizen as worthless, saying that you
would hardly trust him with Cesena—or wine taverns.[34] After
Cicero's day, Pliny includes a *vinum Caesenaticum* among the noted
wines of Italy.[35] When Cesena was in the grip of civil strife, it was
sacked by the Bretons in A.D. 1338, in a show of obedience to the
church of Rome.[36]

Further inland on the course of the Savio is the village of 16
Mercato Saraceno, and a little above it in the foothills of the

tas, quae in Bois nobilissima Plautum comicum civem habuit, quem Eusebius tradit: 'propter annonae difficultatem ad molas manuarias pistori se locasse; ibi, quotiens opere vacaret, fabulas scribere et vendere solitum fuisse.' In eiusque urbis ruinis episcopium est, cuius dioceseos et dominii sunt castella et oppida ad viginti, 'Bobio' pro Boio vetusto nomine appellata.

17   Ad Sapis vero fluvii fontem vel paulo infra oppidum est Sanctae Mariae, a balneis quae intus habet latericio opere conclusis dictum, *quod Gherardus obtinet Gambacurta Pisanus, litteris adeo delectatus, ut erudiendis ea in montium asperitate filiis nostrum doctissimum Trapezuntium magno impendio annuerit praeceptorem.*[19] Et secundum amnis eiusdem decursum Vallis est Balinea, castellis vicisque plurimis frequentata. Obtinuerunt vero Boi a principio omnem eam nunc Romandiolae regionem, quae a Sassina Bononiensem includit agrum. Perhibetque Plinius Bononiam pro Boionia dictam esse, quamquam non modo Bononiensem agrum Boi sed eos qui nunc Mutinensis Regiensisque dicuntur complexi fuisse videntur. Quod indicat Livius libro XXII his verbis: 'Q. Minucius inde in agrum Boiorum legiones duxit. Boiorum exercitus haud ita[20] multo ante traiecerant Padum iunxerantque se Insubribus et Cenomanis, quod ita acceperant, coniunctis legionibus, consules rem gesturos, ut et ipsi collatas in unum vires firmarent. Postquam fama accidit alterum consulem Boiorum urere agros, seditio extemplo orta est. Postulare Boi ut laborantibus universi opem ferrent. Insubres negare se sua deserturos. Ita divisae copiae, Boisque[21] in agrum suum Tannetum profectis.' Si itaque Tannetum fuit Boiorum, Mutina

Apennines, Sarsina, a very ancient city and the best known of the towns of the Boii. Among its citizens was the comic poet Plautus, of whom Eusebius says: "Owing to difficulties in getting a supply of corn, he hired himself out to a baker at a hand-operated mill; there, whenever his work spared him, he would write and sell his plays."[37] There is a cathedral in the ruins of this town; it has about twenty castles and towns under its diocesan jurisdiction, called Bobium after the ancient name Boius.

At the source of the river Savio, or a little below it, is the town 17 of Santa Maria in Bagno,[38] so called from the brick-faced baths within the town. *It was obtained by Gherardo Gambacurta of Pisa, who delighted so much in literature that at great expense he summoned our most learned Trebizond to educate his children in the middle of these rugged mountains.*[39] The Valdibagno with its multitude of castles and villages follows the course of the river downwards. From the beginning the Boii occupied this region, now called Romagna, starting at Sarsina and including the territory of Bologna. Pliny says that it was called Bononia for Boionia, [40] although the Boii possessed not only the territory of Bologna, it seems, but what are now known as the territories of Modena and Reggio as well. Livy supports this in Book XXII: "From there Minucius led his legions into the country of the Boii, whose army had not long before crossed the Po. They had heard that the consuls intended to attack with their united legions, and in order that they too might consolidate their strength by union they had formed a junction with the Insubres and Cenomani. When a report reached them that one of the consuls was burning the fields of the Boii, a sharp difference of opinion arose; the Boii demanded that all should render assistance to those who were hard pressed, the Insubres declared that they would not leave their own country defenseless. Their forces were accordingly divided, and the Boii went off to their own territory, Tannetum."[41] So if Tannetum belonged to the Boii, then Modena

pariter et nunc Regium, ultra quam civitatem Tannetum esse ostendemus, in Bois fuere.

18   Fuerunt autem potentissimi bellacissimique populi, quod innuit Livius, libro XXI: Boi sollicitati ab Insubribus defecerunt, nec tam ob veteres in Romanum populum iras quam quod nuper circa Padum Placentiam Cremonamque colonias in agrum Gallicum deductas aegre patiebantur. Triumviri ad deducendas colonias missi, Placentiae moenibus diffisi, Mutinam confugerunt. Legati ad Boios missi violati sunt, Mutina obsessa. Et simulatum de pace agi. Missique ad eam tractandam a Gallis comprehensi. L. Manlius imperator effusum agmen ad Mutinam ducit. Caesi sunt Romanorum octingenti. Sex signa militaria adempta. Item Livius XXXVI: P. Cornelius Scipio Nasica cos., vir optimus a senatu iudicatus, Boios Gallos victos[22] in deditionem accepit, de quibus triumphavit.

19   Prima post Sapis ostia in Adriatici litore loca describi digna sunt parva Candiani, sive vallis sive stagni ostia: documento prudentibus rerumque peritis futura quam[23] in rebus humanis omnia fluxa, omnia sunt caduca. Sapis fluvius, quem octavo miliario descriptum post terga linquimus, ad annum hinc plus minus sexcentesimum ipsam illabebatur Candiani vallem efficiebatque portum in primis Italiae celebrem.[24] In quo, sicut Suetonius Tranquillus Vegetiusque et plerique vetustiores scripserunt, Octavius Augustus, primus Romanorum imperatorum,[25] classem instituit, quae sinum Adriaticum, Illyricum, Dalmatiam, Graeciam, Pontum, Armeniam, Asiam, Aegyptum, et omnem Mediterranei maris oram tueretur. Scribitque Plinius in eius portus ostiis turrim fuisse Phaream, omnium maximam quas Romanum ubique habuit

and what is now Reggio (which lies beyond the town of Tannetum, as I shall show) were in Boian territory as well.

As Livy suggests in Book XXI, the Boii were a very powerful   18
and warlike people: provoked by the Insubres (he says) and moti-
vated not so much by old resentment against the Roman people as
by the outrage they felt at the recent settlement of colonies in Gallic territory around the Po, such as Piacenza and Cremona, the
Boii rose up in revolt. The three commissioners for founding the
colonies fled to Modena, not feeling themselves safe behind the
walls of Piacenza. Envoys sent to the Boii were maltreated, and
Modena laid under siege. The Boii made a pretense of suing for
peace, but those sent to negotiate it were seized by the Gauls. The
commander Lucius Manlius led his army to Modena. Eight hundred Romans were killed, and six standards lost.[42] And Livy again,
in Book XXXVI, says that the consul P. Cornelius Scipio Nasica,
judged best and worthiest in the commonwealth by the senate, received the surrender of the defeated Boian Gauls and celebrated a
triumph over them.[43]

Just after the mouth of the Savio on the Adriatic coast is a   19
small area worth describing, Candiano, the name of a valley and a
lagoon: for the wise and informed student of history it provides a
lesson on the mutable and transient nature of all human enter-
prises. Some 600 years ago, more or less, the river Savio (described above, eight miles behind us now) used to flow into the
valley of Candiano and formed a harbor, among the most celebrated in Italy. We have it on the authority of Suetonius, Vegetius,
and many other ancient authors that Augustus, the first Roman
emperor, established a fleet [classis] there to protect the Adriatic
Gulf, Illyria, Dalmatia, Greece, Pontus, Armenia, Asia Minor,
Egypt, and the whole Mediterranean coast.[44] Pliny writes that at
the harbor mouth there was a lighthouse, the greatest in the entire
Roman empire.[45] Shortly after the harbor was brought into service, it happened that a town [Classe] was built there by naval units

imperium. Et brevi ab instituto eo portu factum est ut a navalibus turmis convenientibus undique mercatoribus civitas ibi sit aedificata et quidem opulentissima, de qua Aelius[26] Spartianus in *Didii Iuliani vita* scribit: 'Sed dum haec agit Iulianus, Severus Classem Ravennatem occupat.' Ea vero civitas cum antea tum maxime Beati Gregorii temporibus episcopum habuit. Capta vero fuit a rege Longobardorum Luthprando atque direpta, unde et urbe sublata et, quod magis crediderim, fluvio Sapi in remotum averso cursum, videmus factum ut nec urbis moenium nec turris Phareae neque portus, nisi minima ex parte, aliquod appareat vestigium, praeter Sancti Apollinaris in ipsa Classe civitate basilicam variis ornatam marmoribus, ceterisque aequiparandam quas Italia ubique habet[27] vetustae magnificentiae speciosiores, quae Theoderici Ostrogothorum primi regis opus fuit.

20   Influunt vero ipsam Candiani vallem, qui et tanti olim portus tenues conservant reliquias, parvi torrentes Avesa et Bevanus appellati, quorum primus latera abluit Fori Pompilii[28] civitatis olim nunc oppidi nominis vetusti. Quod in via Flaminia unum fuit ex quattuor foris quae Plinius illa in regione simul enumerat. Quam civitatem ad annum salutis septingentesimum, Vitaliani pontificis Romani natione Signiensis temporibus, Grimoaldus Longobardorum tyrannus, dum Sabbato Sancto conficeretur chrisma, furto occupatam diripuit, ac solo aequavit, et a Forliviensibus postea instauratam, iterum destruxit ararique fecit ad annum salutis millesimum trecentesimum sexagesimum Aegidius Sabinensis Romanae ecclesiae cardinalis *hispanus, pugil Ecclesiae*[29] celeberrimus.

21   Supra eminenti in colle est Bretonorium civitas in quam destructi Fori Pompilii[30] episcopalis dignitas est translata. Fuitque id oppidum quod Plinius vetustiora repetens Brintum appellat, Umbriae apud Ravennam ultimum et postea inter quattuor fora enumeratum dicit esse forum Brintanorum. Sub Bretonorii colle imminet torrenti Avesae Polenta oppidum paucis habitatum colo-

for the merchants that descended upon the place from all sides,
and a very fine one too. Aelius Spartianus in his *Life of Julian* says
of it: "While Julian was engaged in these activities, however,
Severus seized the town of Classe by Ravenna."[46] This city had a
bishopric, notably in the time of Gregory the Great, but also before.[47] It was captured by the Lombard King Liutprand, however,
and destroyed.[48] And so we see that the city's destruction and
(more importantly, I think) the diversion of the Savio further away
brought it about that none but the slightest trace is now visible of
the city wall, the lighthouse, or the harbor, except only the Basilica of Sant'Apollinare in Classe, embellished with various carven
marbles. The work of Theodoric, first king of the Ostrogoths,
Sant'Apollinare can match any other basilica anywhere in Italy for
the beauty of its ancient splendor.

The little streams known as the Ausa and the Bevano flow into   20
the valley of Candiano, and they too still preserve some slight rel-
ics of that once great harbor. The Ausa washes the flanks of the
ancient town (formerly a city) of Forlimpopoli. It lies on the
Flaminian Way, one of four "Forums" in the region listed together
by Pliny.[49] About the year A.D. 700, in the time of Pope Vitalianus
of Segni, while ointment was being prepared on Holy Saturday,
Grimoald, the king of the Lombards, seized the town by a trick,
pillaged it and razed it to the ground. It was afterwards restored
by the men of Forlì, but again destroyed in A.D. 1360 by the famous cardinal of Santa Sabina, Gil Albornoz *of Spain, the champion
of the Church*,[50] who had it plowed under.[51]

On a high hill above Forlimpopoli is the town of Bertinoro,   21
where the former's episcopal see was transferred when it was destroyed. It was this town that Pliny, in seeking to recover older
usage, calls Brintum,[52] the last town of Umbria near Ravenna,
and later he lists it among four "Forums," calling it Forum Brintanorum.[53] Overlooking the Ausa beneath the hill of Bertinoro is
the town of Polenta, inhabited by a few farmers. Here, as I

nis, ad quem locum ostendimus in *Historiis* proelium illud Romae et Italiae infelicissimum fuisse commissum, in quo lacessiti magis quam clade aliqua confecti Visogothi, omissa ad Gallias quam intendebant profectione, arma in urbem Romam victricia converterunt.[31] Et ea capta direptaque ac alicubi incensa, *Romani imperii inclinatio*, nostrae *Historiae* titulus initiumque, inchoavit.

22   Post Classensem Candiani portum prima sunt Bedesi amnis, ostia Ravennae portum efficientia. Estque inde secundo miliario Ravenna urbs vetusta quam diximus fuisse oppidum Sabinorum. Unde Livius libro XXI: 'Cornelius cos., cum audisset a Bois ante suum adventum incursiones in agrum sociorum factas, duabus legionibus subitariis tumultus eius causa scriptis additisque ad eas quattuor cohortibus de exercitu suo, C. Appium praefectum suum hac tumultuaria manu per Umbriam, qua tribum Sabinianam vocant, agrum Boiorum invadere iussit.' Fuit itaque ager Ravennas haec tribus Sabiniana. Et infra addit Livius: 'deinde ad castrum Mutillum,' quae nunc dicitur Mutiliana.[32]

23   Cinxit Ravennam muris nunc exstantibus Tiberius imperator, quod litterae docent cubitales ad portam eius clausam, quae Aurea dicitur, quadrato lapide speciosam. Auxit vero ipsam Ostrogotha gens: cuius rex Theodericus, Italiae omnis, Dalmatiae, Hungariae, Germaniae et partis non parvae Galliarum dominus, annis duo de quadraginta eam incoluit civitatem et, quod constat, superbas in illa aedes basilicasque construxit. Visitur eius regis monumentum ab Amalasuntha filia positum extra Ravennae moenia, in quo Sanctae Mariae monasterium est aedificatum 'in Rotundo' ea ratione appellatum, quod altare maius ecclesiae chorusque, viginti capax monachorum ordine, ut est moris, in stallo psallentium,

showed in my *Histories*, there was the battle that proved disastrous for Rome and Italy. Provoked rather than overwhelmed by defeat, the Visigoths discarded their plan to make for Gaul and turned their conquering army on Rome.[54] And with the capture, pillaging and later burning down of the city, the *Decline of the Roman Empire* (the title and beginning of my *Histories*) set in.

After the harbor of Classe in Candiano we come first to the 22 mouth of the river Ronco, which forms the harbor of Ravenna. Two miles from Classe is the ancient city of Ravenna, which, as we said above, was a Sabine town [Umbria §2]. Livy speaks of it in Book XXI: "When the consul Cornelius heard that the Boii had been making raids into the territory of the allies prior to his arrival, he hastily raised a force of two legions in view of this disturbance and strengthened it with four cohorts from his own army. He ordered his prefect C. Appius to take this improvised force and to invade the territory of the Boii through the part of Umbria they call the Tribus Sabiniana."[55] And so the territory of Ravenna was this Tribus Sabiniana. Further on, Livy adds: "Thence to Castrum Mutillum," the place now called Modigliana.[56]

The emperor Tiberius built the walls around Ravenna that are 23 still there today, as an inscription attests in eighteen-inch high letters on the city gate called the Porta Aurea, handsomely built of squared stone and now blocked off.[57] The Ostrogoths enlarged the city, and their king Theoderic—ruler over the whole of Italy, Dalmatia, Hungary, Germany and no small part of France—lived in the city for 38 years and, as is well known, built splendid palaces and basilicas there. The king's mausoleum can still be seen, erected by his daughter Amalasuntha outside the walls of the city, where the monastery of S. Maria in Rotondo stands.[58] The monastery was so named because the church's high altar and choir (the stalls can accommodate a line of twenty monks at their psalms, as tradition dictates) are covered by a dome made of a single block of

unico atque integro rotundo lapide conteguntur. Praeestque illi monasterio abbas Matthaeus Blondus nobis frater germanus, *mera Beati Benedicti militia nequaquam degenerans.*[33]

24 Populo nunc Ravenna est infrequens; olim autem viros habuit cum sanctos tum etiam doctos: Apollinarem, Vitalem eiusque filios Gervasium et Prothasium, ac Ursicinumque medicum, omnes martyrio coronatos; Iohannem quoque nominis ordine XVII pontificem Romanum; Petrum quoque Ravennatem Fori Cornelii episcopum qui multas sacri eloquii scripturas eloquentissime dilucidavit; et Cassiodorum urbis Romae senatorem regumque Ostrogothorum epistularum scriptorem et postea monachum qui praeter scripta saecularia nequaquam contemnenda libros de sacris literis[34] gravissime ac eruditissime scriptos reliquit. Videtur etiam Ravenna genuisse Faustinum ad quem Martialis poeta multa scripsit: 'quos, Faustine, dies qualem[35] tibi Roma Ravennam abstulit.'

25 Genuit quoque superiori saeculo Guilielmum physicum quem Petrus Paulus Vergerius notissimum amicissimumque sibi hominem magnis effert laudibus. Genuit eodem tempore Iohannem grammaticum rhetoremque doctissimum, quem solitus dicere fuit Leonardus Arretinus, omni in re sed potissime in hac una gravissimus locupletissimusque testis, fuisse primum a quo eloquentiae studia — tantopere nunc florentia longo postliminio — in Italiam fuerint reducta: digna certe cognitio quae a nobis nunc illustranda Italia in medium adducatur.

26 Vident atque intellegunt qui Latinas litteras vero et suo cum sapore degustant, paucos ac prope nullos post doctorum ecclesiae Ambrosii, Hieronymi et Augustini ⟨tempora⟩, quae et eadem inclinantis Romanorum imperii tempora fuerunt, aliqua cum elegantia scripsisse, nisi illis propinqui temporibus beatus Gregorius ac venerabilis Beda et, qui longo his posterior tempore fuit, beatus Bernardus in eorum numerum sint ponendi. Primus vero omnium Franciscus Petrarcha, magno vir ingenio maiorique diligentia, et

stone. My brother, abbot Matteo Biondo, is in charge of the monastery, *preserving undiminished the pure standards of Benedictine monastic life.*[59]

Ravenna has few inhabitants now, but she once had men notable not just for their piety but for learning too: Apollinaris, Vitalis and his sons Gervasius and Protasius, and Ursicinus the physician, all with the martyrs' crown; Pope John XVII; Petrus Ravennas, the Bishop of Imola, who interpreted many texts of holy scripture with great eloquence; and Cassiodorus, senator of Rome and secretary of the Ostrogoth kings, later a monk who, apart from his not inconsiderable secular writings, has left us a learned and important book *On Sacred Letters.*[60] Ravenna seems also to have produced the Faustinus to whom the poet Martial often wrote: "What days, what a town in Ravenna has Rome stolen from you, Faustinus!"[61]   24

In the last century Ravenna bore the physician Guglielmo, highly praised by his dear and intimate friend Pietro Paolo Vergerio.[62] At the same time she bore the learned grammarian and rhetorician Giovanni Malpaghini,[63] who was the first to bring back to Italy the study of eloquence, now so flourishing here after its long exile, as Leonardo Bruni used to say — a most solid and reliable authority on all matters, but specially on this one. It is a subject that certainly merits discussion here in my illustration of Italy.   25

Those who have developed a sure and true taste for Latin literature realize and appreciate that few authors, indeed hardly any, wrote Latin with any measure of elegance after the time of the doctors of the Church, Ambrose, Jerome, and Augustine — the very period of the decline of the Roman empire — unless we are to include in their number St. Gregory and the Venerable Bede, who came just afterwards, and St. Bernard, who was much later. The very first to revive Latin poetry and eloquence was Francesco   26

poesim et eloquentiam excitare coepit. Nec tamen eum attigit Ciceronianae eloquentiae florem quo multos in hoc saeculo videmus ornatos, in quo quidem nos librorum magis quam ingenii carentiam defectumque culpamus. Ipse enim etsi *Epistulas* Ciceronis Lentulo inscriptas Vercellis reperisse gloriatus est, *aliud non vidit volumen earum quae, Ad Atticum inscriptae, sic grandiorem habent eloquentiam sicut maiora et auctorem magis anxium attentumque habentia continent.*[36] Tres tamen[37] Ciceronis *De oratore* et *Institutionum oratoriarum* Quintiliani libros non nisi laceros mutilatosque vidit, ad eiusque notitiam *Oratoris maioris* et *Bruti de oratoribus claris*, item Ciceronis libri, nullatenus pervenerunt.

27   Iohannes autem Ravennas Petrarcham senem puer novit nec eos aliter quam Petrarcha vidit libros neque quod sciamus aliquid a se scriptum reliquit. Et tamen suopte ingenio et quodam dei munere, sicut fuit solitus dicere Leonardus, se Petrum Paulumque Vergerium, Omnebonum Scolam Patavinum, Robertum Rossum et Iacobum Angeli filium Florentinos, Poggiumque et Guarinum Veronensem, Victorinum Feltrensem, ac alios qui minus profecerunt, auditores suos, si non satis quod plene nesciebat docere potuit, in bonarum ut dicebat litterarum amorem Ciceronisque imitationem inflammabat. Interea Emanuel Chrysoloras Constantinopolitanus, vir doctrina et omni virtute excellentissimus, cum se in Italiam contulisset, partim Venetiis, partim Florentiae, partim in Romana curia quam secutus est, praedictos paene omnes Iohannis Ravennatis auditores litteras docuit Graecas; effecitque eius doctrina paucis tamen continuata annis ut qui Graecas nescirent litteras, Latinas minus viderentur edocti.

28   Et cum magnus bene discendi ardor multos in Italia apprehendisset conciliumque apud Constantiam Germaniae ab universo populo Christiano haberetur, quaerere ibi et investigare coeperunt ex nostratibus multi si quos Germaniae loca Constantiae proxima

Petrarca, a man of great talent and even greater industry, even if he never attained the full flower of Ciceronian eloquence that we see gracing so many men of our own time: but we do not criticize in him want or defect of genius so much as lack of books. Though he boasted of finding Cicero's *Letters to Lentulus* at Vercelli,[64] *he never saw the other volume of the Epistles, the letters To Atticus: they have a larger eloquence, just as they have grander themes and show an author taking more pains and care.*[65] Nor did he ever see the three books of Cicero's *On the Orator* or Quintilian's *Institutes of Oratory* except in imperfect and mutilated copies, and he did not know that Cicero's books *The Orator* and *Brutus, on Famous Orators* even existed.

Giovanni Malpaghini as a boy knew Petrarch in his old age, 27 and saw those books no more than Petrarch did, nor did he leave anything in writing, so far as I know. And yet by dint of his natural talent and (as Leonardo used to say) the grace of God, he managed to kindle in his students a passion for "good letters" (as he put it) and for the imitation of Cicero, even if he was unable to teach subjects he was entirely ignorant of: and they included Pietro Paolo Vergerio, Ognibene Scola of Padua, the Florentines Roberto Rossi and Jacopo di Angelo da Scarperia, Poggio, Guarino da Verona, Vittorino da Feltre, and others who didn't advance quite so far.[66] At the same time, Manuel Chrysoloras of Constantinople came to Italy, a man pre-eminent in scholarship and all the virtues; he taught Greek to nearly all those students of Giovanni Malpaghini, in Venice, in Florence and in the Roman Curia, with which he was associated. His teaching lasted only a few years, but it had the effect that those who did not know Greek appeared ignorant in Latin.[67]

While this great enthusiasm for acquiring knowledge had taken 28 hold of many people in Italy, all Christendom convened at a council in Constance in Germany: a number of our countrymen began to conduct searches there and enquire whether any of the lost books of the Romans and old Italy were hiding in the recesses of

ex deperditis Romanorum et Italiae olim libris in monasteriorum latebris occultarent. Quintilianusque integer repertus a Poggio primum transcriptus in Italiam venit. Secutaeque sunt, incerto nobis datae libertatis patrono, Ciceronis *Ad Atticum epistulae*. Cumque his in Quintiliani *Institutionibus* et *Ad Atticum epistulis* nostrorum Italiae adulescentium ingenia desudarent, Gasparinus Bergomensis, grammaticus rhetorque celeberrimus, Venetiis meliori solito doctrina nonnullos erudivit, plurimos ad ea imitanda studia incitavit. Florebantque iam et fama celebrabantur Petrus Paulus Vergerius, Omnebonum Schola natu maiores, Leonardus Arretinus, Robertus Rossus, Iacobus Angeli, et Poggius ac Nicola Mediceus, quem praeceptor domi assiduus erudierat Arretinus.

29 Guarinusque Venetiis et Victorinus Mantuae multos coeperant erudire, cum Philippus Mediolanensis dux III Gasparinum patria Bergamo subditum hominem invitum Mediolanensibus edocendis Padua et Venetiis[38] evocavit, ubi id maxime adiumenti studiis eloquentiae attulit, quod repertus Laude a summo viro Gerardo Landriano, tunc ibi episcopo, multis maximisque in ruderibus codex,[39] pervetustus et cuius litteras vetustiores paucissimi scirent legere, ad eius perveniens manus interitum evasit. Continebat is codex, praeter *Rhetoricorum novos* et *veteres* qui habebantur, tres quoque *De oratore* integerrimos, et *Brutum de oratoribus claris Oratoremque ad Brutum*, M. Tullii Ciceronis libros. Unde liberatus est bonus ipse vir Gasparinus ingenti quem assumpserat labore supplendi quoad poterat librorum *De oratore* defectus, sicut diu antea in Quintiliani *Institutionibus* multo labore suppleverat. Et cum nullus Mediolani esset repertus qui eius vetusti codicis characterem nosset,[40] Cos-

monasteries in that part of Germany.[68] A complete Quintilian was discovered by Poggio and when transcribed made its way to Italy for the first time. Cicero's *Letters to Atticus* followed Quintilian, though I do not know the master that emancipated that particular slave. While the talents of our Italian youth were exerting themselves on Quintilian's *Institutes* and Cicero's *Letters to Atticus*, the famous grammarian and rhetorician Gasparino Barzizza instructed a number at Venice with his uncommonly good teaching, and roused many more to follow his example in these studies.[69] The most notable figures now winning themselves a reputation were Pietro Paolo Vergerio and Ognibene Scola of the older generation, Leonardo Bruni, Roberto Rossi, Jacopo di Angelo, Poggio, and Nicola de' Medici, who had intensive teaching at home from Bruni.[70]

Many boys had begun to receive an education at the hands of Guarino in Venice[71] and of Vittorino in Mantua, when Filippo Maria Visconti, the third duke of Milan, summoned his unwilling subject Gasparino of Bergamo from Padua and Venice to teach in Milan. While he was there he rendered this extraordinary service to the study of eloquence: an extremely old manuscript was found at Lodi amid a mass of ruins by Gerardo Landriano, a great man, and at that time the local bishop. Its script was so ancient that very few could read it, and it was only saved from destruction by coming into Gasparino's hands. In addition to the *Rhetorics* (the *New* and the *Old Rhetoric*, as they are called), the manuscript also contained three books *On the Orator* absolutely complete, *Brutus on Famous Orators*, and *The Orator to Brutus*—all books by Marcus Tullius Cicero. As a result of the discovery, the good Gasparino was delivered from the vast labor that he had taken upon himself of filling in the gaps, so far as he could, of *On the Orator*, just as long before he had laboriously filled in the gaps in Quintilian's *Institutes*. Since no one could be found in Milan who could read the script of the old codex, a man of outstanding talent, one Cosimo

29

mus quidam egregio ingenio Cremonensis tres *De oratore* libros primus ex eo descripsit.[41] Multiplicataque inde exempla omnem Italiam desideratissimo codice repleverunt. Nos vero cum publicis patriae tractandis negotiis adulescentes Mediolanum adissemus, *Brutum de claris oratoribus* primi omnium mirabili ardore ac celeritate descripsimus,[42] ex quo primum Veronam Guarino, post Leonardo Iustiniano Venetias misso omnis Italia exemplis pariter est repleta.

30   Quo ex tot librorum, ipsius eloquentiae fomitum, allato nostris hominibus adiumento factum videmus ut maior meliorque ea quam Petrarcha habuit dicendi copia in nostram pervenerit aetatem. Nec parvum fuit cum adiumentum ad discendum eloquentiam tum etiam incitamentum Graecarum accessio litterarum, quod, qui eas didicere — praeter doctrinam et ingentem historiarum exemplorumque copiam inde comparatam — conati sunt multa ex Graecis in Latinitatem vertere, in quo usu aut assiduitate scribendi, aut reddiderunt eam quam habebant eloquentiam meliorem aut qui nullam prius habuerant inde aliquam compararunt. Hinc ferbuerunt diu magisque nunc ac magis fervent per Italiam gymnasia. Plerique sunt in civitatibus ludi, in quibus pulcherrimum iucundumque est videre discipulos, non solum postquam sunt dimissi, sed quousque etiam sub ipsa ferula declamant et scribunt, praeceptores dicendi scribendive elegantia superare.

31   Ex his autem quos Iohanni nostro Ravennati diximus fuisse discipulos duo aetate priores Guarinus et Victorinus, hic Mantuae, ille Venetiis, Veronae, Florentiae et demum Ferrariae, infinitam paene turbam, et in his Ferrarienses Mantuanosque principes, erudierunt. Georgius Trapezuntius publico Romae gymnasio Hispanos, Gallos Germanosque multos, in quis nonnulli aliquando sunt magni praestantesque viri, simul cum Italicis oratoriae ac poe-

of Cremona, was the first to transcribe the three books *On the Orator*, and copies of his transcription filled all Italy with that most sought-after of all books. When I myself was in Milan as a young man, carrying out official business on behalf of Forlì, I was the very first to copy the *Brutus*, which I did with extraordinary excitement and speed, and from my transcription (sent first to Guarino in Verona, then to Leonardo Giustiniani in Venice) the whole of Italy was similarly filled with copies of the book.[72]

We can see that the benefit brought to our countrymen by so   30
many books—the tinder of eloquence itself—resulted in our age having richer and finer resources of expression at its disposal than Petrarch enjoyed. The arrival of Greek letters was no small help in the acquisition of eloquence; and it was actually a stimulus to doing so, because, quite apart from the sheer knowledge and the huge supply of historical and moral material they gained from it, those who knew Greek attempted a good many translations into Latin, and so by constant practise in composition, their skill in writing improved, if they had any to begin with; or if they hadn't, they acquired some. And so academies all over Italy have long been hives of activity, and they are more and more active now with each passing day. The schools are generally in the cities, where it is a fine and pleasant spectacle to see pupils surpassing their teachers in the polish of their speech or writing, and not just when the class is dismissed but while they are actually declaiming and composing under the teacher's very rod.

Two of Giovanni Malpaghini's pupils that I mentioned as being   31
of an older generation, Guarino and Vittorino, have educated a whole host of students almost without number, the former at Venice, Verona, Florence and finally Ferrara, the latter at Mantua, and among their pupils were the princes of Ferrara and Mantua. At the University of Rome, George of Trebizond has alongside Italian students many Spaniards, French, and Germans, some of them important and distinguished men, for his courses on rhetoric

ticae auditores habet. Franciscus vero Philelphus ab ipsa gente
Chrysolora Constantinopoli eruditus Venetiis, Florentiae, Senis,
Bononiae et demum Mediolani plurimos Graecas litteras docuit et
Latinas. Quid quod Valla Laurentius non modo suis *Elegantiis*
quosdam Neapoli implevit sed eas quoque per omnem Italiam dis-
seminari obtinuit?[43] Petrusque Perleo Ariminensis Mediolani primum, dehinc Genuae, Iacobus frater eius Bononiae, Porcellius
Romae et Neapoli et Thomas Pontanus Perusiae, variisque in civitatibus Seneca Camertinus, Italiam bonis litteris implere pro viribus enituntur.

32   Sed iam ad Ravennam.[44] Auctor est Plinius, dum[45] nebulas nu-
trire uvas disputat, Ravennae vina praesertim Vermicula haberi
optima. Sed Martialis contra sentit his versibis: 'Sit cisterna mihi
quam vinea malo Ravennae. Nam possum multo vendere pluris
aquam.' Et alibi dicit nullo in solo gratiorem gigni asparagum iis
quos vidit in hortis Ravennatium. Quod Martialis confirmat his
versibus: 'Mollis et aequorea quae crevit spina Ravenna non erit
incultis gratior asparagis.' Et alio item loco scribit Plinius in Ravennatium mari rhombum esse optimum. Martialis vero indicat
Ravennae semper, alias sicut nunc, ranas fuisse multas: 'cum com-
parata rictibus tuis ora, Niliacus habeat crocodillus angusta me-
liusque ranae garriant Ravennates.'

33   Cingunt Ravennam amnes duo Bedesim facientes, quorum qui
ad dextram Montonus, qui ad sinistram olim Vitis nunc Aquae-
ductus dicitur, ortum in Apennini iugis propinquo Tiberis fonti
loco habens. Adiacetque illi intus Meldula oppidum, et superius
Galeata primum, deinde Sancta Sophia.[46]

34   Proxime vero ad Montoni fluminis sinistram in via Flaminia est
Forum Livii civitas vetusti nominis, tertium obtinens locum inter

and poetry.[73] Francesco Filelfo, himself educated by Chrysoloras' own progeny at Constantinople, has taught a great many people Greek and Latin letters in Venice, Florence, Siena, Bologna, and finally at Milan.[74] Lorenzo Valla's *Elegances* have not only brought satisfaction to people at Naples, but he has managed to broadcast them throughout Italy.[75] Pietro Perleone of Rimini, first in Milan and later in Genoa, and his brother Jacopo at Bologna, Porcellio at Rome and Naples, Tommaso Pontano at Perugia, and Tommaso Seneca da Camerino in a number of cities are striving might and main to fill Italy with good letters.[76]

But now on to Ravenna. While describing the nurture of the 32 grape in foggy areas, Pliny is our authority that the wines of Ravenna, especially its Vernaccia, are reputed to be of the finest quality.[77] But Martial expresses a contrary opinion in these lines: "I'd rather have a cistern at Ravenna than a vineyard, since I can get a far better price for water."[78] Elsewhere Pliny says that no soil produces better asparagus than the one he saw in the gardens of Ravenna.[79] Martial confirms this in the following couplet: "The soft stalk that grew in seaside Ravenna will not be more palatable than wild asparagus."[80] And in another place Pliny says that the finest turbot is found in the waters of Ravenna.[81] Martial shows that the frogs at Ravenna were always numerous, just as they are now: "Compared with your jaws, the Nile crocodile has a narrow mouth, and the frogs of Ravenna chatter more agreeably."[82]

Two rivers flow around Ravenna and form the Ronco, the 33 right-hand one being called the Montone; the one on the left was formerly known as the Vitis but is now the Acquedotto, rising in the Apennines near the source of the Tiber. Further inland the town of Meldola lies on the Acquedotto, and higher up Galeate, then Santa Sofia.[83]

Next, to the left of the river Montone along the Flaminian Way 34 is Forlì, a city of ancient foundation that Pliny puts third among the four "Forums" that he lists in that region, as I said above.[84] I

quattuor fora quae[47] Plinium ea in regione diximus posuisse. Videmus autem Eusebium *De temporibus* dicere Gallum poetam, cuius saepe Vergilius et Horatius meminerunt, fuisse Forliviensem. Et Plinius in vinis Italiae optimis Liviense enumerat. Fuit vero ea civitas, quod procul a vanitate mendacii de patria nostra sit dictum, viris praestantissimis praesertim litteratis fecunda. Nam praeter Gallum poetam habuit Guidonem Bonactum astrologorum principem, habuitque Rainerium Arsendum iureconsultum celebrem, Bartoli Saxoferratensis praeceptorem. Et eisdem ferme temporibus Checho Rubeo et Nereo Morando, viris doctissimis et Francisco Petrarchae, sicut ipse in *Epistolis* saepe meminit, amicis, ornata fuit. Excelluit vero per aetatem nostram Iacobus de Turre Forliviensis cunctos philosophiam medicinamque professos. Et Iacobi Allegretti Forliviensis bucolicum carmen exstare videmus ceteris post Vergilianum eo in genere scriptis carminibus facile, ut periti iudicant, praeponendum. Quid quod Ugolinus cognomine Urbevetanus Forlivii genitus et nutritus omnes aetatis nostrae musicos sine contradictione superat, editusque ab eo de musica liber haud secus omnium qui ante se scripserunt labores obscurabit quam Bonacti opera vetustissimorum scripta astrologorum seponi faciunt? Obiitque nuper Ludovicus Forliviensis et episcopus et civis, philosophorum aetatis nostrae theologorumque facile princeps. Rei autem bellicae gnaros et eo in munere claros habuit patria nostra Iohannem Ordelaphum, Brandolinum, *cuius nepos abneposque supersunt comes*,[48] et Tibertum Brandulos ac Mostardum. Nunc quoque ornata est Nicolao Hasteo Recanatensi ac Maceratensi episcopo, litteris, moribus et bonitate conspicuo, *Manfredoque Maldente qui iuris civilis scientiae, in qua plurimum excellit, eloquentiam et bonarum artium studia haud mediocriter coniunxit, pariterque Stephano Nardino eius pronepote camerae apostolicae clerico doctrina virtutibusque decorato.*[49] Magnam item spem dei munere constitutam videmus in quinque Blondis natis nostris qui litteris omnes pro aetate sunt pleni.

note that Eusebius in his *Chronicle* says that the poet Gallus, often mentioned by Vergil and Horace, was from Forlì.[85] Pliny lists a *vinum Liviense* among the best wines of Italy.[86] It may be said of my home without empty boasting that the city has been prolific in men of talent, in authors in particular. Apart from the poet Gallus, she bore the leading astrologer Guido Bonatti and the famous jurist, Rainerio Arsendi, the teacher of Bartolo da Sassoferrato.[87] About the same time she was adorned by the learned Cecco Rossi and Neri Morando, friends of Petrarch that he often mentions in his letters.[88] In our own time Giacomo della Torre of Forlì has outstripped all professors of philosophy and medicine.[89] We also note that a pastoral poem of Jacopo Allegretti of Forlì is extant, which in the opinion of experts is superior to anything else written in that genre since Vergil's *Eclogues*.[90] And what shall I say of Ugolino Urbevetano?[91] Born and raised in Forlì, by universal consent he surpasses all the musicians of our time, and the book he has published on music will eclipse the labors of all who have written before him, just as the works of Bonatti have caused the writings of the ancient astronomers to fall into neglect. Ludovico, bishop and citizen of Forlì, has recently died, easily the foremost philosopher and theologian of our time. Our city has also had men skilled in the art of war and famous for its practice: Giovanni Ordelaffi, Brandolino, *whose grandson and great-grandson survive as counts*,[92] and Tiberto Brandolini, and Mostarda da Forlì. The city even now is ornamented by Niccolò dall'Aste, Bishop of Recanati and Macerata, and notable for his learning, character, and goodness,[93] *and by Manfredo Maldenti, who has joined to his profound knowledge of civil law the study of the liberal arts and no small eloquence and by Stefano Nardini likewise, dall'Aste's grand-nephew, a clerk of the Apostolic Chamber and graced by learning and virtue*.[94] And by the grace of God I see high hopes lodged in my five Biondo sons, all well-stocked in literature, so far as their years allow.[95]

35 Feracissimi etiam et in multis naturae benignitate praecipui est
patria nostra soli. Nam praeter communes ceteris Italiae urbibus
fruges, vini, olei, frumenti, seminibus quoque abundat aromaticis
nulli in Italia alteri solo quam Apulo concessis: aneso,[50] carda-
momo, fenograeco, cimino, coriandro. Eam civitatem IV Martinus
pontifex Romanus murorum munitione spoliatam in vici rurisve
formam redegit. Quam ignominiam honestissima populo et male a
pontifice existimata praecessit causa. Cum enim Galli, ecclesiae soliti[51] militare, Guidone Appiensi ductore, urbem durissima ac diutina pressissent obsidione, cuius meminit vulgaris poeta Dantes,
populus Forliviensis, Guidone Bonacto hortante, armis correptis,
facta eruptione, magnam in illis edidit occidionem. Sed qui armis
resistendo fortes fuerant cives, suasionibus postea mollissimis se
decipi permiserunt, in quos pontifex immerito iratus in moenium
urbis demolitione desaeviit.

36 Ad Montoni dexteram Castrum Carum est oppidum, prius
Salsubium a scatente ibi salso fonte dictum, inde Dovadula, post
Cassianum. Dehinc arduo in colle est Porticus, item oppidum,
eloquentissimo et Graece Latineque doctissimo Ambrosio Camal-
dulensium principe monacho quem genuit clarum, ut non immerito nos aliquando gloriari soleamus quod vetusti patriae nostrae
agri oppida, ius a Forliviensi praetore patrum nostrorum memoria
petere solita, Plautum Sassina, Ambrosium genuerunt Porticus.

37 Ravennae moenia secus Montonum amnem fossa attingit, a vetustissimis, ut inquit Plinius, Messanicus[52] appellata, duodecim
milibus in Padum navigia perferens. Padusaque ad eam fossam incipit palus vetusti nominis et quam geographi unicam in Italia paludem esse volunt. De qua in *Georgicis* Vergilius: 'piscosove amne
Padusa.' Complectitur vero quicquid lacunae aut stagnorum aut

Among the gifts that a kindly nature has given my home town   35
is a quite unusually fertile soil; apart from the produce it shares
with the other cities of Italy—wine, olive-oil, grain—it has an
abundance of aromatic spices which are given to no other soil in
Italy, save only Apulia: aniseed, cardamom, fenugreek, cumin, and
coriander. Pope Martin IV stripped Forlì of its walls and reduced
it to the appearance of a village or bare countryside. The underly-
ing cause of this humiliation was honorable to the Forlivesi but
taken amiss by the pope: the French (the usual forces of the
Church) under Guido d'Appia had put the city under a long and
hard siege, as the *volgare* poet Dante recalled.[96] Urged on by Guido
Bonatti, the people of Forlì seized arms, broke out of the city, and
massacred them. But the citizens who had been stout in resisting
aggression later allowed themselves to be taken in by talk of reconciliation, and the pope vented his unreasonable anger on them by
destroying the walls of their city.

On the right bank of the Montone is the town of Castrocaro,   36
earlier called Salsubium from a salt-water spring that wells up
there; then comes Dovadola, and after that Rocca S. Casciano. Set
on a steep hill, the town Portico comes next, to which its famous
son Ambrogio Traversari lent luster, the general of the Camaldulensian monks and eloquent and learned in Greek and Latin.[97]
We are accustomed on occasion to take a justified pride in the fact
that towns in our ancestral territory (in our fathers' day they
would look to the magistrate of Forlì for justice) have borne such
sons as Sarsina has in Plautus and Portico in [St.] Ambrose.

Along the Montone, a canal called Messanicus by the ancients   37
(Pliny says) touches the walls of Ravenna, carrying shipping up
the Po for twelve miles.[98] The Padusan marsh begins at the canal,
according to the geographers the only marsh in Italy. Vergil says of
it in the *Georgics*: "or the stream of Padusa teeming with fish."[99]
The term embraces all the lagoons, swamps and marshes that we
see lying between the Po and the territory of Flaminia (or Emilia)

palustris soli ab ea Ravennate fossa quinquaginta ferme miliaribus Padum inter et Flaminiae aut Aemiliae agros intercedere videmus. Anomoque fluvius nec Adriaticum mare nec Padum attingens in eam primus delabitur paludem. Cui fluvio primus in sicco adiacet Traversaria, Ravennatium vicus, et pari spatio ad dexteram Bagnacavallum novi nominis oppidum, prius Tiberiacum et aliquando Ad Caballos appellatum.

38   Interius autem Anomo diluit Faventiam vetusti nominis civitatem, cuius tamen factam primo mentionem invenimus apud Livium libro LXXXVIII: 'Sulla Carbone cum exercitu ad Clusium, ad Faventiam, Fidentiolamque caeso, Italia expulit.' Et Aelius Spartianus in *Vita Hadriani:* 'interfecti insidiatores Hadriani consulares, Palma Terracinae, Nigrinus Faventiae.' Idemque Spartianus: 'Ceionius Commodus qui et Helius Verus natus est, maioribus Faventinis.' Et Iulius Capitolinus Lucii Veri Helii imperatoris vitam scribens sic habet: 'Origo eius paterna ex Etruria fuit, materna ex Faventia.' Eam urbem Gothi sustulerunt et postea, reaedificatam sed male habitatam,[53] Federicus cognomine Barbarossus reddidit immunitam, et anno abinde vixdum ducentesimo Brittones in Italia tunc militantes diripuerunt. Nuper vero Guidatius Manfredus, post eumque Astorgius frater, praestantes rei militaris duces illam vicariatus ecclesiae titulo gubernantes, muro cingere praevalido inceperunt. Ornata autem fuit Faventia nuper Martino praestanti rei militaris ductore, *ac Stephano Viarraneo, astrologiae magis quam medicinae, cui deditus erat, peritia noto.* Tradi videmus a multis Octavium Augustum, M. Lepidum, et M. Antonium de scelestissimo triumviratu suo apud Confluentiam prope Bononiam[54] convenisse. Abesse autem non potest quin aut Faventia[55] aut proxime apud Bagnacavallum, Cutignolam et Lugum, ubi flumina Anomo, Sennius et Vatrenus ac Padus in mare unis ostiis

for nearly fifty miles from the canal at Ravenna. The river Lamone, which reaches neither the Adriatic nor the Po, is the first
to flow into the marsh. The first place on dry land beside the
Lamone is Traversara, a village in the territory of Ravenna, and on
the right bank at the same distance is the town whose modern
name is Bagnacavallo, earlier Tiberiacum, and sometimes called
Ad Caballos.

Further inland, the Lamone washes the city of Faenza. It is an   38
ancient name, though the first mention we find of it is in Livy,
Book LXXXVIII: "With Carbo's army defeated at Chiusi,
Faenza, and Fidenza, Sulla drove him out of Italy."[100] Aelius
Spartianus says in his *Life of Hadrian* that the consular conspira-
tors against Hadrian were killed, Palma at Terracina, Nigrinus
at Faenza.[101] And Spartianus again: "Ceionius Commodus, who
was born Helius Verus, his forebears being of Faenza."[102] Julius
Capitolinus writes in the *Life of the Emperor Lucius Verus Helius*:
"His paternal roots were in Tuscany, his mother's in Faenza."[103]
The Goths destroyed the city and, later, when it had been rebuilt but was underpopulated, Frederick Barbarossa once more
tore down the walls. Scarcely two hundred years after that, Breton
mercenaries fighting in Italy destroyed it again. But recently Guidaccio Manfredi, followed by his brother Astorre, two outstanding
military leaders who govern the place as vicars of the Church, have
begun to encircle the city with massive walls.[104] The city was lately
distinguished by Martino da Faenza, an outstanding captain of
war,[105] *and by Stephanus Viarraneus, known more for his knowledge of
astrology than for practicing medicine.*[106] We know from numerous authorities that it was at a "Confluence" near Bologna that Octavius,
Lepidus, and Mark Antony came to an understanding about their
criminal triumvirate. It can only be that that "Confluence" was at
Faenza (or nearby at Bagnacavallo, Cotignola, or Lugo), where the
rivers Lamone, Senio, Santerno, and Po come together and flow
through a single mouth into the sea. In Book CXIX Livy writes

confluunt, ea fuerint Confluentia. De quo nefario scelere in hanc sententiam scribit Livius libro CXIX: in triumviratu proscriptio facta est in qua plurimi equites, senatores CXXX vicissim concessi. Lepidus enim L. Paulum fratrem, Antonius L. Caesarem avunculum, et Octavius M. Ciceronem, qui a Popilio legionario milite cum haberet annos LXIIII occisus est, caputque cum dextra manu in Rostris posita ubi multos defenderat. Plinius de lino Italiae tractans Faventinum in Aemilia via miris effert laudibus. Et alio loco eos numerans quos Vespasianus imperator, facta Italiae descriptione, excellenter inveteratos repperit, unam dicit mulierem Faventiae inventam fuisse quae annos centum viginti quinque nata esset.

39   Interius quarto supra Faventiam miliario Aureolum est oppidum ecclesiae Ravennatis amoenissimo in colle situm. Sub quo in Anomonem defluit Martianus torrens, qui latera abluit Mutilianae vetustissimi oppidi, cuius Mutilli tunc appellati Livius in principio belli Macedonici, sicut in Ravenna ostendimus, meminit; fuitque ante quingentos annos nobilis familiae comitum, qui Guidi cognomine in Flaminia et Etruria floruerunt. Supra Faventiam ad Anomonis fluenta convallis est, fluvii nomen retinens, populis frequentata, in qua Brasgella, Rontana, Gattaria, Castilionum castella, Marratae et Bifurcus vici, et sub Apennino Crispinus.

40   Post Anomonem Padusam paludem influit Sennius amnis, cui ipsa in palude et in silva quam Lugi dicunt adiacet Fusignanum oppidum. *Et quinto inde miliario abest Lugum, a luco cui adiacet appellatum, frequens populo oppidum.*[56] Et ad dexteram Senii ripam Cutignola est oppidum, unde ex Attendula gente fortiori Sfortiorum familia fluxit in Italis[57] nunc clarissima. Adiacet Lugo Zagonaria castellum acceptae a Florentino populo cladis in Philippensi bello

about their wicked crime in the following terms: during the triumvirate, a proscription was carried out in which a great many knights and 130 senators were traded between them: Lepidus gave up his brother L. Paulus, for example, Antony his uncle Lucius Caesar, and Octavius Marcus Cicero. Cicero was killed in his sixty-fourth year by a legionary soldier named Popilius, and his head and right hand were set up on the Rostra where he had defended so many.[107] When Pliny discusses Italian linen, he is most complimentary about the linen of Faenza "on the Aemilian Way."[108] Elsewhere he records those who Vespasian's census disclosed had lived to a quite remarkable old age, and mentions the discovery at Faenza of a woman who was 120 years old.[109]

Four miles above Faenza is Oriolo dei Fichi, a town of the church of Ravenna set on a delightful hill. Beneath it the stream Marzeno flows down into the Lamone, brushing the flanks of the ancient town of Modigliana, which Livy records (as Mutillum) at the beginning of the *Macedonian War*, as I mentioned in describing Ravenna.[110] Five hundred years ago Modigliana belonged to the noble family of the Conti Guidi, who flourished in Flaminia and Tuscany. Above Faenza on the course of the Lamone is a well-populated valley of the same name as the river, where the castles of Brisighella, Rontana, S. Martino in Gattara, Castellina, and the villages of Marradi, Biforco, and (under the Apennines) Crespino are to be found.

After the Lamone, the river Senio flows into the marshes of Padusa. The town of Fusignano lies on the Senio, in the actual marshland and in a forest called the forest of Lugo. *Five miles away is the populous town of Lugo itself, so named from a nearby wood.*[111] On the right bank of the Senio is the town of Cotignola, where originated from the powerful Attendola clan the family of the Sforza, now so famous among Italians.[112] Hard by Lugo lies the castle of Zagonara, celebrated in history for the Florentine defeat in the war with Filippo Maria Visconti and for the capture of Carlo

39

40

et capti in eo proelio Caroli Malatestae, quod in *Historiis* diffuse
ostendimus, memoria celebratum. Et intra secundum inde miliarium ad Senii ripam excisum est oppidum Cunium, ex quo operis
huius principio diximus familiam nobilem Cunii comitum originem duxisse, quae multos habuit belli duces: non itaque duximus
omittendum quod maxime ad praesentem facit rationem,[58] Albricum Cunii comitem, qui primus hoc nomine in ea familia fuit,
fato quodam illum fuisse qui maximam in re militari Italica fecit
mutationem.

41   Ut enim remotiora omittamus tempora rei publicae et imperatorum qui ad inclinationem usque imperium et Romae et in Italia
integrum tenuerunt; ut etiam illa praetereamus quae annis ferme
quadringentis malo suo Italia Visogothorum, Herulorum, Ostrogothorum et Longobardorum temporibus vidit, accurate in nostris
Historiis narrata, magnam quietem Italia sub Carolo Magno et eius
filiis ac nepotibus Romae imperantibus per annos circiter centum
habuit. Sed mox ad pristinos paene labores sub Italicis tribus tyrannis Berengariis redacta, paulo post Germanorum regum imperii titulo ornatorum temporibus varia uti fortuna coepit. Nam aliquot ex ipsis tyrannos, aliquot inertes aut malignos, passa nil
minus mali vidit quam cum inter se ipsam divisa est. Tunc enim
parte oppressa, pars astu, dolis aut fortitudine usa calamitatem ad
tempus potuit declinare.

42   Unicum vero tantis malis remedium aliquando excogitatum est,
cum implorata Romanorum pontificum auxilia aliquos a mali regis
sive imperatoris Germani saevitia tutabantur—quamquam tempora saepe fuerunt in quibus magis ipsa pontificum dissidia cum
malis principibus nocuere. Cum itaque id Romanorum pontificum
aliquando inefficax remedium esset visum, coepere urbes in Italia

Malatesta in the battle, as I described at length in my *Histories*.[113] Within two miles of Zagonara is the ruined town of Cunio on the banks of the Senio. I said at the beginning of this work that the noble family of the counts of Cunio, which has had many military leaders, came from here.[114] So I do not think I should pass over something that bears directly on the plan of the present work, namely that Alberigo, Count of Cunio (the first of the family to bear the name), was somehow destined to change the face of warfare in Italy.[115]

Leaving aside the distant times of the republic and of the emperors who kept the empire in one piece at Rome and throughout Italy right up to the fall, and passing over too those events (of which I gave a careful account in my *Histories*) which Italy witnessed to her cost over nearly four hundred years in the days of the Visigoths, Heruli, Ostrogoths, and Lombards, the land enjoyed a long period of peace under Charlemagne, his sons and his grandsons, who ruled at Rome for about a hundred years. But Italy was soon enough reduced almost to her original wretchedness under the three Italian tyrants named Berengar, and not long after that, she experienced mixed fortunes under the Germans kings who assumed the title of emperor. Suffering under these kings — some of them tyrannical, others just lazy and perverse — Italy saw no less misery than when she was divided upon herself. At that time parts of Italy were crushed by oppression, but others were able to stave off disaster for a while by cunning, trickery, or courage.

The only remedy that was at length devised for this dreadful state of affairs was to beg help of the Roman pontiff, which afforded some people protection from the savagery of a bad king or emperor — though there were often times when more harm was done by the pope's own differences with bad rulers. When it was realized that the remedy of seeking papal assistance was ineffective, the stronger Italian cities, in Lombardy and the March of

potentiores, praesertim Lombardiae et Marchiae Tarvisinae, sese in libertatem erigere et, societatibus initis, invicem se tueri.

43 Irruerunt vero aliquotiens Germani reges, Otto tertius, tres Henrici (tertius et quartus et postea septimus), deinde primus Fredericus et secundus, et demum Ludovicus Bavarus, et hinc pontificibus sociisque bello populis, inde regibus vel impugnantibus vel iniuriam propulsantibus, strages ubique, caedes, direptiones, incendia in Italis sunt commissa: ut ausim affirmare plus aliquando calamitatis sub hac gente a nostris acceptum quam raro alias a barbaris omnino Christianae fidei hostibus perpessi fuissent.

44 In tantis autem malis ultimo paene Bavari tempore coeperunt Romani pontifices atque etiam aliquae bellorum sociae civitates adversus Germanicam tyrannorum rabiem externos milites, Francos, Hispanos, Anglicos Brittonesque mercede conductos in Italiam vocare; quin etiam quotiens orta inter electores imperii, quod saepe contigit, aut aliter inter Romanos principes discordia † visum est tutum esse, † Germanorum electo imperatori inimicorum praesidia pretio sunt accita. Unde factum est ut annos circiter centum, a Martini IV pontificatu usque ad Gregorii XI tempora, diversis in regionibus Italia aut Teutonicos aut Brittones aut Anglicos habuerit mercede conductos. Nulla enim erat Italiae civitas quae Italico homini stipendia penderet, sed singuli populi inter se centuriati suae rei publicae munera gratis obibant et post vexilla curru vecta, quod appellarunt 'Charrotium', in expeditiones et proelia ducebantur. Acciditque dimissos aliquando aut alias cum praedandi libido incessit huiusmodi mercenarios milites plura maioraque damna nostratibus quam eos a quibus timebatur intulisse.

45 Dicunt hoc maximo suo damno experti Perusini, clade ingenti XII milium vel ferro caesorum vel Tiberi immersorum[59] a Britto-

Treviso in particular, began to claim independence for themselves and form communes for mutual protection.

German kings invaded Italy on a number of occasions — Otto 43
III, the three Henrys (III and IV and, at a later stage, VII), then Frederick I and II, and finally Louis of Bavaria. What with the popes and his military allies on the one side, and the German kings on the attack or repelling attack on the other, there were massacres and murder, fire and pillage all over Italy.[116] I dare say that our people suffered greater calamities then at the hands of the Germans than they ever had from the barbarian enemies of Christendom.

In view of such widespread misery, towards the end of the reign 44
of Louis of Bavaria, the popes and some of the cities in military alliance with them began to invite foreign mercenaries into Italy — French, Spanish, English, and Bretons — to counter the ferocity of the German rulers;[117] and not only that, but whenever the imperial electors were at odds with one another, as often happened, or the Roman princes were, [and it seemed safe to do so],[118] bodyguards of Germans hostile to the emperor elect were hired. And so it happened that for about a hundred years, from the pontificate of Martin IV to the time of Gregory XI, the various regions of Italy hired German, Breton or English mercenaries.[119] There was no city in Italy that would hire Italian soldiers, but the people of individual cities would organize themselves into regiments and offer their services to the state for nothing. Their standards would be led on expeditions and into battle carried behind on a cart called the *carroccio*. It turned out on occasion that the mercenaries of that sort who had been laid off or succumbed to the lust for plunder inflicted more frequent and more extensive damage on our cities than those from whom such damage had been feared.

This is said by the Perugians, who experienced the greatest loss 45
when they suffered a terrible disaster at the hands of Bretons and

nibus Anglicisque afflicti. Testantur Caesena Faventiaque crudeliter direptae et omnis regio affirmat urbi Romae adiacens, in qua ferunt, qui interfuerunt, supra LX oppida et castella partim funditus, ut nunc manent, excisa, partim habitatoribus pulsis spoliata fuisse, ut felices habiti sint ex ipsis qui nihil rerum amissione durius ab Anglicis Brittonibusque fuerunt passi.

46   Crescebat interim Vicecomitum in Lombardis potentia, Benedicti XI pontificis Romani auctoritate in Bavari damnum dedecusque Luchino Vicecomiti et Iohanni eius fratri, Mediolanensi archiepiscopo, attributa. Et varie per aliquot tempora inter Lombardos, quod diffuse in *Historiis* diximus, est certatum; quibus in bellis cum Brittones Anglicique contraria Bernabovi Vicecomiti sentirent, armavit ille cum alios in Italia tum in primis Albricum, de quo dicere coepimus, Cunii comitem, qui externo militi saepe congressus superior victorque evasit. Et tamen, variante ut fit fortuna, exercitu Bernabovis fracto fugatoque, Albricus est captus quem ut militari aetatis nostrae more dimitterent cum illi precibus rationibusque aliis adduci non possent, Bernabos, argento trutinam quanti ponderaret dato, eum redemit. Isque praestantissimus ductor gentem illam externam brevi expulit Lombardia quae Vicecomiti erat subdita.

47   Bernabove postmodum a nepote in carcerem coniecto, Albricus stipendio dimissus Italis omnibus qui arma ferre coeperant sese ducem ea ratione exhibuit ut coacti eam in militiam praestantiores quique, inito foedere, quod sacramento firmatum est, una essent societas Sancti Georgii appellata: qua cum societate adeo ardenti celsoque animo externos Albricus est insectatus ut nullus qui pa-

English, twelve thousand of them put to the sword or drowned in
the Tiber. The cruel plunder of Cesena and Faenza bears witness,
and every district around Rome affirms it: those who were present
say that of more than sixty towns and castles, some were completely destroyed, and so they remain to this day, while others
were plundered and their inhabitants driven off, so that those of
them that suffered nothing worse at the hands of the English and
Bretons than the loss of their property are reckoned to have been
lucky.

In the meantime the power of the Visconti in Lombardy was   46
growing, Benedict XI having granted authority to Luchino Visconti and his brother Giovanni, the Archbishop of Milan, to damage and discredit Louis of Bavaria.[120] There were for some time
various internal struggles among the Lombards, as I described in
detail in my *Histories*. The Bretons and English opposed Bernabò
Visconti in these wars, so among other Italians he enlisted
Alberigo da Barbiano, Count of Cunio, with whom we began this
section. In his frequent engagements with the foreign soldiers
Alberigo emerged victorious, and yet as fortunes changed, as they
will, Bernabò's army was smashed and routed, and Alberigo captured. When the enemy could not be prevailed upon to release
him by entreaty or other tactics, as is the military custom of the
day, Bernabò ransomed him for his weight in silver. And in a short
while that outstanding general drove the foreigners out of all of
Lombardy that was under Visconti sway.

When Bernabò was subsequently thrown into prison by his   47
nephew,[121] Alberigo lost his hire and accordingly offered himself as
the leader of all those Italians who had begun to take up soldiering, with the plan that the best fighters should be organized into a
unit to form a military company, known as the Company of
St. George and formally bound by oath. With this company,
Alberigo harried the foreigners with such ferocity that no one not

terna avitaque origine in Italia genitus non esset arma per eam cir-
cumferre sit ausus.

48   Fuisse autem ad quadraginta externorum equitum milia Italia
tunc pulsa audivimus, cum Albricus sua in societate repentino tumultu congregata vix duodecim milia habuerit. Fomesque id et
origo quaedam fuit ea res omnium rei militaris ducum quos audivimus et ipsi vidimus administrandorum bellorum gloria excel-
luisse. Nam Braccius Montonensis domi apud Albricum servivit;[60]
et Sfortia cum Laurentio Attendulo consanguineo prima ductu
Brandolini Forliviensis in Albrici exercitu tyrocinia fecit; Paulus
item Ursinus Mostarda Forliviensis Tartaliaque Lavellensis et
Thomasinus Cribellus Mediolanensis aeque atque illi ductu, auspiciis disciplinaque Albrici militiam sunt secuti.

49   Institutae autem in Italia militiae Albricus novum addidit ornamentum, qui ubi thoraces, ocreas, bracchialiaque ex corio, quod
nos vidimus, vel externi vel cives in tumultibus patriae militantes
induebantur, ferro ipse et chalybe totum armari hominem primus
edocuit et in sua societate curavit. Externis Italia pulsis, Albricus
in Neapolitanum se conferens regnum Ladislao regi, a quo magni
comestabilis dignitate ornatus fuit, talem praestitit operam ut non
solum regno a multis potentissimisque invasoribus occupato sit
potitus, sed talia per Italiam iecerit fundamenta, ex quibus apparuit eum, nisi morte post Albricum praeventus fuisset, regni Italici
atque imperii dignitates in Italiam reducturum fuisse.

50   Sentiant vero quicquid alii volunt: nostra fert opinio tanti fuisse
externos milites Anglos, Brittones, Germanosque Italia pulsos esse
ut postea et opibus magis abundaverit et maiorem, certe tutiorem

born in Italy of ancestral stock dared to hawk their arms round the country.

I understand that about forty thousand foreign knights were   48
then expelled from Italy, at a time when Alberigo had scarcely twelve thousand in his company, and those mustered in a hasty and confused fashion. And this was the tinder and wellspring, so to speak, of all the military captains who attained glory in fighting wars that I have heard of, or seen for myself:[122] Braccio da Montone was in Alberigo's household and a familiar of his; and Muzio Attendolo Sforza, along with his kinsman Lorenzo Attendolo, took his first steps in soldiering under Brandolino's command in the army of Alberigo; Paolo Orsini, Mostarda da Forlì, Tartaglia da Lavello, and Tommasino Crivelli of Milan all likewise followed the profession of soldier under the command, leadership, and instruction of Alberigo da Barbiano.

Alberigo added an original embellishment to the military cus-   49
toms practised here. Soldiers, be they foreign mercenaries or citizens involved in civil strife, used to wear breastplates, greaves, and armguards made of leather, as I have myself seen. Alberigo was the first to tell his men to use total body armor of iron and steel, and he made sure this was done in his company. Once the foreigners had been expelled from Italy, he went over to the Kingdom of Naples, and worked to such good effect for King Ladislaus (by whom he was honored with the title of High Constable) that he not only got control of a realm occupied by many powerful invaders but even laid the foundations for the return to our land of a "Kingdom of Italy" and the dignity of empire—something that Ladislaus would clearly have brought about had he not been forestalled by his death, which followed that of Alberigo.[123]

Others may feel differently, but my own opinion is that the ex-   50
pulsion of foreign soldiers from Italy (the English, Bretons, and Germans) was of such importance that her wealth increased and she had greater peace—certainly a more secure peace—ever after-

quietem [postea] semper habuerit. Nam etsi in bellis quae post eam externorum eiectionem sunt gesta[61] urbium oppidorumque direptiones committuntur, ab excidio tamen incendio et sanguine nostri saepius temperant et quod uni in expilatione damno est opes alteri Italico accumulat — quas externus barbarusque asportasset.

51   Quin etiam econtra factum videmus ut, cum multi ex Italicis magna conducti mercede Francis atque Anglicis coeperint militare, spolia inde et pecuniae in Italiam deferantur. Nullusque mihi ostendet[62] aedificandi, vestiendi, ornandi et ceteram omnem vitae huius nostrae quam hoc saeculo vivimus luxuriam, lauticiam, ceterosque magnificos apparatus, his qui superioribus saeculis fiebant certe maiores, aliunde quam ab hac securitate et tutela originem habuisse, quae omnia Albrico nostro Cunii alumno, quod excisum nunc aratur, non immerito laudem gloriamque perpetuam accumulant.

52   Nec tamen negamus Romanae curiae in Italiam ab Avinione reversionem opulentiam Italiae plurimum adauxisse. Nam cum annos LXX Avinione Romani pontifices curiam tenuissent, Gregorius XI natione Lemovicensis eandem ad annum salutis LXXX supra millesimum et trecentesimum in Italiam reduxit.

53   At postquam dei munere eloquentia per viri Romandioli Ravennae geniti virtutem reviviscere coepit et nova tutiorque rei militaris forma in Italia, externis eiectis, per Albricum item Romandiolum est reddita, eandem quoque Romandiolam per nostras manus tertiam in rebus maximis gloriam Italiae speramus dedisse, qui latentem supra mille annos historiam tanta attingimus diligentia ut omnem non solum Italiae, sed totius olim Romani imperii provinciarum regionumque statum, ad quorum vel regum vel principum vel nationum manus pervenerit, clare magis et quam fieri posse videretur diffuse ostenderimus, cum *Roma* interim *instaurata,*

wards. It is true that in the wars that have been waged after the foreigners were thrown out, the pillaging of towns and cities does take place, but our people commonly restrain themselves from wholesale destruction, burning, and murdering. And what is lost as plunder to one Italian piles up as wealth for another, which the barbarous foreigner would have made off with.

In fact we see the reverse has happened: since many Italians 51 have taken to serving in the French and English armies as expensive mercenaries, money and spoils are being transferred from those countries to Italy. No one will convince me that the sumptuousness, elegance and other magnificent paraphernalia of our buildings, dress, and decoration, and all the rest of the life we live in this world—surely pitched at a higher level than was customary in the past—originated from anything other than this sense of security and being protected. All of this redounds to the deserved honor and glory of Alberigo, scion of that Cunio which is now destroyed and plowed over.

Not that I would deny that the return of the Roman Curia to 52 Italy from Avignon greatly increased the wealth of Italy. For after the Roman pontiffs had held court in Avignon for seventy years, Gregory XI of Limoges brought it back into Italy in A.D. 1380.

But now, by God's grace, eloquence has begun to revive thanks 53 to the talent of a Romagnolo born at Ravenna, and following the expulsion of the foreigners, a new and safer form of warfare has been introduced in Italy by Alberigo, another man of the Romagna. Following these, I hope that the same Romagna has given Italy a third glory in a great enterprise through this work of mine. I am putting my hand to a history that has been hidden for more than a thousand years with such care that I have revealed the whole situation, not just of Italy, but of all the provinces and regions of the former Roman empire as it passed into the control of the various kings, princes or nations; and this with greater clarity and detail than seemed possible, since by *Restoring Rome* in the

Italiam quoque, abstersa errorum obscuritatumque multa rubigine, noverimus *illustrare*.

54　　Sed ad institutum. Interius via Flaminia Sennium iungit pons Proculeius et ad dexteram in eadem via Bolognesium est novi nominis oppidum, quod patrum nostrorum memoria Bononiensis populus a fundamentis aedificavit. Supra sunt Sosenana et in Apennino Palatiolum castella, olim Ubaldinae genti rei militaris gloria clarissimae subdita, quae superiori saeculo simul cum vicis, castellis et oppidis longissimo Apennini tractu sitis, ab eadem gente possessis, populus Florentinus vi cepit. In Padusam item influens Vatrenus sequitur amnis, quem Plinius scribit solitum fuisse ostia Padi nunc Primaria, quod Spineticum appelleretur, augere. Sed nunc, averso paene viginti milibus cursu, novi nominis ostium in Padusam et Padum habet Zaniolum appellatum, apud quod clarae memoriae Nicolaus Estensis Marchio magnifici operis arcem et postea Leonellus filius successorque viam fecit, quae duodecim miliaribus Lugum perducit.

55　　Intus ad Vatreni dexteram in via Flaminia est Imola, Forum Cornelii a priscis appellatum, ad quod erat Aemiliae regionis initium. Martialisque coquus poeta hanc urbem inhabitasse videtur, sicut his in versibus innuit: 'Si quibus in terris qua simus in urbe rogabit, Cornelii referas me licet esse Foro.' Ea civitas a Narsetis militibus, sicut in *Historiis* diximus, diruta et paulo post a Clephi immanissimo Longobardorum rege sub novo hoc Imolae nomine, ut Ravennatibus fidem populo Romano servantibus opponeretur, aedificata est. Habuitque paulo supra aetatem nostram Benvenutum, qui grammaticus et ludi magister tunc in Italia primarius; cum historias nosset, aliqua scripsit *iam paene obliterata*.[63] Claruit etiam diebus nostris Iohannes Imolensis pontificii et civilis iurium

meantime, I have been able to *Illustrate Italy* by scraping away the rusty accretions of error and obscurity.

To return to the subject: further inland on the Flaminian Way, 54 the Ponte di San Procolo crosses the Senio,[124] and on the right bank of the river on the same road is Castel Bolognese, a new foundation built from the ground up by the people of Bologna in our fathers' day.[125] Higher up the Senio is the Badia di Susinana and, in the Apennines, Palazzuolo sul Senio, castles once subject to the famous military family of the Ubaldini. In the last century, the Florentines took them by force, along with the villages, castles, and towns of a considerable stretch of the Apennines that had been owned by the same family.[126] The next river flowing into the marsh of Padusa is the Santerno, which Pliny says used to swell the mouth of the Po, at what is now the Po di Primaro but used to be called the Spina mouth.[127] But the course of the Santerno has shifted nearly twenty miles, and the river has a new mouth into Padusa and the Po called Zaniolo. Here the famous Marquess Niccolò d'Este built an elaborate fortress, and his son and successor Leonello later constructed a road to Lugo twelve miles away.[128]

Inland on the Via Aemilia, on the right bank of the Santerno, 55 is Imola, called Forum Cornelii by the ancients, where the region of Emilia began. It seems that the poet Martial lived in this city, as he suggests in these lines: "If she asks what land, what town I am in, you may tell her that I am at Forum Cornelii."[129] I mentioned in my *Histories* that the city was demolished by the soldiers of Narses; not long afterwards it was rebuilt under the new name of Imola by Cleph, the monstrous king of the Lombards, to serve as a bulwark against the people of Ravenna, who were still loyal to Rome.[130] A little before our time it had in Benvenuto Rambaldi, the foremost grammarian and schoolmaster of the age; since he was acquainted with history, he composed some works, *now almost forgotten*.[131] Giovanni da Imola was famous in our time as an expert in civil and canon law,[132] *and the doctor Baverio of Imola is also famous,*

peritissimus, *prout etiam claret Baverius Imolensis medicus, non modo doctissimus, sed humanitate modestia et bonitate conspicuus, quo summus pontifex Quintus Nicolaus medico et Romani gymnasii doctore utitur.*[64] Est interius ad Vatreni sinistram septimo ab Imola miliario Tausignanum oppidum, quod decimum Iohannem Romanum pontificem genuit, ingentis certe virtutis et famae virum, a quo Sarraceni mediam ferme Italiam obtinentes in fugam conversi, dehinc ad Lirim fluvium magna occisione profligati Italiam reliquerunt. Fuit quoque Tausignanum superiori saeculo ornatum Petro excellenti medico. Et nuper ex vico Codregnano, qui Tausignano mille quingentis passibus abest, originem habuit Iohannes Ferrariensis episcopus, vir cum doctus tum omnis generis vitae sanctimonia redundans. Supra ad Vaterni dexteram Coderonchum et superius sub ipsis Apennini radicibus est Florentiola, novum oppidum a populo Florentino cui subest aedificatum.

56   Proximo item in Padusae loco oppidum est Caput Silicis appellatum, ex quo transmissa lintribus septimo miliario Padusa per Zaniolum navigatur in Padum. Via quae ab eo oppido Imolam duodecim ducit miliaribus Silicis nomen retinet, inde olim inditum quod silicibus Roma avectis strata fuerit. Cum enim, Romano imperio florente, aliqua belli aut pacis usibus necessaria in Aemiliam deferri esset opus, ea mari advecta per Padi ostia et inde per Padusam huc loci comportabantur; unde viam natura soli et paludis propinquitate caenosam et raro tunc, sicut et nunc, etiam aestate plaustra perferentem sterni necessitas adegit. Silices autem Roma avectos fuisse, ut dicamus facit Plinius, qui genus id lapidis nullo alio quam circa urbem et mare Etruscum loco reperiri dicit. Dispersos vero per Ferrariam, Imolam, ac circumstantia loca silices

noted for his kindness, modesty and goodness as well as his learning. Pope Nicholas V uses him as his doctor and as a teacher at the University of Rome.[133] Further inland, seven miles from Imola on the left bank of the Santerno, is the town of Tossignano, where Pope John X was born, a man of great virtue and renown. He put the Saracens to flight at a time when they held sway over almost half of Italy, and then routed them with great slaughter at the river Garigliano, causing them to quit Italy.[134] Tossignano was also adorned in the last century by the notable physician Pietro.[135] More recently Giovanni, Bishop of Ferrara, was born in the village of Codrignano, a mile and a half from Tossignano, a man both learned and blessed with a manner of life in every respect holy.[136] Above Tossignano on the right bank of the Santerno is Codronco, and higher up, under the very base of the Apennine ridge, is Firenzuola, a new town built by the Florentines and subject to them.

In a place bordering the marsh of Padusa is a town called   56
Conselice. From here the marsh can be crossed in boats by way of Zaniolo to the Po seven miles away. A road which leads from Conselice to Imola twelve miles away has kept the name Via Selice, given it in the past from its being paved with flint brought from Rome.[137] In the days of the Roman Empire, when they needed to transport raw materials for use in war or peace to Emilia, they would be taken by sea through the mouth of the Po and from there through Padusa to Conselice. From that point they were obliged to pave the road, since owing to the nature of the terrain and the closeness of the marsh, it was covered in mud and rarely capable of supporting carts even in the summer, then as now. The reason I say the flint was shipped from Rome is that Pliny tells us that that sort of stone is found only in the vicinity of the city and the Tyrrhenian Sea.[138] In fact the flint we see scattered around Ferrara, Imola, and neighboring places was taken from the paving of this road and came from the same source as

ab hac nunc spoliata via acceptos videmus esse ex his qui nunc in stratis circa urbem Romam viis passim conspiciuntur.

57   Sequitur torrens in Padusam labens Siler, cui intus apposita sunt agri Bononiensis oppida Sancti Petri ad dexteram et Ducia ad sinistram. Superius vero in montibus est Flagnanum oppidum secundo Honorio pontifice Romano ibi genito decoratum. Torrens inde habetur Claterna Padusam iuxta, vicum Ad Caballos petens; ad cuius nominis pontem via Flaminia oppidum fuit Claterna, cuius modica apparent fundamenta, de quo Cicero *Ad Lentulum*: 'erat Claternae noster Hirtius, ad Forum Cornelii Caesar'. Parvo inde spatio a Padusa absunt oppida, hinc Medicina, inde Butrium populo et quidem divite frequentissimum. Supra est in collibus Varagnana.

58   Idex inde habetur fluvius apud Mulinellam vicum Padusam attingens, unde vigesimo stadio ad Padi ripas lintribus navigatur.[65] Ad sinistramque Idicis primo in colle castellum est Brittonum sub Apennino, ad sinistram Visanum, ad dexteram Caburatium. Amni Savenae Padusam illabenti Bononia adiacet. Suntque intus ad eius amnis sinistram via Florentina vici Planorum primo, dehinc in montibus Loianum, inde Scarcalasinum, et in Apennino Caprennum. Deinde est Rheni Bononiensis pars, fossa manu facta per urbem ducta, quae Avesam torrentulum urbem dividentem ad pomerium augens lintres per Padusam dimittit in Padum. Secundum huius navigationis sinistram Padusae adiacet Ocellinum turris in Ferrariensi via, ad limitis agri Bononiensis custodiam communita, *nunc villa fortissimi et animis pleni equestris ordinis Galeatii Marescotti Bononiensis quinti Nicolai romani pontificis dono habita*.[66] Apud Ocellini

that which paved the roads that can be seen everywhere around Rome.

The stream of the Sillaro comes next, which flows into the 57 marsh of Padusa. Inland it has towns of the territory of Bologna on either side, Castel S. Pietro on the right bank and Dozza on the left. Higher up in the mountains is the town of Fiagnano, its glory the Roman pontiff Honorius II, who was born there.[139] Then comes the stream Quaderna beside the marsh, which makes its way to the village "Ad Caballos"; at a bridge of the same name [Ponte a Cavallo] on the Flaminian Way was the town of Claterna, some modest foundations of which may still be seen. Of this town Cicero writes in his *Letters to Lentulus:* "Our friend Hirtius was at Claterna, Caesar at Forum Cornelii."[140] A short distance from the marsh are the towns of Medicina on this side of the Quaderna, and on the other Budrio, which is populous and wealthy. Above, in the hills, is Varignana.

Then comes the river Idice, which reaches the marsh at the vil- 58 lage of Molinella; from there one can take a boat to the banks of the Po, twenty stades away. On the first hill under the Apennines on the left bank of the Idice is Castel dei Britti, with Bisano to the left and Caburaccia to the right. Bologna lies beside the river Savena which flows into the Padusa. Inland on the left bank of the river along the road to Florence are the villages of Pianoro first, then Loiano in the hills, then Scaricalasino and in the Apennines Cavrenno. Next is a section of the Bolognese Reno, here canalised in its passage through Bologna and then augmenting the little stream Avesa at the point where it runs through the boundary of the city. The Reno carries boats through the marsh of Padusa to the Po. On the left bank of the canal beside the marsh lies the tower of Ocellino, on the road to Ferrara, a fort set there to guard the borders of Bolognese territory, *now the villa of Galeazzo Marescotti of Bologna, a courageous and spirited knight, given to him as a gift by Pope Nicholas V.*[141] The ancient course of both rivers shows

turrem Padusae finem olim fuisse et Rhenum Bononiensem eo in loco aut propinquo Padum influxisse indicant pervetusti utriusque amnis alvei. Indicantque pariter Ptolemaei ac aliorum geographorum descriptio ac pictura. Cum vero Padus quatuor fere milia passuum retrocesserit, quicquid praesentem Padi ripam et Ocellinum intercedit Padusae accessit; nec, ut ante consueverant, Padum illabuntur Rhenus et Scultenna, sed Lavinio et Samogia auctus Rhenus, Scultennae et Formigini torrentulo iungitur, coactaque huiusmodi aquarum moles per ultima Padusae ostia ad Bondenum illabitur Padum.

59 Id vero Bononiensis agri quod Rhenum, Padusam et ipsam intercedit urbem plurimis vicis, oppidis et castellis frequentatur: Podio Lambertinorum, Prosperio Platesiorum, Venantio, Galleria, Peretulo, Centhio, et Plebeio.

60 Bononiam urbem vetustam scribit Plinius, urbium quas Etrusci ultra Apenninum habuere primariam, Boiorum postea caput fuisse, ut pro Felsina credatur primum Boionia, post Bononia, esse dicta. Eam Livius XXXVII dicit coloniam a Romanis deductam agrumque eum fuisse captum de Bois Gallis, qui ager prius fuerat Etruscorum. Quam Augusti et aliquot imperatorum temporibus trium opulentissimarum Italiae civitatum supero mari adiacentium unam fuisse cum alii dicunt scriptores tum affirmat Plinius. Suetonius autem dicit Octavianum Bononiensibus, quod in Antoniorum clientela antiquitus fuissent, gratiam fecisse coniurandi cum tota Italia pro partibus suis. Idemque Suetonius scribit Neronem imperatorem orasse Latine pro Bononiensibus ad consulem et ad senatum. Iuliusque Capitolinus in *XXX Tyrannorum gestis rebus* de Censorino dicit: 'Erat eius sepulchrum grandibus litteris circa Bononiam incisi sunt eius honores. Ultimo tamen ascriptum est: "Felix, per omnia infelicissimus."'

that the marsh once ended at this tower and that the Bolognese Reno flowed into the Po at that point or close by, and this is like-wise borne out by the descriptions and maps of Ptolemy and the other geographers. But now that the Po has receded about four miles, whatever lies between Ocellino and the present course of the Po has been absorbed into the marsh. Nor do the Reno and Scoltenna flow into the Po as they used to: the Reno now is swol-len by the Lavino and Samoggia and then joined by both the Scoltenna and the little stream of Formigine, and this concen-trated mass of water enters the Po through the last reaches of the marsh at Bondeno.

This portion of the territory of Bologna that lies between the 59 Reno, the marsh, and the city itself has a great crowd of towns, villages, and castles, such as Poggio Renatico, San Prospero, San Venanzio, Galliera, Peretolo, Cento, and Pieve di Cento.

Pliny writes that the ancient city of Bologna was the chief 60 Etruscan city on the other side of the Apennines, later becoming the capital of the Boii, and so named Boionia, instead of the Etruscan Felsina, and subsequently Bononia or Bologna.[142] In Book XXXVII Livy says that Bologna was a Roman colony and that its territory had been taken from the Gallic Boii, having ear-lier belonged to the Etruscans.[143] Pliny, like a number of other writers, states that Bologna was one of the three wealthiest Italian cities on the Adriatic in the age of Augustus and several later em-perors.[144] Suetonius says that Octavian excused the community of Bologna from rallying to his side with the rest of Italy, since they had traditionally been dependents of the family of Antony.[145] He also says that the emperor Nero pleaded the case of Bologna in Latin before the consul and senate.[146] Julius Capitolinus in *The History of the Thirty Tyrants* says of Censorinus: "His tomb was near Bologna, inscribed with his honors in large letters. But in the last line is added: 'Fortunate in every respect, but most unfortu-nate.'"[147]

61   Ad annum salutis octingesimum quadragesimum Sergii pontificis Romani (Os Porci prius appellati) temporibus, cum Lotharius
tunc imperator Ludovicum filium Romam cum copiis mitteret,
Bononienses illum multis incommodis damnisque affecerunt.
Quamobrem ille, converso qui iam praeterierat exercitu, ultionis
modum excessit, quod post agri vastationem factamque inson-
tium per vicos villasque repertorum caedem, obsessam urbem cap-
tamque reddidit immunitam. Et tamen illam ad annum salutis
septuagesimum primum supra millesimum ducentesimum tam scimus fuisse potentem ut adversus Venetos, liberam mari Adriatico
navigationem prohibentes, tribus annis bello contenderit, in quo
Bononiae praetor castra habens apud primaria Padi ostia, ubi Bononienses castellum aedificaverant, quadraginta milia equitum peditumque in exercitu tenuerit. Repulsique Veneti, copiarum parte
amissa, cum ducis Venetiarum Laurentii Teupoli ductu paratiores
redissent, inter Bononienses Venetosque pax firmata est in qua
actum est ut, Padi ostiorum custodia Venetis relicta, possent Bononienses per ea sal et frumenta absque vectigali ad libitum depor-
tare.

62   Sequenti anno orta civili dissensione, Bononienses factionem
civium, ut dicebant, imperialem patria eiecerunt: Lambertatios et
eorum partes secutos Asinellos, De Andalo, comites Panici, Car-
bonesios, Storletos, Albaros, De Villanova, De Principibus, De
Abbate, comites Butrii, Fuscardos, De Albesio,[67] De Fratta, De
Lamola, De Rusticanis. Exinde cum pars quae in civitate victrix
manserat extorres animosius insecuta Forum Livium, in quam illi
se receperant civitatem, obsedisset, Bononiensis exercitus caesus[68]
est et fugatus. Quo in proelio legi in Venetorum monumentis octo
milia Bononiensium cecidisse. Quoquo autem modo res postea se
habuerint, Bononiam, anno nonagesimo vixdum elapso, fuisse a

About the year 840, in the time of Pope Sergius (formerly 61
known as "Pig's Snout"),[148] when the emperor of the day, Lothair,
sent troops against Rome under his son Louis, the Bolognese
caused him great difficulties and damage.[149] The army had already
passed Bologna, but Louis turned it back and took disproportionate revenge. He laid waste to the fields and killed any people he
found in villages and farms, blameless though they were, then laid
siege to Bologna, captured it and razed its fortifications. Yet we
know that by the year 1271, the city was once again strong enough
to conduct a three-year war against the Venetians, who were trying
to restrict open shipping in the Adriatic. In the course of these
hostilities, the Bolognese commander had a camp at the mouth of
the Po di Primaro (where they had built a castle) and kept there a
force of forty thousand horse and infantry. The Venetians were
beaten back with the loss of some troops; when they returned
better prepared under the leadership of the doge Lorenzo
Tiepolo,[150] a peace was concluded between the two cities with the
provision that the mouth of the Po would be left in Venetian possession but the Bolognese could import salt and grain through it
without restriction and free of tolls.

The following year there was civil strife in Bologna and the 62
Bolognese exiled the so-called "imperial" party of citizens: the
Lambertazzi and those that followed them: the Asinelli, the De
Andalo, the counts of Panico, the Carbonesi, the Storleti, the
Albari, the De Villanova, the De Principi, the De Abbate, the
counts of Budrio, the Foscardi, the De Albesi, the De Fratta, the
De Lamola, the De Rusticani. In their vindictive persecution of
the exiles, the victorious party that had remained in Bologna laid
siege to Forlì, where they had taken refuge, but the Bolognese
army was cut down and put to flight. I read in Venetian annals
that eight thousand Bolognese fell in the battle.[151] However things
were in the aftermath of the battle, we know that scarcely ninety
years later the church authorities enclosed Bologna with a new

Romanae ecclesiae magistratibus hoc novo, quem nunc habet, circumdatam muro scimus. Constatque eam non muro magis per id temporis ac diu postea quam opibus amplificatam fuisse.

63   Habuit Bononia, sicut tradit Eusebius, L. Pomponium Bononiensem Atellanarum scriptorem et paulo post M. Tullii Ciceronis temporibus, sicut ipse in *Bruto* dicit, C. Rusticellum oratorem minime contemnendum. Et fuit praeterea secundo Lucio pontifice Romano, Alberti filio, cive ornata. Martialis vero eam urbem Rufo ornatam fuisse dicit his versibus: 'Funde tuo lacrimas orbata, Bononia, Rufo et resonet tota planctus in Aemilia'. Pliniusque refert cum Vespasiani imperatoris edicto Italiae census haberetur, L. Ternutium,[69] Marci filium, Bononiensem centum viginti quinque annos fuisse natum. Idemque Plinius dicit nullos calamos aptiores esse sagittis quam Bononienses, et speculares lapides breves maculososque complexu silicis in Bononiensi agro reperiri.

64   Habuit autem paulo supra aetatem nostram Bononia Iohannem Andreae Calderinum, iure consultorum aetatis suae celeberrimum. Gaudeamusque aetatem nostram tulisse Nicolaum Albergatum, qui primo Cartusiae monachus, dehinc Bononiae episcopus, demum Romanae ecclesiae cardinalis, vir fuit cum celebris sanctimoniae, tum etiam sapientiae singularis. Nuper quoque Antonius claruit Bentivolius, vir nobilium aetatis suae in Bononia potentissimus et potentium sui saeculi bonarum artium ceterarumque virtutum, praesertim liberalitatis, gloria celeberrimus. Obiitque proximis temporibus philosophorum sui saeculi praestantissimus Nicolaus Faba Bononiensis.

65   Supersunt autem Gaspar nunc episcopus Imolensis et philosophus insignis et multi iuris civilis et pontificii philosophiaeque ac medicinae studiis ornatissimi: Ludovicus de gente Ludovisia, sacri palatii Apostolici causarum auditor, Baptista Floriani iure consultissimi filius, Gaspar Arrengherius et noster Bornius Salensis, *et*

wall, which it still has today; it is well known that at the time and for long afterwards the city grew in power as much by its wealth as by its walls.

Bologna had, as Eusebius tells us, a writer of Atellan farces in 63 Lucius Pomponius,[152] and a little later in Cicero's time, as he himself says in the *Brutus*, the respectable orator, Gaius Rusticellus.[153] She was further ornamented by her citizen Pope Lucius II, the son of Alberto.[154] Martial tells us that the city was also graced by Rufus in these lines: "Pour forth your tears, Bologna, bereaved of your Rufus, and let lamentation sound all along the Aemilian Way."[155] Pliny reports that when a census was carried out by order of the emperor Vespasian, Lucius Termicius of Bologna, son of Marcus, was found to be still alive at the age of 125.[156] Pliny likewise tells us that there are no better reeds for arrows than those of Bologna,[157] and that small and streaky transparent stones are found embedded in the hard rock in Bolognese territory.[158]

A little before our own day, Bologna bore Giovanni Calderini, 64 son of Andrea, the most distinguished jurisconsult of his time.[159] And let us rejoice that our age has borne Niccolò Albergati, successively a Carthusian monk, Bishop of Bologna, and finally cardinal of the Roman church, and a man not just of celebrated piety but of singular wisdom.[160] Antonio Bentivoglio has also found renown in recent years, the most powerful noble of his time in Bologna and the most distinguished of the important men of the century for his fame in the liberal arts and the other virtues, specially his generosity.[161] A short while ago Niccolò Fava of Bologna passed away, the leading philosopher of his age.[162]

Living still are Gaspare, the present Bishop of Imola and a dis- 65 tinguished philosopher, as well as many others noted for their study of civil and canon law, philosophy, and medicine: Lodovico Ludovisi, Auditor of the Sacred Palace, Battista, son of the famous jurisconsult Floriano, Gaspare Aringhieri, and my friend Bornio da Sala, *and Alberto Zambeccari, no minor ornament of his*

non parvo patriae est ornamento Albertus Zanbecharius, bonarum artium studiis deditissimus.[70] Matrem vero studiorum Bononiam tam paucis nunc ornari eleganter doctis nullus mirabitur, qui meminerit (quod cum horrore dicimus) civiles discordias plures ferro aetate nostra Bononiae abstulisse praestantes cives his quos nunc ipsa et duae similes in Italia habeant civitates.

66 Ad Rheni sinistram interius Olivetum, ubi convallis Rheni incipit, vicis, villis, castellisque habitata; et qua Lavinius torrens illam influit, est Panicus vicus; ad dexteram sub Apennino, Casium; in Apennino, Granariolum[71] arx altissima. Inter Samogiam torrentem et Scultennam amnem sunt oppida et castella: Crevalcorium, Persicetum et Francum, ubi olim fuit Forum Gallorum, apud quod oppidum M. Antonium Hirtius et Pansa coss. proelio superarunt; de quo proelio sic habet Livius libro CXIX: 'Cum Pansa cos. male adversus Antonium pugnasset, Hirtius cos. cum exercitu superveniens, fusis Marci Antonii copiis, fortunam utriusque partis aequavit. Victus deinde ab Hirtio et Caesare Antonius in Galliam confugit. At Hirtius qui post victoriam in ipsis hostium castris ex vulnere ceciderat et L. Pansa ex vulnere defunctus in Campo Martio sepulti sunt.' Intus vero sunt Plumatium, Bazanum, Mons Velius, agri Bononiensis castella. Est etiam in Bononiensi agro in paludem Padusam vergenti Nonantula, oppidum monasterio insigni ornatum quod gloriosae Matildis comitissae opera impensaque aedificatum est. Sed iam Scultennae ripa, ad quam pervenimus, Cispadanae Romandiolae finis, ad Transpadanum transeundum esse nos admonet.

67 Ad prima Padi ostia Spinam urbem Diomedeis opibus fuisse conditam scribit Plinius, sed eius nunc parva exstant vestigia par-

country, utterly devoted as he is to the study of literature.[163] No one will be surprised that Bologna, the "mother of universities," now has so few men of polite learning when it is borne in mind that in our time civil strife at Bologna (I shudder to say it) has carried off by the sword more distinguished citizens than she—and two other cities of like size—nowadays possesses.

Further inland on the left bank of the Reno is Oliveto, where 66 the valley of the Reno begins, an area of villages, farms, and castles; and where the Lavino flows into the Reno is the village of Panico; on the right bank, beneath the Apennine ridge, lies Cassio, and high up in the Apennines the fortress of Granarolo. Between the stream Samoggia and the river Scoltenna are the towns and castles of Crevalcore, San Giovanni in Persiceto, and Castelfranco Emilia—the site of Forum Gallorum, where Mark Antony was defeated in battle by Hirtius and Pansa. Of this battle, Livy writes in Book CXIX: "After the consul Pansa had unsuccessfully fought Antony, the consul Hirtius arrived with his army, defeated the troops of Mark Antony and brought the fortunes of both sides in balance again. Antony, defeated by Hirtius and Octavian, fled to Gaul. Hirtius, who had been killed in the camp of the enemy after his victory, and Caius Pansa, who died from his wounds, were buried on the Field of Mars."[164] Then inland there are the castles of the Bolognese, Piumazzo, Bazzano, and Monteveglio. Also in the territory of Bologna, where it meets the marsh of Padusa, is the town of Nonantola, distinguished by the famous monastery that was built at the commission and expense of the glorious countess Matilda.[165] But now we have reached the banks of the Scoltenna, which mark the boundary of Romagna on this side of the Po, and they remind us to pass over into the Transpadane region.[166]

Pliny writes that the city of Spina was founded by the wealth of 67 Diomedes at the mouth of the Po di Primaro,[167] but scant traces of it remain now—places here and there called Valle Spina and

tim Vallis, partim Dorsum Spinae appellata, unde propinquum
Padum veteres Spineticum appellant. Quo in Spinetico tradit
Suetonius Claudium imperatorem de Britannis triumphaturum
navem aedificasse omnium maximam, quae potius magna domus
potuerit appellari. Primum ea dextera Padi ripa vicum habet Sanctum Albertum ubi anno hinc centesimo septuagesimo nono Veneti
castellum aedificarunt, Marcomama appellatum, ut Bononiensibus
resisterent hostibus, qui aliud castellum in adversa Padi ripa, sed
inferius iuxta mare magnis sumptibus communiverant. Estque is
Sancti Alberti locus unde per fossam Padusae, Messanicum, XII
miliaribus Ravennam itur. Ea in Padi ripa frequentes et prope
contigui intra viginti milia sunt vici: Humana, Fossa, Putula, Lon-
gastrinum, Filum, a Padi perpetua sex miliarium rectitudine dictus, Rupta, Blasianum in quo villam habemus locupletem e regione Zanioli sitam, et horum partem scripsimus; Argenta quoque
oppidum simul cum Ferraria a Smaragdo exarcho, sicut in *Historiis*
diximus, primum moenibus communitum, duodeviginti milibus
passuum distans a Ferraria civitate. Quo in spatio secundum Padi
ripam distat ab Argenta tribus passuum milibus Cosandula, villa
marchionum Estensium magnifici operis aedibus ornatissima.

68   Ad eamque villam rectus et primarius Padi cursus qui praeterlabitur[72] anno nunc centesimo tortuosiore veniebat alveo, quem
nunc a vici incolis Codeream corrupte pro Capite Eridani dictum,
secus villam Belreguardam desiccatum videmus. Nam pictura
Italiae quam in primis sequimur, Roberti regis Siciliae et Francisci
Petrarchae eius amici opus, Vicuentiam Vicueriamque et Conam
vicos profluenti Pado appositos habet. Quare partes ipsas Padi a
Ferraria Cosandalum et a Coderea in mare nunc defluentes a centesimo anno initium habuisse non dubito.

69   Supra Cosandalum alia est villa Sancti Nicolai appellata, et secundo abinde abest Monasteriolum, *quam pulchre ornavit et saepe in-*

Dosso Spina—which is why the ancients called the Po near Spina the Padus Spineticus. On this Padus Spineticus, Suetonius tells us that when the emperor Claudius was preparing to celebrate a triumph over the Britons, he built a massive ship, so big that one might rather have called it a palace.[168] The first village on the right bank of the Po is Sant'Alberto, where 179 years ago the Venetians built a castle called Marcomama as a bulwark against their Bolognese enemies: on the opposite bank the Bolognese had built another castle and fortified it at great expense, but lower down, beside the sea. From Sant'Alberto, one can travel the twelve miles to Ravenna through the Padusa marsh by the canal called Messanico. Crowded along this bank of the Po and almost contiguous for twenty miles are the villages of Umana, Fossa, Putola, Longastrino, Filo (named for the straight six-mile stretch of the Po), La Rotta and San Biagio, where I have an ample country home opposite Zaniolo, and where I have written some of this. And also the town of Argenta, eighteen miles from Ferrara, which was first given walls at the same time as Ferrara by the exarch Smaragdus, as I mentioned in my *Histories*;[169] in this area, three miles from Argenta along the banks of the Po, is Consandolo, an estate of the marquesses d'Este embellished with fine buildings.

The channel of the Po di Primaro that runs straight to Consan- 68 dalo used to take a more winding course a hundred years ago, running from Codrea (a local corruption of Caput Eridani) to the villa of Belriguardo, though we see it now dried up. The map of Italy on which I chiefly rely, the work of King Robert of Sicily and his friend Petrarch, has the villages of Voghenza, Voghiera, and Cona set alongside the free-flowing Po; and so I can say with confidence that those stretches of the Po that now extend from Ferrara down to Consandolo and from Codrea to the sea originated within the last hundred years.

Above Consandolo is another country estate called San Nic- 69 colò, and then two miles further on there is Monestirolo, *which the*

habitat generoso vir animo reverendissimus Meliadusius Estensis, claris-
simo Nicolao marchione Estense, cuius effigiem simillimam refert, natus,
qui laudatissima visendi orbis cupiditate ductus et Egypti Charras, amplis-
simam omnium civitatem, et Hierosolymam honesto cum comitatu adiit et
Graeciae, Epiri, Dalmatiae ac omnes Italiae oras accuratissime perlustra-
vit.[73] Et paulo supra est Gaibana. At secundum maris litus distant
a primariis Padi ostiis passuum quindecim milibus stagni, quod
prisci Capresiam dixere, ostia, nunc Magna Vaca vulgo appellata.
Ad quod stagnum supra duodecim milia passuum in circuitu pa-
tens Comaclensis sita est vetusta civitas, quam Gothorum Longo-
bardorumque temporibus classem armare solitam Veneti, ab
Alberto Berengarii regis filio Comaclensium auxilio iniuria lacessiti, ad annum salutis nongentesimum tricesimum secundum destruxerunt, ut semper postea sicut et nunc a paucis fuerit incolis
habitata. Mirum vero est cernere quantam[74] id stagnum praestet
piscium copiam, quod anguillarum cephalorumque sale condito-
rum vis maxima inde habita, magnum Estensibus marchionibus
vectigal praebens, omni propemodum Italiae satisfaciat. Scimus
vero vidimusque hac in piscatione contingere quod Plinius de Benaco Mincioque scribit his verbis: 'In Benaco Octobri mense glo-
meratae anguillae volvuntur mirabili multitudine, ut in excipulis
eius fluminis Mincii ob hoc ipsum fabricatis singulorum milium
globi capiantur'.

70   Volana sequuntur vetusti praesentisque nominis ostia, quae ramus auget a Pado veteri apud Coderam sive Caput Eridani scissus. Suntque ea in insula, quam bifurcatus hac scissura Padus,
mare Adriaticum ac palus Capresia efficiunt, vici populis frequentissimi et villis civium ac omni agresti cultu amoenissimi in quibus
praecipui sunt inferius Massa et *Fossadalbarum,*[75] Miliare Miliari-
numque et Medelana; et supra, Portus ac Belreguardum, ingentia

*most reverend and noble-spirited man Meliaduse d'Este, offspring of the fa-
mous Marchese Niccolò d'Este (whom he closely resembles), adorns and
where he often dwells. Drawn by a most laudable desire of seeing the
world, Meliaduse went with an honorable escort to Cairo in Egypt, the
largest of all cities, and to Jerusalem. He has travelled around, in the most
studied way, the coastlines of Greece, the Epirus, Dalmatia and all of Italy.*[170] A little higher up is Gaibana. Along the coast, fifteen miles
from the mouth of the Po di Primaro, is the mouth of a lagoon
which the ancients called Caprasia, now commonly called Magna-
vacca.[171] The ancient city of Comacchio is situated in the lagoon,
which has a circumference of more than twelve miles. It regularly
fitted out a fleet in the times of the Goths and Lombards, but because King Berengar's son Alberto had attacked them with the
help of the men of Comacchio, the Venetians destroyed it in the
year 932; and so it was sparsely populated ever after, as it is today.
It is a wonder to see the great quantities of fish provided by the
lagoon; the enormous supply of salted eels and mullet taken from
there (providing a large revenue for the Marquess of Ferrara)
would satisfy pretty much all of Italy. Having seen it, I know that
what Pliny writes of the fishing in Lake Garda and the Mincio actually happens here: "In the month of October the eels of Garda
are heaped together in incredible numbers, so that balls containing
thousands of them are caught in receptacles placed in the river
Mincio for the purpose."[172]

The mouth of the Po di Volano (the ancient and modern   70
name) comes next, augmented by a river that branches off from
the old Po at Codrea, or Caput Eridani. On the island created by
the Po (here two-pronged owing to the fork), the Adriatic, and the
lagoon Caprasia, there are villages full of people and the villas of
the Ferrarese—most attractive landscape with agriculture of all
sorts. Towards the sea, Massa Fiscaglia, *Fossa d'Albero*,[173] Migliaro,
Migliarino, and Medelana are prominent among them; and inland,
Portomaggiore and Belriguardo. The sumptuous and vast palaces

cuius villae magnificentissimi operis palatia a praeclaro praestantissimoque principe Nicolao marchione Estensi in veteri vico Vicoeria aedificata ceteris aequiparari possunt omnibus, quae in civitatibus alios Italiae principes aedificasse viderimus. Hicque Volanae
ramus vigesimo supra mare miliario dextrorsum se in alterum
scindit ramum, cuius ostia appellant Ghorum. Sunt quoque in insula inde facta Codeghorium et Massentia vici populis refertissimi.
Est etiam ditissimum aedificiisque superbissimum Pomposiae monasterium. Quartus dehinc habetur ramus Padi, quem contra Ficarolum diximus primum ab eo scindi; eiusque ostium 'Ad Fornaces' a vico vel potius ab hospitatoria taberna denominatur. Idque
ultimum Padi ostium limitem efficit quo Romandiola secundum
mare dividitur a Venetiis.

71   In ea vero insula, quam duo hi rami a veteri Pado quindecim secundum ripam superiorem distantem miliaribus efficiunt, Ferraria
est, ad secundum ramum veteri Pado apposita. Quam civitatem in
Historiis primum fuisse moenibus circumdatam a Smaragdo patricio et Italiae exarcho ostendimus. Nominis causam hanc afferunt
vetusta Ravennatum ecclesiae monumenta quod urbis illius archiepiscopi tria iurium ecclesiae suae loca a tribus metallorum nominibus appellaverint: Aureolum Forliviensis agri in amoeno colle situm ab auro; et Argentam Pado primario appositam ab argento;
Ferrariamque a ferro. Ob eam autem quae in Padi ramorum scissura et alveorum mutatione facta est locorum confusionem, non
satis iudicare[76] possumus utrumne in hoc Ferrariae loco an supra,
ubi ramus est Ficaroli, incoluerunt Assarigi, quos populos Etruria
oriundos vult Plinius Assagiam fossam in Adrianorum paludes derivasse et inde urbis Adriae submersionem inchoasse. Sed vetera
haec ut sunt dubia relinquentes ad nostrum redeamus institutum.

72   Cum Ferraria urbs ab ipso condicionis initio in partibus Ravennatium Romanorumque simul adversus Longobardos durasset, il-

of the estate of Belriguardo were built by that eminent and distinguished prince, Niccolò d'Este, Marquess of Ferrara, in the old village of Voghiera,[174] and can rival any other princely palace in Italy. Here on the island, twenty miles from the sea, the branch of the Po di Volano forks again to form a second stream branching to the right, whose mouth is called the Po di Goro. On the island so formed there are likewise populous villages, Codigoro and Massenzatica, and also the wealthy monastery of Pomposa with its proud buildings.[175] Here there is a fourth arm of the Po, which, as I said, first broke through opposite Ficarolo. This branch of the Po is called at its mouth "Ai Fornaci" after the neighboring village, or rather the inn. This last mouth of the Po forms the boundary on the coast that separates Romagna from Venetian territory.

These two arms that branch off from the left bank of the old 71 Po are fifteen miles apart, and on the island that they form is Ferrara, set on the second arm beside the old river.[176] As I described in my *Histories*, the patrician Smaragdus, the exarch of Italy, was the first to enclose the city with a wall.[177] Old records of the church of Ravenna assert that it was so named because the archbishops of Ravenna called three places under their jurisdiction after metals: Oriolo dei Fichi, set on a pleasant hill in the territory of Forlì, after gold; Argenta, on the Po di Primaro, after silver; and Ferrara, after iron. Owing to the confusion arising from the branching of the Po and its changing channels, I cannot be sure whether the Assarigi lived here at Ferrara or further up, where the Po di Ficarolo branches off. Pliny maintains that the Assarigi (originating in Etruria) channeled the "Assagian ditch" into the marshes of Adria, and so began the submersion of the city of Adria.[178] But let us leave aside these matters of ancient history as beyond resolution, and return to the business at hand.

From the very moment that Ferrara assumed the status of a 72 city, she held out against the Lombards on the side of the Ravennates and the Romans alike; but once the Lombards had been

347

lis a Carolo victis post donationem de exarchatu Ravennate factam Romanae ecclesiae in eius oboedientia perseveravit. Tandem quo tempore Germani imperatores ecclesiae adversari coeperunt, ipsa quoque civitas sub alterutris vacillavit. Sed ad annum salutis undecies centenum Matildis comitissa Venetorum Ravennatumque auxilio eam ab Henrico III, ecclesiae hoste, occupatam sibi subegit. Et anno abinde centesimo et vicesimo primo cum marchiones Estenses amicitiis divitiisque potentissimi in Ferraria essent, Salinguerra quidam Ferrariensis per eorum et Ecelini de Romano amicitiae occasionem, perfidia usus, Frederici Barbarossi instigationibus auxilioque Ferrariae dominium occupavit—quem Innocentius IIII pontifex Romanus Venetorum auxilio ad annum salutis millesimum ducentesimum quadragesimum expulit. Et marchiones Estenses Ferrariam sibi paulo post subigere inceperunt. Sed anno abinde sexagesimo octavo Veneti, ipsis marchionibus vi pulsis, Ferraria sunt potiti; eamque ut dimitterent adduci non potuerunt, licet Clemens quintus pontifex Romanus civitatem Venetiarum ecclesiastico supposuerit interdicto, unde omnia eorum bona per Gallias Britanniamque direpta fuerunt. Nec paruissent iussionibus papae Veneti, nisi legatus ecclesiae in Italiam Avinione veniens, marchionum Estensium et Ferrariensium extorrum auxilio fretus, Venetos vi et armis Ferraria primum, dehinc castello Thealdo, quod ad pontem retinebant, magna utrinque caeda commissa, deturbasset. Fuitque postea semper Ferraria sub Estensis familiae gubernatione pontificibus oboedientissima et adeo tali dominio felix ut cum opibus et potentia creverit per singulos annos, tum maxime proximis XX annis mirabile habuerit incrementum, quod tamen augeri fecit concilium a quarto Eugenio pontifice Romanorum ibi celebratum.

73   Cui interfuerunt Iohannes Paleologus imperator Constantinopolitanus et quicquid praesentis temporis Graecia Christianis subdita virorum habuit excellentium. Inchoata namque est Ferrariae,

defeated by Charlemagne, from being part of the exarchate of Ravenna she was given by him to the Church of Rome, and continued thereafter in obedience to the Church. When eventually the German emperors began to oppose the Church, the city came under the sway of each in turn. The city had been occupied by the enemy of the Church Henry III, but in the year 1100 the countess Matilda took control of Ferrara with the aid of the men of Ravenna and Venice.[179] One hundred and twenty-one years later, when the marquesses d'Este had grown powerful in Ferrara through their wealth and connections, one Salinguerra of Ferrara siezed control of the city by treachery, exploiting his friendship with the Este and with Ezzelino da Romano, and egged on and helped by Frederick Barbarossa.[180] With the assistance of the Venetians, the Roman pontiff Innocent IV drove Salinguerra out in the year 1240, and the d'Este began to make themselves masters of Ferrara soon after that. Fifty-eight years further on, however, the Venetians expelled them by force and took possession of the city. They could not be prevailed upon to give it up, despite Clement V's imposing an ecclesiastical interdict on Venice by which all their merchandise in France and Britain was distrained.[181] Nor would the Venetians have obeyed the commands of the pope had not a papal legate come from Avignon to Italy and with the help of the Este and the Ferrarese exiles expelled them by force of arms, first from Ferrara, then from Castel Tealdo (which the Venetians retained as far as the bridge), with great slaughter on both sides. Under the rule of the Este family the city was thereafter faithful to the popes. So successful was she under these masters that her power and wealth increased year by year, and in the last twenty years in particular she has enjoyed astonishing growth, to which the Council held there by Eugenius IV only added.

The emperor of Constantinople Johannes Paleologus took part 73 in the Council, along with all the leading men of the parts of Greece still under Christian control. This was in connection with

quam Florentiae conclusam fuisse diximus, orientalis ecclesiae unio cum ecclesia occidentali.

74   Habuit etiam Ferraria per aetatem nostram praestantissimum principem Nicolaum Estensem, cui ad summam gloriam nihil praeter litterarum ornamenta defuit—quam felicitatis partem additam vidimus principi Leonello, quem nuper amisimus. Novus vero marchio Borsius etsi litterarum ornamento caret, humanitate tamen liberalitate et prudentia genitorem Nicolaum nobis reddet. Quod vero praeteritis temporibus novae sed splendidissimae civitati defuit praesens supplevit saeculum, in quo viros habemus nobiles studiis[77] humanitatis ornatos: *Feltrinum Boiardum, Paulum Costabilem*, Nicolaum, Laurentium, Robertum et Titum fratres Strozzas, *Andream Perundulum*, Lippum Platesium et, qui peritissimus etiam est medicus et philosophus, Hieronymum Castellum, *qui vir magni nobilisque ingenii Graecis ac Latinis literis plenus non magis in medicina, cui est addictus, quam in oratoria poeticaque excellit.*[78]

75   Difficilis nunc nobis restat limitum huius regionis designatio—praesertim Adriam exarchatui Ravennae subiectam simul cum Ferraria in Romandiola claudere cupientibus. Pado, quem Ficaroli diximus appellari, decimo supra mare miliario ad dextram, ubi primum tellus habetur solida et aratri patiens, adiacent Corbulae vici duo, aliquot passuum milibus inter se distantes, dehinc Crispinum. Post hos est fossa Pelosella cui intus adiacet Orachanum, speciosa villa praedictorum Nicolai, Laurentii, Roberti et Titi Strozzarum, doctrina aeque ac nobilitate gentis ornatorum. Multas ab ostio fossae Pelosellae Padus alienas accipit aquas. Nam parvo ducta tractu ipsa fossa paludes exonerat amplissimas, utpote quas magna pars Athesis fluvii Veronensium et totus Tartarus totusque Menacus torrentes adeo late longeque augent ut maris sinum amplitudine ac sublatis quandoque fluctibus imitentur. Sunt in his paludibus complura castella et vici, quorum ad dexteram primum est Fratta oppidum, in quo ad annum salutis duodecies centenum atque vicesimum quartum magna ac prope universalis

the union of the Eastern and Western Churches, which began at Ferrara and, as I mentioned, was concluded at Florence.[182]

In our day Ferrara has also borne that excellent prince Niccolò 74 d'Este, who wanted only the ornament of letters to scale the heights of glory—an element of felicity with which the Marquess Lionello d'Este, recently lost to us, was amply endowed. And even if he lacks the adornment of literature, the new marquess Borso yet recalls his father Niccolò in his humanity, generosity and wisdom.[183] What this modern but very grand city lacked in times past, the present century has certainly supplied, and we now have men of high birth distinguished in the humanities: *Feltrino Boiardo, Paolo Costabile*, the brothers Niccolò, Lorenzo, Roberto, and Tito Strozzi,[184] *Andreas Perundulus*, Lippo Platesi,[185] and Girolamo da Castello, also an accomplished physician and philosopher, *a man of great and noble mind, replete with Greek and Latin letters, who excels no less in oratory and poetry than in his chosen calling of medicine.*[186]

There remains the difficult task of drawing the boundaries of 75 the region, particularly because I should like to include in the Romagna the town of Adria, as subject to the exarchate of Ravenna, alongside Ferrara. Ten miles from the coast up the Po (what I called the Po di Ficarolo), where the land first becomes solid and able to take the plow, are the two villages of Corbola, some miles apart from one another, and then Crespino. Afterwards comes the Polesella canal, on the landward side of which lies Raccano, the attractive country villa of the Strozzi brothers mentioned above, Niccolò, Lorenzo, Roberto and Tito, distinguished in equal measure for their learning and their gentle birth. The Po receives many different waters from the Polesella canal, for though it is short, it drains very large marshes: a large part of the Veronese river Adige and the whole of the streams Tartaro and Menago give the marshes such access of water over such a wide area that they look like a stretch of sea in point of size—and waves actually form sometimes. In these marshes there are a great

populi utriusque sexus caedes facta est ab Azzone Novello marchione Estense partes Salinguerrae Ferrariensis tyranni acrius insequente. Ad sinistramque paludem Pelosella ingredientibus est silvestris domus, unde Patavina via in Arquatam, vicum peninsulae Rodigiensis, est passuum duorum milium traiectus. Mediaque in valle sunt Tresienta et oppidulum Guilielmum ac ipsius vetustae Adriae fundamenta — inter quae vicus est ecclesia una et aliquot domibus, sed casis fere piscatoriis, frequentatus. Ea urbs olim praeclarissima, quam mari Adriatico nomen dedisse ostendimus, vel a Graecis Lydis, sicut vult Iustinus, vel ab Etruscis, sicut Livius Pliniusque scribunt, originem habuit, et nunc quoque civitatis titulum ac diocesim retinet.

76   Oritur Menacus torrens ad Magnanum, agri Veronensis vicum, Ceretamque et Praetellas vicos praeterlabitur. Tartarus item ex agro Veronensi ad Graecianum oriundus Micarolum,[79] Insulam Porcariciam[80] ad sinistram et Gagium ad dexteram vicos habet. Athesis autem pars, quae dictas illabitur paludes, sub Liniaco et Villa Bartholomaea primam ad Castagnarium scissuram facit. Trium vero huiusmodi fluviorum per contiguam regionem Marchiam Tarvisinam delabentium ideo in hac cursum descripsimus ut peninsulam Rodigiensem Adriensium dioceseos ac regionis quam claudunt, sicut par est, in partibus Romandiolae colligamus. Estque ea in peninsula Rodigium, nobile oppidum Bartholomaeo ornatum Roverella, archiepiscopo Ravennate, studiis eloquentiae ac humanitate plurimum decorato, *et Laurentio Roverella, episcopo Ferrariensi, sacrae theologiae et medicinae doctore excellentissimo.*[81] Est et Venetium castellum antiquae Venetiae nomen servans. Sunt quoque oppida Lendenaria et Abbatia populis frequentata. Supra

many castles and villages, of which the first on the right bank is the town of Fratta Polesine. Here in the year 1224 a great massacre — almost total — of the people of both sexes was carried out by the Marquess Azzo Novello d'Este in his ferocious pursuit of the supporters of the Ferrarese tyrant Salinguerra.[187] As one enters the marsh from the Polesella, there is on the left a rustic house from which one can take the Padua road to Arquà Polesine, a village of the peninsula of Rovigo two miles away. In the middle of the valley are Trecenta, and the little town of Castelguglielmo, and the remains of ancient Adria itself, among which is a thriving village with a church and some houses, fishermen's cottages for the most part. This was once a famous city which, as I mentioned, gave its name to the Adriatic Sea: either it originated with the Lydian Greeks (as Justin believes),[188] or the Etruscans (as Livy and Pliny write),[189] and even now it keeps the title of 'city' and diocese.

The Menago stream arises at Magnano, a village in Veronese 76 territory, and flows by the villages of Cerea and Pradelle. The river Tartaro also rises in the territory of Verona, at Grezzana, and has on its left the villages of Nogarola and Isola Rizzo, and on the right Gazzo. The part of the Adige which flows into the marshes mentioned above, first forks off at Castagnaro, below Legnago and Villa Bartolomea. I have described here the course of three rivers which actually flow through the neighboring region of the March of Treviso so as to bring into the territory of the Romagna, as is only proper, the peninsula of Rovigo in the diocese and district of Adria, of which these rivers form the border.[190] Rovigo itself is on this peninsula, a well-known town graced by the Archbishop of Ravenna Bartolomeo Roverella, a man honored for his pursuit of eloquence and his humanity,[191] *and by Lorenzo Roverella, the bishop of Ferrara and a most excellent doctor of theology and medicine.*[192] There is also the castle of Venezio, which preserves the name of ancient Venetia. Also on the peninsula are the bustling towns of Lendinara and Badia Polesine. Further up the river, above the mouth

fossae Pelosellae ostium sunt ad sinistram Francolinus, ad quem via Paduana profecti Ferraria Padum transmittunt, et ad dexteram Pontis Lacus Obscuri vicus.

77   Supraque pervenitur ad Padi integri ripam, unde ramus scinditur Ficaroli, ab eoque loco integer Padus. Hunc vero Ficaroli ramum intra annos centum proximos inchoasse ideo non dubitamus quia Roberti regis Neapolitani et Francisci Petrarchae pictura Italiae, quam nos sequi supra diximus, ipsum non habet ramum. Praeterea monasterium Sancti Salvatoris in quo arx Ficaroli aedificata fuit et eius vices obtinens Sancti Laurentii de Casellis ecclesia, monasterio Sancti Marci Ferrariensis annexa, iurium suorum vetusta habet annorum quadringentorum monumenta, in quibus facile intellegitur: ubi Padus ipse nunc est Ficaroli dictus fuisse agros. Confirmantque nos in hac novitatis huius rami opinione appositi singulis praediis singulisque iuribus monasterii ultra citraque Padum nunc existentibus fines—quibus designandis nulla umquam ipsius rami mentio facta est. Sunt ea in Padi integri ripa Seravallae et Castrum Novum arces, Massa, Brigantinus et Melaria vici cum opulentissimi tum etiam populis frequentissimi. Deinde terra et per Padi ripam euntibus Lombardiae et ad contiguas Melariae ac Brigantini agro paludes Tarvisinae Marchiae limites habentur.

of the Polesella canal, are Francolino on the left, where the road to Padua from Ferrara crosses the Po, and the village of Ponte-lagoscuro on the right.

Above these villages one reaches the undivided Po: an arm 77 branches off at Ficarolo, and then from that place onwards the Po is undivided. I am sure that this branch of the Po at Ficarolo was formed in the last hundred years, because the map of Italy of King Robert of Sicily and Petrarch (which as I said, I am following) does not have it.[193] Added to which, the monastery of San Salvatore, on which the fortress of Ficarolo was built, and the church of San Lorenzo of Caselle (attached to the monastery of San Marco in Ferrara) which took its place, have old records of their legal titles going back four hundred years: it is easy to see from them that where the Po di Ficarolo now is was once fields. In support of my belief in the recent origin of this branch of the Po are the boundaries set to the individual properties and titles of the monastery as they exist today, on both sides of the Po, in defining which no mention is ever made of this branch. On the banks of the undivided Po are the fortresses of Serravalle and Castelnovo Bariano, and Massa, Bergantino, and Melara, very prosperous and populous villages. Then on land and along the bank of the Po are set the boundaries of Lombardy, and at the marshes abutting the territory of Melara and Bergantino, those of the March of Treviso.

Note on the Text

❦❦❦

The Latin text of the *Italy Illuminated* survives in some twenty-seven manuscripts and six printed editions of the fifteenth and sixteenth centuries.[1] New material not found in the editions but extracted from various MSS has been published by Nogara (1927), Campana (1938), Lucarini and Pontari (2001) and Pontari (2003).

The text of the *Italia illustrata* is an extremely unstable one, reflecting Biondo's decades of revising the text, a process which continued to the end of his life (see Introduction, pp. xxi–xxii). The text was circulated in a number of redactions, disclosing the various stages in the evolution of the work, but there is also contamination between redactions, and despite recent work the interrelationships of the various manuscript witnesses and the *editio princeps* is still far from clear.[2] It is to be hoped that Paolo Pontari's text being prepared for the Edizione Nazionale delle Opere di Flavio Biondo under the auspices of the Istituto storico italiano per il Medio Evo in Rome will sort out the complexities of the tradition and produce a definitive edition of this work of central importance to Renaissance studies.

For the present edition I have principally relied, with some hesitation, on the posthumous *editio princeps* of 1474 prepared by Flavio's son, Gaspare Biondo.

r   The *editio princeps*, published in Rome by Johannes
          Philippus de Lignamine in 1474.

In the preface to this edition, Gaspare claims that he produced his edition from materials inherited from his father, and that, regarding his father's writing as *sacrosanta*, he has changed nothing but obvious scribal errors.[3] At an earlier stage of my research, I expressed the suspicion that Gaspare's intervention in the text was more radical than this pious disclaimer would suggest, a view which has recently been echoed by Paolo Pontari, though without presenting any concrete evidence.[4] I was led to this view by the large number of stylistic changes introduced into the text

357

of the *princeps*, not all of them improvements, as well as by the numerous impossible readings and banal errors, to say nothing of typographical slips. However, closer comparison of the manuscripts and the *princeps* shows that a number of these stylistic improvements are anticipated in early manuscripts having no connection with Gaspare. Moreover, Massimo Miglio has recently drawn attention to the parallel case of the *Roma instaurata*, which Gaspar also prepared for publication in 1471, the twin as it were of the *Italia illustrata*. In this case the manuscript used as the copytext for printing the edition has survived (Ottob. lat. 1279 in the Vatican Library), and comparison of the manuscript with the printed edition shows that autograph changes made seemingly in Flavio's own hand entered Gaspare's edition of 1471.[5] Furthermore, the provisional recension recently done by Lucarini (2003) shows that the *editio princeps* of the *Italia illustrata* is intimately related to the latest redactions of the text made in Flavio's lifetime, and also shows contamination from an earlier stage of the tradition, as though Gaspare was confecting his edition from a number of manuscript sources. Finally, there is the fact that there are numerous readings, sometimes entire lines, found in the *princeps* but not in the MSS collated, which are obviously correct and improbably of Gasparine origin. So even if it is the case that Gaspare intervened stylistically in his father's text, something that has yet to be proven, there is still clearly authorial material contained in the *princeps*, possibly uniquely so, which cannot be disregarded.

In order to have some control over Gaspare's editorial work, however, I collated in addition five important witnesses against the 1531 Froben edition, as follows:

B   Vatican City, Biblioteca Apostolica Vaticana, MS Ottob. lat. 2369. Mid-15th century (see Introduction). Contains the dedication to Nicholas, and numerous marginal and interlinear additions in the author's hand. After Nicholas' death in 1455, the author scored the dedication and all passages relating to him.

C   Ravenna, Casa Cavalli, s.n. Mid-15th cent. Has the Nicholas dedication and many of the passages

scored by Biondo in the text and margins of *B,* but also several of the *additiones* of *E.*

E Florence, Biblioteca Riccardiana, MS Ricc. 1198. Mid-15th century (see Introduction). Contains new *supplementa* to Liguria and Tuscany, new marginal *additiones,* and author's letter to Pius II. The source of the new material in Nogara (1927).

H Vienna, Österreichische Nationalbibliothek, MS Series Nova 2960 (*olim* Staatsarchiv 711). Dated 1466. Has the *supplementa* of *E,* the letter to Pius II, and the *additiones* of *E* incorporated into the text.

Q̰ Vatican City, Biblioteca Apostolica Vaticana, MS Pal. lat. 948. Late-15th cent. Lacks the distinctive material of *BC* and *EH.*

I also cite indirectly, via the passages printed in Lucarini-Pontari, "Nuovi passi inediti," pp. 233–238, and Pontari, "Ancora su passi inediti," pp. 363–370, three witnesses to the earliest redactions of the *regiones Etruria* and *Romandiola:*

F Florence, Biblioteca Nazionale Centrale, MS Magl. XIII 38. Early sixteenth century.

R Ravenna, Biblioteca Classense, MS 203. Dated 1460.

W Florence, Biblioteca Medicea Laurenziana, MS Plut. LXV 17. Mid-fifteenth century.

In short, the text printed here in roman type is in principal that of the author's final recension as transmitted by his son Gaspare, but corrections have sometimes been imported from earlier redactions where these offered a better text. Since the final recension omitted a number of passages found in earlier redactions, these have been included in italics for the reader's convenience, with notes to indicate their source.

Poetical passages in the Latin and English texts are printed as prose, following Biondo's own practice, and I have not attempted to reduce to grammatical order the many sentence fragments quoted by Biondo. In accordance with the preference of this series, spelling has been modernized, and modern conventions of punctuation and capitalization have

been followed. In the Latin text, editorial additions are indicated by angle brackets, deletions by square brackets; in the translation, editorial additions are indicated by square brackets.

I am grateful to dott. Maurizio Campanelli and dott.ssa Maria Agata Pincelli, the editors of the *Roma Triumphans* for the Edizione Nazionale, whom I consulted when trying to evaluate the status of the *editio princeps*; their information and advice was invaluable in preparation of this edition.

NOTES

1. I studied twenty-six MSS of the *Italy Illuminated* in "Towards a Critical Edition"; Bianca in her review of Cappelletto, p. 341, adds Bernkastel-Kues, Hospitalbibliothek, MS 157. For the editions, see the Bibliography.

2. Some significant progress has been made by Lucarini, "La tradizione manoscritta."

3. The text is in Miglio, "Incunaboli come fonte," pp. 127–128, at 127: "Igitur ut primum licuit subducere publicis negociis, quibus ut nosti iam dudum dies et noctes distringor, successiva aliqua tempora exemplaria *Italiae* quae apud me hereditaria erant recognovi, non quo aliquid ex ipsius scriptis mutarem. Non enim tantum mihi arrogo ut eius scripta, quae mihi pene sacrosanta sunt, temerario ausu pervertam, etsi scio ipsum quod ad eius operis editionem immaturam ab amicis impulsus fuit, nonnulla fuisse mutaturum. Verum mihi id solum curae fuit ut si quae essent in ipso opere librariorum negligentia errata, emendare quoad possem, ne cum vitio multiplicaretur."

4. White, "Towards a Critical Edition," p. 282, note 50; Pontari. "Ancora su passi inediti," p. 367, note 22. Pontari asserts that "Gaspare ha consapevolmente operato un processo sistematico di revisione stilistica del testo paterno assolutamente arbitrario e personale."

5. Miglio, "Incunaboli come fonte," esp. p. 122. At the request of James Hankins, General Editor of this I Tatti series, dott.ssa Maria Agata Pincelli was kind enough to collate a few folios from the beginning and middle of MS. Ottob. lat. 1279 with the *editio princeps* (1471) of the *Roma instaurata* also edited by Gaspare. The comparison showed that the only

differences between the MS used by Gaspare and the imprint are almost certainly simple printing errors. The second corrector of the MS, possibly to be identified with Gaspare, apparently did not introduce any important changes; dott.ssa Pincelli in a private communication writes: "In verità gli interventi di questa seconda mano mi sono sembrati di scarso rilievo e comunque del tutto estranei ad un' opera di riscrittura e di abbellimento della prosa di Biondo."

Notes to the Text

❧❧❧

PREFACE

1. Omitted in *CEHQr, deleted by second hand in B*
2. historiam *BC*
3. quinte pontifex Romane *added superscript by a second hand in B*
4. nil *C*
5. Stephani quoque *C*
6. decoratique *C*
7. *added superscript by a second hand in B*
8. decorasti *C*
9. *italicized portion omitted in EHQr, deleted in B*

I. LIGURIA

1. Blondi Flavii Forliviensis Italiae illustratae liber primus et regio prima Liguria incipit *r*
2. Omitted in *BEHQr*
3. Salluvios *Livy:* Salvios *mss., r*
4. Salluvii . . . Oxybii et Briniates *Livy:* Salturi . . . Exubii et Buriates *mss., r*
5. Helii *CQHr:* Helli *E:* Helis *B*
6. Albingatum *mss., r*
7. Salturios . . . Exubios et Buriates *BCEHQ.:* Oxybios et *om. r*
8. Flisca *H² (recte)*
9. Ferior *mss., r*
10. Buliascum *mss., r*
11. procurrit *Lucan*

363

12. Tigultiam *mss., r*

2. TUSCANY

1. Blondi Flavii Forliviensis Italiae illustratae libri primi regio secunda incipit feliciter *r*

2. *italicized portion from the earliest redaction found in FW (= Lucarini-Pontari, p. 233); see Note on the Text.* Etruriae] Eius *BCEHQr*

3. dicta *mss.*

4. potuerint *Livy*

5. *omitted in EHQr, deleted by a second hand in B*

6. Macrae *omitted in EHQr*

7. *added by a second hand in B; omitted by the other witnesses*

8. *The earliest version of this paragraph, found in FW (=Lucarini-Pontari, p. 233), reads:* Sunt ad Macre dexteram supra Lunam oppida Caput Pontis, Castianus, Monzones, Vianum, Marciasium, Sanctus Terrentius, Tendula, Bibblola, Ponzanellum, Mons Clarus, Chomanum, Verrucula, Castrum Aquile, Olivola, Groppa Sancti Petri, Mons Cigoli, Agnum, Castrum Novum, Fossa Novi, Sanctus Stephanus, Carpignuola, Laula, Terrarossa, Villafrancha, Torrens Bagnonus cum oppido eius nominis Filectum, Malgratum, Filectica et, in Apenino, Pontremulum, Francisco Sfortie novo duci Mediolani subiectum.

9. violatorum *EH*: violatum *BCQ*: Voliatum *r*

10. *omitted in r*

11. Macram *Livy*: Meram *mss., r*

12. *so Livy*: autem *mss., r*

13. eversum *Juvenal*

14. et eiectum . . . montem *not in the mss.*

15. *scil.* Auser: Auxeris *r, possibly an authorial error*

16. vellent *mss., S.H.A.*: nollent *r*

17. *omitted in r, probably owing to an eyeskip*

18. Volaterranorum *mss.*

19. *the italicized portion from FW* (=*Lucarini-Pontari, p. 234*)

20. *from FW* (=*Lucarini-Pontari, p. 234*)

21. *from FW* (=*Lucarini-Pontari, p. 234*)

22. *omitted in r*

23. Cervertere *EHr*

24. Agelinae *r*

25. *corrected:* cui *BCEHQr*

26. appellatio *mss.*

27. *omitted in r*

28. advectos *BCEHQ:* avectas *(!) r*

29. Auxeris *mss, r: see* §13, *note 15*

30. Lomelicus *BCE:* Lumelicus *HQr, possibly an authorial error*

31. *from FW* (=*Lucarini-Pontari, p. 234*)

32. *from FW* (=*Lucarini-Pontari, p. 235*)

33. *corrected from* quod *mss., r*

34. ceperint *BHr*

35. hic . . . aequiparandum] hic Florentinis parentibus Florentiae natus patria exul Ravennae obiit, ille patre Florentino sed exule apud Arretium natus et Arquade inter Euganeos colles mortuus ac sepultus est. Famaque est nullo nobis confirmata auctore Claudianum poetam fuisse Florentia oriundum. Pauloque post Florentia Iotum Bondonem et Taddeum Gaddum habuit pictores celeberrimos insimul socios Eracleonti Zeusi equiperandos: *from the earliest version found in F and with slight variations in W* (=*Lucarini-Pontari, p. 235*)

36. scripserit *EH*

37. *omitted in r*

38. auctae *r*

39. patriarchis] Iosep maximo patriarca *F*

40. *FW adds* patre tuo (=*Lucarini-Pontari, p. 235*)

41. Cumulantque . . . Carolus] Cumulatisque eius felicitatem tu et

Iohannes *FW* (*=Lucarini-Pontari, p. 236*): et Carolus *omitted in r; cf. also Lucarini-Pontari, pp. 251–52*

42. *The sense has become confused in revision; BCEHQ have:* monasterium celebre Sancti Marci, cum superbae sunt et, ut aiunt, insanae exstructiones ceterae, tum maxime bibliotheca alias superat omnes quas nunc habet Italia.

43. *FW adds* vestrae (*=Lucarini-Pontari, p. 236*)

44. assidua *r*

45. *italicized portion from FW* (*=Lucarini-Pontari, p. 236*)

46. Inde *r*

47. quamusque *r*

48. offendebatur *BCEQ*

49. iacerent *r*

50. oppidum nobile] oppidum, ut in montibus, nobile delabente *BCEHQWr*

51. *italicized portion from FW* (*=Lucarini-Pontari, p. 236*)

52. *italicized portion from FW* (*=Lucarini-Pontari, p. 236*); ornamentum *to be emended to* ornatum

53. duo milia *Livy:* duum milium *BCEHQr*

54. *C adds the name* Marino Soçinoque

55. Clano *r*

56. *italicized portion from FW* (*=Lucarini-Pontari, p. 236*)

57. *corrected:* litteras . . . vetustissimas *BCEHQr; see Lazio §20.*

58. ostendemus *BCEH*

59. *italicized portion from FW* (*=Lucarini-Pontari, pp. 236–237*)

60. ornata est etiam] Antonio etiam Rosello et Angelo Gambiono iureconsultissimis *FW* (*=Lucarini-Pontari, p. 237*)

61. Romani pontificis] Nicolai V Romani pontificis *added by another hand in the margin of B:* tuae Sanctitatis *main scribe of B, C*

62. gloriam *r:* nobilitatem *BCEHQ, Pliny*

63. Clanes r; *see note 55*

64. Clanes r: *see notes 55 and 63*

65. XXIII *Livy (Periochae)*: XXIIII BCEQr: XIIII H

66. *italicized words from FW (=Lucarini-Pontari, p. 237)*

67. *italicized portion from FW (=Lucarini-Pontari, p. 237)*

68. primum . . . dicemus] et Braccius de Fortebraciis F *(=Lucarini-Pontari, p. 237)*

69. fusum BCHQ: fusam r

70. Deinceps BCHQ

71. Magno . . . munitissima] Et nuper tu, pater sancte quinte Nicolai pontifex, magno instaurasti impendio qui obviaturus ne cives ulterius in se ipsos saeviant, arcem ibi aedificasti munitissimam BC; *intermediate variations in EH; omitted in Q (see Introduction)*

72. continebant BCHQr

73. videretur r

74. apud Pontianum . . . Fiano propinquum] apud Fianum ipsum, patriam suam, quod oppidum Fianum corrupte pro Veianum nunc appellatur C

75. -que *omitted in* r

76. -que *omitted in* r

77. arces habent BCEHQ

78. Carminum Q: Odarum E

79. *italicized portion from FW (= Lucarini-Pontari, p. 237)*

80. *italicized portion from FW (=Lucarini-Pontari, p. 237)*

81. XXVIII r

82. XXVIII r

83. praevecti C, *Livy*: provecti BEHQ: profecti r

84. et ceteri r: et cetera C: *omitted* BEHQ

85. habita r

86. adiacet EH

87. Sutrium] Lutrium vero *r*

88. olim *after* lacus C, *second hand in* B

89. *italicized words from* FW (=*Lucarini-Pontari, p. 238*)

90. lancea *r*

91. Illeque *BCEHQ:* Ille qui *r:* Ille *Livy*

3. LAZIO

1. Blondi Flavii Forliviensis Italiae illustratae liber secundus incipit et Latina regio III *r*

2. iis quae] is quae *r:* quaequae *mss.*

3. divum virum *r*

4. tamen *r*

5. praesens *Horace*

6. maris *mss:* montis *r*

7. nunc a Civita . . . miliarium] nunc a Lavinio oppido in maris litora duo de viginti milia passus *mss.: see the relevant Note to the Translation*

8. Neque . . . Lavinia] Estque haec non Lavinia, sicut multi opinantur *mss.*

9. Lanuviis *Livy (as in the next line)*

10. cardinalis Columnae Prosperi oppidum *after* Lanuvium *mss.*

11. Quin potius . . . celebre habetur *omitted in* BC

12. caprisque *r*

13. *omitted in* r

14. Palumbae *mss., r, but see below*

15. *so* Pliny: sicute *r (sic)*

16. columbi *r*

17. Aphrodisim *mss., r*

18. lucus Iovis *Pliny:* locum Solis *mss., r*

19. Turni *mss.*

20. *so Vergil:* Acrisona Isdana *(!) r:* Acrisioneis damne *Q:* Ausoniis demum *BCEH*

21. magnum *Vergil:* magna *r*

22. magnis *mss.*

23. Amiternae *mss.*

24. eos *r:* ex eo *Servius*

25. corybanti *BCHQr*

26. *so Pliny:* Danne *BCHr:* Damne *EQ*

27. *omitted in r*

28. licebit *BCQ*

29. conflixisset *r*

30. *so Servius and BCQr:* fluvius *H:* livius *(?) E*

31. *so Servius:* Aetheus *r:* cerces *E (for 'Circeis?):* cereris *HQ:* ceteris *BC. Biondo's text of Servius is quite corrupt in this quotation.*

32. asseruit *r:* astruat *Augustine*

33. Clitarchus *B:* clithargus *C:* dithargus *EHQr*

34. *so Pliny:* magistratui *mss., r*

35. tradidit *r*

36. *omitted in r*

37. quasi axiros [*sc.* aveu xurou] id est sine novacula] a verbo graeco quod sine novacula interpretatur *mss.*

38. et colebatur . . . dicebatur *omitted by the mss.*

39. Astura *Servius*

40. *Italicized portion added by a second hand in E and in the text of H.*

41. *omitted in the mss.*

42. *omitted in r*

43. Minturnam *r:* Minturnum *mss.*

44. *sc.* εὔορμον

45. quondam *r*

46. parataque *Br, H before correction*

47. Vitruvius *Livy*: Vitrubus *r (but* Vitrubius *below)*

48. mustum *BEQ, Martial*: mulsum *CHr*

49. nedum *mss.*

50. ut nostri citrea appellant *omitted in the mss.*

51. *so Cicero*: sileta *BEQr*: syleta *C*: silera (?) *H*

52. *sc.* Pandaria

53. Caecubum montem *r*

54. patre Concordio *omitted in r*

55. proxime *r*

56. interesse *r*

57. nequivimus *r*

58. alicubi . . . alicubi] alicui . . . alicui *r*

59. *corrected*: litteras . . . maiusculas *mss., r; cf. Tuscany cap. 46.*

60. *italicized portion omitted in BEHQr*

61. *italicized portion omitted in r*

62. pubes *BCEHr: corrected in Q and by the second hand in B*

63. nutrici *r*

64. *corrected*: inferentes *mss., r*

65. affluens *r*

66. reddit *r*

67. *so Livy*: Lavici *r*: Lavicanum *mss. (changed to* Lab- *from* Lav- *throughout §§30 and 56)*

68. sistas *Martial*

69. construenda *E*

70. servos *mss.*

71. *sc.* Marsorum: *see Notes to the Translation, Lazio, no. 184.*

72. *The 1531 Froben edition adds the italicized phrase, missing in BCEHQr*

73. *so Livy (Periochae)*: L. Pinna et Caecilio Pinna *mss., r*

74. *correctly* LXI: LXII *CHQr*: XXII *BE*

75. Apetiti *mss*: apetitus *r*

76. *the cognomen added only in* C

77. Celanum . . . limes *CHr, second hand in E: an earlier version read* comitatus titulo ac opibus praecipuum est Celanum, nostrae hac in parte Latinorum regionis limes *BEQ*

78. Rugate *r*: Riute *(?) B*

79. Olibanum . . . oppidum] Olibanum est Piscianum oppidum et Sanctus Vitus *r*

80. Tiburam et Praenestam *mss.*, *r* (*Biondo writes both* Preneste *and* Prenesta, *and writes* Tibur *inconsistently as neuter or feminine; the spelling has been regularized to* Praeneste *and neuter* Tibur *throughout*)

81. ruber *r*

82. positam *mss.*, *r*

83. Anthonius *BCEr*

84. Poncilietti *Q*: Porcelletti *r*

85. *so Livy*: Manilius *CEQr*: Manlius *BH*

86. eodem . . . fuerat] *r gives a text even further from Pliny*: ad Romanos transfugens simili honore ornatus eodem anno triumphavit de eis quo ipsorum consul populi Romani hostis fuerat

87. cavae fossae . . . relictum *r*: quem in cava fossa habent, nunc Odoardi Columnae oppidum, Petrus Columna per secundi Paschalis Romani pontificis tempora possedit paterna (sicut Pandulfus Hostiarius scriptor tradit) hereditate *mss.*

88. *italicized passage omitted in* r

89. operire *r*

90. quater *r*: duos *C*

91. a maioribus] amatoribus *r*

92. complexa *r*

93. Vallis . . . obtinet] Vallem enim concavam duo [quinque *C*] in circuitu mille [*sic*] passus complexam hic lacus dimidiam obtinet *mss.*

94. augmentum *r*

95. *omitted in* r

96. lariceis *r*: larice ligno *BEH*: larice ligneo *Q*: cipreseis *C*

97. *omitted in* r

98. auctorum *r*

99. suumque *r*

100. *italicized passage added in the margin of B by a second hand, afterwards deleted by the same hand.*

101. Et Virgilius] Unde Vergilius 'simplicibus Gabiis' et in VII *r, perhaps incorporating an incomplete reference to Juvenal 3.192 (see Notes to the Translation, Lazio, note 255)*

102. eos conditos *r*

103. detracto a Gallo *r*: tracto a Gallo *H*: detracto Gallo *BECQ*

104. maxime *r*

105. Nero *mss.*

106. fuisse coniicimus . . . temporibus optavit *CEHQr, added in the margin of B*

107. *So Livy, BEHr*: iterum *CQ*

108. *italicized portion omitted in* r

4. UMBRIA

1. Blondi Flavii Forliviensis Italiae illustratae liber III et IV regio incipit: Umbria ⟨sive⟩ Ducatus Spoletanus *r*

2. fuerant *CEHr*

3. -que *om.* r

4. *italicized words omitted in* r

5. productam *r*

6. *omitted in mss.* r; *word supplied from the 1559 edition* thesauris claram, *influenced apparently by Pliny's* ut Delphicis creditum est thesauris

7. non erit . . . asparagis *the second line of the epigram is omitted in the mss.*

8. instituemus *r*

9. *corrected:* arcibus *in mss,* r

10. *omitted in* r

11. quam longe *mss.*

12. approprinquamus *mss.*

13. magis nostrae regionis distantia *mss.*

14. *properly* Tinia: *Biondo writes alternately* Tinium, Tenium *and* Tennium

15. *The witnesses spell alternately* Chiesium *and* Chiasium

16. in IX Decius *omitted in* EHQr

17. eam *r*

18. Spelium *BCHQ*

19. *italicized portion omitted in* r

20. inde *r*

21. *italicized portion omitted in* r

22. *italicized portion omitted in* r

23. depopulato *BEH*: perpopulato *Q*

24. lag(o)enis *r*: lacunis *mss.*

25. quae curavit] Narsetemque eunuchum refici curavisse *r*

26. *corrected from* curantem *in BC*

27. *italicized portion found in BC*: EHQr *and the second hand in B have*: quae aedificiorum pulchritudine nuper ornatissima est reddita.

28. distantia *mss.*

29. itur *EQ*

30. quibus *mss.*

31. Unde Silus (!) Italicus . . . tauros *omitted in BCEQ: italicized portion omitted in* r

32. in primo] supra *mss.*

33. Spolitium *mss.,* r

34. *corrected:* suique *in mss.,* r: famique *Froben (1531)*

35. Et ex eadem . . . celeber habetur *omitted by the first hand in B; added by the second hand and in CEHQr*

36. *corrected:* genti *in mss., r*

37. *corrected:* Jovinus *in BCHQr:* Joannes E *(perhaps correctly)*

38. ad *r*

39. Corvus *BCEr*

40. Corvus *BCE:* Corvuus *r*

41. torrens *r*

42. Corvum *BCE*

43. alumno . . . patre] beato Benedicto monachorum patre alumno *mss.*

44. Quod . . . docet] Quod enim ipse docet effectus *mss.*

45. physicae *mss.*

46. Nursinum agrum] Nursiam *BCEH*

47. Conissa *r:* Comissa *E:* Leonessa *BCHQ (see Note to the Translation)*

48. sub ipsis . . . remotum] sub ipsa . . . recedens *r*

49. *italicized portion omitted in r:* -que *omitted EHQ*

50. *corrected:* XXXI *mss., r*

51. propinquum *BCHQr*

52. is fluvii *mss.*

53. locum Italiae umbilicum] medium Italiae *mss.*

54. Venusiae *r*

55. et *mss., r*

56. *the italicized portion, not in Pliny, is found only in C*

57. superius *omitted in EHQr*

58. Cicero *BEHQr*

59. Persicum *r*

60. septuaginta *BHQr*

61. singulariter *mss.*

62. Nequinam *EHQr*

63. oppidum *r*

64. habeat *r*

65. Numentano *mss.*

66. tu Paestanis] Tupestanis *r*

67. Storconum *r*

68. Curresii *CH*: Curtesii *BEr*

69. *italicized words omitted in r, probably owing to an eye-skip*

70. ut videtur *omitted in r*

71. *omitted in r*

72. Crustumerii *CH*

73. Crustumiis *r*

74. *omitted in r*

75. Crustumenus *mss., r*

5. PICENO

1. Blondi Flavii Forliviensis Italiae illustratae regio quinta Picenum sive Marchia Anconitana incipit *r*

2. eum *BEHQ*: eam *C*

3. prosperitate *r*

4. easdem *BCH*

5. arrepta *BHQ*

6. quod *BCEHr*

7. nactam *CHQr, second hand in B*

8. agri *r*

9. Vitelliensi *mss.*

10. prout etiam nunc gubernat idem Federicus *mss.*

11. et Livii . . . victoria . . . narrata *r*: per Livii . . . victoriam . . . narratam *mss.*

12. durissimi saxi *mss.*

13. Carda *r*

14. gravissimus *omitted in r*

15. habens *r*

16. devotus *Hr*

17. Samnitumque *BC*

18. conflixere *EHQr*

19. *corrected:* antesignariis *in mss., r*

20. eaque *Hr*

21. Fabrianum Romanae curiae] Fabrianum Quinti Nicolai pontificis ac Romanae curiae *B*: tua Quinte Nicolae pontifex Romane atque etiam Romane curiae *C*

22. accumulabat *r*

23. cantant *r*

24. cistellam . . . ornatissimam *EHQ*: ornatam *r*

25. Fabriani nuper (*om. EH*) degens pontifex accuratius persequitur: *EHr*: Fabriani degentes accuratius persequuntur *Q, second hand in B*: tu, Pater sancte, Fabriani degens accuratius persequaris *BC*

26. *So Pliny:* Cymera *EHQ*: Cymeria *BCr*

27. centralem *mss.*

28. Siciliae accolis] ut Iuvenalis, aut, ut Plinius, a Siculis *mss.*

29. defendat *r*

30. ceteris tribus *r*: ceteris lintribus *E*

31. *Following Pliny:* Cymericum *or* Cimericum *mss., r*

32. habeat *r*

33. *omitted in r*

34. *corrected:* Casaurius *mss., r*

35. excellentia *mss.*

36. Quod *r*

37. Chientinem *r*

38. Sernanam *EH*

39. Terrinum *r*

40. Terminus *Q:* Terinus *r*

41. primo . . . collationem] militia primum et tribunorum collationem detrectarunt *r*

42. *omitted in r*

43. *corrected:* Petridum *in mss., r*

44. fuerit *r*

45. mali . . . nostri] mali quod *mss.*

6. ROMAGNA

1. Blondi Flavii Forliviensis Italiae illustratae liber IIII et VI regio Romandiola sive Flaminia incipit *r*

2. *italicized portion from the earliest redaction, found in R (= Pontari, pp. 363–64)*

3. Pariter *mss.*

4. XXXVIII *mss.*

5. Q. Flaminium] L. Q. Flaminium *BEHr*

6. Lurum] Iurum *BCHQr; italicized portion from the earliest redaction, found in R (= Pontari, p. 364)*

7. *The place names in italics in caps. 5–6 are found only in R (Pontari, pp. 364–65)*

8. sequitur *EH*

9. *omitted in EHQr*

10. cui *BC*

11. et nunc . . . subjecta] et nunc est subiecta Sigismondo Pandulpho Malatestae, germano fratri tuo, praestanti bellicae rei ductori vicariatus ecclesiae titulo *R (Pontari, p. 365)*

12. Siciliae *CEHQr*

13. partes *r*

14. *italicized words found only in R (Pontari, p. 365)*

15. *italicized words found only in R (Pontari, p. 365)*

16. *italicized words found only in R (Pontari, p. 366)*

17. urbem *r*

18. quae praedicti Malatestae . . . innuerit] quae per tuam administrationem talis est reddita, ut pateat quod maiores sapientissimi prodidere: beatos fore populos quorum princeps contigisset sapientiae studere. Nunc enim multo pluris videtur facienda quam innuere voluit: *the version found in the earliest redaction, R (Pontari, p. 366)*

19. *italicized passage found only in R (Pontari, p. 366)*

20. *omitted in Hr*

21. -que *omitted in BCHr*

22. *omitted in BC*

23. qua *B*

24. celeberrimum *mss.*

25. imperator *BCQ*

26. *Biondo spells alternately* Helius *and* Aelius; *his spelling has been regularized throughout*

27. habeat *BCEH*

28. Popilii *r*

29. *italicized words from the earliest redaction R (Pontari, p. 366)*

30. Popilii *r*

31. convertunt *BC*

32. Mutilliana *BH*: Mutillana *E*

33. *italicized words from the earliest redaction R (Pontari, p. 366)*

34. de sacris literis] De anima *mss.*

35. quales *BCHQr*

36. *italicized passage omitted in r*: auctorem] Ciceronem *R*

37. *omitted in the mss.*

38. Venetia *BCEHr*

39. Ciceronis *after* codex *mss.*

40. characterem nosset] literam sciret legere *mss.*

41. ex eo descripsit] transcripsit *mss.*

42. transcripsimus *mss.*

43. sed . . . obtinuit] sed ipsum quoque Aragonum regem in meliorem literarum nostrarum cognitionem duxit? *R (Pontari, p. 367)*

44. Sed . . . Ravennam *omitted in the mss.*

45. olim *E*

46. Galeata . . . Sophia] in Apennino, Rundinaria primo, post Cotulus, quam supra diximus aeream arcem esse Tiberis fonti propinquam *R (Pontari, p. 368)*

47. innominata *after* quae *BCE:* in nominata *HQ: omitted in r*

48. *italicized passage from the earliest redaction R (Pontari, p. 368)*

49. *italicized passage omitted in r:* Manfredoque . . . coniunxit *omitted in BCQ:* pariterque . . . decorato *deleted by a second hand in E, omitted in H*

50. annisio *BCHQ:* annisis *E*

51. solit(a)e *r*

52. *corrected from* Messanius *mss., r*

53. sed male habitatam] male habitam *after* Barbarossus *mss.*

54. prope Bononiam] Ariminum inter et Bononiam *R (Pontari, p. 369)*

55. Abesse . . . Faventia] suntque qui opinentur eum locum fuisse Faventiam, quia par prope ab Arimino Bononiaque distantia eum infamem locum *R (Pontari, p. 369)*

56. *italicized portion omitted in EHQr*

57. Italia *B:* italicis *E*

58. intentionem *mss.*

59. evectorum *C:* enectorum *BEH:* eiectorum *Q*

60. domi . . . servivit] domesticus Albrico familiarisque fuit *mss.* (-que *om. BE)*

61. geruntur *r*

62. ostenderet *BCE*

63. *italicized words from R (Pontari, p. 369)*

64. *italicized passage from R (Pontari, p. 369)*

65. pervenitur *r*

66. *italicized passage from R (Pontari, p. 369)*

67. Abbaesio *BCH*

68. fractus *mss.*

69. Termicium *E*: Terentium *Pliny*

70. *italicized passage from R (Pontari, p. 369)*

71. Granaionum *BHQr*: Gravarionum *E*

72. rectus . . . praeterlabitur] qui recto et primario cursu praeterlabitur Padus *r*

73. *italicized passage from R (Pontari, pp. 369–70)*

74. quantum *r*

75. *omitted in r*

76. indicare *BEHQ*

77. litteris *mss.*

78. *italicized words and phrase from R (Pontari, p. 370)*

79. Nucardum *r*

80. Porcariam *HQr*: Procariam *E*

81. *omitted in BEHQr*

Notes to the Translation

ॐঔৎঔ

ABBREVIATIONS

Biondo, *History*	Biondo Flavio, *Historiarum ab inclinato Romanorum libri XXXII*, in *Blondi Flavii De Roma triumphante libri X* . . . (Basel: Froben, 1559)
Bruni, *HF*	Leonardo Bruni, *History of the Florentine People*, James Hankins, ed. and tr., 2 vols. to date (Cambridge, Mass.: Harvard University Press, 2001–2004), cited by book and paragraph number
CIL	*Corpus inscriptionum latinarum* (Berlin: G. Reimer, 1894–)
DBI	*Dizionario biografico degli italiani* (Rome: Treccani, 1960–)
LP	*Liber pontificalis*, L. Duchesne, ed. (Paris: E. de Boccard, 1981)
R.I.	Biondo Flavio, *Roma instaurata*, in *Blondi Flavii De Roma triumphante libri X* . . . (Basel: Froben, 1559).
RIS	Rerum italicarum scriptores
S.H.A	Scriptores Historiae Augustae

PREFACE

1. A somewhat fanciful though traditional idealization of the early third-century emperor M. Aurelius Severus Alexander and his (Christianized) mother Julia Avita Mamaea. Cf. S.H.A. *Aurelius Severus* 3.1–5 and 16, and see Clavuot, *Biondos Italia Illustrata*, p. 24f. with notes. The ruler with a generous appreciation of the learned is a recurring humanist *topos*, of course. Cf. also Lazio §52 (below).

2. Biondo will vary "Octavius" with the name "Octavianus" the future emperor took when adopted by Julius Caesar.

3. This formal dedication (Preface §§5–7) survives in only one of the work's (at least) three recensions.

4. Perhaps an allusion to his unemployment under the new pontiff.

5. Fulsome but not disproportionate observations on Nicholas' learning and his powers to reward it in others — as also on his building programs, in §§6 and 7, for which, see Ludwig Pastor, *The History of the Popes from the Close of the Middle Ages*, tr. F. I. Antrobus (St. Louis: Herder 1949), 2: 173–191. The "catalogue of the most learned men of this age" is perhaps an oblique reference to Nicholas' most famous work of learning, the library catalogue he compiled for Cosimo de'Medici when he was still an obscure cleric called Tommaso Parentucelli; see Vespasiano da Bisticci, *Vite*, ed. Aulo Greco (Florence: Sansoni, 1970), 1: 46.

6. Sta. Maria Maggiore.

7. San Stefano Rotondo.

8. Sta. Maria Rotonda.

I. LIGURIA

1. Biondo is probably referring to Virgil, *Georgics* 2. 236–276; Pliny the Elder, *Natural History* 3.38–42, and Petrarca's famous canzona *Italia mia* (*Canzoniere* 128).

2. Solinus, in Th. Mommsen, ed., *Collectanea rerum memorabilium* (Leipzig, 1893), *De terminatione provinciarum Italiae*, pp. 137–141.

3. I.e., *Vitalia*, from *vitellus*.

4. Virgil, *Aeneid* 7.3.

5. Servius, *In Aeneidem* 7.3.

6. Justin 43.1, 3–5.

7. Pliny the Elder, *Natural History* 3.43.

8. Cicero, *On Consular Provinces* 34.

9. Pliny the Elder, *Natural History* 3.43–44.

10. Ibid. 3.48–49. The land of the Bruttii (a pre-Roman people) is the part of lower Calabria facing Sicily.

11. In 299 B.C. Ibid. 3.110. And see Piceno §2.

12. Ibid. 3.138.

13. That Italian military weakness was a result of its political divisions was a common complaint of Biondo's contemporaries.

14. Geographus Ravennas, in M. Pinder, G. Pathey, eds., *Ravennatis Anonymi Cosmographia et Guidonis Geographica* (Berlin, 1860; repr. Aalen, 1962), 4.30 (p. 249.12).

15. Modern Palestrina.

16. See Tuscany §1.

17. Modern Basilicata.

18. Justin 20.1, 11.

19. Ibid. 43.3, 4

20. Livy, *Periochae* 47.

21. Ibid. 60.

22. Jordanes, in Theodor Mommsen, ed., *Iordanis Romana et Getica* (Berlin, 1882), *Romana* 177. Cf. Florus 1.18, 1.

23. See note 59.

24. See Florus 1.19, 4–5.

25. Livy 39.1, 1–2.

26. Ibid. 39.1, 5–6.

27. Ibid. 39.1, 7–8.

28. In December 218 B.C.

29. A loose paraphrase of Livy 28.46, 7–12.

30. Vergil, *Aeneid* 11.700.

31. Servius, *In Aeneadem* 11.700.

32. Vergil, *Georgics* 2.168.

33. Lucan 1.442–443.

34. "Breeches-wearing Gaul."

35. The identification of the Latin place-names with these modern towns is far from certain.

36. Virgil, *Aeneid* 6.830.

37. Servius, *In Aeneadem* 6.830. "Monoecus" is Greek for "dwelling alone."

38. Lucan 1.405–408, of Caesar's passage into Italy.

39. Barbarossa recognized the dominion over Monaco of the Genoese in 1162, which was confirmed by his son Henry VI, by cession, in 1191; the second date would fit Biondo's chronology.

40. *Tropaea Augusti*, after the monument or trophy (whose impressive ruin remains) commemorative of Augustus' victories over the Ligurians. Biondo conceived §11 and §§17–38 after Giacomo Bracelli's *Description of the Ligurian Coast* (*Descriptio orae ligusticae*), with wholesale appropriations from Bracelli's text (see note 57).

41. S.H.A., *Pertinax* 1.2.

42. Ibid. 3.3–4.

43. See Pliny the Elder, *Natural History* 3.48.

44. Modern Roya.

45. Lit. "two milestones". A milestone indicates a distance of 1000 *passus* or a Roman mile.

46. S.H.A., *Firmus* 12.1.

47. They are not the same: the Centa is a *fiume*, the Merula (see Pliny, *Natural History* 3.48) a *torrente*.

48. Albenga was brought (along with Genoa) under the control of Filippo Maria Visconti in 1421, and both cities rose up against the Milanese in 1436.

49. I.e. Finarium, supposedly related to the Italian *fin'aria*, "pure air".

50. The Fregosi (or Campofregosi) were a Genoese mercantile and (eventually) ducal family (see Tomasso below, and, in §30, Lodovico and Giano), rising to prominence in the thirteenth century. The Marquises Del Carretto of Savona were their bitter rivals.

51. Livy 28.46, 10.

52. Pliny the Elder, *Natural History* 3.48.

53. Pomponius Mela 2.4, 72.

54. Tommaso, son of Battista and nephew of Tommaso (1402–85) Fregoso was governor of Savona from 1450–58; he was beheaded in 1459 for treason.

55. Varazze, in Biondo's Latin Virago, but usually Vorago (also Viraggio), was the city of the Dominican hagiographer Jacopo de Voragine (d. *ca.* 1298), who may have been, in his *Legenda Sanctorum* (or *Legenda Aurea*), the source of the legend of the Virgin of Varazze (though Biondo's spelling suggests he may have thought association with the Blessed Virgin comes from the similarity of *virgo* to *Virago*). Jacopo is also the source, in his *Chronicon Genuense* (*RIS* 9.5–56), of the story (which Biondo contemns in §24) that the god Janus was the founder and eponym of Genoa.

56. See Pliny the Elder, *Natural History* 3.48.

57. Bracelli, *Descriptio orae Ligusticae*, in G. Andriani, *Atti della Società Ligure di Storia Patria* 52 (1924): 235.

58. See note 55.

59. See §12. Cf. Pliny the Elder, *Natural History* 3.47.

60. Livy 21.32, 5.

61. Livy 30.1, 10.

62. Roman practice was to reward soldiers of long and distinguished service with public lands; groups of soldiers assigned to particular lands were often organized legally as "colonies", and thus became administrative subdivisions of the Roman Empire.

63. See §25, with note 61.

64. Rothari, king of the Lombards (636–56 AD), pacified Liguria and took Genoa out of the Byzantine orbit.

65. Count Ademar of Genoa launched his expedition against Corsica in 806.

66. Hugh of Arles (Hugh of Provence) was king of Italy from 926–45, when he was expelled by Berengar II, Marquis of Ivrea. Berengar was king from 950–963.

67. Biondo must mean the Berbers, but his use of the term "Poeni"

(Carthaginians) recalls the ancient rivals of the Romans, no doubt intentionally.

68. Pope from 928–931.

69. Andrea Dandalo, *Chronica*, in RIS 12, 171.5–10. Dandalo was Doge of Venice from 1343–54, took part in Clement VI's crusade against the Turks, fought with Genoa throughout most of his term of office, and gave Petrarch a Venetian residence at public expense. In Region 8 (Veneto), Biondo's dependence on Dandalo's *Chronica* is very extensive.

70. Innocent IV (Sinibaldo Fieschi), canon lawyer, author of the *Commentary on the Decretals* (*Apparatus in quinque libros decretalium*) and rival of Emperor Frederick II, was pope 1243–54. Adrian V (Ottobono Fieschi), made cardinal by Innocent (his uncle), was pope for a month in the summer of 1276. Giorgio Fieschi was Bishop of Palestrina from 1449–55, participating in the conclave that elected Callixtus III in April 1455.

71. Giano, son of Bartolomeo Fregoso and Caterina Ordelaffi, died in office as doge in 1447, and was succeeded by his brother Ludovico (d. 1489).

72. Ceba (Grimaldi) (fl. mid-fifteenth century), active commercially in the Levant (Adrianople, Chios, Pera), had as friends and correspondents Giacomo Bracelli, Cyriac of Ancona, Leonardo Bruni (who thought highly of his Latin), and Francesco Filelfo.

73. Giacomo Bracelli (d. *ca.* 1466), lawyer, later chancellor and secretary of the Republic of Genoa. Friend of Francesco Barbaro, Biondo, Giovanni Maria Filelfo, Poggio Bracciolini. Wrote *On Famous Genoese* (*De claris Genuensibus*), *Description of the Ligurian Coast* (*Descriptio orae Ligusticae*), *Four Books on the Hispanic War against the King of Aragon* (*De bello Hispano adversus regem Aragoniae libri V*).

74. Gottardo Stella, Ludovico Fregoso's secretary; see Nogara, *Scritti*, p. 168f.

75. See Pliny the Elder, *Natural History* 3.48.

76. In §30.

77. Ptolemy of Alexandria, *Geography*, 3.1, 3.

78. Pliny the Elder, *Natural History* 3.48.

79. The famously beautiful Cinque Terre.

80. Now, as then, known as Soave (sweet).

81. Pliny the Elder, *Natural History* 14.68.

82. Persius 6.9.

83. Lucan 2.426–427.

84. Patron of lighthouse keepers.

85. See, e.g., Pliny the Elder, *Natural History* 8.48.

86. Facio (d. 1457) studied in Genoa and Ferrara. Friend of Francesco Barbaro, Panormita, Poggio, Biondo. Wrote *On Illustrious Men* (*De viris illustribus liber*), and *Ten Books of the Deeds of Alfonso I, King of Naples* (*Rerum gestarum Alphonsi primi regis Neapolitani libri X*), as well as a Latin translation of Boccaccio's Ruggieri tale from the *Decameron*.

87. The Marquis Malaspina di Mulazzo (see Dante, *Purgatorio* 8.109–39).

88. E.g., Pliny the Elder, *Natural History* 3.49.

89. Off Albenga, the Isola Gallinara; off Noli, the Isola di Bergeggi.

2. TUSCANY

1. The italicized portions are added in the earliest redaction; see Introduction, pp. xxi–xxii, and the Note on the Text.

2. Justin 20.1, 6–9.

3. Bruni, *HF* 1.13.

4. Livy 5.33, 7–11.

5. At Servius, *In Aeneidem* 2.278, 8.65, and 8.475, they have the status of *reges*, but likelier Biondo has in mind term officers like the *principes* of Livy 2.44, 8, for example.

6. Livy 10.7, 9; 1.8, 3.

7. Livy 9.36, 3–4.

8. See §63. A.U.C. stands for 'ab urbe condita', the traditional dating system of Rome from its supposed founding in 753 B.C.

9. Livy 29.36, 10–11.

10. Biondo, *History* 102f.

11. Berengar II, marquis of Ivrea, was joint king over Italy with his son, A.D. 950–966.

12. S.H.A., *Hadrian* 19.1.

13. Reigned 275–283. Little is known of him. The phrase "born of an eminent father" derives from a misreading of *ex patre Marino*, "born of a father named Marinus" in this pope's biography in the *Liber Pontificalis*.

14. Lucan 1.584–86: Arruns in fact dwelt in Lucca, not Luni.

15. Martial 13.30, 1–2

16. Tommaso (d. 1485), three times doge of Genoa; see Liguria §23.

17. Nicholas V (Tommaso Parentucelli) was pontiff 1447–1455: he took his papal name from Niccolò Albergati (1357–1443), learned Carthusian bishop of Bologna and cardinal, whom he served as secretary for many years. Nicholas V's half-brother, Filippo Calandrini, was one of eight men he elevated to cardinal. Pietro da Noceto, of Bagnone (1397–1467) was Nicholas' great friend and esteemed advisor. This passage was deleted from editions of the *Italy Illustrated* after the death of Nicholas; see Introduction, pp. xxi–xxii.

18. See note 22.

19. Livy 39.32, 1–4.

20. Juvenal 3.257–258.

21. Pliny the Elder, *Natural History* 36.135.

22. Biondo relied on a faulty reading of Livy in §11, which refers rather to the river Magra (*in Macram fluvium*) and not the nonexistent Mera, attested by one branch of the tradition of Livy. The Serchio was anciently always known as the Auser, though Biondo writes *Auxeris*.

23. It was actually taken from the Pisans in 1266, and remained in the hands of the Lucchesi for half a century. The fortress built in 1166 was sometimes called the Tempio d'Ercole, though not itself an ancient monument.

24. S.H.A., *Aurelian* 48.1–2.

25. Vergil, *Aeneid* 10.179.

26. Pliny the Elder, *Natural History* 3.50: Pliny speaks of the Greek tribe of "Teutani," not "Territani."

27. Justin 20.1, 11.

28. Lucan 2.401.

29. Livy 21.39, 3.

30. Bernardo Pignatelli, pope from 1145 to 1153.

31. Pliny the Elder, *Natural History* 3.50.

32. Ibid. 3.51.

33. Ibid. 3.52: actually *Volsienses* or *Volsinienses*.

34. Ibid. 3.51.

35. *LP* 724.514–515.

36. The two italicized passages in this paragraph are preserved only in the earliest redaction, the version dedicated to Piero de'Medici.

37. Cf. the river "Prile," at Pliny, *Natural History* 3.51. This is the *Prilius* (or *Prelius*) *lacus*.

38. Livy 30.39, 1–2.

39. Vergil, *Aeneid* 10.172.

40. Pliny, *Natural History* 3.51. Biondo runs together Pliny's *Telamo, Cosa*.

41. Matilda of Canossa, Countess of Tuscany (d. 1114), abetted Gregory in his church reforms, supported and protected him, and, in 1077, ceded to the Roman Church under him her lands from Ceperano to Radicofani. Biondo dates the donation from the countess' death.

42. Vergil, *Aeneid* 10.184: *intempestaeque Graviscae*, is in fact some way to the south of Montalto, on the coast at Porto Clementino. The river Minio is mentioned at 10.183.

43. Pliny, *Natural History* 32.21.

44. Ptolemy, *Geography* 3.1, 4; Pliny, *Natural History* 3.51; Pomponius Mela 2.4, 72. Corneto was renamed Tarquinia in 1922.

45. Churchman, condottiere, considered a cruel and arbitrary adminis-

trator. Eugenius IV (who had made Vitelleschi cardinal and whom he served) countenanced his murder in 1440. Biondo had served him in 1432 (see the Introduction).

46. The italicized portion is preserved only in the earliest redaction.

47. Pliny the Younger, *Letters* 6.31, 1–3. "Centumcellae" means "one hundred chambers."

48. In fifteen books, written over 400–416. According to tradition, it was composed in the hermitage of La Trinita, near Cencelle (the medieval replacement of the destroyed *Centumcellae*) in the Tolfa mountains.

49. Vergil, *Aeneid* 10.184.

50. Valerius Maximus 1.1.10.

51. Livy 1.2, 3.

52. Martial 13.54, 1. That the poet Martial was a cook was a common conception from the tenth and eleventh century on. It probably arose from his poetical preoccupation with food and gluttony.

53. Cf. §3.

54. Keen missionary pope (891–896) in an age of political turbulence; his body was exhumed and outraged, his decrees annulled.

55. The passage does not seem to be in either Pliny.

56. Livy 21.59, 10.

57. Biondo, *History*, 96g.

58. Or "Cadalous," bishop of Parma (d. 1072), chosen pope (Honorius II) in Basel by an anti-Gregorian council after the election of the legimate pope, Alexander II. Cadulus seized St. Peter's, was excommunicated (1063) and driven off, but persisted in his claim. Lucius III was pope from 1181–1185.

59. A favorite contemporary example of the reversal of fortune: Guinigi (d. 1432 in Pavia) ruled Lucca from 1400–1430 with spectacular success, but finally was left isolated politically, defeated, imprisoned, ruined in all ways with his sons.

60. Biondo, *History* 455c–457c.

61. Also a student of Francesco Filelfo at Florence, Gian Francesco da Lucca translated parts of Isocrates and Plutarch into Latin. A physician, he taught humanities at Venice, where he died of plague in 1457.

62. Bruni, HF 3.57. The great humanist historian was Biondo's model and source, particularly in this region. Bruni places the destruction of Pescia in 1281.

63. Italicized portion only in the earliest redaction.

64. Italicized portion only in the earliest redaction.

65. Bruni HF. Florence's origins are treated in Book 1, her subsequent history from 1250 to 1402 in Books 2–12.

66. Alcuin did not write a *Life of Charlemagne*; Biondo is perhaps thinking of Einhard, whose *Life of Charlemagne* does not mention his visit to Florence. Here he follows Bruni HF 1.77, who had doubted Giovanni Villani's report that Charlemagne rebuilt Florence; Bruni says that the emperor only rebuilt the walls.

67. Bruni HF 2.69–71. Bruni is in effect commenting on Dante's description of Farinata in *Inferno* X.

68. The earliest version adds the name of Taddeo Gaddi, saying Taddeo and Giotto are to be compared with Zeuxis of Heraclea. Biondo's perfunctory treatment of Florence's cultural giants Brunelleschi (1377–1446), Dante (1265–1321), Petrarch (1304–1374), and Giotto (1267/75–1337) may be compared with his more enthusiastic reaction to Gentile da Fabriano at Piceno §14.

69. Francesco Accorso (d. 1260) is meant, professor of law at Bologna and great compiler of legal commentary.

70. Claudius Claudianus (c. 370–c. 404), court poet of Honorius and Stilicho, was born in Alexandria; the erroneous tradition that he was born in Florence goes back at least to Filippo Villani.

71. Coluccio Salutati (1331–1406), humanist chancellor of Florence (1375–1406), was a transitional figure in the development of the new humanism, and Biondo's assessment of his Latin enforces this. He was among those responsible for bringing Chrysoloras to Florence. Niccolò Niccoli (1364–1437) was an early friend, later an enemy of Leonardo

Bruni; a purist about Latin style, he was a brilliant collector (and copyist) of MSS, Latin and Greek. His books became the nucleus of the public library of San Marco.

72. The earliest version specifies patriarch Joseph.

73. See Romagna §73 (with note).

74. Carlo de' Medici (1430–92), the natural son of Cosimo by a Circassian slave; the name was suppressed in the final redaction of the text as well as in the earliest redaction, a separate publication of the Etruria region dedicated to Piero de'Medici (see Introduction, pp. xxi–xxii.).

75. The earliest version read: "And you and Giovanni crown his good fortune" etc.

76. Cosimo de' Medici "Il Vecchio" (1389–1464) was the wealthiest private person in the Europe in his day, the unofficial ruler of Florence, a devout Christian, a builder of libraries, and a champion and lover of the new humanism in all its literary and artistic expressions.

77. Italicized passage found in the earliest redaction. Matteo Palmieri (1406–75) was a Florentine humanist; his *De temporibus suis* was a supplement to Eusebius's *Chronicle*, covering the thousand years from 449 to 1449.

78. Palla Strozzi (c. 1373–1462) was a wealthy banker and humanist and a student of Chrysoloras; exiled by his rival Cosimo de'Medici, he spent the years after 1434 mostly in Padua, where he assembled a great collection of Greek manuscripts. Angelo Acciaiuoli (d. 1470), was a Florentine statesman from a prominent family with humanist interests. Andrea Fiocchi (d. 1452) was a humanist in the Roman Curia with Biondo, the author of *De magistratibus Romanorum* (1425). Giannozzo Manetti (1396–1459), Florentine orator, diplomat and humanist, knew Latin, Greek, Hebrew and was the author of many works of history, philosophy and scholarship. Leon Battista Alberti (1404–1472), humanist and polymath from an exiled Florentine family, most famous as a writer on the theory of art and architecture; see Lazio §§47–49. For Donatello, or Donato di Niccolò di Betto Bardi (1386/7–1466), was the greatest Italian sculptor of the Quattrocento, who worked primarily in Florence and Padua.

79. Vergil, *Aeneid*, 6.848.

80. Livy, *Periochae* 102.

81. In A.D. 405. Biondo, *History* 8g–9a.

82. Dinus de Rossonibus (d. after 1298), a great jurist, taught civil law in Bologna, and worked for a time in the Roman Curia. The Medici villa is called Cafaggiolo.

83. Jacopo di Angelo da Scarperia (d. 1411), disciple of John of Ravenna, Salutati and Chrysoloras and rival of Leonardo Bruni; he was most famous for his Latin translation of Ptolemy's *Geography*.

84. Biondo *History* 566g.

85. Livy 22.2, 10–11.

86. Livy 22.2, 1.

87. Livy 22.2, 2.

88. Livy 22.2, 5–9.

89. Livy 22.3, 3.

90. Livy 22.3, 5–7.

91. Bruni, *HF* 2.8–9.

92. Bruni, *HF* 4.46.

93. Poggio Bracciolini (1380–1459), a humanist who worked mostly in Florence and at the papal court, most famous as a discoverer of lost ancient works, especially Cicero and Quintilian; see Romagna §28.

94. See §47, with note 132.

95. Italicized portion found in the earliest redaction.

96. Boccaccio (1313–75), most famous as the author of the *Decameron* and other vernacular works, but also a Latin humanist strongly influenced by Petrarch. See his *Famous Women*, ed. Virginia Brown (Cambridge, Mass., 2001), in this I Tatti series.

97. Pliny, *Natural History* 2.227.

98. Livy 10.12, 4–5.

99. Gaspare da Volterra was a humanist who worked for Cardinal Bessarion.

100. Bruni, *De primo bello punico* (Augsburg, 1537), f. IIv. Bruni's work was a compendium based mostly on Polybius.

101. Livy, *Periochae* 89.28–29.

102. See note 97. Pliny says that fishes grow in the hot springs of *Vetulonia*.

103. Bruni, *HF* 2.12–13. Bruni says the battle happened in 1254.

104. Martial 6.42, 1–2.

105. Italicized portion from the earliest redaction. The astrologer Peter of Montalcino has not been identified.

106. Livy 10.4, 5–6; 10.5, 11–12.

107. Livy 10.37, 3–4.

108. Livy 10.37, 4.

109. Orlando Bandinelli (c. 1100–1181), pope from 1159; he was a celebrated canonist.

110. Gratian, *Decretum*, Distinction 23, cap. 1. Nicholas II (ca. 1010–1061), pope from 1058, a champion of church reform much influenced by Hildebrand and Peter Damian.

111. See Bruni, *HF* 2.53–60.

112. Ugo Benzi was a famous teacher of medicine (1376–1439) who taught at Bologna, Pavia, Ferrara; his principal work is his *Trattato utilissimo circa la conservazione della sanità*. For Giacomo della Torre, see Romagna §34.

113. San Bernardino, of the family of the Albizzeschi (1380–1444), a famous Franciscan preacher, later vicar-general of the Observant Franciscans, beatified by Nicholas V in 1450.

114. The humanist Enea Silvio Piccolomini (1405–64), later Pope Pius II (1458–64), had been a student of Francesco Filelfo, attended the Council of Basel (1432), became secretary to the antipope Felix V, and to the Emperor Frederick III, who crowned him with the laurel; he transferred his allegiance to Eugenius IV in 1445; became bishop of Siena in 1450 and

cardinal in 1456. The first volume of his autobiographical *Commentaries* has been published in this I Tatti series, ed. and tr. Margaret Meserve and Marcello Simonetta (Cambridge, Mass., 2003).

115. Patrizi (1413–92) humanist poet and political theorist. An early redaction includes the name of Mariano Sozzini here; Sozzini (1401–1467) was a Sienese lawyer and student of the arts.

116. See §53.

117. Pliny, *Natural History* 8.221 (?), who does not mention "Carmon."

118. Ibid. 36.91.

119. Ibid. 3.53, 56: Pliny calls the river the *Glanis* (Chiana).

120. Italicized portion from the earliest redaction.

121. See §19 with note 41.

122. Alberto da Sarteano (1385–1450), an itinerant preacher, later Franciscan vicar-general; composed letters and orations in the humanist manner and engaged in controversy with Poggio.

123. Livy 9.37, 12.

124. Pliny, *Natural History* 3.52.

125. Livy 27.24, 1–2, 5–8.

126. Possibly *CIL* 11.1849.

127. Livy 28.45, 13–16.

128. Macrobius 2.4, 12.

129. Horace, *Carmina* 3.29, 1–3.

130. Cornelius Nepos, *Atticus* 14.3.

131. Italian Benedictine monk (c. 990–1050), a theorist of plainchant and polyphony who developed a system of musical notation.

132. Tarlati (d. 1328), of the Ghibelline Pietramala and enemy of John XXII, was bishop of Arezzo and *signore a vita* from 1313 on. With his brother Pietro Saccone, he established for his family control over all the Valdarno, which brought him into conflict with the Florentines.

133. I.e. Castiglion Fiorentino.

134. See §51, with note 155.

135. Italicized portion from the earliest redaction. On Bishop Guglielmino at the battle of Campaldino see Bruni, *HF* 4.5–10; for the suspension of his helm and shield in the Baptistery see 4.13.

136. Leonardo Bruni (1370–1444), papal secretary and later Chancellor of Florence, humanist historian and translator from the Greek; the most important humanist of his day. Carlo Marsuppini (1399–1453), humanist and Greek scholar; he succeeded Bruni (1444) as Chancellor of Florence, and later worked as a papal secretary; his most famous work was a translation of Book I of the *Iliad*.

137. Benedetto Accolti (1415–66), jurisconsult and chancellor of Florence from 1458, most famous for his humanist histories of the Crusades. Francesco (1416/17–88), Benedetto's younger brother, studied with Filelfo and taught law at Ferrara, Siena, Pisa; was secretary to Francesco Sforza at Milan; translated Bruni's *De bello Italico adversus Gothos* into Italian. The earliest redaction adds the names of Antonio Roselli and Angelo Gambioni, jurisconsults.

138. Tortelli (1400–66) studied Greek in Constantinople, helped Nicholas V to establish the Vatican Library, and became its first librarian. His most famous work was his treatment of orthography, the *De orthographia* of c. 1450.

139. Pliny, *Natural History* 35.160.

140. Martial 1.53, 6.

141. Florus 1.22.

142. Isole Polvese, Maggiore, Minore.

143. Justin, *Epitome* 20.1, 11–12.

144. Livy 9.40, 18–20.

145. Livy 10.31, 1–4.

146. Livy 10.37, 4.

147. Livy, *Periochae* 125.5–9.

148. Livy *Periochae* 126.1–4.

149. Petrus Baldus de Ubaldis (1327–1406) of Perugia, famous jurist,

taught law at Bologna, Perugia, Pisa, Florence, Padua, and Pavia. Bartolus of Sassoferrato (1314–57), a famous jurist, taught mostly at Perugia; he was the author of many works on civil law, most famously the *De regimine civitatis*.

150. Italicized words from the earliest redaction.

151. The first is Ivone Coppoli, teacher of civil law, fl. 1430; the second Sallustio Sallusti, a teacher of civil law, fl. 1400; the third Giovanni di Petruccio Montesperelli, teacher of civil and canon law at Perugia c. 1420–59.; the fourth is Benedetto Barzi, teacher of civil law, fl. 1398–1407.

152. Italicized portions from the earliest redaction.

153. Biordo (d. 1398) and Ceccolino (d. 1419) Michelotti, Perugian nobles and condottieri; Biordo was Florentine captain-general after Hawkwood and later established himself as lord of Perugia. Niccolò Piccinino (d. 1444) served with Braccio da Montone, whom he succeeded as captain; he was the great enemy of Eugenius IV and the rival of Francesco Sforza in the service of the Duke of Milan; his sons, Jacopo (d. 1465) and Francesco (d. 1449) took over his forces at his death

154. Braccio da Montone or Andrea Fortebraccio (see Romagna §48), comrade in arms of Braccio Baglioni's father, Malatesta Baglioni, restored the Baglioni family's control of Perugia after they had been driven out in a popular uprising (1393). Fortebraccio was the captain-general of papal forces under John XXIII. Braccio Baglioni the son (d. 1479), a cultivated and refined patron, consolidated the family's rule over Perugia.

155. Biondo, *History* 571c-572g.

156. Pope Gregory VII, born Hildebrand, (ca. 1020–85), among the greatest of Roman pontiffs, leader of the church reform movement of the High Middle Ages, and humbler of Emperor Henry IV at Canossa.

157. Livy 10.37, 1–2.

158. Florus 1.16.

159. Not found in Pliny.

160. Bruni *HF* 1.61. The Isola Martana. Amalasuntha (Amalaswintha, d. 535) was Theodoric's daughter; her son, Athalarich, for whom she was

regent, died in 534. In most accounts, it was her cousin, Theodahad, who had her (or countenanced her being) killed. Cf. Romagna §23.

161. Paolo di Castro or Paulus Castrensis (d. 1441), studied under Baldus of Perugia, taught canon and civil law at Florence, Bologna, Ferrara, Padua, among other places; was vicar-general of Cardinal Zabarella of Florence.

162. Bruni says nothing of the sort.

163. In fact begun by Urban IV in the 1260s; the Latin text should perhaps be emended.

164. The suppressed earlier version read: "And you, Holy Father Nicholas, have recently restored at great expense the stout citadel that you built there to put an end to further savagery among the citizens." (See Introduction, pp. xxi–xxii.)

165. Vergil, *Aeneid* 7.716: 'Ortinae classes.'

166. The Ponte d'Augusto on the Via Flaminia just above Narni, in fact over the river Nera, a tributary of the Tiber.

167. The modern site is about a mile distant from the ancient city, on a hill, as Leandro Alberti noted (cited by Castner, "Direct Observation," p. 93 and note 3).

168. Ammianus Marcellinus 16.10, 4: cf. Cappelletto, *Recuperi*, pp. 35–36.

169. Pliny, *Natural History* 3.52; Florus 1.22, 4.

170. Pliny, *Natural History* 3.53.

171. Francesco da Fiano (d. 1421), Roman humanist and churchman, a student of the ancient Latin poets, wrote *Against the Ridiculous Insulters and Mistaken Detractors of the Poets* (*Contra ridiculos oblocutores et fallitos detractores poetarum*).

172. Livy 1.28, 7–11.

173. Livy 2.49, 1–12.

174. Suetonius, *Nero* 39.2.

175. Vergil, *Aeneid* 7.696.

176. Pliny, *Natural History* 31.27.

177. Prospero Colonna (d. 1463) of the wealthy and influential Colonna family with extensive estates in the Papal State and in the Kingdom of Naples; perpetual rivals of the Orsini, the family produced many high-ranking churchmen, condottieri and patrons of culture. Prospero was appointed cardinal (1430) by his uncle Martin V (Oddone Colonna).

178. Horace, *Carmina* 1.9, 1–4. Soracte has now reverted to its ancient name (Monte Soratte) and the village of San Silvestro is present-day Sant'Oreste.

179. Italicized portion from the earliest redaction.

180. St. Gregory I ("the Great") was pope from 590–604, and is known as one of the four Doctors of the Roman church.

181. Pope for about four months in 897, then deposed and sent to a monastery. The italicized portion is found only in the earliest redaction.

182. Livy 27.9, 7.

183. Livy 29.15, 5–8.

184. Livy 5.27. See also Plutarch, *Camillus* 10.1–7.

185. Pliny, *Natural History* 2.230.

186. Pliny, *Natural History* 7.19.

187. Vergil, *Aeneid* 7.697.

188. Livy 9.35, 1–2, 7–8; 9.36, 1–2; 9.39, 5–11, heavily abbreviated

189. In 1420: Martin V (Oddone Colonna), pope 1417–1431. Alberigo da Barbiano was a condottiere who defeated the Breton mercenaries of the antipope in 1379; see Romagna §§46–53.

190. Sabinianus was pope from 604–606, Paschal I from 817–824.

191. Livy 9.35, 1–8.

192. See §56.

193. Italicized words from the earliest redaction. Petrarch does not mention Savelli's role in his account of the coronation in *Seniles* 18.1, nor is it mentioned in the early biographical literature on Petrarch.

194. The lake is now named after the larger town on the opposite shore,

Lago di Bracciano. Orso dell'Anguillara crowned Petrarch in Rome, in 1341, on behalf of Robert King of Naples

195. Lacus Vadimonis is now thought to be the Laghetto di Bassano in Teverina (just west of Orte), now almost disappeared, rather than Biondo's Lago di Monterosi.

196. In fact in 309 B.C. (A.U.C. 470 would be 283 B.C.). Livy 9.39, 5–11.

3. LAZIO

1. Vergil, *Aeneid* 8.319–323.

2. Servius, *In Aeneidem* 7.716; also, Pliny the Elder, *Natural History* 3.68–69.

3. Livy, *Periochae* 72.7–9.

4. Biondo probably knew Strabo in the Latin translation of Guarino Veronese.

5. Strabo 5.3, 4; 5.3, 2.

6. S.H.A., *Hadrian* 19, 1.

7. Servius, *In Aeneidem* 7.31.

8. Strabo 5.3, 5.

9. Livy, *Periochae* 79.12–14.

10. S.H.A., *Marcus Aurelius* 45, 2–3.

11. S.H.A., *Clodius Albinus* 11, 3.

12. Livy 27.38, 1–5. Livy in fact says that Ostia and Anzio preserved their exemption (which was granted to the coastal colonies because their men were needed for ships' crews and maintenance and provisioning) on that occasion. Biondo's reference to the bad air as the motive appears to be his own invention, arising from the malaria that infested the coastland in post-classical times. See R. Meiggs, *Roman Ostia*, 2nd ed. (Oxford, 1973), p. 26, for the exemption.

13. Leo IV was pontiff 847–55: the Saracens had destroyed Rome in 846: Leo rebuilt Ostia (Portus) and settled the Corsicans there after 849. Martin V (Oddone Colonna) was pontiff 1417–31: in 1420, he had the Tor Boacciana, in origin a Roman lighthouse, rebuilt.

14. Livy 8.14, 8.

15. Livy 8.14, 12.

16. A *stade* is a little less than 1/8th of an English mile.

17. Strabo 5.3, 5.

18. Horace, *Carmina* 1.35, 1–4.

19. Livy, *Periochae* 80, 5–6.

20. Suetonius, *Nero* 9.4.

21. See note 101 to §20. Prospero Colonna, cardinal deacon of S. Giorgio (d. 24 March 1463) was one of Biondo's patrons; see Etruria §57 and note 177.

22. Livy 8.14, 2–3. Livy writes 'Lanuviis' rather than Laviniis, i.e. the citizens living at Lanuvium, a town in the Alban hills south of Rome, not to be confused (as Biondo has done) with Lavinium (called Lavinia by Biondo), the town in Latium said to have been founded by Aeneas.

23. Biondo would know of the Murenae from Cicero's speech in defense of L. Licinius Murena, which mentions Murena's Lanuvium at c. 90 as *municipium honestissimum*.

24. Pliny the Elder, *Natural History* 10.65–66.

25. It is of storks that Pliny says (ibid. 10.61): *nec venire sed venisse cernimus*. At 10.110, he says that the largest pigeons are produced in Campania.

26. Pliny the Elder, *Natural History* 10.21–28 on hawks, but no such word appears in Pliny.

27. Ibid. 10.78 ("in agrum *Volaterranum*").

28. Ibid. 10.72.

29. Ibid. 10.70.

30. Ibid. 3.67; Strabo 5.3, 5. The two cities are Ostia and Anzio. By *panegyris* he means the national assembly of the Latin tribes.

31. Pliny the Elder, *Natural History* 3.56. The Numicus is now the Rio Torto

32. Vergil, *Aeneid* 7.409–412.

33. Ibid. 7.629–631.

34. Servius, *In Aeneidem* 7.412. Ovid, *Metamorphoses* 10.54. *Ardea* means 'heron."

35. Servius, *In Aeneidem* 7.796.

36. Pliny the Elder, *Natural History* 3.56.

37. Livy 27.9, 7. The accurate figure of *twelve* colonies is quoted at Etruria §58.

38. Leo V, pope for about a month in 903, was born at Priapi near Ardea.

39. Strabo 5.3, 5.

40. Vergil, *Aeneid* 7. 242.

41. Ibid. 7.150.

42. Servius, *In Aeneidem* 7.150

43. Antonio Colonna (d. 1472) was the son of Martin V's brother Lorenzo.

44. Vergil, *Aeneid* 10.181.

45. Plutarch, *Cicero* 47.1–48.4.

46. Conradin (Conrad V, Conrad the Younger), Duke of Swabia and King of Jerusalem and Sicily, and last of the Hohenstaufen, was the son of Conrad IV (who was poisoned) and brought up by his uncle Louis II. He entered Italy to reclaim Sicily from Charles I of Anjou, who had it by papal grant. His army was defeated by Charles at Tagliacozzo on 23 August 1268: he escaped to Rome, then to Torre Astura, where he was betrayed, and was brought to Naples. Charles had him beheaded there. See Bruni, *HF* 3.14.

47. Strabo 5.3, 6.

48. Servius, *In Aeneidem* 7.10, where Biondo has read *errore*, "wandering," instead of *horrore*, "the dread" with which travelers regarded the promontory.

49. Augustine, *City of God* 18.17, 1–3 (paraphrased).

50. Ibid. 18.18, 12–19.

51. Livy 1.56.3

52. *LP* 735, 229–230.

53. Strabo 5.3, 6; Pliny the Elder, *Natural History* 3.57: now the Ninfa, actually between Anzio and Monte Circeo.

54. Strabo 5.3, 5; Pliny the Elder, *Natural History* 3.57.

55. Strabo 5.3, 5.

56. Pliny the Elder, *Natural History* 3. 57–59.

57. Livy, *Periochae* 46, 23–25.

58. Strabo 5.3, 6.

59. Livy 4. 59, 3–11.

60. Livy 7.39, 7; 9.23, 4.

61. Servius, *In Aeneidem* 7.799.

62. Servius, *In Aeneidem* 7.801; Vergil, *Aeneid* 7.802.

63. Suetonius, *Tiberius* 39.2

64. Ibid. 40.2, but see §53.

65. Suetonius, *Caligula* 31.1, and see §53, with notes 264 and 265. The italicized portion is preserved in an early redaction.

66. S.H.A., *Hadrian* 7, 1–3.

67. S.H.A., *Antoninus Pius* 8, 3.

68. Actually Livy 27.38, 3–4. See note 12.

69. Actually Livy 22.15, 11–12.

70. Lucan 3.84–85.

71. Martial 10.51, 7–8. Quoted again at §21.

72. Martial 10.58, 1.

73. Vergil, *Aeneid* 10.564.

74. Servius, *In Aeneidem* 10.564.

75. Strabo 5.3, 6.

76. Erasmus (St. Elmo), Bishop of Formia, was martyred under Diocletian.

77. Gregory was pope 827–844.

78. This seems to be an erroneous reading of Servius, *In Aeneidem* 7.799, "Iuno virgo, quae Feronia dicebatur."

79. Livy 8.14, 10–11. See §14, with note 85. Livy describes a shared experience of Fondi and Formia.

80. Strabo 5.3, 6.

81. Strabo 5.3, 6.

82. Vergil, *Aeneid* 7.1–2.

83. S.H.A., *Antoninus Pius* 8, 3.

84. S.H.A., *Marcus Aurelius* 19, 7. This Faustina was actually the daughter of Antoninus Pius, wife of Marcus Aurelius.

85. Livy 8.14, 10–11.

86. Livy 8.19, 4–20, 6.

87. Martial 13.113.

88. Suetonius, *Galba* 4.1.

89. The line is not found in Horace; *Lemurnae* is not attested in Latin and is probably a corruption.

90. Strabo 5.3, 6.

91. Cicero, *On the Orator* 2.22–23.

92. Cicero, *On the Agrarian Law* 2.36.

93. In 1378, the Count Onorato I Caetani held in Fondi the conclave that elected antipope Clement VII.

94. Livy 9.28, 7.

95. Strabo 3.5, 6.

96. Strabo 3.5, 6.

97. Pliny the Elder, *Natural History* 17.31.

98. Gelasius II (Cardinal John of Gaeta) was pope 1118–1119, St. Soter 167–175.

99. Pliny the Elder, *Natural History* 3.70.

100. Cicero, *For Murena* 90.

101. See §6. On Biondo's correction of his earlier mistake using inscriptional evidence provided by his patron, Prospero Colonna, see Martino Filetico, *In corruptores latinitatis*, ed. Maria Agata Pincelli (Rome, 2000), pp. 48–50.

102. Livy 8.14, 5–8.

103. Servius, *In Aeneidem* 7.672.

104. Vergil, *Aeneid* 7.670–672.

105. Martial 10.51, 7–10 (and see §12 and note 71).

106. Pliny the Elder, *Natural History* 14.61.

107. Martial 13.112, 1–2.

108. Martial 6.86, 1–2.

109. The town was actually destroyed by the Saracens.

110. Vergil, *Aeneid* 7.803.

111. Servius, *In Aeneidem* 7.803.

112. Livy 8.21, 4.

113. Vergil, *Aeneid* 7.685.

114. Ibid. 11.546–547. The italicized passage is preserved only in a single manuscript, an intermediate redaction.

115. Ibid. 1.7. Alba Longa was on the site of the modern Castel Gandolfo. The Castel Savelli mentioned below was a stronghold of the family just outside neighbouring Albano.

116. Livy 40.46, 12; 1.33, 2.

117. Vergil, *Aeneid* 8.48.

118. Henry III, King of Germany (1039–56) and Holy Roman Emperor (1046–56), invaded Italy in 1046.

119. Honorius III, born Cencio Savelli (pope 1216–1227) was the earliest distinguished representative of this wealthy and powerful family. Ludovico Trevigiano, a Venetian, rose from being Eugenius IV's physician to the rank of cardinal.

120. Livy 8.14, 3–4: Livy has "Lanuvini,'" not "Lavinii."

121. Vergil, *Aeneid* 7.629–631. The italicized passage was suppressed in the *editio princeps*.

122. Servius, *In Aeneidem* 7.630. Vergil and Servius both speak of "Atina," not "Aricia." In §8, Biondo quotes "Atina" correctly. Servius derives the name from the Greek *atai*, bane or ruin.

123. Servius, *In Aeneidem* 7.762. The charge of toadying is Biondo's.

124. Suetonius, *Augustus* 4.1. Octavian was the name of Augustus before that title was conferred on him.

125. Vergil, *Aeneid* 7.761–762.

126. Ovid, *Metamorphoses* 15.479–547; also, Servius, *In Aeneidem* 7.761.

127. Servius, *In Aeneidem* 7.761.

128. Livy 2.14, 5–9.

129. Livy, *Periochae* 80.5–6.

130. Pliny the Elder, *Natural History* 19.140–141.

131. Martial 13.19,1.

132. A Benedictine foundation, it had been a Cistercian abbey from the twelfth century. On the present river Ninfa, see note 53.

133. Livy 2.19, 1–20, 13.

134. Died after 1503; the son of Lorenzo, brother of Cardinal Prospero.

135. Martin V was born Oddone Colonna at Genazzano.

136. Vergil, *Aeneid* 7.684.

137. Servius, *In Aeneidem* 7.684.

138. Ibid.

139. Livy 9.42, 11.

140. Livy 9.43, 7.

141. Livy 9.43, 24.

142. Innocent (Lotario de' Conti) was pope 1198–1216.

143. Boniface (Benedetto Caetani), pope 1294–1303, successor of Celestine V, instituted in 1300 the custom of the Jubilee, a celebration attracting enormous numbers of pilgrims to Rome. Nicholas V's Jubilee of

1450 was marked by the tragedy of several hundred crushed to death on the bridge of Sant' Angelo, in addition to the plague.

144. Celestine V, holy but inept hermit-pope (1294), resigned the papacy and was imprisoned by his successor Boniface VIII (reigned 1294–1303). The masterful Boniface more than made up for Celestine's indecisiveness and inactivity, and succeeded in alienating the Colonna, the French, and much of Christendom; Dante found a prominent place for him in Hell. Clement V was pope 1305–1314.

145. Pliny the Elder, *Natural History* 2.224. Pliny merely observes that river water floats over the surface of the Lacus Fucinus without being mixed with it.

146. Livy 2.38, 1. Biondo seems to be confusing the town Ferentinum with the river Ferentina here.

147. Livy 7.9, 1.

148. Livy 9.43, 23.

149. Livy 10.17,9–10.

150. Suetonius, *Otho* 1.1.

151. Livy 10.1, 3.

152. Pope Hormisdas reigned 514–523, his son Silverius 536–537. The king of the Ostrogoths Theodatus was supposed to have used his influence to slide Silverius by the Empress Theodora's candidate. Another tradition holds that Silverius bought Theodatus' involvement himself.

153. Livy 9.43, 23.

154. Ibid. Bauco, once *Babucum*, is now once more Boville (Boville Ernica).

155. Livy 4.45, 3–6; 4.47, 4–7. A *iugerum* was about two-thirds of an acre.

156. Lucido de' Conti (d. 1437), cardinal deacon of S. Maria in Cosmedin, participated in the Conclave of 1417 that elected Martin V; also in the Conclave of 1431 that elected Eugenius IV. Giovanni de' Conti (d. 1493) was Archbishop of Cosenza and from 1483 cardinal.

157. S.H.A., *Clodius Albinus* 11, 3. For another gustatory feat of the emperor see §4.

158. Pliny the Elder, *Natural History* 14.65–66.

159. Martial 13.116, 1–2.

160. St. Vitalian, pope 657–672.

161. Strabo 5.3, 11.

162. Vergil, *Aeneid* 7.670–672 (see note 103).

163. Ibid. 7.629–30

164. Servius, *In Aeneidem* 7.630.

165. Vergil, *Aeneid* 7.82–83.

166. Servius, *In Aeneidem* 7.83. Servius connects *Albunea* with *albus*, white, from the white sulphurous deposits of the spring.

167. Pliny the Elder, *Natural History* 36.46 and 167. The phrase "paving, adorning and preserving Rome" (*consternanda, ornanda et conservanda Roma*) is often found in inscriptions.

168. Horace, *Carmina* 1.18, 1–2.

169. S.H.A., *Hadrian* 26, 5.

170. Strabo 5.3, 11.

171. St. Simplicius, pope 468–483.

172. Frederick I Barbarossa (d. 1190) rewalled and enlarged the town in 1155.

173. Vergil, *Aeneid* 7.746–747.

174. Livy 9.45, 8, 17–18.

175. Influential aristocratic family in Rome and the region from the twelfth century on, from which came popes Celestine III (d. 1198) and Nicholas III (d. 1280); inveterate enemies of the Colonna, the family produced many soldiers and churchmen.

176. An Italian phrase; cf. Ariosto *Orlando Furioso* 3.77, 8.

177. Suetonius, *Claudius* 20, 1–3.

178. Livy 10.13, 1.

179. Livy 27.9, 7. There were thirty colonies in all. Livy writes that twelve of them (*ex iis duodecim*) said that they could not manage contributions, leaving eighteen who could and did.

180. Giovanni Berardi di Tagliacozzo, died 1449.

181. Livy 22.9, 5.

182. Livy 26.11, 10–11.

183. With the emperor Phocas' permission, St. Boniface (pope 608–615) converted Agrippa's Pantheon into the church of S. Maria ad Martyres (S. Maria Rotonda) in 609.

184. Pliny the Elder, *Natural History* 3.108. It appears that Biondo thinks that there was a place called "Marsi," based on Pliny's *oppidum Marsorum*, which in fact means "a town of the Marsi" (named by Pliny as Archippe).

185. Vergil, *Aeneid* 7.750.

186. The phrase in italics is found only in the 1531 Froben printing, not in any of the witness collated for this edition, but may derive from an unknown manuscript source.

187. Servius, *In Aeneidem* 7.750.

188. Pliny the Elder, *Natural History* 7.15.

189. S.H.A., *Heliogabalus* 28, 2.

190. Ps. 57.7.

191. Augustine, *Enarrationes in Psalmos* 57.7. The asp stands for those who will not only not do the word of the Lord but who will not even listen to it.

192. Livy, *Periochae* 72.2.

193. Livy, *Periochae* 76.5–7.

194. Cicero did serve in the Marsic War, 90–88 B.C.; see Plutarch, *Cicero* 3.1 and Cicero, *Philippics* 12.11, 27.

195. Livy 1.1, 1–2. See §34.

196. Livy 27.9, 7.

197. Strabo 5.3, 13: Strabo's point is rather that, of all the cities of Lazio,

Alba Fucens is the *furthest* inland. The Lago di Fucino was drained in the nineteenth century.

198. *R. I.* 255c.

199. Pliny the Elder, *Natural History* 2.224; 31.41. Biondo supplies the river's name.

200. Pliny the Elder, *Natural History* 9.73.

201. Strabo 5.3, 13.

202. Livy, *Periochae* 61.

203. Conte di Celano, of whom are extant several letters to the Milanese humanist Pier Candido Decembrio. His surname (italicized) is added only in an early redaction.

204. The noble family from Capranica Prenestina became prominent in the fifteenth century. Paolo was archbishop of Benevento in 1435. Domenico (d. 1458) was made apostolic secretary (1423) and cardinal (1430) by Martin V; he collected a large library and founded the Collegio Capranica in Rome. Angelo was made cardinal by Pius II in 1460. The three were brothers. Their nephew Niccolò, a friend and correspondent of Bessarion, was bishop of Fermo in 1458.

205. Sveva Caetani, the parent (with Lorenzo Colonna) of Prospero, Antonio, and Odoardo.

206. Pliny the Elder, *Natural History* 3.109.

207. Benedict of Nursia (d. 543), the father of Western monasticism, was in Subiaco (where he organized twelve monasteries and founded his Rule) until *ca.* 530, when he left for Monte Cassino.

208. Vergil, *Aeneid* 7.678.

209. Servius, *In Aeneidem* 7.678: "*apo tōn prinōn*, id est ab ilicibus"; the ilex or holmoak, another name for the *arbor prinus* of the Vulgate.

210. Strabo 5.3, 11, who makes no mention of Sulla here.

211. Pliny the Elder, *Natural History* 33.61–62.

212. Ibid. 36.189.

213. Strabo 5.3, 11.

214. Stefano Colonna rebuilt and fortified Palestrina in 1448 after its destruction by Cardinal Vitelleschi.

215. Strabo 5.3, 11.

216. Strabo 5.3,11.

217. Livy, *Periochae* 87.1–2.

218. Ibid. 88.10–11.

219. Lucan 2.134.

220. Lucan 2.193–195.

221. Livy, *Periochae* 88.11–16.

222. S.H.A., *Marcus Aurelius* 21, 3–4.

223. Pliny the Elder, *Natural History* 33.16.

224. Livy 23.17, 8–12; 23.18, 1–9; 23.20, 2.

225. Strabo 5.3, 11.

226. The *condottiere* Niccolò Fortebraccio (d. 1435) was the nephew of Braccio da Montone. *Urbi infestorum* must mean "dangerous to papal interests."

227. Strabo 5.3, 11.

228. Strabo 5.3, 12.

229. At Lake Regillus in 496 B.C.: Octavius Mamilius was son-in-law (*gener*), and Tarquin the Proud his father-in-law (*socer*).

230. Livy 8.14, 4–5.

231. Pliny the Elder, *Natural History* 7.136–137 (L. Fulvius in Pliny).

232. Livy 26.9, 11–12.

233. Strabo 5.3, 13.

234. Paschal II, who launched the First Crusade, was pope 1099–1118.

235. Pandulphus Hostiarius was a contributor to the *Liber Pontificalis* and supposed author of the life of Paschal II (*LP* 2: xxxiii-xxxv, and p. 298 for Colonna's possession of Cave).

236. Lucius Licinius Lucullus, a general of legendary extravagance and Pompey's rival; on his Tusculan properties, see Plutarch, *Lucullus* 39.4.

237. Biondo is thinking of Frontinus 1.10. The conduit of Agrippa's aqueduct was in use in Biondo's time (and still is today, supplying the Trevi Fountain).

238. Probably some time between 1155 and 1158.

239. As belonging to the *gens Porcia*

240. Biondo has the papal and regnal numbers slightly adrift. Benedict VIII (d. 1024) crowned Henry II at Rome in 1014. His brother John XIX reigned 1024–1032 and their nephew Benedict IX 1032–1044. They were members of the family of the Counts of Tusculum.

241. Bessarion (1408–72), a leading figure in the attempted union of the Greek and Latin churches; he converted to Latin Christianiaty and was made Bishop of Tusculum in 1449, papal governor of Bologna (1450–55), later a cardinal. He was an advocate of the Platonic revival and his famous library, now part of the Biblioteca Marciana in Venice, was a major venue for the transferral of Greek culture to the Latin world. The italicized phrase was dropped in the *editio princeps*.

242. To this pre-Christian site (and name) became attached part of the Pauline legend—of his severed head bouncing thrice and forming three springs—an event commemorated by the Church of S. Paolo alle Tre Fontane.

243. Livy 5.15, 4–5, 11–12.

244. Suetonius, *Caesar* 46.2.

245. Vergil, *Aeneid* 7.516.

246. Servius, *In Aeneidem* 7.515 and 516.

247. To Genzano (di Roma).

248. The events described in §§47–50 occurred in 1446. The lake was drained and the ships retrieved whole in 1928–31, but they were destroyed in May 1944.

249. On Leon Battista Alberti, see Tuscany §32. His work in twelve books *On Architecture* was finished about 1450.

250. Italicized passage deleted from later redactions. On Nicholas' Roman rebuilding and maintenance program, see the Preface §§6–7.

251. The ancient Volscian name of Terracina (§11).

252. Lucan 3.84–88.

253. Lucan 3.91–92.

254. Livy 1.53, 4–54, 10.

255. Vergil, *Aeneid* 7.682. The edition of 1474 reads "Whence Vergil "simplicibus Gabiis" and in VII", etc. Gaspar Biondo has perhaps clumsily incorporated here a reference to Juvenal 3.190–91 that his father had not yet fully worked out. "Who at cool Praeneste, or at Volsinii amid its leafy hills, was ever afraid of his house tumbling down? Who in modest Gabii (*simplicibus Gabiis*), or on the sloping heights of Tivoli?" Lorenzo Colonna was Martin V's brother and the father of Antonio, Odoardo, and Cardinal Prospero.

256. Servius, *In Aeneidem* 7.682–683.

257. Ibid. 6.773.

258. Ibid. 7.683.

259. Pliny the Elder, *Natural History* 3.109 (i.e. Sublaqueum, "under the lake").

260. Livy 6.42, 5–7; 7.9, 6–10, 14.

261. Not apparently in the *LP*. Ponte Mammolo was named after the Emperor's mother Julia Mamaea according to Biondo's source. But a derivation from *marmor* is likelier: see S. Delli, *I ponti di Roma* (Rome 1977), pp. 194–5.

262. Narses and Belisarius were rival generals of Justinian I in Italy. Belisarius took Rome back from the Ostrogoths in 547 A.D. He was replaced by Narses in 548, who campaigned against the Ostrogoths and defeated their last king Totila in 552. Totila had captured Rome in 550.

263. *CIL* 6.1199: "Narsim . . . qui potuit rigidas Gothorum subdere mentes."

264. Suetonius, *Tiberius* 40.2: spectators at a gladiatorial show in an amphitheater that collapsed. See §12, where the collapse is wrongly placed at Terracina. Fidenae was located at the present Villa Spada five miiles north of Rome.

265. In earlier redactions Biondo had confused Nero with Caligula; this mistake was corrected in the *editio princeps*: cf. Suetonius, *Caligula* 31.1.

266. Pliny the Elder, *Natural History* 10.78.

267. Pliny the Elder, *Natural History* 36.167.

268. Vergil, *Aeneid* 6.773.

269. Biondo cobbles these details from Livy 4 into a sort of narrative whole: 4.17, 1–2; 4.17, 6; 4.30, 6; 4.31, 7; 4.34, 1–4.

270. Livy 26.8, 10–11. The italicized sentence was omitted in the *editio princeps*.

271. Setia in §22, and Lanuvium in §20.

272. Livy 26.9, 2–3.

273. This identification was made in §18, but in fact Fregellae is the modern Ceprano.

274. Livy 26.9, 11.

275. Livy 8.22, 1–2.

276. Livy 9.28, 3.

277. Livy 27.10, 3. A loose paraphrase.

278. Livy 26.9, 11.

279. Livy 26.9, 12.

280. Livy 26.9, 12.

281. Livy 26.9, 12.

4. UMBRIA

1. Biondo, *History* 102c. "Exarchs" under the reforms of Diocletian (emperor 284–305) were administrators of territorial districts; under the Byzantine emperors, the "Exarch of Ravenna" was the provincial governor, at least theoretically, of Italy

2. Livy 9.41, 6 (summarized)

3. Pliny the Elder, *Natural History* 3.112–113. The italicized phrase is not in Pliny and was dropped in one late redaction.

4. Pliny the Elder, *Natural History* 3.120; Justin, *Epitome* 20.1, 11. Pliny does not mention Umbria, in which indeed Spina never was, though Justin's epitome of Trogus speaks of "Spina in Umbris," as here.

5. Martial 13.21, 1. An unconventional interpretation identifying the thornbush grown in Ravenna with the town upon which Ravenna was built.

6. For Guido Tarlati da Pietramala, see Etruria §37 and §47, with notes 132 and 135.

7. Pliny the Younger, *Letters* 5.6, 7. The younger Pliny's estate is now believed to have been at a place called Colle Plinio, between Sansepolcro and Città di Castello in the Tiber valley.

8. Niccolò Vitelli of Città di Castello (1414–1486), a mercenary often in the service of (or opposed to) the popes.

9. See Pliny the Elder, *Natural History* 3.53.

10. Federigo da Montefeltro (1422–1482), Duke of Urbino, condottiere, scholar (he was a pupil of the humanist schoolmaster Vittorino da Feltre), statesman, patron of the arts and letters, and at one time captain-general of papal forces.

11. Nuceria Alfatena is in Campania; the Umbrian Nuceria was called "Camellaria." Biondo calls Nocera Umbra *Nuceria Alphatena* again at Piceno §18, with note 65.

12. Livy 9.41, 3–4, italicized words omitted in the *editio princeps* and some earlier mss.

13. Gentile Gentili, physician and anatomist (d. 1348, a victim of the Black Death), studied medicine at Bologna and Padua, and practiced and taught at Bologna, Siena, Padua, Perugia; he was a prolific medical writer in Latin.

14. Pliny the Elder, *Natural History* 3.113. The correct reading in Pliny is *Hispellum*.

15. Francesco di Bernadone (d. 1226), founder (in spite of himself) of the Franciscan Order.

16. Italicized portion dropped in the *editio princeps*.

17. Propertius 4.1, 125–126. The poet, apostrophizing himself, speaks of the augmentation of the city's *fame* in his poetry.

18. Fratta is the medieval name of the present Umbertide, north of Perugia on the Tiber and seven miles south of Montone.

19. For Braccio da Montone (d. 1424), mercenary captain and lord of Perugia, see Tuscany §50, with note 154, and Romagna §48; on Piccinino and his sons, Tuscany §50, with note 153; on Niccolò Fortebraccio, Lazio §41, with note 226.

20. Servius, *In Aeneidem* 7.711.

21. Martial 5.71, 1–2 (i.e. June and July).

22. Vergil, *Aeneid* 7.706–711. Trebula Mutusca is now reckoned to be the present Monteleone Sabino, 45 miles to the south.

23. Livy 9.41, 13.

24. Italicized portion dropped from the *editio princeps*.

25. Nonius Marcellus 169.32. Propertius was known in the Middle Ages as Propertius Aurelius Nauta, the last from a corruption in his MSS.

26. Propertius 1.22, 9–10.

27. Propertius 4.1, 121–125.

28. Propertius 4.1, 63–64. Biondo seems to have misunderstood Propertius, who here too speaks of himself. The figment of the Umbrian Callimachus appears again in §11.

29. Lucan 1.473–474. Italicized portion dropped from the *editio princeps*.

30. Livy, *Periochae* 20.2.

31. Livy 22.9, 1–3.

32. Livy 24.10, 10.

33. Eusebius, *Ecclesiastical History* 250.25–26. C. Maecenas Melissus, grammarian and poet of the time of Augustus; on his birth, see also Suetonius, *On Grammarians* 21.

34. Martial 13.120.

35. Biondo, *History* 34g.

36. *Caesar Lucensis*, identified as Cesare de' Nobili in Nogara's index. The

italicized portion was omitted in later redactions. The *arx* is the Rocca Albornoziana, still the most imposing fortress in Umbria, and is covered with Nicholas V's coat of arms.

37. Vergil, *Georgics* 2.146–148.

38. This is not a quotation of Pliny but derives from Servius on the above passage of the *Georgics*, where Servius wrongly says that Pliny places the white oxen at Clitumnus, whereas Pliny (*Natural History* 2.230) has them in Faliscan territory (as in Etruria §59, with note 164).

39. Silius Italicus 4.544–546. Italicized portion omitted in the *editio princeps*, and the reference to Silius ("Silus") Italicus omitted in all but a single late manuscript.

40. See note 29.

41. See note 27.

42. Propertius 2.19, 26.

43. The parasite of Terence's *Eunuchus*.

44. Lodovico Pontano (1409–39), protonotary of Eugenius IV and representative of Alfonso of Aragon at the Council of Basel, where he died of plague. Wrote a commentary on Justinian's *Code* and *Pandects*.

45. Called "Ceretanus."

46. Giovanni Gioviano Pontano (1426–1503), the greatest Latin poet of the fifteenth century, was also famous for the purity of his Latin prose. He made his life in Naples, from 1448 on, where he was head of the Accademia Pontaniana, based at the Aragonese court.

47. Livy 28.45, 13–14, 19.

48. On the founder of the order of Benedictines, see Lazio §39, with note.

49. Quintus Sertorius (d. 73 B.C.), an able, anti-Sullan politician, mercenary and guerrilla, created abroad a counterweight to Pompey and the Senate. There is a life of Sertorius in Plutarch.

50. Vergil, *Aeneid* 7.715–716.

51. Servius, *In Aeneidem* 7.715.

52. Successively physician of Eugenius IV and Francesco Sforza, Duke of Milan. As Benedict of Nursia, the author of a frequently printed tract *De conservanda sanitate*.

53. Martial 13.2

54. Now Leonessa. The original name Gonessa (*Connexa*) is attested alongside the newer name of Leonessa at least from the end of the fourteeth century, and both names are found in Biondo's manuscripts; it is not clear whether Biondo believed that this Gonessa was a place distinct from the Leonessa mentioned later.

55. Italicized phrase dropped from the *editio princeps*.

56. Vergil, *Aeneid* 7.517.

57. The ancient Lacus Velinus is now largely drained. Biondo means the largest of the remaining lakes, Lago di Piediluco.

58. Livy 26.11, 10–11.

59. Suetonius, *Vespasian* 2.1. In Suetonius' text, the village is *Falacrina* (or, a variant, *Pherine*), perhaps near the modern Cittareale, and *in Samnio* is a variant of *in Sabinis*.

60. Tommaso Morroni da Rieti (d. 1476), soldier, humanist, philosopher, rhetorician, magician, and *volgare* poet.

61. Not found in Pliny.

62. Pliny the Elder, *Natural History* 31.12.

63. I.e. the dead center of the country: Pliny the Elder, *Natural History* 3.109, where the title is given to the *Cutiliae lacus*.

64. Pliny the Elder, *Natural History* 2.226. The Cascate delle Marmore where the Velino drops into the Nera, a famous waterfall even today.

65. Vergil, *Aeneid* 7.563–570.

66. Usually *Venusia*, the birthplace of Horace; the reading *iuxta Venusium* is an interpolation in Biondo's text of Servius, or by Biondo into his own text.

67. Another uncanny association: see Tuscany §59.

68. Servius, *In Aeneidem* 7.563.

69. Vergil, *Aeneid* 7.712.

70. Italicized portion (not part of the quotation) found only in an early redaction.

71. Servius, *In Aeneidem* 7.712.

72. Pliny the Elder, *Natural History* 17.32.

73. Servius, *In Aeneidem* 7.565.

74. Livy 27.9, 7–8.

75. Pliny the Elder, *Natural History* 18.263.

76. Humanist, jurist, and papal governor, whose Palazzo dei Mazzancolli survives in Terni; he left a large humanistic and legal library at his death, c. 1473.

77. Pliny the Elder, *Natural History* 3.114. Rome's war with the Macedonian king began in 171 B.C.

78. Vergil, *Georgics* 1.265.

79. Servius, *In Georgica* 1.265.

80. See Cicero, *For Roscius Amerinus* 15–32.

81. Plutarch, *Cicero* 3.4.

82. Biondo has confused the two unrelated Roscii, both defended by Cicero, the Amelian in *For Roscius Amerinus* and the famous actor in *For Roscius the Comic Actor*.

83. Pliny the Elder, *Natural History* 3.113.

84. Actually, Martin I (649–653).

85. Livy 10.10, 5; Pliny the Elder, *Natural History* 3.113.

86. Livy 27.9, 7–8.

87. Pliny the Elder, *Natural History* 31.51.

88. Martial 7.93, 1–2.

89. Martial 7.93, 7–8.

90. Erasmo da Narni (d. 1443), known as Gattamelata, a condottiere now best known for Donatello's equestrian statue of him at Padua; he served Florence, the papacy, and finally Venice. His feat of transporting a

flotilla over the mountains from Torbole to launch it on Lake Garda (1438–39), is touched on by Biondo at Lombardy §19, without mentioning his name.

91. Berardo Eroli of Narni, Bishop of Spoleto, later (1460) elevated by Pius II to become Cardinal of Spoleto, trained in both laws.

92. Livy 9.41, 20.

93. Livy 22.11, 5–6.

94. Vergil, *Aeneid* 1.532 and 3.165.

95. Vergil, *Aeneid* 7.85 and Servius, *In Aeneidem* 7.85.

96. Servius, *In Aeneidem* 7.709.

97. Vergil, *Aeneid* 7.709.

98. Servius, *In Aeneidem* 7.709.

99. Vergil, *Aeneid* 7.713–714. Vergil's *Casperia* and *Foruli* are identified with modern Aspra and Civitatomassa respectively.

100. Vergil, *Aeneid* 8.50–51.

101. Ibid. 7.714.

102. Horace, *Epistles* 1.10, 49.

103. Ps. Acron, in O. Keller, ed., *Pseudacronis Scholia in Horatium vetustiora* (Stuttgart 1904), *ad Epist.* 1.10, 49, quoting Varro. "Those with time for philosophy" (*qui sapientiae vacant*) is Varro's etymological explanation of the goddess' name.

104. Gregory the Great, *Registrum* 3.20. The ancient Sabine town of Cures is now placed some 12 miles to the south of Torri in Sabina, near the abbey of Farfa.

105. Seneca, *Moral Epistles* 104.1.

106. Martial 13.119. In modern texts "If Quintus loves you," i.e. *amat* not the *emat* of Biondo's reading.

107. Martial 9.60.

108. Where he was hanged in 998 by Otto III. This was Crescentius II Nomentanus of the Roman family of the Crescenzi, *consul, senator,* and *patricius:* he imprisoned John XV (pope 985–86), whom he had put in

office. But Eugenius III was pope from 1145–53, Eugenius II from 824–27.

109. Horace, *Epistles.* 1.18, 104–106.

110. Ps. Acron, *In Epist.* 1.18, 105. The *Digentia* is the modern Licenza, a tributary of the Aniene. Mandela (a name reassumed in 1870, in Biondo's time Bardella) is a village at the southern edge of Sabina, next to Vicovaro.

111. Pietro Odo of Montopoli (d. 1463), poet and teacher at the University of Rome (Pomponio Leto was his student); verses on Biondo by Odo are found in at least two Biondo MSS and in the *editio princeps* of *R. I.*, 1471. See Gemma Donati, *Pietro Odo da Montopoli* (Rome, 2000).

112. Servius, *In Aeneidem* 7.715.

113. Ovid, *Metamorphoses* 14.330, the reading now *opacae Farfarus umbrae*, "the dark shades of Farfa," though Biondo's source Servius has the first word as *amoenae*, as here. The quotation from a lost play of Plautus (frag. 171 Lindsay) also comes from Servius, ibid.

114. Farfa was a seventh-century Benedictine foundation with enormous economic and political power in the Middle Ages.

115. The Allia is in fact the modern Fosso della Bettina, which enters the Tiber eleven miles north of Rome.

116. Italicized portion omitted in the *editio princeps*, probably inadvertently.

117. Horace, *Epistles* 1.16, 4–10.

118. Horace, *Carmina* 1.17, 1–4. The area just to the north of Horace's farm is known as the Monti Lucretili. Lycaeus is a mountain in Arcadia. "Apparently" was deleted in the *editio princeps*.

119. Ps. Acron, *In Carmina* 1.17, 1.

120. Horace, *Carmina* 1.20, 1–4.

121. Ibid. 1.22, 9–12. "As follows" was deleted in the *editio princeps*.

122. Ibid. 3.1, 47–48.

123. Ibid. 3.13, 1–3.

124. Ibid. 3.13, 9–16.

125. Horace, *Epistles* 1.7, 1–2.

126. Pliny the Elder, *Natural History* 3.53–54. The town is alternately called Crustumium or Crustumerium. The italicized words were omitted in the *editio princeps*.

127. Vergil, *Aeneid* 7.717.

128. Servius, *In Aeneidem* 7.717. See note 115.

129. Livy 6.28, 6.

130. 18 July 390 B.C. See Livy 6.1, 11.

131. Tradition tells us very little beyond the fact that Pope Lando (d. 913, after ruling less than a year) was a man of the Sabine country.

5. PICENO

1. *Liber pontificalis*, second recension, in U. Prerovsky, ed., *Liber Pontificalis nella recensione di Pietro Guglielmo, OSB, e del Cardinale Pandolfo, glossato da Pietro Bohier, OSB, Vescovo di Orvieto* (Rome, 1978), pp. 689, 328–690, 334. Robert Guiscard was a Norman freebooter and the conqueror of southern Italy (d. 1085). Gregory excommunicated him in 1074 for his attacks on papal Benevento, but then ceded the March of Fermo to him in 1080, needing his help against Henry IV.

2. Biondo's compass points here are more or less 90 degrees different from ours.

3. Livy 22.9, 3.

4. Pliny the Elder, *Natural History* 3.110.

5. Livy 22.9, 3.

6. Livy 23.32, 19.

7. Livy 27.43, 12.

8. Martial 13.36.

9. Martial 13.47.

10. Martial 13.35.

11. Livy 39.55, 7.

12. Eusebius, *Chronicle* 226.22–227.3.

13. Biondo, *History* 74e. Many of the historical events catalogued over §§3–15 (as here) belong to the violent ebb and flow in the process of recovering Italy from Germanic peoples (like Totila, d. 552), undertaken by the Byzantine emperor Justinian I (527–65) through commanders like Belisarius (d. 565), Narses (d. 573), and Conon (see §15).

14. The Malatesta ruled over Pesaro until 1444, Malatesta di Pandolfo dying in 1429. For Paola, see Lombardy §18.

15. Lucan 2.406: *et iuncto Sapis Isauro*, i.e. the junction of the river *Savio* and the Foglia. The present *torrente* Apsa (Biondo's *Idaspis*) does join the Foglia at Montelabbate, but is far removed from the Savio.

16. Tacitus, *Histories* 3.62, 1, recounting the death at Urbino of Fabius Valens.

17. After the river Metauro which passes by Urbino to the south: see Pliny the Elder, *Natural History* 3.114.

18. Biondo, *History* 62h.

19. See Umbria §3 and note 10.

20. Among his cultural accomplishments, he prompted Rinuccio Aretino's translation of Lucian's *Charon*.

21. *Argilla* means "clay."

22. See Umbria §3 and note 10. Federigo bought Fossombrone from the Malatesta in 1445.

23. Lucan 2.405.

24. Livy 27.47, 1–49,4.

25. The name *Forulus* coming from *forare*, "to bore."

26. CIL 11.6106.

27. Biondo, *History* 91a.

28. Ibid. 121a.

29. Hasdrubal haunts the locale in Biondo's cultural imagination: he was defeated here in a great battle at the Metauro and killed by the Romans in 207 B.C. (Livy 27.43–49).

30. Casteldurante is now Urbania. Guillaume Durand the Younger (ca. 1235–1296) was a Frenchman who studied law in Bologna and taught canon law. His very influential *Speculum iuris* (1271) synthesized civil and canon law; he was made auditor general of the Roman Rota by Clement V and performed several other high-level functions in papal administration.

31. See note 22.

32. Giovanni d'Azzo degli Ubaldini (d. 1390) was one of the most prominent condottieri of the fourteenth century. The Ubaldini formed a dynasty closely intertwined with the fortunes of the Montefeltro; Ottaviano was Federigo's right-hand man in the administration of the Duchy of Urbino.

33. Ugone dei Conti di Montevecchio, abbot of the ancient Benedictine abbey of S. Lorenzo in Campo, fl. 1398–1428. His family were feudal lords of S. Lorenzo for most of the fifteenth century.

34. Angelo della Pergola, soldier of fortune and captain, died 1428; a condottiere trained by Alberico da Barbiano.

35. In 383 B.C.: Diodorus Siculus 14.113; Livy 5.35.

36. See Romagna §7, with note 18.

37. With a reminiscence of Ennius' self-epitaph, "Volito vivus per ora virum." On Bartolus of Sassoferrato, see Tuscany §50 and note 149.

38. Alessandro Oliva da Sassoferrato (d. 1463), Augustinian, taught at Perugia for twenty years, rising to become Prior General of his order and in 1460 Cardinal of S. Susanna. Niccolò Perotti (d. 1480) studied with the humanist schoolmasters Vittorino da Feltre and Guarino Veronese, and worked in the learned entourage of Cardinal Bessarion at Bologna and Rome. He wrote the *Cornucopia* (a commentary on Martial) and various works on Latin grammar and prosody.

39. Cf. Livy 10.27, 3, 10.28, 12–18.

40. These are not Livy's figures ("25,000 of the enemy were killed in that day's fighting and 8000 made prisoners," 10.29, 17).

41. Livy 10.30, 3.

42. Livy 10.27, 8–9.

43. Rocca Priora.

44. Gentile da Fabriano (1385–1427), great exponent of the International Gothic style, will appear again shortly in §14.

45. On the Feast of the Ascension, 1435, in the cathedral of San Venanzo. Battista Chiavelli appears as the protagonist of the dialogue *De institutione regiminis dignitatum* by the Fabriano author Giovanni Tinti.

46. John XXII (an Avignon pope, 1316–1334), supporting Robert of Naples, excommunicated the emperor Louis IV of Bavaria. Louis had Pietro Rainalducci of Corvaro elected as Nicholas V in 1328. The antipope renounced his position in 1330, when Louis left Italy, and was imprisoned in Avignon. Contemporaries mockingly called Nicholas V Louis' "idol."

47. The strain of the Fraticelli that Biondo follows here was an heretical independent order of Franciscans, organized by Fra Francesco da Clareno c. 1318. They denied the validity of the papacy of John XXII, his decrees and appointments, and his successors. The Franciscan saint and preacher, Giovanni da Capistrano (d. 1456) was given inquisitorial powers to deal with the Fraticelli by Martin V in 1426.

48. Ovid, *Amores* 3.1, 2.

49. The "Polittico di Valle Romita," removed in 1811 and today in the Pinacoteca di Brera in Milan.

50. Pliny the Elder, *Natural History* 3.113.

51. Ibid. 3.111 speaks only of Ancona set opposite the *promunturio Cunero* ("the promontory of Cunerus") *in ipso flectentis se orae cubito*. Ancona was in fact named for its natural harbor in the shape of an elbow (Greek *ankōn*).

52. The manuscripts, instead of saying "who dwelt in Sicily," with the *editio princeps*, read "according to Juvenal, or by the Siculi according to Pliny." See Juvenal 4.40 and Pliny the Elder, *Natural History* 3.111. Biondo is correcting his original misunderstanding of the foundation by Dorians from Syracuse in Sicily.

53. Such as *CIL* 9.5894.

54. Biondo, *History* 61b–c.

55. Ibid. 87d–88e.

56. Ibid. 175c–d. Sergius II was pope 844–47. Lothair (emperor 840–55) questioned the legitimacy of his election. The Saracens came in 846. However, it was Sergius IV (pope 1009–12) who was famous for his gluttony and gout, hence the sobriquet.

57. Of these two, Francesco was a friend of Cyriac of Ancona and wrote a life of his townsman, *Vita viri clarissimi et famosissimi Kyriaci Anconitani*, ed. and tr. Charles Mitchell and Edward W. Bodnar (Philadelphia, 1996).

58. An accurate self-summary (see Sandys 2.40, with note 4). Ciriaco de' Pizzicolli (1391–1452), humanist, antiquarian, and unwearied traveler, shared with Biondo an uncommon appreciation of antiquities in general, and inscriptions in particular, for reconstructing the past. See Cyriac's *Later Travels*, ed. Edward W. Bodnar (Cambridge, Mass., 2003), in this I Tatti series.

59. In Biondo's time, because of earthquakes. It regained its ancient name of Numana in 1868, having been Umana in the Middle Ages.

60. For example, Caesar, *Civil War* 1.12–13.

61. Biondo, *History* 63d.

62. Caesar, *Civil War* 1.15. Titus Labienus came from Picenum.

63. Biondo calls the city and emperor Helia/Helius rather than Helvia/Helvius. Its remains can still be seen on the river Potenza some three miles north-west of Macerata.

64. Bishop 1440–1469. See Romagna §34.

65. A confusion of *Nuceria Alfatena*, Nocera Inferiore in Campania, with *Nuceria Camellaria*, Nocera Umbra.

66. Biondo's Montecchio and Montesanto have both been renamed, reverting to the names of neighboring Roman cities, the former becoming Treia (1790), the latter Potenza Picena (1862).

67. Francesco Sforza (1401–66), condottiere and captain, was Eugenius

IV's vicar in Piceno, though distrusted, and in 1450 became Duke of Milan. Montolmo, modern Corridonia, was sacked by him in 1433.

68. San Nicola da Tolentino, an Austin friar and charismatic preacher, particularly in Tolentino where he died (1305). Eugenius IV completed Nicola's canonization in 1446.

69. Condottiere (ca. 1350–1435), captain-general of the Florentine forces; his burial in Florence cathedral was attended by Eugenius IV; his painted funerary monument there is by Andrea del Castagno.

70. See Romagna §31, with note: Filelfo was born at Tolentino in 1398.

71. Umbria §9.

72. Livy 9.36, 2–8.

73. Livy 28.45, 20.

74. See §11. The carnage at Camerino took place in 1433–34. Rodolfo and Giulio Cesare da Varano, infant cousins, survived it.

75. In a rather abrupt jump, Biondo has moved from Caldarola in the middle of Piceno to two towns near the mouth of the Chiento. S. Elpidio Mare has in fact the Torrente Ete Morto (north of the Tenna) flowing by it, not the Ete Vivo (south of the Tenna). San Giusto is some way from both. It appears from §23 on the Ete Morto that Biondo has the two confused.

76. Pliny the Elder, *Natural History* 3.111 and Biondo, *History* 330f.

77. Biondo hankers after a town named for the river, as often, and the association may be genuine. But modern texts of Caesar read *Iguvium* (Gubbio), some MSS., among which presumably Biondo's, giving *Tiguium*.

78. Caesar, *Civil War* 1.12, 1–3.

79. Livy 27.9, 7.

80. Giovanni Visconti da Oleggio (d. 1366), soldier, lord of Bologna and of Fermo, which he held for the Church (1360–66) and where he died. See Bruni, *HF* 7.55–59

81. The glacial Lago di Pilato, named for Pontius Pilate, whose body supposedly rests in its depths. Leandro Alberti also describes the lake.

82. Giacomo della Marca (d. 1476) studied civil law at Perugia, then theology with Bernardino of Siena, and was ordained a Franciscan priest in 1420: preacher, miracle-worker, crusader, inquisitor of the Fraticelli.

83. Livy, *Periochae* 72.3.

84. Ibid. 76.7.

85. Cicero, *Brutus* 169.

86. Aulus Gellius 15.4, 3.

87. Francesco degli Stabili, 1259–1327: astrologer, physician, poet in the *volgare*, controversialist, burned at the stake for heresy.

6. ROMAGNA

1. The italicized portion is a dedicatory passage found in the earliest redaction and later excised. The dedication was to Malatesta Novello (1418–1465), the lord of Cesena, who belonged to a famous family of condottieri. He was the the founder of one of the great Renaissance libraries, the Biblioteca Malatestiana of Cesena, and a patron of Leon Battista Alberti, Pisanello, and Piero della Francesca.

2. Vergil, *Aeneid* 7.696 (some MSS read *Flaminiaque* for the correct *Flaviniaque*).

3. *R. I.* 265d.

4. Livy 24.44, 3.

5. Livy 39.2, 10–11.

6. Livy 39.43, 2–3 and *Periochae* 20.17.

7. Biondo, *History* 163d.

8. Italicized portion from the earliest redaction. Niccolò Piccinino and Francesco Sforza were famous condottieri; see Tuscany §50, note 153, and Piceno §18, note 67.

9. Lucan 2.406.

10. From 1938, Tavullia.

11. On Malatesta, see note 18.

12. The italicized place names in caps. 5–6 are found only in the earliest redaction.

13. Chancellor of Carlo Malatesta and correspondent of Salutati.

14. Nowadays the Ausa; the sentence was omitted in later redactions.

15. Livy, *Periochae* 15.5.

16. Eusebius, *Chronici canones*, ed. C. J. Fotheringham, *Chronici Canones* (London, 1923), p. 211, 4–5.

17. Biondo, *History* 60f–g, referring to the siege of A.D. 538. Witigis, son-in-law of Amalasuntha and murderer of Theodahad, was the last king of the Ostrogoths (536–540). He died in Constantinople, reconciled ultimately with Justinian.

18. Sigismondo Pandolfo Malatesta, bastard son of Pandolfo III, condottiere, 1414–1468. Renaissance lord of Rimini, cultured but despised by Pope Pius II, who famously "canonized" him to Hell.

19. Livy 21.51, 7.

20. Livy, *Periochae* 109.2, merely remarking that Curio came over to Caesar at the beginning of the Civil War.

21. Caesar, *Civil War* 1.10 ff. and Lucan 1.231.

22. Jerome does not say he attended the Council, held in 359 to settle the Arian question, but that he consulted the official acts: *Altercatio Luciferiani et orthodoxi*, ed. A. Canellis, Sources Chrétiennes, 473 (Paris, 2003), §18.51–53 (p. 156).

23. Ammianus Marcellinus 27.3, 9.

24. Biondo, *History* 416f. Carlo (d. 1429), a learned but unlucky warrior prince, friend of humanists such as Biondo and Bruni, ally of Cosimo de'Medici.

25. Italicized words found only in the earliest redaction.

26. Italicized words found only in the earliest redaction.

27. Galeotto Roberto (d. 1432, at twenty-one), a family exception (called "the Blessed"); he was the nephew and successor of Carlo.

28. Italicized words found only in the earliest redaction. Roberto Val-

turio was a Romagnole humanist who worked in the court of Sigismondo Malatesta, lord of Rimini, and was the author of a well-known book on military science.

29. Pietro Perleone or Parleone studied Greek with Argyropulos, and taught at Venice, Genoa, Milan. Filelfo was his teacher, too, and friend. His brother Jacopo taught at Bologna.

30. *CIL* II, 1.30*, a Renaissance forgery. It was quoted with variants by Cyriac of Ancona in various of his MSS. Clavuot, *Biondos Italia Illustrata*, p. 194 f., observes, following *CIL*, that Ognibene Leoniceno originated it, inspired by Lucan, *Pharsalia* 1.185.

31. Cicero, *Philippics* 3.13.

32. Pliny the Elder, *Natural History* 3.116.

33. Malatesta Novello (d. 1465) completed the Biblioteca Malatestiana in 1452; it is the most perfectly preserved of Quattrocento libraries.

34. Cicero, *Familiar Letters* 16.27, 2, actually from Cicero's brother Quintus to Tiro.

35. Pliny the Elder, *Natural History* 14.67.

36. The "Sacco dei Brettoni," a savage slaughter carried out under the English *condottiere* John Hawkwood (in 1376); see Bruni, *HF* 8.117–118..

37. Eusebius, *Chronici canones*, pp. 217.24–218.4.

38. Today Bagno di Romagna.

39. Italicized passsage found only in the earliest redaction. For George of Trebizond see §31 and note 73.

40. Not in Pliny.

41. Livy 32.30, 1–4. Modern texts read at the end *tutandum*, 'to protect their country', not *Tannetum* (a Celtic settlement between Reggio Emilia and Parma on the Via Aemilia).

42. Livy 21.25, 2–13, telegraphically compressed.

43. Livy 36.40, 8–11.

44. Suetonius, *Augustus* 49.1 and Vegetius 3.31.

45. Pliny the Elder, *Natural History* 36.83.

46. S.H.A., *Julius* 6.3. The author probably meant "the fleet stationed at Ravenna," but Biondo has evidently taken it as referring to the town of Classe.

47. Pope Gregory I (reigned 590–604).

48. See Lombardy §9.

49. Pliny the Elder, *Natural History* 3.116.

50. Italicized words found only in the earliest redaction.

51. St. Vitalian of Segni was pope 657–72. Grimoald was king of the Lombards from 661–71. Gil Albornoz (d. 1367), soldier-cardinal, was charged by Innocent VI with the reimposition of papal authority over the papal states of Italy.

52. Not in Pliny.

53. Pliny the Elder, *Natural History* 3.113.

54. Biondo, *History* 9b–10e. After defeat at *Pollentia* (in fact modern Pollenzo south of Turin) in 403, Alaric and the Visigoths sacked Rome in 410.

55. Livy 31.2, 5–6.

56. Livy 31.2, 7.

57. *CIL* 11.7 (the text given by Cyriac of Ancona in a letter of 1449: see *Later Travels*, ed. Bodnar, p. 358). The gate was demolished in 1582.

58. See note 17. Also Tuscany §52, with note 160.

59. Italicized words found only in the earliest redaction.

60. Apollinaris, Bishop of Ravenna (and patron of the city), was beaten to death by a mob in the time of Vespasian. In the fictitious martyrologies, a family of saints: Vitalis (father), a consular, was martyred in Ravenna under Nero, and Gervasius and Protasius (sons) under Antoninus Pius. The doctor Ursicinus of Ravenna was a first-century martyr, too. Pope John XVII (d. 1003) was supposed to have been a Roman named Sicco, who owed his five-month papacy to Otto III. St. Peter Chrysologus (406–450), named for his exceptional eloquence, was ordained by the bishop of Imola and consecrated Bishop of Ravenna in 433; his homilies were collected and survive. The *De anima* of Cassio-

dorus' (c. 490–c. 585) was appended, as Book XIII, to his *Variae* after 540.

61. Martial 10.51, 5–6.

62. We find in §27 that Vergerio (d. 1444) had been a student of Giovanni Malpaghini. In Florence, he studied Greek with Chrysoloras; he was an influential teacher and educational theorist himself; see *Humanist Educational Treatises*, ed. C. Kallendorf, (Cambridge, Mass., 2002), in this I Tatti series. He also studied medicine at Padua, possibly accounting for his introduction to the physician Guglielmo da Ravenna.

63. On the shadowy Giovanni Malpaghini (on whom more in §27), see *DBI* 10.551 and Nogara, *Scritti*, p. XXIX.

64. The first nine letters of the *Ad Familiares* are written to P. Cornelius Lentulus, and Biondo is doubtless referring here (as in §15 and §57) to those letters. But what Petrarch found at Verona in 1345 was *Ad Atticum*, *Ad Quintum Fratrem*, and *Ad Brutum*, and he did not know the *Ad Familiares*, recovered by Salutati from a Vercelli codex after Petrarch's death.

65. Italicized passage dropped from the *editio princeps*.

66. An impressive group, most of whom reappear in §28, where they are Chrysoloras' pupils.

67. Manuel Chrysoloras (ca. 1350–1415), Byzantine nobleman, Greek teacher and diplomat. An intimate of the emperor Manuel II, he came from Constantinople to Florence at Salutati's invitation in 1397 as professor of Greek. Bruni, Niccolò Niccoli, Guarino da Verona, Palla Strozzi, Vittorino, Vergerio were among his students, and §30 is a statement of the fruits of his labors.

68. The Council ran from 1414 to 1418, and comprehended a papal interregnum of almost three years, facilitating, for example, the papal secretary Poggio's spectacular successes in recovering ancient MSS.

69. Gasparino Barzizza of Bergamo (ca. 1360–1431) taught at Pavia, Padua, Ferrara, Bologna, Milan, and Venice. An ardent Ciceronian. Biondo mentions him at Lombardy §27, and sketches his role in the recovery of the *codex Laudensis* of Cicero's rhetorical works (§29): Barzizza

had supplied filler of his own composition for the gaps in Quintilian's *Institutes* and, more usefully, had divided the text of Cicero into *capitula*. Among his many pupils were Vittorino, Filelfo, George of Trebizond, and Leon Battista Alberti.

70. Nicola de' Medici (1385–1454), a distant cousin of Cosimo, banker and humanist, friend of Poggio, Bruni, Alberti; he appears frequently in Bruni's letters.

71. Guarino da Verona (d. 1460) studied Greek in Constantinople with Chrysoloras. He taught at Florence, Venice, and for many years at Ferrara, where he enjoyed a close relationship with the Este. A correspondent and friend of Biondo, the copy of the transcription of Cicero's *Brutus* that Biondo made for him survives.

72. On the history of the transmission of the text of the *Rhetorica* from the famous *Codex Laudensis*, see R. Sabbadini, *Storia e critica di testi latini* (Padua, 1971), pp. 84–108; *Texts and Transmission*, ed. L. D. Reynolds et al. (Oxford, 1984), pp. 107–9; and the Introduction, p. viii.

73. George of Trebizond (1396–1472), from Venetian Crete, taught Greek at Vicenza, Venice, Rome, and worked alongside Biondo at the Curia. Remembered for his Aristotelian partisanship and feud with the Platonist Bessarion, as also for his ambition to convert the Sultan Mehmed II to Christianity.

74. Francesco Filelfo (1398–1481) was taught in Constantinople by Johannes Chrysoloras (nephew of Manuel) and married his daughter. A great collector of Greek MSS, he taught Greek and Latin in several Italian cities, above all Milan. Famous for his *Sphortias*, a Latin epic composed in honor of his Sforza masters in Milan.

75. Biondo has in mind the *De elegantiis linguae Latinae* of Lorenzo Valla (1407–57), humanist, professor at the University of Rome, and the most famous philological critic of the Renaissance. The earliest redaction substitutes for the second half of the sentence: "but he has also led the king of the Aragonese himself into a better knowledge of our [Latin] literature."

76. On Pietro and Jacopo Perleone see note 29. Porcellio (Giovanni Antonio dei Pandoni, d. after 1485), itinerant poet, laureated by Freder-

ick III in 1452, teacher of grammar, rhetoric, and poetry; he was an enemy of Eugenius IV but Biondo's friend. Tommaso Pontano, a pupil of Guarino, was professor of eloquence at Perugia in 1440–1450. Tommaso Seneca da Camerino, another itinerant poet and teacher (of Cyriac of Ancona among others), and associate of Porcellio; he succeeded Barzizza at Pavia.

77. Pliny the Elder, *Natural History* 14.34.

78. Martial 3.56.

79. Pliny the Elder, *Natural History* 19.151.

80. Martial 13.21. Biondo applied this epigram to quite another purpose in Umbria §2.

81. Pliny the Elder, *Natural History* 9.169.

82. Martial 3.93, 6–8.

83. The earliest redaction read: "and higher up in the Apennines, first Rondinaia, then Cotulus, which, as we said above, is the airy citadel near the source of the Tiber."

84. Pliny the Elder, *Natural History* 3.116.

85. Eusebius, *Chronici canones*, p. 246.6. Gaius Cornelius Gallus, the inventor of Roman elegiac love poetry, is thought to have been born rather in Forum Julii (Fréjus in southern France). Often mentioned in Vergil's *Eclogues* (6.64, 10.2, 10.6, 10.22, 10.73), but not in Horace.

86. Not in Pliny.

87. Guido Bonatti died c. 1300. His *Decem tractatus astronomiae* were published at Augsburg in 1491. Rainerio Arsendi (1292–1358) taught law at Bologna and Padua. On his most famous pupil, Bartolo da Sassoferrato, see Tuscany §50 and note 149.

88. See Vittorio Rossi's edition of Petrarch's *Familiari*, IV (Florence, 1942) *ad indicem*.

89. Della Torre was a teacher of the humanist schoolmaster Vittorino da Feltre. His copious commentaries on medical texts (Hippocrates, Galen, Avicenna) were often printed in the fifteenth century under the name of Jacobus de Forlivio.

90. Allegretti (c. 1326–1393), Latin poet, imitator of Catullus; he lived in Rimini at the court of Galeotto Malatesta. See Diego Rossi, *Le egloghe Viscontee di Jacopo Allegretti* (Hildesheim, 1984).

91. Ugolino was probably Forlivese, despite his name (d. 1457). Priest, music theorist, and composer. Biondo must mean his *Declaratio musicae disciplinae*, completed in exile at Ferrara, a speculative integration of music into the *quadrivium*.

92. Italicized passaged found in the earliest redaction.

93. See Piceno §17 and note 64.

94. As papal governor of Rome under Paul II, he built the palace (1477) which survives as the Palazzo del Governo Vecchio. Under Sixtus IV a cardinal and Archbishop of Milan (d. 1484). The italicized portion was omitted in the *editio princeps* and other late redactions.

95. The only one to achieve distinction was Gaspare (d. 1493), papal secretary in his father's footsteps and editor of his *Roma instaurata* and *Italia Illustrata*.

96. Dante, *Inferno* 27.43–44. The siege lasted from 1281 to 1283. Guido da Montefeltro, advised by the astronomer Bonatti of §34, organized the defense of Forlì. The French captain was actually *Giovanni d'Appia* (Jean d'Epée).

97. Traversari (1386–1439), humanist and General of the Camaldulensian Order. Largely self-taught in Greek, he was Eugenius IV's representative at the Council of Basel, and also prominent in the Council of Florence (it was he who drew up the decree of Union of the Churches in 1439). Biondo would have known his *Hodoeporicon*, the account of his tour of his convents, and his translation of Diogenes Laertius. Giannozzo Manetti was among his students.

98. Pliny the Elder, *Natural History* 3.119.

99. The *Aeneid* in fact, 11.457.

100. Livy, *Periochae* 88.1–2.

101. S.H.A., *Hadrian* 7.1–3.

102. S.H.A., *Aelius* 2.7–9.

103. S.H.A., *Verus* 1.9.

104. A very old Guelph family, the Manfredi, lords of Faenza, are mentioned in Dante's *Inferno* (32.122–123); Guidaccio (Guidantonio) died in 1448, Astorre in 1468.

105. Martino dei Bernabucci, also known as Martino Manfredi, condottiere, d. 1418.

106. Italicized passage found only in the earliest redaction.

107. Livy, *Periochae* 120.11–16.

108. Pliny the Elder, *Natural History* 19.9.

109. Ibid. 7.163.

110. Livy 31.2, 7, and see §22.

111. Italicized sentence omitted in the final redaction.

112. The Sforza dynasty of condottieri began with Muzio Attendolo Sforza (1369–1424), son of Giovanni Attendolo of Cotignola.

113. In July 1424. Biondo, *History* 414h-415d.

114. See Liguria §8.

115. The great condottiere Alberigo da Barbiano (1348–1409), founder of the Compagnia di San Giorgio, learned the arts of war chiefly from John Hawkwood (Giovanni Acuto) and in the service of Bernabò Visconti, Duke of Milan (1354–1384).

116. Roughly the period 1000–1350.

117. Louis IV became Holy Roman Emperor in 1328: he occupied Rome and had himself crowned in that year. Died in 1347.

118. The bracketed passage is corrupt in the Latin; the English rendering is a guess as to the meaning.

119. Roughly the period 1280–1375.

120. He means Benedict XII (1334–1342).

121. Gian Galeazzo Visconti (1351–1402), Duke of Milan.

122. Biondo prided himself on having met Alberigo in his boyhood (Nogara, *Scritti*, p. 171).

123. Alberigo died in 1409, Ladislaus five years later.

124. Named after St. Proculus, an early bishop of Bologna murdered by Goths in 542.

125. The foundation document shows it was built in 1388–1389.

126. Piceno §8, with note 32.

127. Pliny the Elder, *Natural History* 3.120. See Umbria §2.

128. See §74 with note 183.

129. Martial 3.4, 3–4.

130. Biondo, *History* 103d–104e. Cleph was second king of the Lombards (572–574), succeeding Alboin. His brief rule, from Pavia, ended in his assassination.

131. Benvenuto da Imola (d. 1390) was principally known for his learned commentary on the *Divine Comedy* in scholastic Latin, based on his lectures at Bologna, as well as for his work on Roman history (*Romuleon*, *Liber Augustalis*) and commentaries on Lucan, Valerius Maximus, and his friend Petrarch's *Bucolicum carmen*. The italicized words at the end of the sentence are preserved only in the earliest redaction.

132. Giovanni Nicoletti (c. 1372–1436), teacher of both laws at a number of north Italian universities, chiefly Bologna, and an energetic commentator.

133. Italicized passage preserved only in the earliest redaction.

134. John X (pope in 914, d. 928): an energetic, purposeful foe of the Saracens; by tradition he led the confederated Italian forces that routed them at the mouth of the Garigliano in August 916.

135. Pietro (Curialti) da Tossignano (d. 1407), teacher at Bologna, Ferrara, Padua, and Pavia, personal physician of Gian Galeazzo Visconti, author of medical tracts.

136. Giovanni Tavelli da Tossignano (d. 1446) of the mendicant order of the Gesuati, Bishop of Ferrara in 1431, participated in the Councils of Basel, Ferrara, and Florence.

137. *Via Silicis* means "road of flint [or some other hard stone]." At the end of the road was Conselice or *Caput Silicis*, "the head of the flint."

138. Pliny's discussions of *silices* in *Natural History* Book XXXVI do not seem to have this information (caps. 135, 168 ff.).

139. Lamberto Scannabecchi, pope 1124–30.

140. Cicero, *Familiar Letters* 12.5, 2.

141. Italicized passage found only in the earliest redaction.

142. Pliny the Elder, *Natural History* 3.115. Pliny mentions *Felsina* but not *Boionia*.

143. Livy 37.57, 7–8.

144. Not in Pliny.

145. Suetonius, *Augustus* 17.2.

146. Suetonius, *Nero* 7.6–7.

147. Cf. S.H.A., *Thirty Tyrants* 33.4–5: "Exstat eius sepulchrum circa Bononiam, in quo grandibus litteris incisi sunt omnes eius honores; ultimo tamen versu adscriptum est: 'felix omnia, infelicissimus imperator,'" the last word supplying the point lacking in Biondo that Censorinus was "happy in all things, as emperor most hapless."

148. Sergius II. See Piceno §15, with note 56.

149. Lothair I (Holy Roman emperor, 840–855) gave his son Louis (Holy Roman Emperor Louis II, 850–875) rule over Italy in 844.

150. Doge 1268–1275.

151. Andrea Dandolo, *Chronica*, in *RIS* 12, p. 321, 11–12.

152. Eusebius, *Chronici canones*, p. 232, 9–11.

153. Cf. Cicero, *Brutus* 169 (*Rusticelius Bononiensis*).

154. Lucius II (Gerardo Caccianemici dal Orso) was pope, briefly and unhappily, in 1144–1145.

155. Martial 6.85, 5–6.

156. Pliny the Elder, *Natural History* 7.163.

157. Ibid. 16.161.

158. Ibid. 36.161.

159. Calderini (d. 1365), pupil and adopted son of Giovanni d'Andrea,

was a famous teacher and prolific writer on canon law, much printed in the incunable period.

160. Albergati (d. 1443), a lover of the new learning, was a patron of Enea Silvio Piccolomini and Eugenius IV's legate at the Councils of Basel and Ferrara; his own writings are of a theological and ecclesiastical character. He was the dedicatee of Leonardo Bruni's *Life of Aristotle*.

161. Antonio Galeazzo Bentivoglio (d. 1435), son of the dynast Giovanni I, taught law at the University of Bologna, seized power in the city and was overthrown. He became a condottiere, and was murdered by papal agents.

162. Niccolò Fava (d. 1439), an ardent Aristotelian and anti-Averroist philosopher and physician, he taught medicine and philosophy at the University of Bologna, and was a friend of Filelfo.

163. Italicized passage found only in the earliest redaction.

164. Livy, *Periochae* 119.3–6, events of 43 B.C.

165. The Benedictine Abbey of San Silvestro at Nonantola was founded by St. Anselm of Nonantula in 752 with donations of his brother-in-law the Lombard King Aistulph. It was an imperial monastery until Matilda (see Tuscany §19, with note 41) brought it under the pope's control in 1083.

166. By the Scoltenna, Biondo means what is now called the Panaro, to which, a long way upstream, the modern Torrente Scoltenna is a minor tributary.

167. Compare Pliny the Elder, *Natural History* 3.120, who says that Spina was founded by Diomedes, and was regarded as wealthy on the basis of its treasures deposited at Delphi.

168. A reminiscence of Pliny the Elder, *Natural History* 3.119 ("praegrandi illa domo verius quam nave intravit Hadriam"), rather than Suetonius.

169. Biondo, *History* 102g-h. Smaragdus was sent to Italy as exarch of Ravenna by Phocas (Byzantine emperor, 602–610).

170. Italicized passage found only in the earliest redaction.

171. Pliny the Elder, *Natural History* 3.120.

172. Ibid. 9.75.

173. Italicized words omitted from the *editio princeps*.

174. Niccolò III d'Este (d. 1441). See note 183.

175. Benedictine foundation (on a tract literally "isolated" by the sea, the Po di Goro, and the Po di Volano) of the sixth or seventh century, famous for its now-dispersed library. It was abandoned in 1553 after the Po di Ficarolo, breaking through in 1152 and with its mouth "Ai Fornaci", eventually made a malarial swamp of the vicinity.

176. That is, Ferrara lies at the junction of the main (or "old") Po di Primaro flowing south and the Po di Volano branching off to the east. The Po di Ficarolo, the new channel just mentioned, likewise branched east at the town of that name, some twelve miles north-west of Ferrara.

177. Biondo, *History* 102g-h. See §67, with note 169.

178. A garbled version of Pliny the Elder, *Natural History* 3.120.

179. Henry (d. 1056) was king of Germany from 1039–46, and emperor from 1046.

180. Salinguerra I Torelli (d. c. 1244) was the brother-in-law of Ezzelino, Frederick's general. But the Guelph d'Este and Ghibelline Torelli were bitter rivals, and Innocent IV was pope in the years 1243–1254.

181. Clement (pope 1305–1314) was the first of the Avignon popes.

182. Cf. Tuscany §30. The Council of Ferrara, held in 1438 to discuss the union of the churches, was transferred to Florence at the beginning of 1439. John VIII Paleologus, Byzantine Emperor 1425–1448, was compelled to look to the West for help against the Turks; when it became clear this would not materialize, union failed.

183. Niccolò III d'Este (1383–1441) consolidated and increased his family's power, and began to make his city a vibrant cultural center. His illegitimate sons Leonello, Guarino's pupil (1407–1450) and Borso, Duke of Modena, Reggio, and Ferrara (1413–1471) were equally capable.

184. Ferrarese heirs of the Florentine Strozzi: Tito (d. 1505) was a student of Guarino, scholar, poet, city administrator, whose Latin remains include three eclogues, a fragmentary *Borsias*, and *Erotica*.

185. Lippo Platesi, another student of Guarino, poet (*vates politissimus*), was the dedicatee of Angelo Decembrio's *Epistularum electarum libri tres*.

186. Girolamo da Castello, philosopher, poet, and astrologer. Physician of Leonello and Borso, he gave congratulatory addresses (which survive) on the visits to Ferrara of Frederick III and Pius II. Another student of Guarino. The italicized words and phrases are preserved only in the earliest redaction.

187. Azzo VII Novello (d. 1264). On Salinguerra, see §72 with note 180.

188. Justin 20.1, 6–10.

189. Livy 5.33, 8; Pliny the Elder, *Natural History* 3.120.

190. The rivers form the western border of the "peninsula" of Rovigo, the tongue of land extending to the Adriatic with the large rivers of Adige and Po north and south.

191. Roverella (1406–1476) was secretary to Eugenius IV and was made Archbishop of Ravenna by him in 1445. Created a cardinal by Pius II in 1461, he was an active governor in the states of the Church and frequent papal diplomat.

192. Italicized portion included in an early redaction.

193. In §68. Robert of Anjou, King of Naples (1309–43) patronized writers like Petrarch and Boccaccio and artists like Giotto. In 1340 he invited Petrarch to Naples to receive the laurel crown from him. Petrarch preferred to receive it in Rome, but he dedicated his unfinished *Africa* to the king. We do not have their map. The Po di Ficarolo was in fact formed in 1152 (note 175).

Bibliography

ᏡᏧᏦ

EDITIONS OF THE LATIN TEXT

Rome: Johannes Philippus de Lignamine, 1474. (See Note on the Text.)
Verona: Boninus de Boninis, 1481–1482.
Venice: B. de Vitalibus, 1503.
Venice: G. Gregorius de Gregoriis, 1510.
Basel: *In officina Frobeniana,* 1531.
Basel: Hieronymus Frobenius and Nicolaus Episcopius 1559.

ITALIAN TRANSLATION

There is an Italian translation/paraphrase by "Lucio Fauno" (i.e., Giovanni Tarcagnota) that was printed in the following editions:
Venice: Michele Tramezzino, 1542; reprinted in 1543, 1544, 1548, and 1549.
Venice: Domenico Giglio, 1558.

STUDIES

Bianca, Concetta. Review of Cappelletto, *Recuperi,* as below. *Rivista di filologia e di istruzione classica* 114 (1986): 339–42.
Bruun, Christer. "Frontinus and the Nachleben of his *De aquaeductu* from Antiquity to the Baroque." In *Technology, Ideology, Water: From Frontinus to the Renaissance and Beyond,* C. Bruun and A. Saastamoinen, eds., pp. 41–80. Acta Instituti Romani Finlandiae 31. Rome, 2003. Contains a section on Biondo's use of Frontinus.
Cameron, Alan. "Biondo's Ammianus: Constantius and Hormisdas at Rome." *Harvard Studies in Classical Philology* 92 (1989): 423–436.
Campana, Augusto. "Passi inediti dell' *Italia Illustrata* di Biondo Flavio." *Rinascita* 1 (1938): 91–97.
Cappelletto, R. *Recuperi Ammianei da Biondo Flavio.* Roma, 1983. (Note e discussioni erudite, 18).

———. "Passi nuovi di Ammiano in Biondo Flavio." *Atene e Roma*, n.s. 30 (1985): 66–71.

———. "*Italia Illustrata* di Biondo Flavio." In *Letteratura Italiana: Le Opere*. Vol. I: *Dalle origini al Cinquecento*, a cura di Alberto Asor Rosa, pp. 681–712. Torino, 1992.

Castner, Catherine J. "Direct Observation and Biondo Flavio's Additions to *Italia Illustrata*: The Case of Ocriculum," *Medievalia et Humanistica*, n.s. 25 (1998): 93–108.

Clavuot, O. *Biondos "Italia Illustrata": Summa oder Neuschöpfung? Über die Arbeitsmethoden eines Humanisten*. Tübingen, 1990. (Bibliothek des Deutschen Historischen Instituts in Rom, Band 69).

Cruciani, A., Corbella, G. and others, edd. *Guida d'Italia del Touring Club Italiano*. 16 vols. Revised editions of the several volumes at various dates. Milan, 1969–.

Defilippis, D. *La Rinascita della corografia tra scienza ed erudizione*. Bari, 2001.

Fubini, Riccardo. "Biondo Flavio." In *Dizionario biografico degli italiani*, 10: 536–559. Rome, 1968.

Hay, Denys. "Flavio Biondo and the Middle Ages." *Proceedings of the British Academy* 45 (1958): 97–125.

Husslein, J. C. *Flavio Biondo als Geograph des Frühhumanismus*. Würzburg, 1901.

Jacks, Philip. *The Antiquarian and the Myth of Antiquity: The Origins of Rome in Renaissance Thought*. Cambridge, 1993.

Lucarini, C. M. "La tradizione manoscritta dell'*Italia illustrata* di Biondo Flavio." *Giornale italiano di filologia* 55 (2003): 59–80.

Lucarini, C. M. and P. Pontari. "Nuovi passi inediti dell' *Italia Illustrata* di Biondo Flavio." *Rinascimento*, n.s. 42 (2001): 225–257.

Masius, A. *Flavio Biondo, Sein Leben und Seine Werke*. Leipzig, 1897.

Mazzocco, Angelo. "Some Philological Aspects of Biondo Flavio's *Roma Triumphans*." *Humanistica Lovaniensia* 28 (1979): 1–26.

Miglio, Massimo. "Incunaboli come fonte: il manoscritto utilizzato in tipografia della *Roma instaurata* del Biondo." In Massimo Miglio, *Saggi di Stampa: Tipografi e cultura a Roma nel Quattrocento*, ed. Anna Modigliani, pp. 115–128. Rome, 2002.

Nogara, Bartolomeo. *Scritti inediti e rari di Biondo Flavio*. Vatican City, 1927. (Studi e Testi 48).

Paolo Pontari. "Ancora su passi inediti dell' *Italia illustrata* di Biondo Flavio." *Rinascimento* n.s. 43 (2003): 357–415.

Sandys, J. E. *A History of Classical Scholarship*. 3 vols. Reprinted, New York, 1964.

White, Jeffrey A. "Towards a Critical Edition of Biondo Flavio's *Italia Illustrata*: a Survey and an Evaluation of the MSS." In *Umanesimo a Roma nel Quattrocento*, pp. 267–293. New York, 1984.

Index

🖙🖙🖙

References are by region and paragraph numbers. Pr = Preface. Notes are indexed by the paragraph in which they appear.

Publication of this volume has been made possible by

The Myron and Sheila Gilmore Publication Fund at I Tatti
The Robert Lehman Endowment Fund
The Jean-François Malle Scholarly Programs and Publications Fund
The Andrew W. Mellon Scholarly Publications Fund
The Craig and Barbara Smyth Fund
for Scholarly Programs and Publications
The Lila Wallace–Reader's Digest Endowment Fund
The Malcolm Wiener Fund for Scholarly Programs and Publications